GOSPEL PERSPECTIVES

Studies in Midrash and Historiography

Volume III

Edited by
R. T. France
and David Wenham

JSOT Press

Published by
JSOT Press
Department of Biblical Studies
The University of Sheffield
Sheffield S1O 2TN
England

Printed in Great Britain
by Redwood Burn Limited
Trowbridge, Wiltshire

CONTENTS

PREFACE

The essays published in *Gospel Perspectives* volumes I and
II examined a wide variety of questions on the general theme of
history and tradition in the four gospels. One of the essays
(by David Aune) was a consideration of the genre of the gospels
and in particular of C. H. Talbert's thesis that the gospels
should be considered as hellenistic biographies. The present
volume of essays takes the question of genre further; but,
whereas Aune and Talbert concentrated attention on possible
hellenistic parallels to the gospels, this volume looks at the
possibility of explaining the gospels on the basis of Jewish
literary and historical genres.

The past fifty years has seen increasing attention
being paid to the Jewish background of the New Testament, a
trend encouraged especially by the discovery of the Dead Sea
Scrolls. This study of Judaism has undoubtedly cast much
fresh light on the New Testament, but it has also suggested
many scholarly ideas that are hard to evaluate. One of these
ideas is the hypothesis that the gospels may be compared to
the Jewish 'midrashim', or at least that they contain material,
which though apparently historical is really 'midrashic'
elaboration of tradition. Suggestions of this sort have been
put forward by many scholars, notably by Michael Goulder, John
Drury and - most recently and from a different perspective - by
Robert Gundry.

The proposals of such scholars as these need serious
evaluation. Although some observers may be tempted to dismiss
their ideas as simply one more attempt by sceptical scholars to
explain the gospels away, such a verdict should not be accepted
too quickly. Gundry, for one, is a conservative scholar; and
the primary question at issue is not in fact the question of
the historicity of the gospels, but the question of the nature
of the gospel tradition. Not that the historicity question
and the question of genre are unconnected: if indeed the
gospels are 'midrashic', then elements in the gospels that have
been regarded by many readers of the New Testament as
historical will need to be understood differently, and the
historical base of Christian faith will be narrowed. On the
other hand, the historical basis of the Christian faith will
only be soundly understood and established given a recognition
of the true nature of the gospel tradition; attempts to

establish the historicity of elements in the tradition that were never intended to be understood in that way by the evangelists will not help.

In seeking to establish the nature of the gospel tradition, the student of the gospels must examine both the internal evidence of the documents themselves to see what implicit or explicit claims the evangelists seem to make for their writings and also the external evidence to see what the literary and historical conventions of the time were. But, if that sounds quite a simple process, it is in fact a complex one, as is illustrated by the debate over whether the gospels should be understood as 'midrashic'.

In this debate there is, first, a problem over the use of terms. Terms like 'midrash' and 'haggadah' are used freely by scholars in all sorts of ways, and it is often very difficult to know how a particular scholar is using them. The terminological confusion means that some scholars can categorically deny the relevance of the term 'midrash' to the gospels on the grounds that the term means strictly something that the gospels are not, whereas other scholars may with equal conviction maintain the usefulness of the term because they use it in a much looser sense. Such confusion in the use of terms can hinder the debate of the real issues.

Secondly there is a problem in the dating of comparative materials: the dating of Rabbinic traditions (including the traditions in the midrashim) is notoriously difficult. The final written form of many of the traditions is certainly much later than the New Testament, and this leads some people to deny their relevance for the New Testament. But there is no doubt that some of the traditions go back to New Testament times, and the delicate and debated question is therefore whether particular traditions and tendencies can be traced back to the New Testament period or not.

A third problem concerns the proper understanding of the Jewish traditions in question: what did the writers of Jewish 'haggadah' and 'midrash' consider that they were doing? Were they uninterested in preserving historical tradition? When they elaborate Old Testament history, why do they do so and where do their elaborations come from?

A fourth and very important question is whether the gospels and the Jewish traditions are in any case comparable in any significant way. There is a tendency among biblical scholars to seize on possible extra-biblical parallels to biblical materials and to assume that they are probable and significant parallels; the tendency is to concentrate more on similarities than differences. But caution is in order: it cannot be taken for granted, for example, that the Rabbinic traditions are the natural parallels to the gospel traditions; the gospel traditions could have more in common with popular folk traditions or with Hellenistic literary genres (in so far as these can be distinguished from Jewish literary genres). And, furthermore, there is no question that the Jesus movement was an extraordinary movement, and it is quite possible that the gospels will be equally extraordinary, not corresponding closely with either Jewish or Hellenistic literary genres. The scholarly pendulum may now be swinging away from the idea that the gospels are a unique literary genre, but scholarly pendulums have a tendency to swing too far, and it would be as unwise to assume that the gospels are generically identical to other contemporary documents as to assume that there are no generic similarities between the gospels and any other documents.

It is these sorts of question about midrash, Jewish historiography and the gospels that are addressed in this volume. The essays are not a comprehensive treatment of the subject, but they touch on many of the questions. A number of essays look at Jewish exegetical, historical and literary genres: Bruce Chilton seeks to clarify what Jewish 'midrash' was. Richard Bauckham examines one Jewish writing, the Liber Antiquitatum Biblicarum of Pseudo-Philo, and explains how the Old Testament history has been treated in this document. F. F. Bruce contributes a study of the Qumran texts, and Dick France surveys a broad range of Jewish materials. Leon Morris looks at the question of Jewish lectionaries, and considers the idea that the gospels can be explained on the basis of such lectionaries.

The remainder of the essays look at the gospels themselves in the light of midrash and Jewish historiography. *Gospel Perspectives II* included one essay on this theme - a study of the Matthean infancy narratives by Dick France. That essay is now followed up by an examination of Matthew 27:3-10 by Douglas

Moo, a consideration of Robert Gundry's new commentary on
Matthew by Philip Payne, an article on the so-called Lukan
travel narrative by Craig Blomberg, including consideration of
the ideas of C. F. Evans, Michael Goulder and John Drury, and
finally a study by David Greenwood of F. Kermode's *The Genesis
of Secrecy*, which is a major work by an English literary
critic who invokes the idea of 'midrash' in the aid of a
literary analysis of Mark's gospel.

This book is inevitably more a reaction to the work of
other scholars than a creative new approach.   But, if some
readers are disappointed by this, it must be said that to
analyse and criticise any important scholarly hypothesis is a
positively useful exercise.   To show the weaknesses of a
particular theory must lead either to the reformulation of
that theory or to the adoption of other theories, and in either
case something valuable has been achieved.   To say that is not
to imply that the essays in the volume are simply destructive
of other views;   several of the essays offer new suggestions
and analyses, which will be of positive value to students of
Judaism and of the gospels.

It would be foolish to claim too much for this volume:
the authors of the different essays have not reached unanimity
on exactly how much relevance Jewish 'midrash' and
historiography have for the understanding of the gospels, nor
have they even used their terms in exactly the same way
(though they have tried carefully to define their terms).
But all the authors would agree that much recent discussion has
been simplistic in its appeal to the Jewish background of the
gospels.   And it is our hope that the essays will at least
clarify thinking about the nature of the gospel tradition and
that they will help point the ways forward for future research.
In order to draw together our findings and to suggest where
they may lead, the symposium concludes with a postscript by
Dick France.

Like *Gospel Perspectives I* and *II* this volume is a
team-effort of the Tyndale House Gospels Research Project.
Our thanks go to the Tyndale House Council for their support of
the Project and to all others who have been involved in the
consideration and discussion of the essays in the volume.

R. T. FRANCE & DAVID WENHAM
Tyndale House, Cambridge.

VARIETIES AND TENDENCIES OF MIDRASH:
RABBINIC INTERPRETATIONS OF ISAIAH 24.23

Bruce Chilton,
Department of Biblical Studies,
The University,
Sheffield, S10 2TN

I. Introduction

"Midrash" has a range of meanings. Etymologically, it may
refer to the general process by which one "searches out" the
meaning of scripture, while generically it may refer only to
certain specific rabbinic documents. We refer to the former
as "midrash" with lower case "m", reserving a capital for the
latter. Methodologically, it seems wise to begin any discussion
with Midrash (the literature) in order to give the consideration
a firm documentary basis /1/. No application of the term
"midrash" as a category within New Testament exegesis which
fails to take account of rabbinic usage can claim to be a
responsible application of the available evidence. "Midrash"
is not first of all a genre within the New Testament: it is
definable only within Rabbinica, and may be applied to the
New Testament only when a pronounced similarity to Rabbinica
is evident. All of the extant Midrashim stem from the period
of rabbinic Judaism; that is, they were composed no earlier
than during the second century A.D. /2/. The earliest Midrashim
are, on the whole, halakhic: their concern is with the
development of directions for the Jewish community in the
post-biblical situation. The biblical texts here serve as the
occasion to arrange discussions of a generally ethical nature
(cf. Mekhilta, Sifra, Sifre), and these halakhic Midrashim are
to be compared in purpose and content with the Mishnah /3/.
From a later period, on the whole, and according more with the
purpose and content of the Talmud, we have the haggadic
Midrashim, best represented by Midrash Rabbah (on the Pentateuch
and the five books of the Megillah). In this case, although a
halakhic point is sometimes in view, the overall intent is to

relate the rabbinic ethos to the biblical text through a series
of illustrative stories (haggadoth). Homiletic Midrashim are
also haggadic in content (again, generally speaking), but stem
from a still later period and purport to represent sermons by
rabbis (cf. Tanhuma and Pesiqta Rabbati). An as yet unsettled
question concerns the status of the so-called "narrative
Midrashim". Literature from this genre (including Jubilees,
the Genesis Apocryphon and the Liber Antiquitatum Biblicarum)
is demonstrably earlier than the documents which have so far
been mentioned, and deserve the careful attention of New
Testament scholars, no matter how they are categorized. On the
other hand, such works retell biblical stories, often without
citing the biblical text, and frequently departing from it
substantially. They are not expositions of the Bible, whether
along halakhic, haggadic or homiletic lines, and their lack of
an exegetical programme suggests they are not best treated as
a species of Midrash /4/.

When one applies the word "Midrash" generically, it is
patent that the New Testament does not belong to the category.
Although this is an obvious observation, the looseness with
which the Gospels have been styled as in some sense midrashic
(as other articles in the present volume demonstrate) requires
that it be stated openly. The Midrashim are not simply odd
references to biblical imagery, nor are they accurately defined
merely as literate commentaries: they are exegetical treatments
pursued in the halakhic, haggadic and/or homiletic interests of
the Jewish community.

Behind the genre, however, there does lie a process /5/.
The rabbinic Midrashim are the documents of communities, not of
individual authors, and for this reason each Midrash is
composed of individual midrashim (or chains of midrashim) which
have a history of their own. Some of these may simply be
contemporaneous with the formulation of a given Midrash, but
some may represent interpretative activity at an earlier period.
Conceivably, certain of the constituent readings of the rabbinic
Midrashim may be contemporaneous with, or even antedate, the
New Testament. Moreover, the function of a given interpretation
might have been quite different originally from the purpose of
the entire Midrash in which appears /6/.   Indeed, midrashic
treatments frequently appear in non-midrashic works such as
the Talmud itself. This implies that the student of the New
Testament would better look to individual midrashic treatments
within the rabbinic Midrashim than to complete documents or the

interpretative perspectives of those documents in his
consideration of possible analogies to his text.

The development of the extant Midrashim, then, presupposes
antecedent midrashic activity. Such activity also provided the
occasion on which the rabbis evolved exegetical conventions, the
seven or thirteen or thirty-two middoth /7/. These categories
of deduction, inference and analogy in exegesis are, however,
not systematically or consistently applied in anything like a
self-conscious way in Rabbinica. As in the case of the
principles of the Alexandrian grammarians (with which they
have an affinity), these conventions or standards (not "rules",
except in the sense of "measures") seem more to reflect accepted
midrashic techniques than to prescribe their application /8/.
The observation of individual instances of midrash, therefore,
would seem to be the best way forward for us.

In the present discussion, a passage from the book of
Isaiah (24.23) has been selected, and its interpretation in
rabbinic literature considered. The passage has been chosen
because it is frequently commented upon, although for
introductory purposes there is no need to cite all of these
interpretations. The selection is also influenced by the
interpretation contained in the Targum, which seems to come
from its earliest, Tannaitic, level /9/. Together with the
Septuagint, the Targum will therefore help us to ensure
chronological breadth in our consideration of instances of
midrash, although we will only introduce the examples by way
of appreciating midrashic genres; to discuss the principles of
dating the examples lies outside the scope of our inquiry.

II.   Isaiah 24.23 in midrash

a) Interpretation as translation
Isaiah 24.23 in the Masoretic text reads:

And the moon will be abashed, and the sun will be
ashamed, because the LORD of hosts reigns on mount
Zion and in Jerusalem, and before his elders -
glory /10/.

This straightforward depiction, in cosmological terms, of God's
in-breaking rule acquires fresh meaning in the Targum:

> And the servants of the moon will be ashamed,
> and those who worship the sun will be humiliated,
> because the kingdom of the LORD of hosts will be
> revealed in mount Zion and in Jerusalem, and before
> the elders of his people in glory /11/.

Although, occurring as it does in a purported translation of
Isaiah, this interpretation is simple (peshat), rather than
involved or elucidatory (darash), its substantive deviation
from the Hebrew text in the interests of explanation is
manifest. Precisely for this reason, translational Jewish
literature should be included in a consideration of the general
phenomenon of midrash. Idolaters - "the servants of the moon"
and "those who worship the sun" - appear as the butt of God's
disclosure. Slight deviations from the Hebrew in the verbs
chosen for use, dependent on these more major innovations, can
also be seen. "To be ashamed" (בהת) is normally the Aramaic
counterpart of the Hebrew verb which appears in the second
clause (בוש), and "to be humiliated" (יתכנע) is scarcely a
translation of either of the Hebrew verbs used. Nonetheless,
the use of the verbs in the Masoretic text is already
metaphorical (as applied to the moon and sun), so that our
attention is naturally drawn to the alteration in the
substantives in the Targumic text. The punishment of Israel's
idolatrous enemies (a frequently sounded theme in this Targum),
rather than the cosmic dislocation of which the Hebrew text
speaks, is here linked strongly with the revelation of the
kingdom.

The use of the verb גלא explicitly brings the language of
revelation into play /12/. The entity to be revealed is called
"the kingdom of the LORD"; this phrase is characteristically
used in respect of God's active intervention on behalf of his
people, and its linguistic and substantive correspondence to
Jesus' usage has been discussed elsewhere /13/. Although the
Hebrew verb "to reign" (מלך) has here occasioned the use of the
substantive "kingdom" (מלכותא) in the Targum, the latter is no
mere circumlocution for the former. Elsewhere in the same
Targum, "kingdom" appears when the corresponding verb is not
present in the Masoretic text (31.4; 40.9), and God can be
referred to by the Targumic interpreter with an active verb
(cf. v. 21 and 25.1,2), so that the mere avoidance of an
apparent anthropomorphism does not seem to be a motivation
here. The future passive of the verb "to reveal", as compared
to the Hebrew perfect of "reigns", is noticeable, and tends to

underline the vividness of the expectation at what is to come
in future. (In Targumic Aramaic the distinction between perfect
and imperfect is more emphatically temporal than is the case in
the Hebrew of the Masoretic text.) The same stress is achieved
by saying "in glory" rather than just "glory"; the preposition
eases the rather difficult syntax of the Hebrew and makes
"glory" the means of the divine revelation rather than an
independent affair. The focus of the revelation on Israel
exclusively is evident in the phrase "elders of his people"
instead of the less specific "his elders".

The interpretation represented by the Septuagint takes
quite a different turn:

> The brick will be wasted and the wall will fall, because
> the lord will reign in Zion and in Jerusalem, and he will
> be glorified before the elders /14/.

A few of the elements here are quite similar or identical to
what we find in the Masoretic text, but the Septuagint manifests
a clear tendency to explain almost discursively what the Targum
deals with by periphrasis. The verb "to reign" is used in the
future, as is "to be revealed" in the Targum, and to this
extent the commonly heightened expectation of the two documents
is perhaps indicated, even though the possibility of literary
dependence between them at this point is to be discounted. The
common need to explain the occurrence of "glory" in the passage
is met in different ways, in that a verbal form appears in the
Septuagint. The Greek "translation" of the first two clauses
of the verse is, however, obviously its most striking feature.
But this surprising rendering does suit the context remarkably
well; the description of the punishment of the rebellious kings
precedes our passage (vv. 21f.). It has been suggested that
the Greek translator(s) read a somewhat different Hebrew
original whose first, second and fourth words would be identical
to the Masoretic text except in their pointing וחפרה הלבנה
ונשבה החמה /15/. The third term (ונשבה), however, is quite
different from the Masoretic text reading (ובושה), which is
so straightforward and frequently found as to make the proposed
confusion seem improbable. The reconstructed word is, moreover,
not the usual equivalent of the simple Greek verb, "to fall";
in fact the latter is never used to render the former in the
extant text of the Septuagint. On the whole, then, an
innovative element should be acknowledged, although this
element is much reduced in certain of the variant readings

(cf. the Ziegler edition, cited in n. 14). The points of
contact between the Septuagint and the Targum evidence a desire
to explain the cosmological metaphor of the Hebrew, to make
sense of the "glory" usage, and a tendency to apply the text
to the future. From the point of view of the content of their
renderings, however, the interpreters of the two documents
followed quite different paths.

b) Interpretation as explicit comment

When we shift our attention to Exodus Rabbah (45.5), we
move from interpretation by means of translation (peshat) to
interpretation by means of explicit comment (darash). The
starting point, however, is actually - as we might expect in
this Midrash - the book of Exodus (33.18):

> And he said: Let me see your glory (Exodus 33.18). He
> sought access to the gift of reward for the righteous
> and of respite for the wicked. And where is it written
> of the gift of reward to the righteous as glory? It
> is said: The wise will inherit glory (Proverbs 3.35).
> Similarly, he says: And before his elders - glory
> (Isaiah 24.23) /16/.

This passage (introduced as an alternative view, אחר דבר) is
not formally an interpretation of the clause from Isaiah it
cites, but it employs the clause in order to explicate "glory",
proceeding on the basis of the verbal similarity between the
divine glory spoken of in Exodus and the glory which appears
before God's elders in Isaiah. The positive evaluation of
"glory" in the midrash is such that it reaches beyond the
sphere of God himself to his people, and even includes the
wicked (to whom respite is promised); it should immediately be
mentioned, however, that Psalm 73.24, where glory is promised
after a temporary lapse, is also cited in this context, so that
unrepentant wickedness is probably not in view. Isaiah 24.23
is only used here as a means of understanding "glory" in
Exodus 33.18, and this midrash is a good example of the
incidental interpretation of a passage whose wording or subject
matter is pertinent to the subject at hand. Indeed, the very
concatenation of texts, which may seem unsystematic at first,
is in fact the vehicle for developing a theology of "glory".

The theme of glory is developed far more extensively in
Leviticus Rabbah (11.8) in a comment which is placed to

explicate Leviticus 9.1 (cf. v. 6):

> For Rabbi Simeon ben Yoḥai taught: not in one place, and
> not in two places do we find that the holy one, blessed
> be he, has apportioned glory for the righteous, but in
> many places. At the thorn bush: Go and gather the elders
> of Israel (Exodus 3.16). In Egypt: And you will go, you
> and the elders of Israel (v. 18). On Sinai: Come up to
> the LORD, you and Aaron, Nadab and Abihu and seventy from
> the elders of Israel (Exodus 24.1). In the wilderness:
> Gather to me seventy men from the elders of Israel
> (Numbers 11.16). In the tent of meeting: And to the
> elders of Israel (Leviticus 9.1 cf. v. 5). Even in
> respect of that which is to come, the holy one, blessed
> be he, has apportioned glory to the righteous. This is
> that which is written: And the moon will be abashed and
> the sun will be ashamed; and it is written: And before his
> elders - glory (Isaiah 24.23). Rabbi Ishmael bar Bebai
> and Rabbi Simeon and Rabbi Reuben, in the name of Rabbi
> Ḥanina, say: the holy one, blessed be he, is about to
> establish an academy of the elders who belong to him;
> this is that which is written: Because the LORD of hosts
> reigns on mount Zion and in Jerusalem, and before his
> elders - glory (Isaiah 24.23). It is not written: Before
> elders, but: before his elders - glory /17/.

Rabbi Simeon's compendium of biblical "glory" passages
presupposes, as in Exodus Rabbah 45.5, that the Torah and the
book of Isaiah address the same issue, although Isaiah 24.23
here has a uniquely important role (as the explicit
justification for associating "elders" and "glory"), and is
the only biblical passage outside the Torah which is cited.
Moreover, the basic agreement of the many scriptural "places"
is far more expressly argued in Leviticus Rabbah as compared
to Exodus Rabbah. Nonetheless, Isaiah 24.23 is distinguished
from the other passages, in that its relevance for the future
is asserted. The point is established by reference to the
cosmological language of the Hebrew (not present in the Targum
or the Septuagint), which is cited quite fully, while the Torah
passages are cited only briefly after they are referred to
under shorthand categories borrowed from the story of Israel's
first days. The understanding that Isaiah 24.23 addresses the
future is common to Leviticus Rabbah and Exodus Rabbah, and -
for that matter - the Targum and the Septuagint. But the
emphasis on the idea here is so strong that the focus of the

midrash quite evidently shifts from Leviticus 9.1, its
ostensible base text, to the Isaian passage. Rabbinic
midrash is notoriously flexible in this regard, and the
present example shows that a theological motif, rather than
a single text, sometimes governs the overall structure and
tendency of interpretation. Once having been seen to have a
special meaning for the "glory" theme, Isaiah 24.23 now
becomes the focus of consideration in the observation handed
on in the name of Rabbi Ḥanina. In this observation, based on
a straightforward reading of the biblical text, an opinion is
confuted which is not actually cited. Simeon's compendium,
as cited, can hardly have occasioned the comment, although it
is possible that the form in which we have his midrash has
been accommodated to take account of what Ḥanina said. Ḥanina
may have been a contemporary of Simeon (that is, he may have
lived in the second century A.D.), but then the name is too
common in Rabbinica for much to be made of it. One source we
have already mentioned might be the target of Ḥanina's complaint:
the Septuagint reads only "the elders" (in the best manuscripts;
αὐτοῦ is evidently a later correction), just the generalizing
translation which Ḥanina rather astringently rejects. Rabbis,
at least from as early as the second century, were publicly
dissatisfied with the Septuagint, and the present comment might
well reflect this dissatisfaction.

Isaiah 24.23 is pressed into service in a very different
way in Qohelet Rabbah, the commentary on Ecclesiastes (1.2):

Rabbi Judah, in the name of Rabbi Simeon, said: the
vanities mentioned in the book of Qohelet correspond
to the seven days of creation ... on the fourth day
(God said): Let there be lights, and it is written:
And the moon will be abashed ... /18/.

The use of Isaiah 24.23 in this midrash represents a departure
from what we have seen so far. The "vanities" spoken of in
Ecclesiastes are programmatically related in this rather
developed interpretation to the transient components of the
creation. Genesis 1 provides the list of the components, and
here the citation from Isaiah functions quite consistently as
the biblical support for the assertion that even the heavenly
luminaries are transient. Although the application of the
verse in the Amoraic midrash cannot be said to contradict the
eschatological reading which we have seen in the sources
mentioned above, the emphasis is clearly distinctive here. The

focus is more on the fact of cosmological transience than on what is to follow this transition. Most strikingly, the present passage instances the coordinated use of the Bible in rabbinic comment, with Ecclesiastes, Genesis and Isaiah all used to explicate a single idea. The idea itself is derived and developed from the base text (Ecclesiastes) quite directly.

III.   Midrash as theology

Even within the instances of midrash already surveyed, the prominence of theological ideas has already been observed. In each case, a clear tendency of interpretation informs the midrash. The Targum, by means of several innovative translations, stresses God's glorious vindication of his people at the expense of their idolatrous enemies. The more discursive rendering of the Septuagint dwells more on the destructive aspects of God's glorification. "Glory" as a category of reward for the righteous is the theological theme which is expressed, partially by means of citing Isaiah 24.23, in Exodus Rabbah, while in Leviticus Rabbah the same passage is referred far more precisely to the eschatological vindication of righteous rabbis. On the other hand, the citation in Qohelet Rabbah is applied to the theme of cosmological transience. Examples of the use of Isaiah 24.23 within the Babylonian Talmud permit us further to appreciate the theological tendencies in whose interests this scripture is cited. The first (taking our examples according to the order of the tractates in which they appear) to be considered begins with the observation of an apparent contradiction in scripture (Pesaḥim 68a):

> Rabbi Ḥisda opposed (two passages). It is written: And the moon will be abashed and the sun will be ashamed (Isaiah 24.23). And it is written: And the light of the moon will be as the light of the sun, and the light of sun will be sevenfold, as the light of seven days (Isaiah 30.26). There is no difficulty; the former refers to the world to come, the latter to the days of the messiah. But what is to be said in respect of Samuel, who maintained there is no difference between this world and the days of the messiah except that of the servitude to (foreign) governments alone? Both refer to the world to come, and there is no difficulty. One refers to the camp of the Shekhinah, and the other to the camp of the righteous /19/.

In this passage, the basic contention is consistent as between
Ḥisda and the adjustment made in deference to Samuel: it is
argued that different aspects of eschatology are referred to
in Isaiah 24.23 and Isaiah 30.26 respectively. According to
Rabbi Ḥisda, the first refers to the divine disclosure of a
totally new order ("the world to come"), while the latter
applies to God's messianic vindication of his people. Ḥisda
was an Amora, and he is credited with having made a sound
distinction, but then the question arises: how is this opinion
to be reconciled with the view of an earlier rabbi concerning
the messianic days? If the messianic days differ from the
present order only in political terms, then the cosmological
language of Isaiah 30.26 is scarcely appropriate to them. The
point of the passage is that only a slight adjustment of
Ḥisda's midrash is necessary on the assumption that Samuel
was correct. Isaiah 30.26 would then refer to the camp of the
righteous in the new order, rather than to the Shekhinah /20/;
the basic distinction between a reference to the divine
revelation itself (Isaiah 24.23) and the fruits of that
revelation (Isaiah 30.26) would be preserved.

     In Sanhedrin 91b, virtually the same discussion appears
with virtually the same wording /21/, but - curiously - the
placement of the two Isaian passages in each argument is
reversed. In the case of Ḥisda, mention is made first of the
days of the messiah, and then of the world to come, with Isaiah
24.23 referring to the former and Isaiah 30.26 referring to the
latter. Similarly, "the camp of the righteous" precedes "the
camp of the Shekhinah" in the solution to the potential problem
posed by Samuel's opinion. (The translations of Sanhedrin 91b
and Pesaḥim 68a in the Soncino Talmud obscure their
relationship.) For two reasons, the version of the passage in
the tractate Sanhedrin should be seen as secondary. First,
the language used in Sanhedrin to discuss the difficulty
involved with Samuel's position repeats more nearly than
Pesaḥim 68a that used in describing Rabbi Ḥisda's opinion.
Second, the tendency of the Sanhedrin version to focus more
on the gains to Israel in Isaiah 24.23 than on the divine
self-disclosure corresponds to the Amoraic interpretations we
will see instanced below. Both of these considerations lead
to the judgement that the passage from Sanhedrin is - tradition
critically speaking - later than the passage from Pesaḥim.

     The eschatological application of Isaiah 24.23 has been
evident in all of the midrashim so far discussed, with the

possible exception of Qohelet Rabbah.   One of the shifts in
rabbinic theology during the Amoraic period is to construe
eschatology in an individualistic way.   The promise of reward
in a future life to some extent takes the place of the more
communal expectation of the earlier period.   This can be seen
in the opinion cited in Baba Bathra (10b):

> And Rabbi Abahu said: they asked Solomon, who is a son
> of the world to come?   He said to them, Everyone who
> is as (it says in scripture): Before his elders - glory
> (Isaiah 24.23).

The extent to which this is construed in an individualistic way
can be seen from what follows:

> So Joseph, son of Rabbi Joshua, became ill and lost
> consciousness.   His father asked him: what did you see?
> He said to him: I have seen an inverted world; what is
> above was beneath and what is below was above.   He said
> to him: you saw a purified world, and how did you see
> us?   As we are respected here, we are respected there.
> And I heard those who say: blessed is he who comes here
> with his learning in his hand.   And I heard those who
> say: No one is able to stand in the circle of those
> slain by the government.   Who are they?   If one says,
> Rabbi Aqiba and his companions, apart from being slain
> by the government, is there not another reason for them
> to be here?   Really, the martyrs of Lydda are meant /22/.

This passage instances another common feature of rabbinic
midrash.   Indeed, August Wünsche consistently referred to
"Midrasch Haggadah", and although this designation is no
longer widely current, the haggadic side of interpretative
activity among the rabbis must be acknowledged.   Even the
framework of the initial opinion - explicitly in the name of
an Amora - is imaginary, in that Solomon is pictured as
responding to a question with words taken from Isaiah.   Events
and figures from the past are here being telescoped, a
technique that modern writers of science fiction use, albeit
in reference to the future.   Whether or not the initial hearers
of this haggadic midrash understood that Abahu's claim is,
historically speaking, anachronistic, they would surely have
grasped that the order of statement being made, grounded in
the conviction that God's message through many voices is
essentially coherent, was speculative.   The story about Joseph's

dream (whose visionary orientation may owe something to its
principal's name) represents an obviously more developed form
of haggadah, and in itself cannot be described as midrash, or
even as midrashic (in that the elements of which the story is
composed are not biblical). But the attachment of the story
here is perfectly explicable, given that the haggadic midrash
(Abahu's opinion) which immediately precedes is also governed
by the question which the haggadah itself also poses and
answers: who has a place in the world to come? The world to
come, that is, is the topic which is addressed; Isaiah 24.23
is not the object under scrutiny. The midrash offered is more
the means of inquiry than its subject; it is far from an
instance of method applied in the abstract or an exercise
pursued for its own sake. Because participation in the world
to come, rather than the right interpretation of the biblical
verse, is the issue, the story about Joseph does not represent
as abrupt a transition as might at first sight appear. Haggadic
midrash simply gives way to a haggadah which illuminates the
same subject. The story itself is of some interest, and
presses the question further by addressing the order of the
world to come. It might be an expanded, narrative version
of the principle that many who are first shall be last, and
the last first. The position of scholars is expressly
safeguarded by the presumably angelic audition as well as by
Joseph's own observation of their esteem. The second audition,
however, which guarantees the place of martyrs, implicitly
presents a difficulty. Although their exaltation accords
perfectly with the basic principle of inversion which lies at
the heart of the vision, the question which apparently arises
(although it is not specifically posed) is whether martyrs as
such are above scholars. That is the reason for which Rabbi
Aqiba is brought into the picture: he was both a most learned
and influential academic and a victim of execution during the
Bar Kokhba revolt (at least as rabbinic legend had it /23/).
The point of the discussion which follows is that those of
Aqiba's stature do not require martyrdom to achieve their rank,
so that the angelic voice must pertain to another group. The
logic of haggadah, in a word, can be as complex as that of
midrash, as demanding of associative thinking in order to be
understood, and it is no less informed and influenced by
theological interests.

An even more specific concern with the hierarchical
structure of the world to come is manifest in a midrash
connected with Leviticus 19.1f. in Tanḥuma (קדושים 1.1-7):

> Our rabbis say: what is the order of seating that is
> to come? The holy one, blessed be he, sits, and the
> angels give thrones to the great ones of Israel, and
> they sit. And the holy one, blessed be he, sits as
> a father in the house of judgement, and they judge the
> peoples of the world. This is spoken of (in scripture):
> The LORD will come in judgement with the elders of his
> people and his princes (Isaiah 3.14). It is not written,
> against the elders of his people, but, with the elders ....
> The teaching is that the holy one, blessed be he, sits
> with the elders and the princes of Israel, and he judges
> the peoples of the world. And what are they but the
> thrones of the house of David and the elders of Israel?
> This is spoken of (in scripture): For there they will
> sit (on) thrones to judge, thrones of the house of David
> (Psalm 122.5) /24/.

The interest of this midrash from our point of view is that
Isaiah 24.23 is not mentioned, despite its reference to God's
elders, its eschatological application elsewhere in Rabbinica,
and particularly its connection to the eschatological academy
in Leviticus Rabbah (11.8). The argument of this midrash also
coheres with the haggadah of Joseph's dream in Baba Bathra 10b,
where the Isaian passage also features prominently (albeit only
by context). The omission of a reference to Isaiah 24.23
becomes less perplexing when we observe the innovative feature
in the passage from Tanḥuma: the rabbinic model of judgement
is here said to endure the change in the ages. The judicial
practice of the rabbis in this world, authorized for the
present and the future by means of the promises to David, is
said to continue in the world to come, with God himself sitting
as president in a heavenly Sanhedrin. The continuity of this
view with earlier interpretation of Isaiah 24.23 is obvious,
particularly as it comes to expression in Leviticus Rabbah 11.8,
and yet the specificity of the claim in Tanhuma is bold and
innovative. From a technical point of view, Isaiah 24.23
might have been applied within the new midrash, but this would
have at least bordered on a break with the conventional
interpretation of the verse, which concentrated more on the
glorification of the elders for Israel than on their
glorification for themselves. This reinforces the point
that, among the rabbis, scripture is not cited only according
to mechanical principles of exegesis; the theological ideas
normally associated with the text are also an important
influence on the way in which interpretation takes place.

III.   Summary and conclusions

The title of the present contribution focuses our
attention on what are called the "varieties" and the
"tendencies" of midrash. When using the first term, we refer
to the sort of interpretation a midrash offers, and its method
of proceeding. Under this heading, we pose such questions as
that of how scripture is cited in the midrash, that of what
place it occupies in the statement as a whole, and that of
the weight the citation carries within the logic of the
interpretation. When using the second term, we refer to a
related but distinct matter: what is the direction or aim of
the midrash? Under the heading of "tendency", our concern is
more with the purpose than with the form of the midrash,
although these two aspects obviously cannot be separated
entirely. Initially, the first heading will occupy us, since
the variety of one midrash as compared to another is perhaps
more readily observable than its tendency, which is more a
matter of inference.

The Targum and the Septuagint both belong to the general
category of translation, or peshat rendering, but we have seen
that their apparent simplicity is deceptive. The Targumic
version of Isaiah 24.23 manifests a characteristic procedure
of verbal expansion; the metaphorical language of the Hebrew
text is given a more easily understood, almost pedestrian,
point of reference by "explaining" the mention of the sun and
the moon. Similarly, to speak of the kingdom, a theologoumenon
which occurs frequently in the Targum in the context of God's
intervention on behalf of his people, is a more direct
assertion than the general use of the language of kingship.
The interests of explication are also served by the use of
"in" with "glory". Although the Septuagintal rendering also
appears to be motivated by a desire to explain the Hebrew
text, and - indeed - essentially at the same points that the
Targum expands upon, its procedure is distinctive. There is a
greater freedom evidenced here in the more discursive character
of the rendering. Entire phrases and clauses, as well as
individual words, are the objects of explanation; a noun is
rendered as a verb, and a metaphor is represented only by what
the interpreter thinks it stands for, not by any evident
reference to its original formulation. Where the Targum
explains by expanding on - one might almost say deciphering -
words, the Septuagint transforms entire phrases in what is
technically speaking a more daring technique of translation.

Initially, one must say at the risk of being paradoxical
that midrash proper (that is, interpretation as darash rather
than as peshat) is rather more conservative in its procedure
than peshat renderings in the Targum and the Septuagint.   In
the case of Exodus Rabbah 45.5, the term "glory" in connection
with "elders" occasions the citation of Isaiah 24.23.   The
sophistication of this midrash - which does make it a species
of darash rather than peshat - lies in the way the passage is
associated with Proverbs 3.35 and Exodus 33.18, the base text.
"Glory", whether associated with the wise (as in Proverbs) or
with the elders (as in Isaiah), belongs to the righteous in
the argument of the midrash, and this argument is founded
scripturally.   But the relevance of the argument for the
understanding of the Exodus text, where the glory spoken of
is God's, is far from obvious.   The verbal identity of the
word "glory" in the three passages is not sufficient to
explain their association, because many passages with a
greater degree of verbal similarity could have been adduced
if anything like so mechanical a principle governed the
interpretative procedure of the midrash.   The real point of
departure for this midrash is the meaning of "glory", not
merely the use of the word in this particular text.   The
principle here is thematic, while the citation of Isaiah is
only incidentally important as a support for the basic theme.
As a text, Isaiah 24.23 is not significantly coherent with
Exodus 33.18, verbal similarity aside; their association
depends on the acknowledgement that the two verses illuminate
the same theme in their different ways.   Leviticus Rabbah 11.8
also instances thematic midrash, although here "elders",
together with "glory", is the catchword.   As we saw, Isaiah
24.23 is applied uniquely to the world to come, and as a result
it becomes the centre of gravity in the midrash.   Attention to
details in the Hebrew text - again, including elements which
the Targum and the Septuagint explain away - constitutes the
point of departure for the views mentioned.

In the case of Qohelet Rabbah 1.2 the thematic component
("vanities") is provided by the base text, Ecclesiastes.   Here
again, however, the term is applied in a new way as the midrash
runs its course; as a result, it refers to the creation itself
as transient in its components.   The sophistication of this
midrash lies in the consistent connection of the "vanities" to
the days of creation, but the citation of Isaiah 24.23 is
purely incidental.   The application of the verse in Pesahim 68a
(and Sanhedrin 91b) is of a different order, in that it is

applied in itself to a specific aspect of eschatology. The
midrash proceeds on the supposition that Isaiah 24.23 and
30.26 in some way relate to the world to come, and distinguishes
between their particular points of reference within that
understanding. The assumption that the texts are thematically
similar is antecedent to the task of sorting out their
relationship to one another. The text here is held immediately
to illustrate the theme; it is not incidental to the theme,
nor does the theme depend upon it as completely as it does in
Leviticus Rabbah 11.8. Similarly, the midrash from Tanḥuma
קדושים 1.1-7 illustrates the theme of the order of the world
to come with its citations; the fact that Isaiah 24.23 is not
among them suggests that the innovative idea here expressed
was not thought to be in full accord with the meaning usually
associated with this verse. Baba Bathra 10b provides us with
a classic instance in which scripture is cited incidentally,
in order to introduce a theme which is then developed by means
of haggadah.

        The range of the varieties of midrash is startling, as
even our limited selection has shown. We have observed
translational interpretation (by verbal expansion, as in the
Targum, and by the transformation of words, phrases and
clauses, as in the Septuagint), thematic midrash (in which the
citation is incidental, as in Exodus Rabbah 45.5; Qohelet
Rabbah 1.2, central, as in Leviticus Rabbah 11.8, and
illustrative, as in Pesaḥim 68a and Sanhedrin 91b), and
haggadic midrash (Baba Bathra 10b). The way in which scripture
is cited in a midrash, the place it occupies within the
interpretation, and its relative importance therein are all
largely determined by the genre of midrash in question.
Curiously, peshat rendering is no guarantee of verbatim
citation; although the scripture is here coextensive with the
interpretation and is its centre of gravity, the words used
are meant to convey the very sense the text is thought to have.
In the case of thematic midrash, or darash proper, the words
of scripture might be cited very much more accurately than they
are in a peshat treatment. Even in the case of an incidentally
cited scripture within a thematic midrash, the verbal and
substantive pertinence of the passage is demonstrated by
precise quotation, and this is also the case in our example
of haggadic midrash. In those instances in which the passage
is held illustratively to express the very theme which is at
issue, its exact wording will obviously be crucial to the
investigation of that theme. The same observation obtains in

instances in which the passage is more than illustrative, but occupies the centre of attention to such an extent that it governs the theme treated of, rather than merely affirming or illustrating it. Verbatim citation is therefore characteristic of thematic (and haggadic) midrash. The weight placed on the words cited depends on the place of the scripture in the midrash, incidental, illustrative or central.

If the varieties of the midrashim considered appears bewildering, it is perhaps comforting to consider the substantial continuity in their theological tendencies. An essentially eschatological understanding of Isaiah 24.23 is common to the interpretations we have surveyed. The eschatological perspective is developed in a distinctive way in each of the examples considered, but this development has never appeared to be a mere function of the form of the midrash to hand. The fact that both the Septuagint and the Targum represent peshat renderings in no way implies that their theological tendencies are identical. The Targum emphasizes the eschatological revelation on behalf of Israel, while the Septuagint much more strongly emphasizes the break-up of God's enemies in the face of his future reign. Curiously, a negative application of the imagery of Isaiah 24.23 also emerges in the thematic midrash contained in Qohelet Rabbah 1.2, apparently without any dependence on the Septuagint. Eschatological "glory" is the focus of our thematic midrashim generally. Exodus Rabbah 45.5 establishes the promise of glory to the righteous; Leviticus Rabbah 11.8 speaks of the glorious academy that is to come. The insistence in Pesahim 68a (cf. Sanhedrin 91b), however, is that Isaiah 24.23 is pertinent to the divine revelation itself. Baba Bathra 10b, a haggadic midrash, brings us back to the motif of the promise of glory to the elders which is dominant in the thematic midrashim considered. The thematic midrash from Tanḥuma, although its motif is a further development of thinking instanced in the thematic midrashim generally, gives no citation of Isaiah 24.23, apparently because its claim about the hierarchy of the world to come represented a bolder assertion than was usually made in connection with that verse. Essentially, then, the tendencies conventionally associated with the interpretation of the verse exercised some control on the development of the midrashim which cite it. Theoretically and formally, there was much more diversity in rabbinic interpretation than was theologically (and therefore practically) possible.

Our brief survey cannot, of course, be used to justify
the promulgation of a comprehensive definition of midrash. The
hope is merely that it has served to introduce midrash as a
species of theological discourse. The varieties we have
isolated have all evidenced the importance in rabbinic midrash
of citing scripture in a precise way for the purposes of
interpretation. In the case of peshat renderings, this involved
offering interpretations which were held to be coextensive with
the text, while verbatim quotation is preferred in thematic and
haggadic midrashim, even when scripture is only referred to
incidentally. Indeed, the more developed the midrash, the more
important it becomes to specify the biblical foundation on
which it is constructed. It is particularly noticeable that
in darash interpretations (that is, thematic midrashim)
innovative claims require the most explicit scriptural backing
and the most involved linguistic discussion. Another variable
which determines how a text is treated, however, is its
relationship to the overall assertion which is made in the
midrash. But the formal varieties of the midrashim represent
only one perspective on their development; another is their
theological tendencies. The tendencies appear to transcend
the formal varieties, in the sense that the same or similar
assertions can be made within quite different midrashic genres.
"Midrash", in a word, refers not only to a series of possible
operations on the explicitly cited biblical text, but also
(and at the same time) to the use of that text among the rabbis
in order to express ideas which, they held, God intended the
community and her elders to attend to.

In respect of New Testament exegesis, the most obvious
analogy among the midrashic genres we have discussed is with
haggadic midrash. In this case, the theological tendency of
an interpretation is spelled out by means of narrative. Some
time ago, it was pointed out that the Transfiguration shares
certain key elements with the story recounted in Exodus 24 of
Moses ascending Sinai with Aaron, Nadab and Abihu /25/. The
select group in Exodus have a divine vision (v. 10), and later
in the story there is reference to a cloud (v. 15), glory (v.
16) and a period of six days (v. 16). The actual mention of
Moses in the Transfiguration narrative constitutes another
possible connection with Exodus 24, and the mention of Elijah
might put one in mind of the revelation on Horeb which is
described in 1 Kings 19. When such evidence (a sample of that
presented in the article cited in n. 25) is taken into account,
it seems apparent there is a certain relationship between the

Transfiguration and the Sinai narrative. Does the phrase "a
certain relationship" commit us to saying that the
Transfiguration is a "midrash" on Exodus 24? Within the
terms of reference we have developed in this paper, one would
have to reply negatively to this question. Citation of and/or
comment upon the scripture is simply not a part of the
Transfiguration. What we are dealing with are allusions which
give the account tone and colour, and the account in itself is
obviously of more importance to the narrator than the allusion.
In this sense, the narrative should be seen as an example of
haggadah. That is, the story is a vehicle of theological ideas,
and does not depend on midrash to make its point. ("Haggadah",
of course, is a literary category, and its application implies
nothing in respect of historicity.) There is a certain
similarity between the Transfiguration and the haggadah related
to Isaiah 24.23 in Baba Bathra 10b. Both stories, in themselves,
convey definite theological claims by narrative means (and both
pursue those claims in the discussions which follow the
narratives proper in the stories as we have them). But the
account in Baba Bathra is expressly related to a biblical text,
while the Transfiguration is not. For this reason, while we
have classed the rabbinic passage in the category of haggadic
midrash, we must call the Transfiguration midrashic haggadah,
because the story is the primary vehicle of the ideas involved,
while scripture is used in a subsidiary manner.

If "midrash" is understood as it was developed by the
rabbis, the term will have to be applied with some reserve in
the study of the New Testament. Much that has been called
"midrash" (or, less cautiously, "Midrash") can only be called
"midrashic" because - as in the case of the Transfiguration -
terms and images borrowed from the Old Testament are used to
colour the presentation of haggadoth without serving as
occasions for comment. The distinction between the words
"midrash" and "midrashic" is an important one for the present
discussion. The noun, as applied to the New Testament, implies
that the Evangelists and their predecessors felt themselves
free to develop such theological ideas as appealed to them
with reference to biblical texts. As we have seen, midrash is
a form of active theological thinking; in the hands of the
rabbis, scripture was a part of discourse about God, and not
simply the object of exegesis or interpretation. There are
many cases in the New Testament in which Old Testament texts
are cited and applied in this way /26/. But when the language
and imagery of the New Testament accounts seem to allude to the

Old Testament without making anything of the allusion, we had
better make it clear that we are not dealing with "midrash" in the
proper sense of the word, but with a "midrashic" style of narration

Narratives such as the Transfiguration present us with
haggadoth with midrashic elements, and it would be a
potentially fruitful investigation to see whether Rabbinica
presents precise analogies of the genre. Haggadoth can be
found in the so-called narrative Midrashim, but here the
connection with the biblical text is often even more tenuous
than in the midrashic haggadoth of the New Testament. Because
the narrative Midrashim are presented as re-written Bibles, we
naturally think of their fresh material as related to the
Old Testament text, even though its only substantive association
may be the name of the hero in a given haggadah (or something
even more slender). In the case of such narratives as the
Transfiguration, however, it is the substance of the story, not
its literary setting, which reminds us of Exodus 24. It is
nonetheless striking that the narrative Midrashim seem to
approach the genre of some New Testament passages, and this
similarity underlines the principal finding that "midrash" in
the formal sense ought to be used more carefully in New
Testament study.

Previous discussion of midrash has been hampered by a
tendency to posit a single, all-inclusive model which might be
attributed to Rabbinica and the New Testament generally. The
present contribution is an initial attempt to describe the
various ways the Old Testament might be cited according to the
context and function of the passage in which the citation
appears. The examples of translational interpretation, thematic
midrash and haggadic midrash here offered are only a selection
from a much larger catalogue (cf. n. 4). Fortunately, the
importance of the literary function of midrash has been
increasingly realized in recent discussion /27/, although a
commonly agreed scheme of categorization has yet to emerge.
For this reason, the categories here developed must be regarded
as provisional. Nonetheless, the basic phenomenon of midrash
as a means of discourse about God rooted in the biblical text is
today more and more widely recognized, and the distinction of
midrash from haggadah better appreciated. Hybrid categories such
as midrashic haggadah /28/, however illuminating they might be
for the understanding of the New Testament, require further
investigation.

Notes

/1/ For discussion of these issues, cf. A. Wünsche,
"Einleitung in der Midrasch Rabbot im Allgemeinen" in: *Der
Midrasch Kohelet zum ersten Male ins Deutsche übertragen*
(Leipzig: Schulze, 1880); H.L. Strack, *Einleitung in Talmud
und Midrasch* (Mit einem Vorwort und einem bibliographischen
Anhang von Günther Steinberger) (München: Beck, 1976[6]) and
the English translation (New York: Atheneum, 1972); R. Bloch
(tr. W.S. Green and W.J. Sullivan), "Methodological Notes for
the Study of Rabbinic Literature" in: W.S. Green (ed.),
Approaches to Ancient Judaism: Theory and Practice. Brown
Judaic Studies 1 (Missoula: Scholars, 1978) 29-50 (from
RSR 43 [1955] 194-227); Bloch (tr. M.H. Callaway), "Midrash"
in: Green, *Approaches to Ancient Judaism: Theory and Practice*,
29-50 (from *Supplément au Dictionnaire de la Bible* 5 [Paris,
1957] col. 1263-1281); G. Vermes, *Scripture and Tradition in
Judaism: Haggadic Studies*. Studia Post-Biblica (Leiden: Brill,
1961 and 1973); R. Le Déaut, *Introduction à la Littérature
Targumique: Première partie* (Rome: Institut Biblique
Pontifical, 1966); A.G. Wright, *The Literary Genre Midrash*
(Staten Island: Alba House, 1967); J. Bowker, *The Targums and
Rabbinic Literature: An Introduction to Jewish Interpretations
of Scripture* (Cambridge: C.U.P., 1969); R. Le Déaut, "Apropos
a Definition of Midrash" in: *Interpretation* 25 (1971) 259-282;
M.P. Miller, "Targum, Midrash and the Use of the Old Testament
in the New Testament" *JSJ* 2 (1971) 29-82; D. Patte, *Early
Jewish Hermeneutic in Palestine*. S.B.L.D.S. 22 (Missoula:
Scholars Press, 1975); J. Weingreen, *From Bible to Mishnah: The
continuity of tradition* (Edinburgh: Manchester University Press,
1976); M.P. Miller, "Midrash" in: K. Crim (ed.), *The
Interpreter's Dictionary of the Bible*.   Supplementary Volume
(Nashville: Abingdon, 1976) 593-597; E.E. Ellis, "Midrash,
Targum and the New Testament Quotations" in: *Prophecy and
Hermeneutic in Early Christianity* (Grand Rapids: Eerdmans,
1978) 188-197.
/2/ Cf. A.J. Saldarini, "'Form Criticism' of Rabbinic
Literature" in: *JBL* 96 (1977) 257-274.
/3/ Such Midrashim are commonly styled as Tannaitic, but this
characterization refers to their provenience, which is
contestable (cf. B.Z. Wacholder, "The Date of the Mekilta
de-Rabbi Ishmael" in: *HUCA* 39 (1968) 117-194), not to their
general function, which is the proper focus of an initial
designation.

/4/ For editions of the works cited incidentally, cf. B.D.
Chilton, *The Glory of Israel: The Theology and Provenience of
the Isaiah Targum*. J.S.O.T.S. 23 (Sheffield: JSOT, 1982).
Such works are mentioned here only by way of example, so that
an extended citation of them would not be justified.
/5/ The works cited in n. 1, especially those by Bloch,
Vermes, Le Deaut and Weingreen, amply justify this point.
Cf. J. Mann, *The Bible as Read and Preached in the Old
Synagogue* (Cincinnati: 1940).
/6/ Cf. I. Chernus, "On the History of a Pericope in Midrash
Tanḥuma" in *JSJ* 11 (1980) 53-65.
/7/ Cf. Strack, *Einleitung* (1972), 93-98; H.G. Enelow, *The
Mishnah of Rabbi Eliezer or The Midrash of Thirty-Two
Hermeneutical Rules* (New York: The Jewish Publication Society
of America, 1933); A. Finkel, *The Pharisees and the Teacher of
Nazareth*. Arbeiten zur Geschichte des Spätjudentums und
Urchristentums (Leiden: Brill, 1964) 123-128; Miller,
"Midrash", 595.
/8/ Cf. H.A. Fischel, *Rabbinic Literature and Greco-Roman
Philosophy*. Studia Post-Biblica 21 (Leiden: Brill, 1973).
/9/ For a discussion of the composition history of the Targum,
cf. Chilton, *The Glory* (1982).
/10/ Cf. R. Kittel (and P. Kahle), *Biblia Hebraica* (Stuttgart:
Württembergische Bibelanstalt, 1937).
/11/ Cf. A. Sperber, *The Bible in Aramaic III* (Leiden: Brill,
1962); J.F. Stenning, *The Targum of Isaiah* (Oxford: Clarendon,
1949).   Martin McNamara, in a private communication, has
informed me of his project with an international board of
editors to provide an English edition of all extant Targums,
and I have agreed to prepare the Isaiah Targum for the series,
which is to be published by Michael Glazier in Delaware over
the next few years.
/12/ Cf. G. Dalman (tr. D.M. Kay), *The Words of Jesus*
(Edinburgh: Clark, 1902) 97; G.F. Moore, *Judaism in the First
Centuries of the Christian Era II* (Cambridge: Harvard U.P.,
1927) 374.
/13/ Cf. B.D. Chilton, "Regnum Dei Deus Est" in: *SJT* 31 (1978)
261-270; K. Koch, "Offenbaren wird sich das Reich Gottes" in:
NTS 25 (1979) 158-165; B.D. Chilton, *God in Strength: Jesus'
Announcement of the Kingdom*. Studien zum Neuen Testament und
seiner Umwelt (Monographien) 1 (Freistadt: Plöchl, 1979);
Chilton, *The Glory*.
/14/ Cf. J. Ziegler, *Isaias. Septuaginta Vetus Testamentum
Graecum Auctoritate Academiae Litterarum Gottingensis editum 14*
(Göttingen: Vandenhoeck und Ruprecht, 1967).   Cf. H.B. Swete,

The Old Testament in Greek according to the Septuagint
(Cambridge: CUP, 1905) for a preference for the reading of
other prepositions.
/15/   F. Wutz, *Systematische Wege von der Septuaginta zum
hebräischen Urtext* (Stuttgart: Kohlhammer, 1937) 839.   Cf.
A. van der Kooij, *Die alten Textzeugen des Jesajabuches*.
Orbis Biblicus et Orientalis 35 (Göttingen: Vandenhoeck und
Ruprecht, 1981) 22-73.
/16/   Cf. the Hebrew editions published by Lewin-Epstein in
Jerusalem (1925), and by Javneh in Tel-Aviv under the
editorship of Mirqin (1960);   A. Wünsche, *Der Midrasch Schemot
Rabba*.   Bibliotheca Rabbinica (Leipzig: Schulze, 1882);
S.M. Lehrmann, "Exodus" in: H. Freedman and M. Simon, *Midrash
Rabbah* (London: Soncino, 1939).
/17/   Cf. Lewin-Epstein (1925) and Mirqin (1962);   Wünsche,
Der Midrasch Wajikra Rabba;   and, in the Soncino translation,
J. Israelstam and J.J. Slotki.
/18/   Cf. the offset publication of the Wilna edition by פאר
תורה in Jerusalem; Wünsche, *Der Midrasch Koheleth*;   and
A. Cohen in the Soncino translation.
/19/   Cf. L. Goldsmith, *Der babylonische Talmud II: Erubin,
Pesaḥim, Joma* (Berlin: Harz, 1925) and *Der babylonische Talmud
neu übertragen: Erubin, Pesaḥim, Šeqalim* (Berlin: Jüdischer
Verlag, 1930);   H. Freedman, "Pesahim" in: I. Epstein (ed.),
The Babylonian Talmud (London: Soncino, 1938), and in the
Hebrew-English edition (1967).
/20/   Cf. A.M. Goldberg, *Untersuchungen über die Vorstellung
von der Schekinah in der frühen rabbinischen Literatur -
Talmud und Midrasch -*.   Studia Judaica 5 (Berlin: de Gruyter,
1969).   The conception of the Shekhinah in the passage seems
rather sophisticated.   Normally, the divine presence was seen
as consistently with Israel, even in exile (cf. Targum Isaiah
43.14; Exodus Rabbah 15.16;   23.5;   Leviticus Rabbah 32.8;
Numbers Rabbah 7.10;   Lamentations Rabbah 1.19-20 par. 54;
Song of Songs Rabbah 4.8.1;   Megillah 29a;   jer. Taanith 1.1;
Pesiqta Rabbati 8.4;   28.2;   29/30.1;   32.2.
/21/   Cf. Goldschmidt, *Der babylonische Talmud* VII (1925), and
his revised translation (1935);   J. Shachter and H. Freedman
in the Soncino translation (1935).   It should be noted that
the reading of גלות for מלכיות in the Hebrew-English edition
(1969) is inferior.   Here, as elsewhere, Goldschmidt's text
appears to be more soundly based than the Wilna edition,
which is the foundation of the Soncino project.
/22/   Cf. Goldschmidt, *Der babylonische Talmud* VI (1906), and
his revised translation (1933);   M. Simon and I.W. Slotki in

the Soncino translation (1935), and in the diglot edition
(1976).

/23/ Cf. P. Schäfer, "The Causes of the Bar Kokhba Revolt" in:
*Studies in Aggadah, Targum and Jewish Liturgy in Memory of
Joseph Heinemann* (Jerusalem: Magnes, 1981).

/24/ Cf. S. Buber, *Midrasch Tanchuma. Ein Agadischer
Commentar zum Pentateuch von Rabbi Tanchuma ben Rabbi Abba*
(Wilna: Rome, 1885).

/25/ "The Transfiguration: Dominical Assurance and Apostolic
Vision" in: *NTS* 27 (1980) 115-124.

/26/ Cf. B. Lindars, "The Place of the Old Testament in the
Formation of New Testament Theology" in: *NTS* 23 (1976) 59-66.

/27/ Cf. L.H. Silberman, "Toward a Rhetoric of Midrash: A
Preliminary Account" in: R. Polzin and E. Rothman (eds.),
Biblical Mosaic. Changing Perspectives (Chico: Scholars,
1982) 15-26.

/28/ Cf. B. Gerhardsson (tr. J. Toy), *The Testing of God's
Son (Matt. 4:1-11 & PAR): An Analysis of an Early Christian
Midrash* (Lund: Gleerup, 1966) 11, for the misleading category
"haggadic midrash".   Gerhardsson does not give instances of
the category, and on the same page he refers to "midrash" and
"haggadah" as if they were more or less the same thing.
Actually, his analysis makes it quite plain that the Temptation
is haggadah with midrashic elements.

THE LIBER ANTIQUITATUM BIBLICARUM OF PSEUDO-PHILO AND THE GOSPELS AS 'MIDRASH'

Richard Bauckham,
Faculty of Theology,
University of Manchester,
Manchester M13 9PL

1. Introduction

The *Liber Antiquitatum Biblicarum* (henceforth LAB) is an example of the genre of 'midrashic'/1/ writings which is sometimes called 'the rewritten Bible', a genre which also includes Jubilees, the Genesis Apocryphon, and Josephus' Jewish Antiquities. The majority of scholars have dated it in the period 70-135 A.D.,/2/ and within this period most have opted for the late first century. Recently Harrington/3/ and Bogaert/4/ have argued for a pre-70 date, and Zeron/5/ has challenged the consensus with a proposal for a date in the third century A.D. or even later. On the whole, however, the case for a late first century date/6/ still seems to have the best of the argument. It is widely agreed that LAB is a Palestinian work written originally in Hebrew, though now extant only in Latin./7/ In its present form it covers the period from Adam to the death of Saul, though it is uncertain whether it originally ended at that point. The biblical text, while sometimes followed quite closely in the manner of the Targumim, is usually rewritten, interpreted, summarized and expanded in a very free fashion. A great deal of the material in LAB is additional to the biblical narrative, and much of this paper will be concerned with the nature of these additions and the way in which they have been developed from the biblical text.

The attention which Pseudo-Philo gives to the biblical narrative varies considerably: some parts of the history are treated very summarily, other parts are retold with a great deal of 'midrashic' expansion. The period of the Judges receives especially detailed treatment. The reasons for this selectivity are not easy to determine. It may be that Pseudo-Philo was deliberately supplementing other collections of

'midrashic' material in which the periods of the patriarchs and
the Exodus were already well treated (cf. Jubilees and the
Genesis Apocryphon). Or it may have been primarily his
conviction of the relevance of the history of the Judges for
his contemporaries (see section 2.11 below) which led him to
give so much attention to that part of his period.

Another basic question about the nature of LAB is whether
Pseudo-Philo intended his work as a commentary on the biblical
text, to be read alongside Scripture, or as an independent
narrative, which could in a sense replace the biblical
narrative. The former interpretation is much the more
probable, because Pseudo-Philo constantly presupposes his
readers' knowledge of biblical material which he does not
himself reproduce. It is his habit to omit quite major events
(such as the sacrifice of Isaac) from his own narrative, but
then to refer allusively to these events in other contexts
(e.g. LAB 40:2). Thus, although Pseudo-Philo's work is not
written in the form of text and commentary, and although he is
not interested in making plain the exegetical work by means of
which his material has been derived from the biblical text, LAB
must be regarded as a kind of commentary on the biblical text.

If we follow the usual dating of LAB, it is contemporary
with the Gospels, and this in itself should give it considerable
significance for comparative purposes. It and Josephus'
Antiquities provide the two major examples, from the same period
as the Gospels, of how Palestinian Jews used the Old Testament
in writing the history of Old Testament times. It is therefore
surprising that hardly any attention has been given to LAB in
discussions of 'midrash' in the Gospels./8/ Comparisons of the
Evangelists' narrative technique with that of Chronicles/9/ or
with the rabbinic Midrashim have their usefulness, but they are
not the obvious comparisons to make when there is
contemporaneous material ready to hand. The conviction which
lies behind this paper is that discussion of 'midrash' in the
Gospels is frequently too undisciplined, and needs to be
controlled by careful analysis of comparable Jewish literature
and by insistence on the drawing of precise analogies between
the literary techniques of this literature and those which the
Evangelists are alleged to have used. This paper cannot be
more than a first step towards this in the case of LAB, but it
should be regarded as an exploratory study, needing to be
followed up by others. In the following sections (2-5) we
shall give most attention to those aspects of LAB which are
likely to be of most importance in comparing LAB with the

Gospels, and in the final section we shall make some preliminary observations on that comparison.

2.   Types of Midrashic Material in LAB

The wealth of additional material with which Pseudo-Philo expands and develops the biblical text can be divided into several categories. The following is not an exhaustive list of such categories, but is intended to draw attention to the principal ones.

2.1.   Names and Genealogies

It is very characteristic of LAB to give names to characters who are anonymous in the Bible: Cain's wife is called Themech/10/ (LAB 2:1-2), Sisera's mother is also called Themech (31:8), the king of the Ammonites (Judg 11:12) is Getal (LAB 39: 8), Jephthah's daughter is Seila (40:1), Samson's mother is Eluma daughter of Remac (42:1), the Levite and his host (Judg 19) are Beel and Bethac (45:2), the witch of Endor is Sedecla (64:3). All that LAB 1 adds to the biblical narrative (Gen 5) are the names of all the sons and daughters of each of the patriarchs from Adam to Noah. Caleb, Joshua and Manoah all have full genealogies created for them (15:3; 42:1; apparently Pseudo-Philo ignores the genealogies of Caleb and Joshua in Chronicles). Sometimes anonymous figures are identified as well-known biblical characters: the anonymous Benjaminite of 1 Sam 4:12 is Saul (LAB 54:3); the mother of Micah is Delilah (LAB 44:2). Sometimes two biblical characters are identified: Sarah is Iscah (Gen 11:29)/11/ (LAB 23:4); Ruth's sister Orpah is 'Haraphah' (i.e. 'the giant') the mother of Goliath and his brothers (1 Sam 21:16-22)/12/ (LAB 61:6). The most remarkable of these identifications is that between Phinehas and Elijah (LAB 48:1)./13/ Other relationships between biblical characters are created: Dinah marries Job (LAB 8:8); the Amalekite who kills Saul is Edab the son of Agag (LAB 65:4; cf. 58:3-4).

All these procedures are typical of haggadic midrash. The invention of names, in particular, poses for us, in perhaps its most acute form, the problem of understanding the psychology and intentions of those who created this kind of midrashic material (and in the case of the non-biblical names in LAB we may well be dealing largely with inventions by Pseudo-Philo himself: see section 5 below). What kind of 'historical' value could they have imagined attached to such names? It is possible to begin to understand a great deal of haggadic midrash by

comparing it with the hypotheses and reconstructions which the
modern historian produces. In the attempt to explain
difficulties in the biblical text or to answer questions which
the text suggested to them, the ancient Jewish exegetes used
their imagination. The methods by which they directed and
controlled their imagination and the kinds of explanations which
seemed plausible to them differ greatly from the methods and
hypotheses to which modern historians (including biblical
scholars!) will resort to explain their evidence, but the degree
of imagination used was not necessarily greater. Moreover, the
way in which flights of fancy became accepted exegetical
tradition (without being accorded the same degree of certainty
as the biblical text itself) is not unlike the way in which
highly speculative historical hypotheses in, say, Old Testament
scholarship can come to carry the weight of scholarly
tradition. The analogy should warn us against the assumption
that haggadah was not really concerned with history./14/ It
might be nearer the truth to regard it as a quite different
method of 'historical research' from ours. However, the
difference in the method appears nowhere more obviously than in
the invention of non-biblical names.

The question 'What was his name?' was one of the questions
which occurred naturally to readers and hearers of the biblical
narrative, as it does in all storytelling situations. It
continued to occur to those who studied the Bible until
relatively modern times: medieval Christendom had its own
haggadic traditions about the names of anonymous characters in
the Gospels. The modern biblical scholar has learned to regard
this question as normally unanswerable (though we still ask
about the identity of the beloved disciple and the author of
Hebrews) and, perhaps more importantly, uninteresting (since the
general tendency to ask and answer unanswerable questions about
the Bible persists in biblical scholarship!). The ancient
Jewish exegete could not leave an interesting question
unanswered. If the anonymous figure could be identified with
a named biblical character, well and good. If not, perhaps an
appropriate name could be devised./15/ Finally, in the last
resort the only course was random invention (which seems to be
the case with most non-biblical names in LAB)./16/

2.2. Explanations of problems in the biblical narrative
A great many of LAB's additions to the biblical account are
attempts to explain some problem which the latter seems to
raise. For example, LAB 10:4 inserts a prayer of Moses, not in

the biblical account, because God's words to Moses in Exod 14: 15 (=LAB 10:5) seem to presuppose that Moses is praying. The account in LAB 16:4 of how Korah's sons refused to join his revolt is added to the biblical narrative to explain why, according to Num 26:11, the sons of Korah did not die in the judgment of Korah. In LAB 18:2 a story of Balaam's previous activity, before he appears in the biblical narrative, explains how Balak appears to be already familiar with the efficacy of Balaam's curse (Num 22:6). God's speech in LAB 36:4 explains why Gideon was not punished for his idolatry, a fact which would otherwise be a serious problem in Pseudo-Philo's theological interpretation of history. A similar theological problem is solved by LAB 45:3, which explains that the brutal death of the Levite's concubine was the just reward for her sin, because she had been unfaithful to her husband in a peculiarly reprehensible way - with Amalekites. The puzzling fact that in 1 Sam 17:55-58 neither Saul nor Abner know who David is (which drives modern scholarship to source analysis) LAB 61:9 explains by reference to angelic intervention. LAB 64:1 supplies a motive for Saul's tough measures against witchcraft (1 Sam 28: 3), given that Saul, at this stage of his career, cannot have been acting out of zeal for God's Law. Many other examples could easily be given (see also section 3.10).

2.3. Interpretations of the biblical narrative

Some additions to the biblical narrative function to give it a particular kind of interpretation. For example, the account of the family of Lamech in Gen 4:17-24 seems a relatively neutral account of the beginnings of civilization; Pseudo-Philo's additions (LAB 2:6-10) specify the evil use to which the inventions were put and interpret Lamech's song in a strongly adverse way. He has thus interpreted the material as an account of the corruption of the world under the influence of Cain's descendants, an interpretation which derives from reading Gen 4:17-24 in the light of its sequel in Gen 6 (a rewriting of which immediately follows in LAB): cf. section 2.5 below. He must have seen his additions as making explicit what is implicit in the biblical account.

At many points in LAB, prophecies and divine speeches, added to the biblical narrative, function to give theological interpretations to the narrative (e.g. 44:6-10; 45:6; 47:3-8; 49:7-8).

2.4. Corrections of the biblical narrative

Pseudo-Philo is prepared, on occasions, to do more than add
interpretations to the biblical narratives. Sometimes, usually
for theological reasons, he changes the storyline in a way which
really contradicts the Bible. The story of Josh 22 is
drastically rewritten in LAB 22, and even greater liberties are
taken with Judg 17-21 in LAB 44-48. A minor, non-theological,
example of the correction of biblical narrative occurs in LAB
31:3, where the statement that Sisera fled on his horse
contrasts with the repeated information in Judges (4:15,17)
that he fled on foot. The reason for this correction is not
clear, unless it arises from understanding Judg 5:22 as a
reference to Sisera's flight.

2.5. Connexions between adjacent accounts

A common midrashic principle is that there ought to be a
real historical connexion between events recounted consecutively
in the Bible./17/ Thus, because the law of the fringes is given
in Num 15:37-41, immediately before the story of Korah's revolt
in Num 16, it becomes in LAB 16:1 the actual occasion for the
revolt. The two distinct stories of Micah (Judg 17-18) and the
Levite's concubine and the Benjaminites (Judg 19-21) are brought
into a causal connexion in LAB 44-48. LAB 64:2 finds a causal
link between the death of Samuel (1 Sam 28:3) and the
Philistine attack on Israel (1 Sam 28:4). (For other examples,
see sections 3.2, 3.15.4 (i).)

2.6. Word-play

Some midrashic developments result from punning
interpretations of words in the biblical text. When Balaam is
called 'the interpreter of dreams' (LAB 18:2), the description
reflects a common interpretation of פתר (Pethor) in Num 22:5.
/18/ An interpretation of 'Ur' in Gen 11:31; 15:7 as 'fire'
lies behind the story of Abraham in the fiery furnace (see
section 3.2), and an interpretation of 'Kamon' (Judg 10:5) as
'furnace' lies behind the story of Jair's fiery furnace (see
section 3.12).

2.7. Rewritten speeches and conversations

Like Josephus, Pseudo-Philo rarely reproduces biblical
speech material *verbatim*, as a glance through James'
translation, which prints most *verbatim* quotes from the Bible
in italics, will quickly show. Sometimes he gives quite a
close summary (LAB 3:4; 22:3-4), sometimes he expands in the
manner of the Targumim (3:9; 7:2). Most often, he simply
writes quite freely in his own way a substitute for the biblical

speech or conversation (e.g. LAB 10:2 (cf. Exod 10:11-12); LAB 15:5-7 (cf. Num 14:11-19); LAB 31:1 (cf. Judg 4:6-7,9)). Even for major poetic passages (the prophecies of Balaam, the song of Deborah, the song of Hannah) Pseudo-Philo substitutes fresh compositions which make only rare contact with their biblical models (LAB 18:10-12; 32; 51:3-6).

In contrast to this habitual freedom, the treatment of the Decalogue (LAB 11:6-13), which is the only section of the Law which Pseudo-Philo quotes, should be noticed. Though it has some odd features (omission of Exod 20:3; reversal of the order of Exod 20:13 and 14) it reproduces for the most part the words of Exod 20:1-17, but adds quite extensive interpretative material./19/

2.8. Didactic speeches
As well as rewriting biblical speeches, Pseudo-Philo adds a considerable number of quite fresh speeches. He is especially fond of didactic addresses by the leaders of Israel to the people, and prominent among these are farewell speeches (LAB 28:1-2; 29:4; 33:1-5; also 19:2-5; 23:1-24:3, which are substituted for biblical examples). These belong to the genre of the 'testament' which was so popular in the intertestamental and New Testament periods. The principle involved in the composition of such speeches attributed to historical figures was, of course, that they should be historically appropriate: what the figure might be expected to have said.

2.9. Psalms and lamentations
As well as the substitutes for the songs of Deborah and Hannah, there are several poetic compositions which correspond to nothing in the biblical text (except that the text provides their occasion). There is the beautiful lament of Jephthah's daughter (40:5-7), and there are two new psalms of David (59:4; 60:2-3) and the brief laments for Joshua (24:6) and Deborah (33:6).

2.10. Apocalyptic revelations
In Pseudo-Philo's time it was common practice to attribute apocalyptic revelations to the great figures of the Old Testament, sometimes by finding hints of them in the biblical narrative. Thus, like many others, Pseudo-Philo finds in the revelation to Abraham in Gen 15 a revelation of heaven and hell and of the future course of the history of Israel (LAB 23:6-7). The vision of Kenaz (28:6-9) is also developed from a hint in

the biblical text (Judg 1:15; see 3.7 below), while the
revelation to Moses before his death (LAB 19:10-15) is attached
to the biblical information that God showed him the land (Deut
34:1; LAB 19:10). LAB also seems to include apocalyptic
revelations to Noah (13:8-10), though the text is obscure. It
is noteworthy that, with the exception of this last example,
Pseudo-Philo does not simply insert such revelations into the
biblical history but develops them out of some feature of the
biblical account which is interpreted as implying such a
revelation.

2.11. *Contemporization*
Naturally, Pseudo-Philo's interpretation of the biblical
text is influenced by his own historical context and his desire
to make the biblical narratives relevant to his readers. These
are likely, for example, to have influenced the selectivity and
emphases of Pseudo-Philo's version of the biblical history.
His interest in the Judges period and in the theme of national
leadership may be his reaction to the situation of Jewish
subjection to Rome in his own time./20/ Wadsworth plausibly
relates Pseudo-Philo's repeated emphasis on the threat of
idolatry to the presence of Gentile religions in the cities of
Palestine at the time of writing. The golden nymphs of the
Amorites (LAB 25:10) and the anthropomorphic and zoomorphic
idols which Micah made (44:5; cf. Judg 17:5) may be intended to
represent the kinds of images which Pseudo-Philo's
contemporaries would encounter./21/ A simple instance of
Pseudo-Philo's updating of the biblical text is LAB 44:2, where
he commutes Micah's money (Judg 17:2) into a suitable sum in
contemporary currency.

3.   Interpreting Scripture by Scripture

3.1. *Introduction*
In this section, we examine cases where the narrative in
LAB has been influenced by biblical passages other than those
which tell the story which Pseudo-Philo is actually retelling.
This will include instances where he is rewriting a biblical
narrative but adapts or expands it under the influence of other
biblical passages. It also includes instances where Pseudo-
Philo's story is not in the Bible at all, but where biblical
passages other than the biblical context into which he has
inserted the story have influenced the creation of the story.
The discussion does not exhaust all such instances, but
includes, I hope, most significant ones and is certainly
representative of the range of such material in LAB. The

detailed treatment in this section corresponds to its importance
for the discussion of 'midrash' in the Gospels.

One of the most prominent characteristics of Pseudo-Philo's
work is the way he constantly draws attention to the parallels
between biblical events, usually by the device of speeches which
recall earlier events in the context of later events. Thus, for
example, Jephthah's daughter Seila, faced with death in
fulfilment of her father's vow, recalls the precedent of the
sacrifice of Isaac (LAB 40:2). Samuel, avowing that he has not
robbed or wronged any of the people, recalls the very similar
protest of Moses against the accusations of Korah and his
company (LAB 57:2; cf. 1 Sam 12:3; Num 16:15). A list of such
comparisons in LAB would be very long. The presupposition
behind this practice must be that there is a consistency about
God's acts in the history of his people, so that similar
situations and events constantly recur. One of the exegete's
tasks is therefore to be alert to these correspondences between
biblical narratives and point them out. We need to be open,
therefore, to the possibilities that this interest in the
parallels between biblical narratives may lead to the influence
of one narrative on another and may also lead to the creation of
fresh narratives by analogy with others.

3.2. Abraham in the fiery furnace
The story of Abraham's deliverance from the fire is one of
the most widely known haggadic traditions, but exists in various
forms. The account in LAB is fairly distinctive, though the
medieval Sefer ha-Yashar has a partially similar story./22/

All versions of the story depend on a typically midrashic
play on words (cf. 2.6 above), which interprets אור in Gen 11:28,
31; 15:7 as 'fire' rather than 'Ur'. This interpretation is
embodied in the Targumim (Tg.Neof. Gen 11:28,31; 15:17; Tg.Jon.
Gen 15:7: 'the furnace of fire of the Chaldeans'; Tg.Jon. Gen 11:
28 has a full account of Haran's death in the furnace; Tg.Jon.
Gen 11:31 preserves the simple pun: 'the fire of the Chaldeans';
so also Neh 9:7 Vulg.) and is presupposed in Jub. 12:12-14 and
Apoc.Abrah. 8. The fact that in these latter two passages the
fire is not a furnace into which Abraham is cast by his enemies,
but a fire which burns 'the house of the idols' (in Jubilees) or
Terah's house (in the Apocalypse of Abraham) shows that it is not
not the influence of Dan 3 but the pun itself which lies at the
root of all these traditions./23/ In Jubilees it is only Gen
11:28 which is interpreted by means of the pun (Haran dies in
the fire); in the Apocalypse of Abraham the use of the pun is

extended to Gen 11:31 (Abraham escapes the fire). It is
unlikely that the use of the pun originated from a desire to
explain Abraham's migration from Chaldea to Haran,/24/ since in
the earliest source, *Jubilees*, it is applied only to Gen 11:28,
not yet to Gen 11:31. Probably it was first used, as in
Jubilees, to explain Haran's death in Chaldea (Gen 11:28), and
this use then itself required a similar interpretation of Gen
11:31; 15:7. The pun was a stimulus to the midrashic
imagination to produce a story which would explain Haran's
death in and Abraham's escape from 'the fire of the Chaldeans'.
More than one such story arose. LAB belongs to the dominant
tradition of such stories, which includes the Targumim and
rabbinic tradition (*Gen.Rab*. 38:13; 44:13; *b.*^c*Erub*. 53a; *Pirqe
R.El*. 26;52), in which the fire was interpreted as a fiery
furnace.

In the interpretation of the fire as a furnace and in the
development of the particular story told in LAB 6, two main
factors have been at work:
(i) LAB connects Abraham's deliverance from the furnace with
the preparations for building the Tower of Babel. It is because
Abraham refuses to participate in the idolatrous preparation of
bricks for the Tower (LAB 6:2-4) that he is thrown into the
furnace, and the furnace is in fact the brick-kiln in which the
bricks for the Tower are burned (6:4-5,16). The story is thus
based on the principle of explaining adjacent biblical accounts
by reference to each other (see 2.5 above). Gen 11:3 implies a
furnace for burning the bricks, and the Targumim make this
explicit (*Tg.Neof*. Gen 11:3: 'Come let us make bricks and
throw them in a furnace', perhaps intending a connexion with
11:28,31, though a different word is used for 'furnace'). The
story in LAB therefore identifies this brick-kiln as the 'fire'
of Gen 11:31. Moreover, the connexion of the Tower with
idolatry was a well-established tradition (*Tg.Neof*. and *Jon*.
Gen 11:4; *Gen.Rab*. 38:8), which would link the story with
Abraham's well-known rejection of Chaldean idolatry (Jdt 5:7;
Jub. 12:1-14; Jos. *Ant*. 7:154-157). Thus the interpretation of
Gen 11:31 by reference to Gen 11:3-4 already gives rise to the
fundamental features of the story.
(ii) The story includes features derived from the story of
the three young men in the fiery furnace in Dan 3 (cf. LAB 6:
17a with Dan 3:22; LAB 6:17b with Dan 3:25,27). In fact, the
parallels with Dan 3 are not very close in LAB's version of the
story, but the thesis that Dan 3 has exercised some influence
is confirmed by other versions of the tradition which mention

the parallel explicitly (*Gen.Rab*. 44:13; *b.Pesaḥ*. 118a) and
conform the story more closely to Dan 3 (*Sefer ha-Yashar* 6-9;
/26/ note also the presence of an angel in the furnace in
medieval pictures of the scene/27/).   There is some reason to
suspect that the influence of Dan 3 on the tradition behind LAB
6 has been obscured by further developments in LAB 6.   In *Sefer
ha-Yashar* 8-9, as in Dan 3:22, only a small number of men,
those who throw Abraham into the furnace, are consumed by the
flames; the massive slaughter of all the bystanders in LAB 6:17
is in line with Pseudo-Philo's habitual exaggeration of
numbers.   In other versions of the story Nimrod plays the role
of Nebuchadnezzar in Dan 3 (*Gen.Rab*. 38:13; *b.ᶜErub*. 53a; *Tg.
Jon.* Gen 11:28; *Tg*. Chron 28:3; *Sefer ha-Yashar* 6-9).   In LAB 6,
he plays a relatively minor role (6:14) and Joktan, who is much
less like Nebuchadnezzar, steps into the foreground, probably
because the story of the escape of the eleven righteous men,
which is unique to LAB's account, required a custodian who would
secretly help them to escape.   Joktan's attitude to Abraham is
more like that of Darius in Dan 6 than that of Nebuchadnezzar
in Dan 3.

   In conclusion, we may say that although Dan 3 was an
important influence on the tradition of Abraham in the fiery
furnace, it was not the starting-point for the tradition, nor
the sole factor in the development of the tradition.   As far as
the version in LAB 6 goes, it is unlikely that Pseudo-Philo
himself (as distinct from the tradition he took up) made
deliberate use of Dan 3, and it is certain that the connexion
with Gen 11:3 has contributed more to his version of the story
than Dan 3 has.   It would be quite misleading to call LAB 6 'a
midrash on Dan 3'.

3.3.   The crossing of the Red Sea
LAB 10:5:   'God rebuked the sea and the sea was dried up.
The seas of waters stood upright, and the depths of the
earth appeared, and the foundations of the dwelling-place
(i.e. the world)/28/ were laid bare, at the blast of the
fear of God and at the blowing of the anger/29/ of my
Lord.'/30/

   This passage quotes Ps 106:9 ('he rebuked the Red Sea and
it became dry'); Exod 15:8 ('the floods stood up in a heap');
and then combines Exod 15:8 ('the deeps') with Ps 18:15 (= 2
Sam 22:16) ('the channels of the sea were seen, and the
foundations of the world were laid bare, at thy rebuke, O Lord,
at the blast of the breath of thy nostrils').   The use of Ps 18:

15 has probably been occasioned by the occurrence of the phrase
רוח אפיך ('breath of thy nostrils') in both Ex 15:8 and Ps 18:
15. The implication is probably that Ps 18:15 is considered to
be actually a description of the parting of the Red Sea./31/

   3.4.   The crossing of the Red Sea and the defeat of Sisera
   These two events are explicitly compared (as two
occasions when God employed the forces of nature to defeat
Israel's foes) in LAB 32:17. There are several points at which
it is possible that the two narratives have influenced each
other in Pseudo-Philo's versions of them.

   3.4.1.   Influence on LAB 10
   LAB 10:3: 'Then the children of Israel, considering the
   fear of that time, divided their opinions into three
   divisions of counsels (*in tres divisiones consiliorum
   diviserunt sententias suas*). For the tribe of Reuben and
   the tribe of Issachar and the tribe of Zebulun and the
   tribe of Simeon said, "Come, let us throw ourselves into
   the sea, for it is better for us to die in the water than
   to be slain by our enemies". But the tribe of Gad and the
   tribe of Asher and the tribe of Dan and the tribe of
   Naphtali said, "No, let us return with them, and if they
   are willing to give us our lives, we will be their slaves".
   But the tribe of Levi and the tribes of Judah and Joseph
   and the tribe of Benjamin said, "Certainly not. Let us
   take our weapons and fight them, for God will be with us".'

This passage should be compared with two other extant versions
of the tradition:/32/

   Memar Marqah 4:8: 'They were divided at the sea into
   three divisions. Each class made a statement and the
   great prophet made a reply corresponding to each
   statement.

      The first division said, "Let us ... go back to
   Egypt" (Num. XIV.4) "and let us serve the Egyptians ... for
   it would have been better for us ... than to die in the
   wilderness" (Ex. XIV.12; Targ.). The great prophet Moses
   said, "You shall never see them again" (Ex. XIV.13; Targ.).

      The second division said, "Let us flee from the
   Egyptians into the desert". The great prophet Moses said
   to them, "Stand firm and see the salvation of the Lord,
   which He will work for you today" (ibid. Targ.).

The third division said, "Let us arise and fight against the Egyptians". The great prophet Moses said to them, "The Lord will fight for you, and you have only to be still" (Ex. XIV.14)"./33/

Tg.Neof. Exod 14:13-14: 'The children of Israel were made into four groups at the time they were standing beside the Reed Sea. One said: Let us fall into the sea; and one said: Let us return to Egypt; and one said: Let us set battle-array against them; and one said: Let us shout out against them and confound them. To the group that said: Let us fall into the sea, Moses said: Fear not, stand prepared and see the redemption of the Lord which he does for you this day; and to the group that said: Let us return to Egypt, Moses said: Fear not, because as you have seen the Egyptians this day, you shall see them again no more in bondage for ever; and to the group that said: Let us set battle-array against them, Moses said: Fear not, the Lord himself works your battle-victories for you; and to the group that said: Let us shout against them and confound them, Moses said: Fear not; stand; be silent and give glory and praise and exaltation to our God.'/34/

Unlike LAB, the Samaritan tradition in *Memar Marqah* and the targumic tradition both record Moses' answers to the proposal of each group. These answers are drawn from Exod 14:13-14, divided into three answers in *Memar Marqah* (which like LAB has three groups of Israelites) or divided into four answers in the Targum (which has four groups). It might be suggested that LAB supplies an earlier form of the tradition which was only later elaborated by the addition of answers. In fact, however, it is clear that the three proposals in LAB have been composed in order to correspond to the three answers into which Exod 14:13-14 can be divided (13a, 13b, 14; retaining the biblical order of 13a and 13b, which *Memar Marqah* inverts). This correspondence can hardly be fortuitous. Thus LAB 10:3 presupposes the exegesis of Exod 14:13-14 which is found in the other two forms of the tradition, even though it does not record this exegesis. This is by no means the only occasion on which LAB fails to make explicit the exegetical origins of its haggadic traditions.

The tradition could have arisen *solely* from an ingenious exegesis of Exod 14:12-14, but it is likely that this exegesis was originally prompted by the influence of another text: Judg

5:15b,16b: 'In the divisions (בפלגות) of Reuben there were
great searchings of heart.'/35/ In this case, LAB 10:3 may
have preserved (in its opening sentence) the exegetical clue
which has vanished in the other forms of the tradition. The
'divisions of Reuben' have been taken to mean, not clans or
factions within the tribe of Reuben, but divisions of opinion
among the tribes, of which Reuben the firstborn heads the list.
(The division of the tribes into three groups then follows a
fairly obvious pattern: four of the Leah tribes; the Bilhah and
Zilpah tribes; the remaining Leah tribes and the Rachel tribes.
/36/)

     This influence from Judges 5 cannot be regarded as certain,
but it is plausible. It should be noted, however, that the
tradition Pseudo-Philo follows has not originated solely from
the influence of Judges 5, but from the use of Judges 5 to
explain Exod 14:13-14.

3.4.2. Influence on LAB 31-32

Is there influence in the other direction, from Exodus 14-
15 on Pseudo-Philo's account of the defeat of Sisera? Three
possible points of influence have been suggested. Feldman/37/
suggests a comparison of LAB 31:1 with Exod 14:24. In the
former passage, Deborah, in a prophetic vision of the defeat of
Sisera, says:

> 'I see the stars being disturbed in their order and
> preparing to fight for you. I see also the flashing
> lights (coruscationes),/38/ immovable in their courses,
> setting out to shackle the machinery of their chariots
> (ad impedienda vasa curruum eorum).'

This is an interpretation of Judg 5:20, but the final phrase
may well derive from the obscure Exod 14:24, especially in the
form rendered in LXX: συνέδησε τοὺς ἄξονας τῶν ἁρμάτων ('he
bound the axles of their chariots'). The chariots themselves,
of course, are prominent in Judges 4, and have not had to be
imported from Exodus 14. Moreover, the means by which the
chariots are impeded cannot be the same in LAB 31:1 as it is in
Exod 14:24 (even though the means in Exod 14:24 is not at all
evident). In LAB 31:1 it is the stars who 'shackle the
machinery of their chariots', presumably as an effect of their
heat (cf. 31:2, 4; 32:11)./39/ Thus the phrase borrowed from
Exod 14:24 has contributed only a minor element to the event of
the defeat of Sisera as Pseudo-Philo recounts it.

Secondly, the continuation of LAB 31:1 may perhaps reflect
the influence of Exod 15:9./40/ Sisera says:

'I will surely go down (iens descendam) in the arm of my
strength to conquer Israel, and will divide their spoils
among my servants and take the goodlooking women for
myself as concubines.'

This resembles the words of Pharaoh in Exod 15:9, but the only
phrase in common ('divide the spoils') could as well derive from
Judg 5:30, which also supplies a reference to concubines. In
any case, Exod 15:9 has contributed nothing of substance to the
story in LAB, even if it has influenced the wording.

Finally, it is possible/41/ that Pseudo-Philo's
introduction to the Song of Deborah (32:1), which says not only
that Deborah and Barak (as in Judg 5:1) but also 'all the
people with one accord' sang it 'to the Lord', reflects the
introduction to the song of Moses in Exod 15:1 ('Moses and the
people of Israel sang this song to the Lord')./42/ This
explanation seems preferable to, but is not necessarily to be
regarded as an alternative to, Harrington's suggestion that
Pseudo-Philo (who in 32:1 calls Barak's father 'Abino') read
אבינעם, 'Abinoam', in Judg 5:1, as two words: אבינ, 'Avino',
and עם, 'people'./43/

These two or three possible points of influence are minor
and do not significantly affect Pseudo-Philo's version of the
story of Deborah. It is notable, in fact, that although he sees
a parallel between the two events (LAB 32:17), he retains the
sharply differentiated character of each: one was a miracle in
which the sea was God's agent against Israel's foe, the other
was a miracle in which the stars fought for Israel against her
enemies. Pharaoh's troops were submerged by the sea, Sisera's
burned by the stars (31:2,4; 32:11). Pseudo-Philo
conspicuously fails to take the opportunity offered by Judg 5:
21 to approximate the two events more closely.

Judg 5:1-20 was the haphtarah for Exod 14:30ff. in the
later synagogue lectionary./44/ This does not prove that the
lectionary was already in use when Pseudo-Philo wrote. It only
shows that a traditional association of the two passages, to
which Pseudo-Philo bears witness, influenced the later choice
of haphtarot in the lectionary./45/ Pseudo-Philo associates a
very large number of biblical passages, but few of these

associations correspond to the lectionary./46/

3.5. *Sinai*
LAB contains several elaborate descriptions of the
remarkable phenomena at Sinai (11:5; 15:6; 23:10; 32:7-8),
comparable with similar descriptions in other literature of the
period (*4 Ezra* 3:18-19; *2 Bar* 59:3). These descriptions may
owe something to the influence of other Old Testament theophany
passages, but such influence is not easy to identify (perhaps
cf. LAB 11:5 with Ps 18:7; Judg 5:4). One clear borrowing,
however, is the sentence, 'I bowed the heavens and came down'
(LAB 15:6; 23:10), from Ps 18:9 = 2 Sam 22:10 (cf. Ps 144:5).
(It is also used of Sinai in *4 Ezra* 3:18; *Lev.Rab.* 19:4; *Eccles.*
Rab. 10:18:1,/47/ and must have been already traditionally so
used when Pseudo-Philo wrote.) As in the case of 3.3 above,
this is probably a case of the interpretation of another
scriptural passage as an actual description of the theophany at
Sinai.

3.6. *Moses' anguish*
The description of Moses' anguish in the face of the
episode of the golden calf, in LAB 12:5, is modelled on 2 Kings
19:3 = Isa 37:3 and Jer 4:31. No reason for the use
of these passages can be suggested, except that they furnished
appropriate imagery for a powerful simile.

3.7. *Kenaz (Cenez)*
The long account of Kenaz in LAB 25-28 is the longest and
most remarkable of Pseudo-Philo's excursions from the biblical
narrative. At first sight it may look as though the whole is
free invention, unrelated to the biblical text, but closer
inspection reveals that the material is anchored, even if
sometimes rather tenuously, in the text of the early chapters
of Judges. Kenaz is a substitute for Othniel, the first judge
(so also Jos. *Ant.* 5: 182-184),/48/ and is also identified by
Pseudo-Philo with the 'Judah' of Judges 1:2 (similarly *Cant.*
Rab. 4:7 identifies this 'Judah' with Othniel). The beginning
of LAB 25 is an interpretation of Judg 1:1-2. The 'Canaanites'
of Judg 1:1 become 'Philistines' in LAB 25:1, perhaps because
Pseudo-Philo knows that 'Judah' (i.e. Kenaz) conquered
Philistine territory (Judg 1:18) and he is interested in this
fact (LAB 29:2). The Lord's appointment of 'Judah' (Judg 1:2)
is explained as taking place by lot (LAB 25:2), and it is
coupled with a requirement to uncover the sin of the people
before they can fight the Philistines, because Judg 2:10-14;

3:7-8 indicate that between the death of Joshua and the
election of Kenaz Israel forgot the acts of God on behalf of
their fathers and fell into sin which kindled the Lord's anger
(cf. especially LAB 25:6; 26:1). The emphasis on the sinners
and sins of each tribe (LAB 25:4,9-10,13) may be intended to
explain the account of the failure of each tribe in Judg 1:19-
33. In this way the rest of the legendary material in LAB 25-
26 is at least loosely tied to the narrative of Judges.

LAB 27 is an expansion of Judg 3:9-10 (note especially LAB
27:9-10: the Spirit comes upon Kenaz; 27:7: God delivers the
Amorites into the hands of Kenaz; 27:12-13: the salvation of
Israel by the hands of Kenaz). It is also possible that behind
this narrative, especially the prayer (LAB 27:7), lie Deut 33:7
(about 'Judah') and 1 Chron 4:10 (the prayer of Jabez, who is
identified with Othniel in *b.Tem.* 16a; *Cant.Rab.* 4:7)./49/

Kenaz' vision in LAB 28:6-9 is based on the reference to
'the upper springs and the lower springs' in Judg 1:15 (= Josh
15:19) - a remarkable exegesis which is also preserved in *b.
Tem.* 16a.

No doubt a feeling that the first of the judges, and in
particular the only judge from the tribe of Judah/50/ (cf.
especially LAB 21:5), deserved more attention than Judges
appeared to give him, has led to the development of a full
narrative account of Kenaz out of the hints provided by Judges.
As well as traditional legends, including perhaps some very
ancient ones, and folklore motifs, the development of this
account has probably incorporated ideas from and analogies with
other parts of Scripture, though these are not easy to identify
since verbal allusions are scarce. The following are more or
less probable influences on LAB 25-27:

25:2	1 Sam 10:20-21
25:3	1 Sam 14:39
25:1,4	Josh 7:10-18
25:5	Deut 29:18 (this quotation is discussed section 4 below)
25:8,9 (Elas)/51/	Gen 35:4 (אלה, 'terebinth'); Gen 49:21 LXX (στέλεχος, translating אלה)./52/
25:10 (Shechem) /53/	Gen 35:4
25:11	Gen 2:11-12

26:1,5   Josh 7:15,25-26
26:1; 27:15   Gen 2:11
26:10-11   Exod 28:17-21
26:13   Isa 64:4; 60:19-20; 54:11-12
27:2   2 Sam 11:11
27:5-6   Judg 7:7-8
27:7   Ps 33:16-17
27:9   Judg 7:14
27:10   Judg 7:11,22/54/
27:11   2 Sam 23:10/55/
27:14   Ps 33:16-19.

Clearly some, if not all, of these passages have influenced the
narratives in LAB 25-27. To what extent they have contributed
to the actual creation of the stories it is difficult to tell.

3.8. Zebul

Zebul (LAB 29) corresponds to Ehud in the Judges narrative
(3:15-30), and probably the name Zebul is a faulty transcription
of Ehud,/56/ rather than derived from Judg 9:28-41. However,
nothing in LAB's account of Zebul corresponds to Judg 3:15-20.
The account of the inheritance of the daughters of Kenaz may
have been inspired by Num 36 (in connexion with Judg 1:18;
Josh 15:45-46). The account of the treasury may have been
suggested by 2 Kings 12:9-12; 2 Chron 24:8-11, but why Pseudo-
Philo should have wished to introduce it here is obscure.

3.9. Jael and Judith

LAB 31:3-7 gives an account of Jael's assassination of
Sisera which departs at several points from the story in Judges
4. Two features of LAB's account (Jael enticed Sisera with her
beauty; she made him drunk) are paralleled in later midrashic
works./57/ But there are also a series of close parallels with
the story of Judith, beyond those which result simply from the
fact that the latter is itself partly based on the biblical
story of Jael: LAB 31:3, cf. Jdt 10:3-4; 12:15; 16:7-9;
                   LAB 31:6, cf. Jdt 13:2;
                   LAB 31:7, cf. Jdt 13:9, 4-5, 7, 15.

These resemblances have usually been explained as borrowings
from Judith,/58/ but the possibility should also be considered
that the book of Judith is based not only on the account of Jael
in Judges but also on midrashic developments of the story such
as LAB preserves./59/

3.10.   Aod the wizard

The episode of Aod the Midianite magician (LAB 34) is
introduced at this point in order to account for Israel's
subjection to the Midianites (Judg 6:1-6; LAB 34:5).   According
to the theology of Judges itself (2:11-15), constantly endorsed
by LAB, such subjection to their enemies could only result from
Israel's sin (Judg 6:1a), more specifically from worship of the
Canaanite gods (Judg 6:10).   LAB's account of *how* Israel was
led into idolatry on this occasion was partly suggested by the
strong traditional association of the Midianites with magic (*b.
Sanh*. 91a; *Num.Rab*. 20:8)./60/ Thus it is a Midianite sorcerer
who seduces the Israelites to worship the Midianite gods.   His
magic sign (LAB 34:1,4) is one which the apocalyptic literature
attributes to the eschatological magician, the Antichrist./61/

However, as Wadsworth points out,/62/ Aod is also modelled
on the warning against false prophets in Deut 13:1-5.   Like Aod,
the false prophet in Deut 13:2 performs a sign in order to lead
the people astray after other gods, and God allows this sign in
order to test the people (Deut 13:3; cf. LAB 34:5).   Moreover,
Siphre Deut. 84, commenting on this passage of Deuteronomy,
explains the sign which God allows the false prophet to perform
as causing the sun and the moon to stand still./63/   Clearly
Aod has been invented to exemplify Moses' warning.

In one respect, however, Aod does not conform to the
picture in Deut 13:1-5: he is not an Israelite (cf. Deut 13:1).
This should alert us to the fact that Deut 13:1-5 alone cannot
have been responsible for the creation of the figure of Aod.
Rather, Deut 13:1-5 has been used as an exegetical aid to the
explanation of Judg 6:1.

3.11.   Gideon

In LAB 35, Pseudo-Philo rewrites the conversation between
Gideon and the angel (Judg 6:12-21), as he rewrites most
biblical conversations.   In course of doing so he introduces
reminiscences of other biblical passages.   Two of these (LAB 35:
2, cf. Judg 19:17; LAB 35:6, cf. Gen 18:30) should probably
not be seen as having any great significance beyond the fact
that a writer so intimately familiar with Scripture will tend
to use scriptural phraseology when composing conversations.
Other parallels in this conversation may, however, be rather
more significant.   Gideon's protest (Judg 6:15) is rephrased
(LAB 35:5) in the same words as LAB later uses (LAB 56:6) to
paraphrase Saul's protest in 1 Sam 9:21.   This suggests that

Pseudo-Philo has noticed the resemblance between Judg 6:15 and
1 Sam 9:21, though he does not assimilate the two incidents any
further. The angel's reply to this protest of Gideon is quite
different from the reply of Samuel to Saul in Pseudo-Philo's
account (LAB 56:6), indicating the *dissimilarity* which he sees
between God's choice of Gideon and his choice of Saul. Instead
the reply to Gideon (LAB 35:5) echoes the Lord's words to Samuel
at the time of his selection of David (1 Sam 16:7): Pseudo-
Philo perceives the same principle of divine action at work in
these two cases.

3.12. Jair
The story of Jair (LAB 38) functions to explain the
biblical account in Judges 10 in two ways. In the first place,
Jair becomes responsible for the national apostasy recorded in
Judg 10:6: his function is equivalent to that of Aod in LAB 34.
Secondly, as Ginzberg suggests,/64/ the word בקמון in Judg 10:5
('Jair died and was buried *in Kamon*') has probably been read as
בקמין, 'in the furnace' (קמין is a loanword in rabbinic Hebrew
from κάμινος).

On this basis an appropriate story has been composed
drawing on the analogies of Dan 3 and the corresponding story of
Abraham in the furnace./65/ The role of the angel Nathaniel
corresponds to that of Gabriel in haggadic treatment of Dan 3.
/66/

Once again, we notice that the story has not simply been
created on the basis of Dan 3. It has a startingpoint in the
exegesis of Judges, and Dan 3 has been enlisted to help in the
interpretation of Judges.

3.13. Saul and Jeremiah
In LAB 56:6 Saul's modest protest at Samuel's indication
that he is to be king (1 Sam 9:21) is rewritten/67/ in a way
which makes it resemble Jeremiah's protest in Jer 1:6. This
gives occasion for Samuel to observe (prophetically!) the
resemblance, and to reflect on the tragedy, as he foresees it,
of Saul's early death.

3.14. Deaths and burials
When the biblical accounts provide insufficient or no
details of the deaths and burials of his heroes, Pseudo-Philo
sometimes borrows from the scriptural accounts of the ends of
other characters. Thus, in the case of Joshua, LAB 24:5

borrows a phrase from Gen 49:33 (Jacob 'drew his feet up into
the bed') and one from Gen 46:4 ('Joseph shall place his hand
on your (Jacob's) eyes'),/68/ while LAB 24:6 recalls the
mourning for and burial of Samuel (1 Sam 28:3). Similarly, in
the case of Deborah, whose death is not recorded in Judges, the
seventy days of mourning (LAB 33:6) may be modelled on the
mourning for Jacob (Gen 50:3), unless it is just an appropriate
number./69/ The information that she 'was buried in the city
of her fathers' may, as Jeremias argued,/70/ reflect local
tradition of her grave near Ramah, but may equally well
(especially since Pseudo-Philo does not give the name of her
city) be modelled on the normal practice with other judges
(Judg 8:32; 12:7,10,12,14; cf. LAB 29:4; 36:4; 41:1-2).

3.15. Birth narratives

The birth narratives in LAB are almost the only parts of
LAB which have previously been compared with the Gospels,/71/
since their relevance to the study of the Matthean and Lukan
infancy narratives is rather obvious. It is well-known that
events surrounding the birth and infancy of the great figures
of the Old Testament were a subject of great interest in Jewish
haggadic tradition, in which there tended to develop a series
of stock features which reappear again and again in birth and
infancy narratives. We should therefore expect this area in
particular in Pseudo-Philo's work to be one in which the
influence of one biblical narrative on the retelling of another
will be seen, especially as Pseudo-Philo is plainly interested
in birth narratives and gives considerable space to those of
Moses, Samson and Samuel. His special interest in the subject
seems also to be indicated by LAB 23:7, where in an
interpretation of Abraham's vision (Gen 15) he takes the 'she-
goat' (Gen 15:9) to represent 'the women whose wombs I shall
open and who will bear children'. This is a reference to the
barren women/72/ (beginning with Sarah, and including Rebekah,
Leah, Rachel, and the mothers of Samson and Samuel) whom
special divine intervention would enable to bear great
descendants of Abraham. With this in mind, we consider each of
LAB's birth narratives in turn:

3.15.1. Noah (LAB 1:20)

In connexion with the birth of Noah, LAB shows no trace of
the legends found in 1 Enoch 106-107 and Gen.Apoc. 2-5. He
merely elaborates on Lamech's prophecy at the naming of his son
(Gen 5:29) in such a way as to make the prophecy of the Flood
explicit (cf. 1 Enoch 106:18). A prophecy of the child's
future is a stock feature which occurs in all the birth

narratives in LAB.

3.15.2. Serug (LAB 4:11)
Pseudo-Philo uniquely records a prophecy made by the
mother of Serug, the great-great-grandfather of Abraham (Gen 11:
21), at the time of his birth. This coheres with Pseudo-
Philo's unusual portrayal of the immediate ancestors of
Abraham, from Serug onwards, as godly men who did not
participate in the astral religion of their time (LAB 4:16).
However, in this case, the prophecy is not so much about Serug
as about Abraham, whose own birth LAB only mentions as tersely
as the Bible does (LAB 4:15; cf. Gen 11:27).

3.15.3. Isaac (LAB 23:8)
The brief mention of Isaac's birth refers to his
miraculous conception ('I formed him in the womb of her that
bare him': this sentence seems to have no specific scriptural
source, but cf. Job 31:15; Isa 44:2,24; 49:5) and, without any
biblical basis, puts him into the special category of children
born in the seventh month of pregnancy./73/

3.15.4. Moses (LAB 9)
By comparison with the account in Exodus, Pseudo-Philo's
account contains the following major additional features:
(i) Moses' conception results from Amram's faith in the
face of the Egyptian threat to the Hebrew children. When the
elders of Israel urged that the threat be met by a policy of
remaining childless, Amram opposed the suggestion out of faith
in God's promises and himself set the example when he took his
wife Jochabed (LAB 9:2-9). This midrashic development is an
attempt to explain the connexion between Exod 1:22 and Exod 2:1
(see section 2.5 above): it does not derive from the influence
of another narrative.
(ii) Before Moses' birth, his sister Miriam has a dream in
which the child's future is prophesied; her parents do not
believe the prophecy. Miriam's prophecy is paralleled
elsewhere,/74/ while in other traditions the birth of Moses is
announced to Pharaoh/75/ or Amram./76/ This kind of prophetic
announcement of the birth and the child's future greatness is a
standard feature of birth narratives (with biblical models only
in Gen 17-18; Judg 13). The less common feature of the
parents' disbelief/77/ may perhaps be influenced by Gen 17:17;
18:12; but does not have an obvious biblical origin. More
probably, it is intended to account for Moses' parents' apparent
abandonment of Moses after his birth (LAB 9:12,14); this is the

interpretation which *Gen.Rab.* 1:22 gives to Jochabed's disbelief in Miriam's prophecy.

(iii) The difficult statement in LAB 9:12 that Jochabed 'hid the child *in her womb* for three months' (cf. Exod 2:2) appears to result from the parallel with Tamar in LAB 9:5. Tamar's pregnancy was noticed only after three months (Gen 39: 24) because she was able to conceal it for that long (LAB 9:5). Pseudo-Philo apparently uses this parallel to interpret Exod 2: 2 to mean, not that Jochabed concealed Moses for three months after his birth, but that she concealed her pregnancy for three months, in accordance with the policy suggested by Amram (LAB 9: 5-6). The point of this interpretation, however, is not to provide a parallel between the two stories for its own sake. The interpretation has arisen from a desire to explain a difficulty in the text of Exodus: in view of Pharaoh's strict instructions in Exod 1:22 (cf. LAB 9:12), how could Jochabed have concealed the child after its birth? The Egyptians would have observed that she was pregnant and be ready, when the child was born, to see that it was dealt with./78/ Therefore the words of Exod 2:2 are interpreted to mean only that Jochabed concealed Moses in her womb for the first three months of pregnancy, and the parallel in Gen 39:24 is invoked as scriptural authority for believing that the first three months of pregnancy can be concealed, but no more. Like Tamar, Jochabed could not hide her pregnancy after three months (LAB 9:12), and so she was obliged, when the child was born, to cast him into the river as Pharaoh's decree demanded./79/

(iv) Moses was born circumcised (LAB 9:13,15). This is the first extant reference to a subsequently widespread tradition. /80/ It is mentioned here to explain how Pharaoh's daughter recognized him as a Hebrew child (Exod 2:6; LAB 9:15).

(v) The name Melchiel given to Moses by his mother (LAB 9: 16)./81/

3.15.5. *Samson* (LAB 42:1-43:1)

The narrative follows Judg 13 quite closely, with the following major additions:

(i) Manoah's genealogy and his wife's name Eluma (LAB 42:1).

(ii) The dispute between Manoah and Eluma over which is responsible for their childlessness, and Eluma's prayer that God will disclose the fact of the matter to them (LAB 42:2). As the parallel in *Num.Rab.* 10:5 makes clear, this tradition arose as an explanation of the angel's words, addressed to Manoah's wife, in Judg 13:3.

(iii) The angel's words include: 'But now the Lord has heard your voice and attended your tears and opened your womb' (LAB 42:3).   These words recall Gen 30:22, where God intervenes to end Rachel's barrenness (cf. also Gen 29:31; 30:17, of Leah).

(iv) Samson's name is given by the angel before his birth. In the Old Testament this privilege is limited to Isaac (Gen 17: 20).

(v) Manoah's failure to believe his wife (LAB 42:4) is probably intended to explain the need for a second visit by the angel (cf. Jos. *Ant*. 5:279-280, where a different solution is offered to the same problem).

(vi) The angel touches the sacrifice with his sceptre and it is consumed miraculously (so also Jos. *Ant*. 5:284) - an interpretation of Judg 13:19b by means of Judg 6:21.

3.15.6. *Samuel* (LAB 49-51)

Non-biblical features of the account are:

(i) The non-biblical story of the selection of Elkanah (LAB 49) gives the opportunity for a prophecy of Samuel before his birth (49:7-8).

(ii) Penninah taunts Hannah in words drawn from Isa 56:3 and Ps 128:3 (LAB 50:1).

(iii) It is at passover time that Elkanah goes to Shiloh (LAB 50:2).   This is deduced from the words 'year by year' (1 Sam 1:3), which, since they also occur in Exod 3:10 with reference to the passover, must indicate passover (similarly LAB 48:3).

(iv) An explanation of Hannah's silent prayer is given (50:5).

(v) LAB 51:1 offers a more plausible explanation of the name Samuel ('strong'; i.e. שמו אל, 'his name is strength') than that given in 1 Sam 1:20.

(vi) LAB 51:1 also states that God prophesied Samuel's name.   This cannot refer back to LAB 49:7-8, where the child's name is not given, but must be interpreted by 51:6 as a reference to Ps 99:6.   This is said to have been a psalm of Asaph written in the wilderness,/82/ so that its mention of Samuel is prophetic.   By this means Pseudo-Philo again contrives, this time without inventing the prophecy, to have a child's name given by God before its birth.

(vii) Samuel at two is said to be 'very goodlooking' (LAB 51:1), a detail which may reflect Exod 2:2 (Moses).

(viii) 'The Lord was with him' (51:1) is the phrase used in 43:1 of Samson (where Judg 13:24 has 'the Lord blessed him'; cf. also LAB 59:3, of David).

(ix) Hannah's father is given the name Batuel (LAB 51:6),
perhaps after Bethuel, the father of Rebekah, another of the
barren women whose wombs the Lord opened (Gen 25:20-21). If so,
this is a rare case in which the choice of a non-biblical name
in LAB can be explained.

(x) As befits a child who is to be leader of the nation,
the whole people are involved in installing Samuel at Shiloh
(LAB 51:7).

3.15.7. *Summary on birth narratives*

Pseudo-Philo has certainly elaborated the biblical birth
narratives he rewrites, but much of the elaboration takes the
form of 'midrashic' explanation of details of the biblical
account of each. There are borrowings from one biblical
narrative to another, most notably the motifs of the prophecy
of the child before its birth (in the Old Testament: Isaac and
Samson; in LAB also Moses and Samuel) and the giving of the
child's name before its birth (in the Old Testament: Isaac only;
in LAB also Samson and Samuel). But in these cases only the
motif itself, not the narrative form of the motif, is borrowed.
Other minor borrowings from one birth narrative to another are
3.15.5(iii); 3.15.6(vii),(viii),(ix): these are embellishments
of the narratives, hardly substantial narrative additions. It
should be observed that each of LAB's birth narratives retains
its own highly individual character, derived from the biblical
account, and the individual outlines of each are by no means
obscured by the tendency towards some assimilation of all birth
narratives to a common pattern. Furthermore, it is very
striking that Pseudo-Philo, despite his evident interest in
birth narratives, does *not* provide them for figures whose births
are not recounted in Scripture./83/ He does not compose, on
the analogy of biblical birth narratives, a birth narrative for
Abraham (as later haggadic tradition did)/84/ or for Noah (as
some other traditions had already done) or for David or for any
of the judges in whom Pseudo-Philo is so interested. This is
an impressive illustration of the fact that Pseudo-Philo's work,
despite its appearance of wandering on occasions rather far
from the biblical text, remains on the whole a commentary on
and explanation of the biblical text.

3.16. *Conclusion*

The general pattern of the evidence examined in this
section needs to be rather carefully stated. There is evidence,
of various kinds, for the influence of one biblical narrative
on the retelling of another. In the majority of cases this

amounts to a minor embellishment of the story with a detail
from another (as in the probable influence of the Red Sea
narrative on the account of the defeat of Sisera: 3.4.2; or in
the influence of Judg 6:21 on LAB 42:9: 3.15.5(vi)). In some
cases, the influence of other passages supplies little more than
vocabulary (as in 3.6). In other cases, it helps inspire the
creation of an incident which is wholly absent from the
biblical narrative in question (as in 3.4.1; 3.13; 3.14).
Finally, there are striking cases of complete narratives which
are not in the Bible but have been created partly under the
influence of analogous biblical narratives (3.2; 3.7; 3.8; 3.10;
3.12). In one of these cases a major non-biblical character
has been created (Aod), while in three others a biblical
character has been given a largely non-biblical career (Kenaz,
Zebul, Jair).

It should be noticed, however, that the influence of one
biblical narrative on the retelling of another is in fact, in
the whole scope of LAB, infrequent and restrained. Most of the
correspondences between biblical events which Pseudo-Philo
himself points out have *not* influenced the retelling of either
event. Thus, for example, despite his desire to portray
Jephthah's daughter as a second Isaac, he has not in any way
assimilated her story to that of Isaac. On the whole he is
very careful to preserve the individual features and character
of each narrative as found in the Bible. For example,
comparison of the sacrifice of Jephthah's daughter with that of
Isaac by Abraham, who acted in faith and obedience to God, does
not lead Pseudo-Philo to portray Jephthah's role in the story
as praiseworthy, by analogy with Abraham's. On the contrary,
he is emphatic in his condemnation of Jephthah's vow (LAB 39:
11). Even in cases where there has been some influence of one
narrative on another, we have already observed (3.4.2; 3.11;
3.15.7) how the assimilation is minor and does not obscure the
distinct features of each narrative in its biblical form.
Pseudo-Philo's interest in correspondences between biblical
events is overwhelmingly an interest in correspondences which
exist in the biblical text. Of the many correspondences which
he explicitly points out, very few have a non-biblical element
as one half of the correspondence (LAB 12:1; 25:7; 56:6)./85/
While not denying that this interest has led to some
assimilation between events, we ought to be at least as
impressed by the infrequency with which this has happened.
Even narratives which are not in the Bible have their individual
distinctness: as compared with Dan 3 and with each other, the

stories of Abraham in the fiery furnace and Jair's fiery
furnace each have their own distinct features which derive from
their points of origin in Gen 11 and Judg 10 respectively.

Finally, it must also be stressed that all the material
considered in this section should be classified as
interpretation *of Scripture* by Scripture. In other words,
Pseudo-Philo is always primarily commenting on and explaining
the text of the biblical narrative which he is following in
chronological order from Genesis to 2 Samuel. Other passages of
Scripture are always utilized as a means of explaining and
interpreting *this* narrative. This applies even to the creation
of non-biblical incidents and events, which always have some
kind of starting-point in the biblical narrative which Pseudo-
Philo is rewriting. It is not the case, for example, that
Pseudo-Philo (or a predecessor) was simply inspired by Dan 3 to
create two similar stories of deliverances from fiery furnaces
and insert them at appropriate points in the biblical history.
/86/ The process of creating these stories did not begin from
Dan 3, since we have seen that in both cases the idea of a
furnace was suggested by details in the biblical text (of Gen
11 and Judg 10) which Pseudo-Philo is rewriting, and it is this
suggestion in the text which has prompted the use of Dan 3 to
help develop it into an appropriate story. Even the stories of
Kenaz and Aod are anchored in features of the text of Judges.
Only the account of Zebul's treasury seems unrelated to
anything in Judges, though it is possible that further study
will uncover such a relationship.

4.   Fulfilment of Prophecy

Pseudo-Philo is very interested in prophecy and its
fulfilment. The prominence of this theme in his work is a means
of emphasizing the providential control of history by God. He
(or the tradition he follows) has invented a large number of
non-biblical prophecies, both *post eventum* prophecies of
historical events (within and beyond his own narrative) and
eschatological prophecies. In this section, however, we shall
consider only his interest in the fulfilment of *biblical*
prophecies within the period his work covers. The biblical
narrative of this period of course itself contains a number of
prophecies which it plainly regards as fulfilled by events it
records, and Pseudo-Philo takes over such prophecies and
fulfilments (e.g. Gen 15:12-13: LAB 9:3; 15:5; Judg 4:9: LAB
31:1,7; Judg 14:5: LAB 42:3). In addition to these obvious

cases, however, Pseudo-Philo records the fulfilment of a number of biblical prophecies (or passages he regards as prophecies) whose application to the events with which he associates them is not, to say the least, obvious. These cases witness to his interest in the theme of fulfilment of prophecy and the ingenuity with which he pursues it. They are:

(i) LAB 9:8. Gen 6:3 (setting a limit to human life of 120 years)/87/ is treated as a prophecy fulfilled in Moses (who lived 120 years). Moreover, the text seems to be quoted in a form (different from the form quoted in LAB 3:2) which is adapted to its fulfilment in Moses ('My Spirit will not be *a mediator* among these men').

(ii) LAB 12:3. Gen 11:6 (paraphrased as: 'And now, unless I prevent them, they will go from bad to worse in daring to do whatever they propose to do') is said to be fulfilled in the making of the golden calf./88/

(iii) LAB 21:5. Gen 49:10a is quoted as about to be fulfilled, initially at least, in the figure of Kenaz, a ruler of Israel from the tribe of Judah.

(iv) LAB 25:5. Deut 29:18 ('a root producing gall and bitterness') is quoted as a reference to the sinners whom Kenaz discovers among the tribes.

(v) LAB 51:6. Ps 99:6 ('Moses and Aaron among his priests, and Samuel among them') is quoted as fulfilled in the birth of Samuel. The psalm is attributed to Asaph, who uttered this prophecy 'in the wilderness', and so before Samuel's birth./89/

It should be asked whether in any of these cases the existence of a prophecy has stimulated the creation of an event to fulfil it. This might be suggested in the cases of (iii) and (iv). In the case of (iii), however, Pseudo-Philo has not invented Kenaz or his descent from Judah (cf. Jos, *Ant.* 5:182), though it is certainly possible that Gen 49:10 has contributed to his motivation in giving such prominence to the figure of Kenaz. In the case of (iv), it is true that the context in Deut 29:17-21 is quite suitable to the events of LAB 25-26, but only in a general sense: it could not have contributed any of the detail of the story. It could not, for example, have suggested the idea of a large number of sinners from each of the tribes. It is better to seek the roots of the story elsewhere (see 3.7).

Pseudo-Philo's ingenuity in this field of exegesis is displayed not in creating events to fit prophecies, but in finding prophecies to fit events.

5. Tradition and Originality

To what extent was Pseudo-Philo's midrashic material
already traditional when he used it, and to what extent was he
a creative exegete? Feldman compiled an impressive list of
'unique features of LAB' to show that 'LAB is much more
individual in nature than has hitherto been recognized'./90/
However, the significance of this list needs careful assessment.
Some of the items are rather trivial, and those which involve
numbers should be treated with some caution, since the
transmission of numbers in the text of LAB can rarely be
trusted. Some items in the list can immediately be deleted,/91/
and it is likely that further study will uncover parallels to
some others. Finally, Feldman himself admits that 'many of
these apparently unique features would undoubtedly not be
unique if we had all the midrashic and other literature which
has been lost'./92/ When allowances are made for all these
considerations, the list is less impressive.

Even on a generous estimate of the unique features of LAB,
they would be considerably fewer than the features which are
also found elsewhere in haggadic tradition (mostly to be found
in Feldman's own commentary/93/ and that of Perrot/94/). It
cannot be disputed that a great deal of Pseudo-Philo's material
was traditional. No doubt he also made some creative
contributions of his own, and we may make a reasonable guess
that these were in two areas in particular: (i) the invention
of non-biblical names, since none of the examples in LAB seems
to be paralleled in other sources, either in *Jubilees* or in
later rabbinic literature; (ii) speech material, especially of
a didactic, prophetic or eschatological kind. There are a few
parallels to LAB's non-biblical speech material,/95/ which show
that we cannot automatically ascribe it all to Pseudo-Philo's
entirely free composition, but they are very much less common
than parallels to the narrative material. It is uncertain
whether the psalms he includes were already existing
compositions, as some have argued.

To a large extent we should regard Pseudo-Philo as a
redactor of traditional haggadic material. This is not the
place to discuss his theology and redactional interests, but he
has undoubtedly selected, arranged and adapted his material to
convey skilfully his own understanding of Israelite history and
employed the freedom he allows himself in composing speeches to
voice that understanding explicitly.

6.   LAB and the Gospels

6.1.   Clearly the question of analogies between LAB and the Gospels can be pursued along two lines.   In the first place, it may be asked whether the Evangelists treat their Christian sources (especially any written Gospel materials which they used) in the way in which Pseudo-Philo treats the biblical narrative he follows.   For example, is Matthew a 'midrash' on Mark (as Michael Goulder maintains), or, perhaps, on Mark and Q, in the way in which LAB is a 'midrash' on Genesis-1 Samuel? Secondly, it may be asked whether the Evangelists used the Old Testament in ways comparable with Pseudo-Philo's use (with special reference to the material in section 3).

6.2.   The burden of the answer to the first question, whether the Evangelists treat their sources for the Jesus-tradition in a 'midrashic' way, must rest on study of Matthew's and Luke's use of Mark (for those who maintain Markan priority), and perhaps also on John's use of the Synoptics (for those who think John used the Synoptics).   Pseudo-Philo's treatment of the biblical narrative of Genesis-1 Samuel is such that we could never have reconstructed that narrative or understood how he uses it if we did not have the text of Genesis-1 Samuel. Therefore any analogy with the Gospels must be tested in cases where we have the 'text' on which the Evangelist writes his 'midrash'.

6.3.   Detailed comparison of Matthew's and Luke's treatment of Mark with the exegetical procedures involved in LAB's midrashic material (section 2) cannot be undertaken here.   But such a comparison will have to be alert to differences as well as similarities./96/   I suspect, for example, that although apparent examples of 2.2, 2.3, and 2.4 would be easy to find, examples of 2.5 would be difficult to find, and since 2.5 (connexions with adjacent accounts) is an important feature of LAB this would need explanation.   Partly because of 2.5, the general impression which LAB gives in most parts is of continuous, developing narrative, consisting of relatively long narrative sections which comprise a sequence of events in close historical connexion.   This must be contrasted with the well-known fact that much of the narrative in the Synoptic Gospels comprises independent pericopae which the Evangelists have done relatively little to bind together.   This contrast may suggest that form-criticism still explains features of the Gospels which 'midrash' leaves unexplained.   The observation that in

this respect John resembles LAB more than the Synoptics do may
also have interesting implications.

6.4.   With regard to the second question, the Evangelists'
use of the Old Testament, the analogy of LAB may at least
clarify the possibilities considerably. It suggests that we
should drop the habit of calling a Gospel narrative 'a midrash
on' an OT text or texts. As we have seen in 3.16, LAB is
always primarily 'midrash' on the narrative which is being
followed in Genesis-1 Samuel. LAB 6, for example, is not 'a
midrash on Dan 3' but 'a midrash on Gen 11'. Similarly,
therefore, Matt 4:1-11 cannot be a 'midrash' on texts in Exodus
and Deuteronomy, because it is not a story about Moses and the
Israelites in the wilderness. It could, however, be regarded
as a 'midrash' on Mark 1:12-13, in which texts from Exodus and
Deuteronomy have aided the exegesis of the Markan text. This
point is not a mere quibble about terminology. It means that if
the Evangelists (or their predecessors) used a 'midrashic'
method comparable with LAB's, they can never have created
Gospel narratives *solely* out of Old Testament texts. Any
'midrashic' development using Old Testament material must
always have had a starting-point and stimulus in the traditions
about Jesus. Even though this starting-point might sometimes
have been as tenuous as in the stories of Kenaz (and we must
remember that such tenuous links are the exception rather than
the rule in LAB), we are under obligation, in explaining
Gospel narratives as 'midrashic' developments using Old
Testament material, to offer a plausible identification of such
a starting-point and to explain how it could have stimulated
the use of Old Testament texts to develop it. This is a
methodological point of considerable importance, which has been
ignored in far too much recent work on 'midrash' in the
Gospels. It means that the recognition of the influence of the
Old Testament on Gospel narratives does not in itself exempt us
from the obligation to investigate the historicity of such
narratives.

6.5.   The analogy with LAB could certainly not rule out the
possibility that the Gospels contain substantial non-historical
narratives, comparable with the stories of Kenaz, Aod and Jair,
or significant non-historical incidents, like the division of
opinion at the Red Sea (3.4.1), but it would lead us to expect
that Old Testament influence on the formation of Gospel
narratives would not normally have gone beyond relatively minor
embellishment of stories whose main outlines already existed
(cf. 3.16).

6.6. The discussion in 3.16 should particularly help us
to understand why it is that, despite the more or less probable
influence of Old Testament material on many Gospel narratives,
the result is never a narrative which is a mere copy of an Old
Testament narrative (compare, for example, the feeding miracles
and the raisings of the dead by Jesus with the comparable
stories of Elijah and Elisha). The Gospel narratives always
have their own individual features by comparison with Old
Testament analogies. This results from the same kind of
respect for the given features of each narrative which we find
in LAB, despite Pseudo-Philo's delight in detecting
correspondences between events (which the early Church surely
shared) and the consequent occasional tendency for one
narrative to influence another. In the Gospels the individual
features of each narrative must result from the Jesus-
tradition itself. Even if we may sometimes suspect (say, in
the Matthean infancy narrative) that Old Testament material has
contributed quite considerably to the content of a Gospel
narrative, the practice of LAB indicates that there still must
have been features of the Jesus-tradition which dictated the
choice of Old Testament material and the particular way in
which it has been used, just as Gen 11:3,31 and Judg 10:5-6 have
made the two fiery furnace stories in LAB each a distinctive
story and not mere copies of Dan 3 or of each other. Thus,
methodologically it will be very important not only to identify
in Gospel narratives points of contact with the Old Testament,
but also to look for their distinctive features which the Old
Testament cannot explain.

6.7. LAB's treatment of the fulfilment of prophecy
(section 4) may not be wholly comparable with that of the
Evangelists, who were recounting events of messianic fulfilment
to which they believed the whole Old Testament pointed forward.
Nevertheless, Pseudo-Philo's interest in prophetic fulfilment
makes his material of some comparative importance, and should
at least warn us against too readily concluding that the
Evangelists would have created events to fulfil prophecies. If
they did so, they had, so far as I can tell, no precedent in
Jewish 'midrashic' literature.

6.8. The conclusions in section 5 about the traditional
nature of much of LAB's 'midrashic' material have extremely
important implications for what it would mean to see the
Evangelists as writing 'midrash'. Sometimes, especially in the
work of Goulder and Drury, this is taken to mean that almost

all non-Markan material in Matthew was created by Matthew
himself, through 'midrashic' development of Mark and the Old
Testament, and that special Lukan material was similarly
created by Luke himself. But this is not at all how Pseudo-
Philo worked (see section 5): he was familiar with a wealth of
haggadic traditions which had already gathered around the Old
Testament text and on which he naturally drew. We must suppose
that when he came to a point in the text which called for
explanation or expansion, his first move would not have been to
use his own imagination but to recall the traditions, and only
if he found no traditional material available or satisfactory
would he himself add to the tradition. Jewish haggadic
tradition of the kind we find in Pseudo-Philo was not the
literary creation of occasional great writers, but must have
grown up in the day-to-day discussion of rabbinic schools or
in the week-by-week exposition of the Scriptures in the
synagogues. Of course, each item of tradition had to be created
by someone at some time, but no one individual, not even a
literary redactor like Pseudo-Philo, would do more than add his
own contribution to a much larger body of tradition which he
received. Thus, even if it were plausible to regard, as
Goulder does, almost all non-Markan material in the Gospels as
'midrashic' development from Mark and the Old Testament, it
would be extraordinary if Matthew were the first person to
engage in such 'midrash' and had no 'midrashic' tradition on
which to draw. If this were the case, it could only be because
the early Church in general did not regard 'midrash' as a
legitimate way to treat the Jesus-tradition and Matthew himself
was a radical innovator in this respect: this would be an odd
conclusion for Goulder to reach. It would also mean that
Matthew's procedure in writing his Gospel would not after all be
naturally explained from the 'midrashic' procedure of his Jewish
contemporaries, if Pseudo-Philo is at all typical of this.
Innovative 'midrashic' development on the scale which Goulder
attributes to Matthew would be a far more novel and audacious
enterprise than Pseudo-Philo's. But Goulder's case rests very
heavily on the analogy between Matthew and Jewish 'midrash'.

6.9. It follows that the 'midrash' model for Gospel-
writing does not at all help us to dispense with Gospel sources
or provide a new solution to the Synoptic problem. To take a
small-scale example, it is quite plausible to compare Matthew's
treatment of Mark in Matt 3:13-4:11 with LAB's procedure. The
baptism of Jesus raises an obvious problem, which Matt 3:14-15
serves to explain. Mark's mention of Satan's temptation of

Jesus provokes the obvious question, 'What form did this
temptation take?', which Matt 4:3-10 serves to answer. But the
analogy with LAB does not at all require that Matthew invented
this 'midrashic' material which he adds to Mark. Just as
Pseudo-Philo drew many such explanations of the Old Testament
text from tradition, so Matthew could well have drawn his
explanations of Mark from tradition (even from Q!). The
analogy with LAB does not enable us to tell whether he did so
in any particular instance. It does lead us to expect that he
would have done so more often than not. Thus Goulder's and
Drury's attempt to use the 'midrashic' theory of the Gospels as
an alternative to theories of Gospel sources, whether written
or oral, can be refuted by means of its own appeal to Jewish
analogies.

6.10. The recognition that if Matthew expands on Mark in
a 'midrashic' way, he may be drawing on tradition to do so,
raises a further question: In such instances must the material
have *originated* as a purely 'midrashic' development from the
Jesus tradition which Mark records (even though this origin is
pre-Matthew), or has it any chance of being historical?
Pseudo-Philo's 'midrashic' material has almost always been
created in some way out of the biblical text (though it is
possible that occasionally he incorporates some completely
extra-biblical oral tradition about the Judges period). But
this highlights the difference in the historical relationship
in which Pseudo-Philo and Matthew stood to their respective
historical subjects. Pseudo-Philo, and his predecessors who
created much of his haggadic tradition, had ultimately very few,
if any, resources outside the biblical text itself with which to
explain it: hence the resort to controlled imagination. It
does not follow that had other resources been available to them
they would have refused to use them (and, in fact, Josephus
sometimes illuminates the biblical narrative with information
from non-Jewish historians). If we reject Goulder's implausible
picture of Gospel traditions in the early Church/97/ and
suppose, as all probability suggests, that Matthew wrote in a
situation in which historical traditions about Jesus were
plentiful, then this situation puts a limit on the analogy with
Pseudo-Philo. It may still be the case that Matthew's own
procedure at, say, Matt 3:13-15 is the same as Pseudo-Philo's,
i.e. he encounters a difficulty in the text of Mark, seeks to
offer an explanation of it, and in doing so turns first to the
other traditions available to him. The difference, however, is
in the nature of the traditions available to him: if Matthew did

draw Matt 3:14-15 from tradition, it might, like Pseudo-Philo's
traditions, have been purely 'midrashic' in origin and of no
historical value, but it might have had a historical basis. The
analogy with LAB does not enable us to decide this question,
which can only be decided from examination of the material
itself and from building up a general estimate of how much
historically reliable tradition was available to Matthew. It is
true that an analogy with LAB helps us to understand how non-
historical material could have entered the Gospel tradition,
and the significance of this aspect of the analogy should not be
underestimated. However, it is equally important to notice
that, because the analogy with LAB obliges us to recognize that
writing 'midrash' means using traditions, it also reopens the
door to the possibility that an Evangelist's traditions,
however 'midrashic' his procedure in using them may be, could be
historical in origin. Thus, although the analogy with LAB is
relevant to questions of Gospel historicity, it provides no
short-cut to answering them.

6.11. The same kinds of considerations must affect our
treatment of analogies with Pseudo-Philo's non-biblical names
and genealogies (2.1). The tendency to name anonymous
characters is a well-known tendency of the Gospel tradition,
which can be observed in the canonical Gospels and especially in
the apocryphal Gospels. When John identifies the anonymous
bystander of Mark 14:47 (par.) as Peter and names his equally
anonymous victim Malchus (John 18:10), this looks exactly like
Pseudo-Philo's practice (especially if we can be sure that John
is following one of the Synoptic accounts). Certainly the
desire to name such characters is the 'midrashic' one
explained in 2.1. But, again, the 'midrashic' question, 'What
was his name?', could be answered *either* as LAB does *or* from
genuine historical tradition, if such were available. The
formal analogy with midrashic procedure cannot itself answer
the historical question, which in John 18:10 will depend on how
we estimate John's access to reliable information of this kind.
A name which enters the tradition late may often be fictitious,
but need not be./98/ Similarly, the practice of inventing
genealogies, attested by LAB, has to be weighed, when
considering the genealogies of Jesus, against the probabilities
that Davidic families kept genealogical records and that such
information from the family of Jesus was easily available in
the early Church. However, it will not do to argue, as writers
on the Gospels sometimes do, that the invention of names and
genealogies is psychologically improbable; this modern

psychological judgment must give way before the facts with
which LAB provides us.

6.12. Finally, Pseudo-Philo's free treatment of biblical
speeches and conversations and his free composition of speech
material (2.7-2.10) may provide a parallel to some types of
Gospel material: the four Gospel versions of Peter's denials,
for example, are well within the limits of freedom which Pseudo-
Philo allows himself when rewriting biblical conversations,
while the Lukan canticles find probably their best extra-
biblical analogies in LAB (section 2.9). We should be cautious,
however, about drawing from Pseudo-Philo's freedom with speech
material conclusions as to the Evangelists' treatment of Jesus'
teaching. It is likely that the normal ancient
historiographical conventions about speeches applied less
readily to historical figures who were remembered as
authoritative teachers and whose teaching was preserved.
Pseudo-Philo's treatment of the Decalogue (section 2.7) may be
a better analogy here. However, this paper has been mainly
concerned with narrative material in LAB and the Gospels. A
much more detailed study of the discourse material in LAB will
be needed before its relevance to the authenticity of the
sayings of Jesus in the Gospels can be assessed./99/

Notes

/1/ I am using the word 'midrash' in the extended sense now
common, referring to Jewish exegesis of the NT period, in
contrast to those writers who restrict the word to the rabbinic
midrashim. But the inverted commas are in deference to the
strictly correct usage of the latter. The substance of my
argument in this paper, which entails a direct comparison of
LAB with the Gospels but no comparison of either with the
rabbinic midrashim, is not affected by this terminological
issue.
/2/ See the surveys of opinions in L. H. Feldman, 'Prolegomenon'
to M. R. James, *The Biblical Antiquities of Philo* (reprinted New
York: Ktav, 1971) XXVIII-XXX; Bogaert, in C. Perrot and P.-M.
Bogaert, *Pseudo-Philon: Les Antiquités Bibliques*, vol. 2
(Sources Chrétiennes 230; Paris: Les Editions du Cerf, 1976)
(henceforth *SC* II) 66-67.
/3/ D. J. Harrington, 'The original language of Pseudo-Philo's
Liber Antiquitatum Biblicarum', *HTR* 63 (1970) 503-14; idem,

'The Biblical Text of Pseudo-Philo's *Liber Antiquitatum Biblicarum*', *CBQ* 33 (1971) 1-17.

/4/ Bogaert, *SC* II, 66-74.

/5/ A. Zeron, 'Erwägungen zu Pseudo-Philos Quellen und Zeit', *JSJ* 11 (1980) 38-52.

/6/ Recently restated, against Bogaert, by M. Wadsworth, 'A New "Pseudo-Philo"', *JJS* 29 (1978) 186-91.

/7/ Parts of LAB appear in Hebrew in the Chronicles of Jerahmeel, but these seem to have been translated into Hebrew from the Latin version: see D. J. Harrington, *The Hebrew fragments of Pseudo-Philo's Liber Antiquitatum Biblicarum preserved in the Chronicles of Jerahmeel* (Missoula, Montana: SBL, 1974) 1-5.

/8/ The equally important task of comparing Josephus' technique with that of the Gospels has been well begun by F. G. Downing, 'Redaction Criticism: Josephus' *Antiquities* and the Synoptic Gospels', *JSNT* 8 (1980) 46-65; 9 (1980) 29-48.

/9/ M. D. Goulder, *Midrash and Lection in Matthew* (London: S.P.C.K., 1974) chap. 2.

/10/ I follow the practice of retaining the Latin forms of names in LAB which do not occur in the Bible, but convert biblical names into their usual English biblical forms.

/11/ This is a means of avoiding what Gen 20:12 appears to say: that Sarah was Abraham's half-sister. The same identification is found in Jos. *Ant.* 1:151; *Tg.Neof.* and *Jon.*, Gen. 11:29; *b. Meg.* 14a; *b.Sanh.* 69b.

/12/ Cf. *Ruth Rab.* 2:20.

/13/ See R. Hayward, 'Phinehas - the same is Elijah: The Origins of a Rabbinic Tradition', *JJS* 29 (1978) 22-34.

/14/ I suspect that some kind of rough distinction needs to be drawn between 'historical' works such as LAB, and works such as Tobit and Judith which were probably intended simply as fiction.

/15/ Cf. my suggested explanation of the choice of 'Batuel' for Hannah's father: section 3.15.6(ix). For the appropriateness of the name Seila for Jephthah's daughter, see Perrot, *SC* II, 189.

/16/ Feldman, 'Prolegomenon', XLVI, regards the non-biblical names in LAB as intended apologetically, citing *b.B.Bat.* 91a, which says that such names are important as a reply to the *minim.* But since the practice of inventing such names goes back at least as far as *Jubilees*, this can scarcely be the original motive for it and I doubt if this motive is operative in LAB.

/17/ On this principle in LAB, see M. Wadsworth, 'Making and Interpreting Scripture', in *Ways of Reading the Bible*, ed. M. Wadsworth (Brighton: Harvester Press, 1981) 10-16.

/18/ Cf. G. Vermes, *Scripture and Tradition in Judaism* (SPB 4; Leiden: Brill, 1961) 129.

/19/ Cf. *Tgs.Neof.* and *Jon.* Exod 20:1-17.

/20/ Cf. G. W. E. Nickelsburg, 'Good and Bad Leaders in Pseudo-Philo's *Liber Antiquitatum Biblicarum*', in *Ideal Figures in Ancient Judaism: Profiles and Paradigms*, ed. J. J. Collins and G. W. E. Nickelsburg (SCS 12; Chico, California: Scholars Press, 1980) 49-65.

/21/ M. P. Wadsworth, *The "Liber Antiquitatum Biblicarum" of Pseudo-Philo: doctrine and scriptural exegesis in a Jewish midrash of the first century A.D.* (unpublished D.Phil. thesis, Oxford, 1975), vol. 2, 356-63; vol. 1, 346-57; cf. also Perrot, *SC* II, 199-200.

/22/ See Vermes, *Scripture*, 68-75.

/23/ *Contra* Vermes, *Scripture*, 89.

/24/ Cf. Vermes, *Scripture*, 89.

/25/ So also later Christian tradition (Augustine, *Civ.Dei*, 16:15) and Muslim tradition (Quran 21:69-71; 37:95-96). For representations in Jewish, Christian and Muslim art, see J. Gutmann, '"Abraham in the Fire of the Chaldeans". A Jewish Legend in Jewish, Christian and Islamic Art', *Frühmittelalterliche Studien* 7 (1973) 342-52; pl. XXXIII-XXXVII.

/26/ See Vermes, *Scripture*, 72-73.

/27/ Gutmann, 'Abraham', 345-48; pl. 79-86. However, *b.Pesaḥ.* 118a stresses that God, not an angel, delivered Abraham, whereas Gabriel delivered the three in Nebuchadnezzar's furnace.

/28/ Latin *habitationes* must be a literal translation of τῆς οἰκουμένης (LXX Ps. 17:15).

/29/ אַף, 'nostrils', 'anger', means 'nostrils' in Exod 15:8; Ps 18:15, but LXX renders θυμοῦ (Exod 15:8) and ὀργῆς (Ps 17:15).

/30/ All translations of LAB are my own from Harrington's text in D. J. Harrington and J. Cazeaux, *Pseudo-Philon: Les Antiquités Bibliques*, vol. 1 (Sources Chrétiennes 229; Paris: Les Editions du Cerf, 1976) (*SC* I).

/31/ *Ex.Rab.* 22:2 applies Ps 18:16 to the crossing of the Red Sea; *Cant.Rab.* 1:9:4 applies Ps 18:10-14 to the defeat of Pharaoh at the Red Sea.

/32/ The three versions of the tradition are discussed in W. S. Towner, *The Rabbinic "Enumeration of Scriptural Examples"* (SPB 22; Leiden: Brill, 1973) 119-20, 218-20, 225-27.

/33/ J. Macdonald, *Memar Marqah: The Teaching of Marqah*, vol. 2 (BZAW 84; Berlin: Töpelmann, 1963) 167.

/34/ A. Díez Macho, *Neophyti 1: Targum Palestinense MS de la Biblioteca Vaticana*, vol. 2: *Éxodo* (Madrid/Barcelona: Conseja Superior de Investigaciones Cientificas, 1970) 447 (trans. by M. McNamara and M. Maher). The same tradition, with only minor verbal differences, occurs in *Tg.Jon.* Exod 14:13-14; ʿy.Taʿan. 2:5 (65d); *Mek.R.Ishmael Besh.* 3:128-136 (trans. in Towner,

Enumeration, 119).

/35/ The influence of this text is suggested by James, *Biblical Antiquities*, 104 n. 3; Feldman, 'Prolegomenon', XCIV; R. Le Déaut, *Targum du Pentateuque*, vol. 2: *Exode et Lévitique* (Sources Chrétiennes 256; Paris: Les Editions du Cerf, 1979) 113 n. 13. It is more plausible than Ps 68:17, suggested by L. Ginzberg, *The Legends of the Jews* (Philadelphia: Jewish Publication Society of America, 1911-38) vol. 6, p. 4 n. 23.

/36/ Possibly the unexpected phrase, 'sons of *Leah*' (LAB 10:4), results from the fact that the Leah tribes take the lead in the division of opinion in 10:3.

/37/ Feldman, 'Prolegomenon', CXVII; cf. *SC* I, 239 n.

/38/ James, *Biblical Antiquities*, 171, and Cazeaux, *SC* I, 239, take *coruscationes* to mean 'lightnings', but this cannot be the meaning, since lightnings do not have fixed courses (*immobiles in cursu*). *Coruscationes* must be synonymous with *astra* ('stars') in the first member of the parallelism. (In LAB 15:2 *coruscationes* could mean 'lightnings' (with *tonitrua*) but the phrase *coruscationes astrorum* suggests 'flashing lights of the stars'. In 11:5; 19:16, the unambiguous *fulgura* is used for 'lightnings'.) Thus the meaning of both lines is that the stars are leaving their regular courses in order to fight against Sisera (so also 32:17). Hence this passage does not, as Feldman ('Prolegomenon', CXVI) thinks, explain the defeat of Sisera in terms of a storm. That is Josephus' rationalizing account (*Ant.* 5:205-6), but Pseudo-Philo takes Judg 5:20 as the key to the matter and interprets the battle wholly in terms of the action of the stars, who burn up the army of Sisera (LAB 31: 2,4; 32:11).

/39/ Cf. also *b.Pesaḥ*. 118a; *Lev.Rab.* 7:6.

/40/ Perrot, *SC* II, 37.

/41/ Cf. Feldman, 'Prolegomenon', CLXVI; Perrot, *SC* II, 169.

/42/ Cf. also Jdt 16:1. (The influence of Judith is possible in LAB's version of Jael's assassination of Sisera: see 3.9 below.)

/43/ Harrington, 'Biblical Text', 5.

/44/ Perrot, *SC* II, 37.

/45/ So Perrot, *SC* II, 37.

/46/ A few others which do are noted by Perrot, *SC* II, 37.

/47/ *Tg.Neof.* Exod 12:42 uses it of the Aqedah.

/48/ Kenaz cannot be simply another name for Othniel son of Kenaz, since LAB 20:6 makes him son of Caleb, nor can he be Othniel's father, since LAB 29:1 states that he had no sons. LAB and Jos. *Ant.* 5:182 must be evidence of an alternative tradition about the relationships in the family of Caleb and about which member of the family was the first judge. Another

Kenaz is *grandson* of Caleb in 1 Chron 4:15.

/49/ Cf. the use of the name Iabis in LAB 28:1.

/50/ LAB omits Ibzan the Bethlehemite (Judg 12:8-10). I cannot accept the argument of A. Zeron, 'The Swansong of Edom', *JJS* 31 (1980) 195-97, that Pseudo-Philo regards Kenaz as an Edomite and, as an Idumean himself, gives prominence to Kenaz for this reason. On the contrary, he gives Kenaz a genealogy (LAB 15:3) which, unlike the Bible, leaves no doubt of his descent from Judah.

/51/ It is curious that 1 Chron 4:15 has a Kenaz son of *Elah* and grandson of Caleb. But Pseudo-Philo is unlikely to have borrowed the name of the Naphtalite sinner Elas from the family of his hero Kenaz.

/52/ See A. Zeron, 'Einige Bemerkungen zu M. F. Collins, "The Hidden Vessels in Samaritan Traditions"', *JSJ* 4 (1973) 167 n. 3.

/53/ M. F. Collins, 'The Hidden Vessels in Samaritan Traditions', *JSJ* 3 (1972) 114, regards this verse as polemic against the Samaritan tradition of the sacred vessels buried in Mount Gerizim.

/54/ Cf. also *1 Enoch* 56:7.

/55/ But see also the similar story of Joab in Ginzberg, *Legends*, vol. 4, 100; vol. 6, 258 n. 77.

/56/ Perrot, *SC* II, 165, where he also offers an alternative explanation of the name.

/57/ References in Feldman, 'Prolegomenon', CXVII. Perrot, *SC* II, 168, suggests that תמר ('wine') was read for חמאה ('curds') in Judg 5:25.

/58/ James, *Biblical Antiquities*, 43; Wadsworth, *Liber Antiquitatum Biblicarum*, vol. 1, 274-75, 278; Nickelsburg, 'Good and Bad Leaders', 55.

/59/ Note that the action of pushing Sisera/Holofernes off the bed, which seems somewhat redundant in Jdt 13:18, has an important function in LAB 31:7.

/60/ Further references in Ginzberg, *Legends*, vol. 6, 125 n. 728.

/61/ The closest parallels are *Asc.Isa.* 4:5; *Apoc.Elijah* 3:5-6; *Sib.Or.* 3:64-67.

/62/ Wadsworth, *Liber Antiquitatum Biblicarum*, vol. 2, 195-96.

/63/ Feldman, 'Prolegomenon', CXX.

/64/ Ginzberg, *Legends*, vol. 6, 202 n. 104.

/65/ It is probably unnecessary to recall the seven brothers in 2 Macc 7 in order to account for the *seven* righteous men in LAB 38:1. The number is too natural to require a source. A minor influence on the story may be 1 Kings 18:24 (cf. LAB 38:2).

/66/ *b.Pesaḥ.* 118a. Cf. Wadsworth, *Liber Antiquitatum*

Biblicarum, vol. 2, 151-52.   The blinding of the people by
Nathaniel recalls LAB 27:10.

/67/ The first part of Saul's protest is a rewriting of 1 Sam
9:21 exactly parallel to the rewriting of Judg 6:15 in LAB 35:
5.   See section 3:11 above.

/68/ The phrase, 'slept with his fathers' (LAB 24:5) has no
specific source: it is used throughout Kings and Chronicles.

/69/ It is surprising that Deborah is mourned for seventy days,
but Pseudo-Philo's great hero Kenaz for only thirty days (LAB
28:10).   But it is impossible to rely on the accurate
transmission of numbers in the text of LAB.

/70/ J. Jeremias, 'Das spätjüdische Deboragrab', *Zeitschrift
des Deutschen Palästina-Vereins* 82 (1966) 136-38.

/71/ P. Winter, 'Jewish Folklore in the Matthean Birth Story',
Hibbert J. 53 (1954-5) 34-42; idem, 'The Proto-Source of Luke
I', *NovT* 1 (1956) 184-99; idem, 'The Main Literary Problem of
Luke I-II', *ATR* 40 (1958) 257-64; C. Perrot, 'Les Récits
d'Enfance dans la Haggada antérieure au IIe Siècle de Notre
Ère', *RSR* 55 (1967) 481-518.

/72/ The phrase, 'whose wombs I shall open', seems to be used
with reference to childbearing after barrenness (cf. LAB 42:3;
Gen 29:31; 30:22).

73. In *b.Rosh Hash.* 11a this is given as an interpretation of
Gen 18:14, but this is unlikely to represent the origin of the
tradition.   The idea that miraculously conceived children are
born after seven months of pregnancy seems to be an example of
Greek influence in Judaism: see P. W. van der Horst, 'Seven
Months' Children in Jewish and Christian Literature from
Antiquity', *Eph.Theol.Lov.* 54 (1978) 346-60.

/74/ *b.Meg.* 14a; *b.Soṭa* 12b; *Exod.Rab.* 1:22.

/75/ Jos. *Ant.* 2:205; *Tg.Jon.* Exod. 1:15.

/76/ Jos. *Ant.* 2:215-16.

/77/ Also in *Gen.Rab.* 1:22 (Jochabed).   Contrast Jos. *Ant.* 2:
218.

/78/ The same difficulty seems to be met in different ways in
Tg.Jon. Exod 2:2 (Moses was born after only six months of
pregnancy, and then was hidden for three months) and *Exod.Rab.*
1:20 (Amram and Jochabed were temporarily separated six months
before the birth of Moses; Moses was conceived three months
before this, but the Egyptians calculated from the time Amram
took Jochabed back and so expected the birth three months too
late).

/79/ Note that, unlike Exod 2:3, LAB 9:14 (*proicerent*) makes it
clear that Jochabed was obeying Pharaoh's edict when she put
Moses in the ark in the river.   The interpretation I have

suggested follows the text of LAB 9:12 as we have it, but it may
be that the text should be corrected. As Feldman suggests
('Prolegomenon', XCIII), it is possible that words have fallen
out by homoeoteleuton in LAB 9:12, and that originally the
verse said: '...hid the child in her womb for three months.
When she gave birth, she saw that he was a goodly child, and
hid him for three months. For she could not hide him any
longer...' This suggestion has the advantage of explaining *why*
she concealed the first three months of pregnancy: so that the
Egyptians should miscalculate her pregnancy and expect the
birth three months too late (cf. *Exod.Rab*. 1:20). This
miscalculation would give her three months, but only three
months, after Moses' birth in which she could keep the birth
secret. *Exod.Rab*. 1:20 (see n. 78 above) shows that the
practical improbabilities of this suggestion would not have
deterred Pseudo-Philo from suggesting it.

/80/ *Exod.Rab*. 1:20 gives it as an interpretation of 'she saw
that he was a goodly child' (Exod 2:2).

/81/ On the name Melchiel, see M. Wadsworth, 'The Death of
Moses and the Riddle of the End of Time in Pseudo-Philo', *JJS*
28 (1977) 15-16, with references to other literature.

/82/ This dating of Asaph (in conflict with 1 Chron 15:17; 16:
5,7,37) may derive from Exod 6:24 (Abiasaph the son of Korah,
who is identified as the author of Ps 73 in *Lev.Rab*. 17:1).
But the idea that Asaph prophesied presumably comes from 1
Chron 25:2 (so also *Gen.Rab*. 65:1; *Lev.Rab*. 13:5).

/83/ Serug is scarcely really an exception.

/84/ See Vermes, *Scripture*, 68-70, 90-95.

/85/ In the case of LAB 12:1, Pseudo-Philo cannot have created
the motif of the people's failure to recognize Moses by
borrowing it from the corresponding event in Gen 42:8, because
this motif is the *only* link with Gen 42:8. Unless the motif
were already a tradition about Moses, Pseudo-Philo would never
have thought of Gen 42:8 at this point.

/86/ Nor was he simply creating a 'doublet' (Goulder, *Midrash*,
36-38).

/87/ Cf.also LAB 48:1, where Phinehas is said to have exceeded
this limit.

/88/ A comparison between the building of the Tower of Babel
and the making of the golden calf is made in *Pesiq.R*. 166b.

/89/ Cf. n. 82 above.

/90/ Feldman, 'Prolegomenon', LXX. The list is on pp. LXX-
LXXVII; and a few more items are added in Feldman,
'Epilegomenon to Pseudo-Philo's *Liber Antiquitatum Biblicarum*
(LAB)', *JJS* 25 (1974) 308.

/91/ Delete: 6:4ff. (cf. *Sefer ha-Yashar* (Vermes, *Scripture*,
            72-73), where the brick-kiln is a survival
            of the connexion with the Tower of Babel);
        8:11 (this simply follows from identifying Dinah
            as Job's wife);
        10:1 (accident or textual error);
        12:10 (see Perrot, *SC* II, 115);
        17:4 (see Perrot, *SC* II, 124);
        32:5 (probably textual error);
        39:9 (there is no confusion: 'Amorites' is
            correct, following Judg 11:19-23, and in
            any case is paralleled in Jos. *Ant*. 5:261-
            62);
        42:8 (a quibble);
        42:10 (see Feldman, 'Prolegomenon', CLXVI);
        45:5 (cf. Jos. *Ant*. 5:150);
        50:3 (cf. Wadsworth, *Liber Antiquitatum Biblicarum*,
            vol. 1, 395-98).
/92/ Feldman, 'Prolegomenon', LXX.
    Sometimes there are sufficient hints in other sources to
make us strongly suspect that LAB's material was traditional.
This is especially true in the case of the narratives about
Kenaz, so often regarded as a prime example of Pseudo-Philo's
inventiveness. Previous writers have noted Josephus' reference
to Kenaz (*Ant*. 5:182-84), the material on Caleb and Othniel in
b.Tem. 16a, and the fact that *2 Bar*. 6:7 presupposes a
tradition in which the ark contained more than twelve precious
stones. It should also be noticed that LAB 25 depends on the
identification of Kenaz with the 'Judah' of Judg 1:2 (see
section 3.7 above), which is found in *Cant.Rab*. 4:7 (Othniel =
'Judah'), and that *Ex.Rab*. 3:2 contains a prayer of Othniel
which somewhat resembles LAB 28:5 and is certainly evidence of
non-biblical tradition about Othniel.
/93/ Feldman, 'Prolegomenon', LXXXII-CXLIV, CLXIV-CLXVIII.
/94/ *SC* II.
/95/ E.g. LAB 18:13; cf. Jos. *Ant*. 5:129-130; *Tg.Jon*. Num 24:
14; and LAB 40:2; cf. Jos. *Ant*. 5:265.
/96/ It is a fault of Goulder's comparison of Matthew with
Chronicles (*Midrash*, chap. 2) that it appears to be only
interested in similarities.
/97/ Goulder, *Midrash*, chap. 7.
/98/ I think, for example, that the strong post-NT tradition
that the first name of the apostle Thomas was Judas is likely
to be historically correct.

/99/ As well as my colleagues in the Gospels Project, I should like to thank Dr Philip Alexander and Dr Michael Wadsworth, both of whom read this paper in draft and made valuable comments and suggestions.

BIBLICAL EXPOSITION AT QUMRAN

F. F. Bruce,
The Crossways,
2 Temple Road,
Buxton, Derbyshire,
SK17 9BA.

A. Exegetical Principles

1. Rāz and pēšer

The types of biblical exposition or application discernible in the Qumran texts vary according to the literary *genres* in which they appear. So far as anything in the nature of exegetical principles is concerned, our examination must be confined to the *pēšārîm* or 'commentaries' on biblical books or parts of books. The use of scripture found in other Qumran documents scarcely merits the designation 'exegesis'.

The basic exegetical principle followed in these commentaries envisages divine revelation as given in two stages: *rāz* and *pēšer*. The *rāz* or divine 'mystery' was communicated through the prophets; the *pēšer* or 'interpretation' is supplied by the commentators. Thus the clause 'so he may run who reads it' (Hab. 2:2) belongs to the divine 'mystery' communicated to the prophet: 'its interpretation (*pišrô*) refers to the Teacher of Righteousness (*môrēh haṣṣedeq*), whom God has caused to know all the mysteries (*rāzê*) of the words of his servants the prophets' (1QpHab 7.4).

With this we may compare the two stages by which a divine revelation is communicated in the Aramaic part of the book of Daniel. Whereas the 'mystery' (*rāz*) in the Qumran commentaries is always a text of scripture, it never takes that form in Daniel: in Daniel it is usually conveyed through a dream or a vision. God, for example, decides to make known to Nebuchadnezzar 'what shall be hereafter' (Dan. 2:45) and does so in two stages. First he sends the king a dream; then he sends Daniel to the king with an interpretation of the dream. The dream communicates the divine purpose to a certain extent, but in itself it remains a 'mystery'; it must be provided with an 'interpretation' before it can be understood. In Daniel's Aramaic the 'mystery' is the *rāz* (a word of Iranian origin); the

'interpretation' is the *pēšar* (the Hebrew equivalent of which is
pēšer, as in Eccl. 8:1, 'who knows the *interpretation* of a
thing?'). The king receives the *rāz*; Daniel, thanks to a
further revelation (given 'in a vision of the night'), receives
the *pēšar* and imparts it to the king (Dan. 2:19, 30-45).

The same two words, *rāz* and *pēšar*, are used in connexion
with Nebuchadnezzar's second dream (Dan. 4:6(9)). The pattern
reappears in the story of the writing on the wall at
Belshazzar's feast and in Daniel's account of his vision of the
four world-empires which are superseded by the eternal kingdom
of God. In these last two contexts the word *rāz* does not occur,
but the principle is there: the writing on the wall is a divine
communication, but it remains a mystery until its *pēšar* is
revealed by Daniel (Dan. 5:12, 16f, 26); so too Daniel's night-
vision (Dan. 7:1-14) remains a mystery even to him until the
pēšar is made known to him by the interpreting angel (Dan. 7:
16).

According to the Qumran commentators, then, God conveyed
his purpose to the prophets in the form of a 'mystery'. No one
can understand this mystery unless its interpretation has been
given to him. The interpretation depended on direct revelation
from God as truly as the mystery had done. The Qumran
commentators give the impression that no one before their day
had understood the prophets; they were able to understand them
because the interpretative key was at their disposal.

2. *The interpreter's role*
What was above all essential to the interpretation of the
prophetic oracles was the knowledge of the time at which they
would be fulfilled. Much had been revealed to the prophets, but
this particular knowledge had been withheld from them. (There
was one exception to this rule: Daniel, as Josephus points out
in *Ant.* 10.267, not only foretold future events, as the other
prophets did, but unlike them foretold also the fixed time at
which those events would take place.) The Qumran commentator on
Habakkuk, for example, explains the words 'still the vision
awaits its time' (Hab. 2:3) by saying that 'God told Habakkuk to
write down the things which would come to pass in the last
generation, but did not make known to him the completion of the
epoch' (1QpHab 7.1 f.). The 'completion of the epoch' (*gĕmar
haqqēṣ*) was the commentator's contribution. The commentator was
able to make this necessary contribution because he belonged to
a community which had been initiated into the mysteries of the
divine purpose. The leader of the community, the 'Teacher of

Righteousness', played the part in the interpretation of the
prophets that Daniel played in the interpretation of
Nebuchadnezzar's dreams. The Teacher was the divinely appointed
interpreter of the end-time, the man raised up (as it is put in
the Zadokite work) 'to show to the last generations what God was
about to do to the last generation' (CD 1.11 f.). The rāz was
revealed to the prophets; the pēšer was revealed to the Teacher
and shared by him with the members of his community. They could
accordingly praise God, as they did in their *Hymns of
Thanksgiving*, for disclosing to them his 'wonderful mysteries'
(e.g. 1QH 7.26 f.).

3. Eschatological reference

All the words of the prophets, it was held at Qumran,
related not to their own time but to the time of the end.
References which might appear to be to people and events
contemporary with the prophets were not really so. The Gentile
oppressors of the people of God might be called Assyrians in
Isaiah (10:4-34; 31:8), Chaldaeans in Habakkuk (1:6), Gog in
Ezekiel (38:1-39:20), but these are but varying designations of
the great power which would dominate the Holy Land in the end-
time - the Romans, who in the Qumran texts (as in Dan. 11:30)
are called the Kittim. What the prophets said about the
Assyrians, the Chaldaeans or Gog was really meant to be
fulfilled in the Romans.

This updating of earlier prophecy was not a total
innovation: the prophets themselves had adopted a similar
procedure. Habakkuk probably (compare Hab. 1:5 with Isa. 29:14)
and Ezekiel certainly (cf. Ezek. 38:17) identified the invaders
to whom they pointed with those of whom Isaiah had spoken in his
day.

Again, since the rise of the Teacher of Righteousness and
the formation of the Qumran community betokened the approach of
the end-time, it was natural to find references to the Teacher
and his contemporaries in the prophetic writings. But the
interpretation of those references is expressed in such allusive
terms that it is difficult for the modern reader to divine the
persons or events indicated by the commentators. He feels as
much in need of a key to interpret their comments as they
themselves required one to interpret the sacred text. Among the
contemporaries of the Teacher of Righteousness who are viewed as
subjects of biblical prophecy are his leading opponents, the
Wicked Priest and the False Prophet. The Wicked Priest appears

to have exercised political power; he lost no opportunity of harassing the Teacher. The general opinion is that he was one of the Hasmonaean rulers, all of whom, from the Qumran view viewpoint, occupied the high-priesthood illegitimately - but which of them? Probably Jonathan, the first of the family to exercise the high-priestly office (to which he was appointed by a Seleucid pretender in 152 BC). But earlier and later priests have been proposed, from Menelaus (installed by Antiochus Epiphanes in 171 BC) to Eleazar (captain of the temple at the time of the revolt against Rome in AD 66). The exact date and identity of the Teacher and his opponents are alike disputed.

4. Nearness of the end

God's raising up of the Teacher of Righteousness to interpret the words of the prophets was a sign that their fulfilment was at hand - close at hand. But, as has so often happened in the history of such movements, the fulfilment did not not come as speedily as had been first expected; hence some explanation of its deferment was called for. So the words of Hab. 2:3, 'For still the vision awaits its time ...', are taken to mean that 'the epoch is prolonged, beyond all that the prophets have spoken, for the mysteries of God are wonderful' (1QpHab 7.7 f.) - past finding out, in other words. But it is insisted that the deferment itself was foreseen by the prophets: 'if it seems slow, wait for it' (Hab. 2:3).

This deferment may be regarded as a Qumran counterpart to the 'delay of the Parousia' - a sometimes overrated factor in NT theology. It may be that, as some Christians thought that the beloved disciple would live to witness the parousia (John 21: 23), so it had been expected at one time that the end of the age would come while the Teacher of Righteousness was still alive. If so, his death demanded a reappraisal of the chronology of the end-time. There would be an interval of forty years before the complete winding-up of the present age (we may compare the application in Heb. 3:10,17 of the 'forty years' of Ps. 95:10 in a manner that suggests that the author envisaged an interval of this duration between the enthronement of Christ at the Father's right hand and the coming dénouement). At the end of this period (corresponding to the forty years of fighting in the War Scroll) 'no wicked man shall be found on earth' (4QpPs37 II.8 f.) - a comment based on Ps. 37:10, 'yet a little while, and the wicked will be no more'.

B.   Exegetical Procedures

1. *Atomization*

The biblical text was atomized in the *pĕšārîm* so as to
bring out the relevance of each sentence or phrase to the
contemporary situation, the situation introduced by the ministry
of the Teacher of Righteousness and the emergence of the elect
community.   It is in this situation, not in the logical or
syntactical sequence of the text, that coherence was found.
Thus, in Hab. 1:13 it is the godly members of the community who
are 'of purer eyes than to behold evil', but the protest, 'why
does thou look on faithless men, and art silent when the wicked
swallows up the man more righteous than he?' is directed against
'the house of Absalom and the men of their counsel, who were
struck dumb when the Teacher of Righteousness was chastised and
did not go to his help against the Man of Falsehood' (1QpHab
5.6 -11).

2. *Use of variant readings*

Variant readings were selected or combined so as best to
serve the commentator's purpose.   Thus, in Hab. 2:5 the
commentator quotes the lemma 'Moreover, wealth (*hôn*) is
treacherous', where the traditional Hebrew text has 'Moreover,
wine (*hayyayin*) is treacherous'.   The commentator finds the
reading 'wealth' serviceable because he applies the words to the
Wicked Priest, who 'treated the commandments treacherously for
the sake of wealth' (1QpHab 8.10 f.).   But he knows that wine as
well as wealth has led the Wicked Priest into sin: in verse 16
he reads 'Drink, yourself, and stagger (*hērā'ēl*)' and not with
MT 'Drink, yourself, and be (as one) uncircumcised (*hē'ārēl*)'
(1QpHab 11.9).   (Here the Qumran commentator's variant is
followed in LXX and Peshiṭta, and preferred by RSV and NEB.)   But
the reading 'be (as one) uncircumcised' is not overlooked: the
comment on verse 16 says that the Wicked Priest did not
'circumcise the foreskin of his heart'.

3. *Allegorization*

Where a relation could not otherwise be established between
the text and the situation to which (*ex hypothesi*) it must refer,
the allegorical method is employed.   Thus the town built with
blood in Hab. 2:12 is not a literal city but a rival religious
community, founded by the False Prophet, which involved in
death and destruction those who were misguided enough to join it
(1QpHab 10.9-13).   But allegorization is less common in the
pĕšārîm than in other Qumran documents.

4. Gĕzērāh šāwāh and related devices

Not so much in the regular *pĕšārîm* (where the sequence, if
not the sense, of the biblical text was followed) as in other
documents, widely separated scriptures might be brought
together and given a unitive interpretation on the strength of
some common term or similarity in subject-matter. This
procedure is quite like the rabbinical device of *gĕzērāh šāwāh*
('equal category'). There is a good example of this in the
Zadokite work, where the 'star' of Amos 5:26 is equated with the
'star' of Num. 24:17 and interpreted of the 'Expositor of the
Law' (possibly the Teacher of Righteousness).

C. Exegetical Illustrations

1. From the Habakkuk commentary

Mention has been made above of the interpretation of Hab.
1:13 in terms of 'the house of Absalom and the men of their
counsel' who failed to help the Teacher of Righteousness against
the Man of Falsehood. The personal name Absalom might promise
to provide a criterion for identifying the persons or events in
question, but in almost every relevant generation we find a man
called Absalom associated with Jewish leaders, from an envoy of
Judas Maccabaeus (2 Macc. 11:17) to a lieutenant of the Zealot
Menahem in AD 66 (Josephus, *BJ* 2.448). Apart from that, the
name might be used figuratively, because the 'house of
Absalom' acted in a way reminiscent of the treachery of King
David's handsome son of that name.

Habakkuk's denunciation of the man 'who gives his
neighbour to drink of the cup of his wrath, and makes him drunk
in order to gaze on their nakedness' (Hab. 2:15) is quoted by
the Qumran commentator with the variant reading *môᶜădêhem*
('their sacred seasons') instead of *mᵉᶜôrêhem* ('their nakedness')
and interpreted of 'the Wicked Priest, who pursued after the
Teacher of Righteousness to swallow him up in his hot fury, even
to his place of exile (or 'to the place of his uncovering',
'abbêt gālûtô), and on the occasion of the sacred season of
rest, the day of atonement, he burst in upon them to swallow them
up and to make them stumble on their fast-day, their sabbath of
rest' (1QpHab 11.4-8).

Some important occasion is apparently indicated, but it is
impossible to be sure what it was. Various suggestions have
been put forward, from the tracking down and assassination of
Onias III at Daphne, near Antioch, in 171 BC to the dragging out

and killing of Menahem on Ophel in AD 66. These two suggestions
are chronologically difficult and if, as seems clear from
references elsewhere in the pĕšārîm, the Teacher of
Righteousness was delivered from his enemies, they are ruled out
on that ground also. The occasion is probably one not otherwise
known to us. If it be asked how the Wicked Priest was free to
take hostile action against the Teacher on the day of atonement,
when he should have been officiating in the temple, the answer
is that the men of Qumran observed their sacred seasons
according to a purely solar calendar like that prescribed in the
book of Jubilees and not according to the lunisolar calendar
followed in the temple.

We have referred to the commentator's choice of the reading
hērā‘ēl instead of hē‘ārēl in Hab. 2:16. The command 'Drink,
yourself, and stagger!' is said to be addressed to 'the priest
whose shame was mightier than his glory, for he ... walked in
the ways of drunkenness to quench his thirst. But the cup of
the fever of [stag]gering will overwhelm him, to add to his
[shame and] ignominy' (1QpHab 11.12-15). The imputation of
drunkenness might have helped in identifying this priest, but
there are too many possible candidates: we may think of Simon,
who was assassinated in his cups (1 Macc. 16:16), or of
Alexander Jannaeus, whose last illness is said to have been
caused by heavy drinking (Josephus, Ant. 13.398).

Because of their persecution of the Teacher and his
followers, and because of their general oppressiveness, the
Wicked Priest with his colleagues and successors ('the last
priests of Jerusalem') would incur divine judgment, and the
principal executors of that judgment would be the Kittim. What
Habakkuk says of the Chaldaeans (Hab. 1:6ff.) is applied by the
Qumran commentator to the Kittim. While they were to be the
agents of divine retribution on the oppressive rulers in Israel,
they themselves would be more oppressive still and would incur
due retribution in their turn: their annihilation would be
followed by the new age of righteousness.

The good condition in which the Habakkuk commentary has
been preserved means that we can derive from it much information
about exegetical principles and methods in the Qumran community,
but the allusiveness of the language means that we cannot give a
certain historical setting to any of the persons or events that
figure in the interpretation.

2. From the Nahum commentary

The Nahum commentary from Cave 4, fragmentary though it is,
promises more help in historical identification. For example,
it takes the description of Nineveh as a den 'where the lion
brought his prey, where his cubs were, with none to disturb'
(Nah. 2:12) to be a reference to '[Deme]trius, king of Greece,
who sought to enter Jerusalem by the counsel of the seekers
after smooth things' (4QpNah I.1, 2). The king is most
probably Demetrius III (Eukairos), who in 88 BC invaded Judaea
at the behest of Alexander Jannaeus's rebellious subjects.
Prominent among these were the Pharisees, who appear to be
alluded to here and elsewhere in Qumran literature as 'seekers
after smooth things' or 'givers of smooth interpretations'
(dōrĕšê ha-ḥălāqôt, in reference perhaps to Isa. 30:10.

The commentary goes on: '[Never has that city been given]
into the hands of the kings of Greece from Antiochus to the rise
of the rulers of the Kittim, but ultimately it will be trodden
down ...' (4QpNah I.2, 3). Antiochus here seems to be
Antiochus VII (Sidetes) whose demolition of the walls of
Jerusalem in 133 BC (early in the reign of John Hyrcanus I) was
the last effective action by a Gentile ruler against that city
until Pompey, one of 'the rulers of the Kittim', entered it as a
conqueror seventy years later.

In the prophet's next words, 'The lion tore enough for his
whelps and strangled prey for his lionesses' (Nah. 2:13), the
commentator sees a reference to the 'raging lion (kĕpîr
he-ḥārôn) who smote with his mighty men and his counsellors' and
'took vengeance on the seekers after smooth things, in that he
hanged men alive, [a thing never done] in Israel before, for to
one hanged alive on a gibbet scripture says, "Behold, I am
against you, says the LORD of hosts ..."' (4QpNah I.6-9). In
the biblical text of Nah. 2:14, 'against you' has the feminine
form (ʾēláyik), because a city is addressed, but the commentator
treats it as masculine (ʾēlékāh), because the hanged man is
taken to be the person addressed. What scripture actually says
about a hanged man, albeit with primary reference to the
exposure of a criminal's corpse, is that he is 'accursed by God'
(Deut. 21:23), but the commentator has in view something even
more obscene - hanging men alive, crucifying them. Such a
thing, he says, has never before been done in Israel - that is,
by an Israelite. The first Jewish ruler who is recorded as
punishing his enemies in this way was Alexander Jannaeus, for
when he had crushed his rebellious subjects, he crucified 800 of
their leaders (Josephus, BJ 1.97; Ant. 13.380). Jannaeus is

almost certainly the 'raging lion' of the commentary. The
commentator, like his fellow-members of the Qumran community,
strongly disapproved of the 'seekers after smooth things', but
could not disguise his horror at Jannaeus's atrocious treatment
of them.

3. From a Psalms commentary

Considerable portions have survived of a commentary on
Psalm 37 from Cave 4. We have seen above how the comment on
verse 10 applies the 'little while' of which it speaks to the
end-time period of forty years. Those who 'wait for the LORD'
and 'shall possess the land' are, not surprisingly, 'the
congregation of the elect who do his will' - i.e. the Qumran
community. Those who 'draw the sword and bend their bow, to
bring down the poor and the needy' (verse 14) are 'the wicked
ones of Ephraim and Manasseh who will seek to put forth their
hand against the priest and the men of his counsel in the time
of trial which is coming on them'. The 'priest' (as in 1QpHab
2.8) is the Teacher of Righteousness. But he and his followers
will not be abandoned to their enemies: 'God will redeem them
from their hand, and afterwards they (i.e. their enemies) will
be given into the hand of the terrible ones of the Gentiles for
judgment' (4QpPs37 II.20). The 'terrible ones of the Gentiles',
whether or not they are the Kittim, are the executors of God's
wrath against the Jewish rulers who persecute the Teacher and
his disciples.

There is a further reference to the Teacher and his
enemies in the defectively preserved comment on verses 32, 33:
'the wicked watches the righteous, and seeks to slay him; the
LORD will not abandon him into his hand, or let him be condemned
when he is brought to trial'. This, the commentator seems to
say, 'concerns the Wicked [Prie]st, who [plotted against the
Teacher of Righteousness] to slay him'. But, as appears from
the fragmentary continuation of the comment, the Wicked Priest's
attack on the Teacher was unsuccessful, while he himself
suffered due retribution at the hands of 'the terrible ones of
the Gentiles' (4QpPs37 IV.9 f.).

The 'wicked man' of verses 35, 36, who disappears without
trace, is identified with the 'Man of Lies' who acted 'with a
high hand'; but the manuscript is too mutilated to show what
more was said of him.

4. From the Isaiah commentaries

Some fragmentary commentaries on Isaiah from Cave 4 make further reference to events associated with the community's life and to their expected sequel.

In 4QpIsa[a] the Assyrian invasion of Isa. 10:28-32 is related to the exiles' return from 'the wilderness of the peoples' (cf. 1QM 1.3, where the eschatological war begins when 'the exiles of the sons of light return from the wilderness of the peoples to encamp in the wilderness of Jerusalem') and to the intervention of the 'prince of the congregation' on their behalf.

The statement of Isa. 10:34 that 'Lebanon will fall by a mighty one' (originally denoting the overthrow of Assyria by divine intervention) is related to the 'war of the Kittim' who beat down the house of Israel but will at last be 'given into the hand of his [God's?] great one' (i.e. the Davidic Messiah). This is quite different from Yoḥanan ben Zakkai's interpretation of the same oracle, in which 'Lebanon' is the Jerusalem temple and the 'mighty one' either Vespasian or his son Titus (b. Giṭṭin 56b).

This fragmentary pēšer ends with a comment on the 'shoot from the stump of Jesse' in Isa. 11:1, who is naturally identified with the coming prince of the house of David, ruling over the Gentiles (including 'Magog') and vested in his coronation robes by one of the 'priests of renown'.

In 4QpIsa[b] the denunciations of the drunken nobles of Judah in Isa. 5:11f. are directed to 'the congregation of the men of scoffing who are in Jerusalem'.

In 4QpIsa[d] the promise to the restored Zion, 'I will lay your foundations in lapis lazuli' (Isa. 54:11), is interpreted of the foundation of the 'council of the community', linked with a group of twelve men (possibly leading priests) who 'give light in accordance with Urim and Tummim'.

5. From the Micah commentary

A fragmentary commentary on Micah from Cave 1 provides a good example of allegorical exegesis. The questions, 'What is the transgression of Jacob? Is it not Samaria?' (Mic. 1:5b) are interpreted of 'the False Prophet, who leads the simple astray' (cf. the interpretation of Hab. 2:12 in 1QpHab), while the following questions, 'And what are the high places of Judah?

Are they not Jerusalem?' (Mic. 1:5c), are interpreted of 'the
Teacher of Righteousness, who teaches the law to his people and
to all who volunteer to be gathered in among God's elect,
practising the law in the council of the community; they will be
saved from the day of judgment'. The False Prophet is evidently
the leader of another religious movement, of which the men of
Qumran held no good opinion; but the two rival leaders can be
read out of Micah's denunciation only if they are first read
into it by an allegorical procedure which by our standards
would be called arbitrary. But the Qumran commentators would
have pleaded not guilty to the charge of arbitrariness: by their
interpretative standards all the prophetic corpus had reference
to the period into which they had now entered, and if such
reference could not be established otherwise, then its
extraction by means of allegory was justifiable.

One thing these commentators did not do was to try to
'create' recent history out of the biblical texts. Recent
events and the current situation provided them with their data.
If adaptation was necessary to make the 'mystery' and the
interpretation fit each other, it was the 'mystery' - i.e. the
biblical text - that was adapted, not the data which formed the
raw material of the interpretation.

D.   Other Illustrations of Biblical Use

In this paper the term 'exegesis' is restricted to the
pešārîm, because they are the only Qumran documents in which
anything of the nature of exegetical rules can be discerned. In
other Qumran texts scripture is freely used and applied, but
more loosely and at times in a way marked by internal
contradictions.

1. From messianic testimonia
The end of the epoch of wickedness and dawn of the new age
would see the emergence of three figures foretold in prophecy.
In 1QS 9.11, for example, it is laid down that the regulations
imposed on the community are to be observed 'until the coming of
a prophet and the anointed ones of Aaron and Israel'. The
reference to these two 'anointed ones' or 'messiahs' resembles
references in the Zadokite work to the rise of 'a messiah from
Aaron and from Israel' (CD 20.1) or of 'the messiah of Aaron and
Israel' (CD 12.23-13.1). The Zadokite references might be to
one messiah or two, since the community itself is said to have
sprung 'from Israel and from Aaron' (CD 1.7), i.e. from the

laity and from the priesthood; but in the light of 1QS 9.11 it
is more probable that two messiahs were expected - an anointed
priest and an anointed king. In several biblical and post-
biblical contexts, both historical and eschatological, the
kingship and the high-priesthood are closely associated. But
for the collocation of a prophet with the high priest and king a
specially important witness is 4Q Testimonia, where biblical
authority is presented for expecting all three of these end-time
figures.

The document begins with the text of Exod. 20:21, in the
fuller form known from the Samaritan Bible, incorporating the
logia which appear in Deut. 5:28,29; 18:18,19 MT, including
God's promise to raise up for Israel a prophet like Moses. No
comment is added, but it is implied that the expected prophet of
the end-time would fulfil this promise.

Next comes the quotation of Num. 24:15-17, including
Balaam's oracle: 'A star shall come forth from Jacob and a
sceptre shall arise out of Israel.' The star and sceptre appear
to be understood as referring to the Davidic Messiah; this
understanding would be the more appropriate if the oracle
originally pointed to David. In 1QM 11.6f. the same oracle is
quoted with reference to the final crushing of the sons of
darkness under the onslaught of the sons of light, commanded by
the hero (gibbôr) who leads them to victory (probably the
Davidic Messiah).

The third testimonium in the series is Moses' blessing of
the tribe of Levi (Deut. 33:8-11), beginning 'Give to Levi thy
Tummim, and thy Urim to thy godly one ...'. The statement in
Deut. 33:9 that Levi 'disowned his brothers and ignored his
children' may have been thought specially appropriate to the
priestly leaders of the community, who maintained the exclusive
claims of the house of Zadok to the high-priesthood and severed
their association with the unworthy priests who continued to
minister in the Jerusalem temple. The further statement in
verse 10, that Levi would declare God's judgment to Jacob and
his law to Israel, should be compared with the reference in 4Q
Florilegium I.11 to the Expositor of the Law (dôrēš hattôrāh)
who is to attend the Shoot of David (ṣemaḥ dāwîd) when the
latter stands up in Zion in the last days in fulfilment of the
promise to David in 2 Sam. 7:11-14 and the promise in Amos 9:11
about the re-erection of David's fallen booth. The Expositor of
the Law is probably the great priest of the end-time, who might
be expected to exemplify pre-eminently the ideal set forth in

Mal. 2:7, 'the lips of a priest should guard knowledge, and men should seek *tôrāh* from his mouth'.

The final section of 4Q Testimonia has nothing to do with 'messianic' personages, unless indeed it points to Antichrist. It begins with the quotation of Joshua's curse on the rebuilder of Jericho (Josh. 6:26), but in a form (attested also in LXX) lacking the name Jericho and referring simply to 'this city'. Whereas the three preceding quotations are unaccompanied by any explicit interpretation, the quotation of Josh. 6:26 is followed by a note (appearing also in 4Q Psalms of Joshua): 'And behold, an accursed man, one of the sons of Belial, will stand up, to be a veritable fowler's snare to his people, and destruction to all his neighbours. He will stand up and /make his sons/ rulers, so that they will both be instruments of violence. They will rebuild the /city/ and set up a wall and towers for it, to make a stronghold of his wickedness ... in Israel and a horrible thing in Ephraim and Judah. ... They will work pollution in the land, and great contempt among the sons of ..., and will shed blood like water on the rampart of the daughter of Zion and in the boundary of Jerusalem.'

At first sight, this passage (in spite of its lacunae) might promise to link up with some identifiable historical incident. But on closer inspection it proves to be as elusive in this regard as most of the Qumran *pĕšārîm*. The city which is to be rebuilt is more probably Jerusalem than Jericho - though some might think of the founding of a religious community, in the light of the interpretation given in 1QpHab 10.6-13 to the building of a town with blood in Hab. 2:12.

But when we look for a man with two sons, placed by him in positions of authority, who take a leading part in the building or fortifying of Jerusalem or some other Judaean city, and cause great bloodshed in the precincts of Jerusalem, we find an embarrassing wealth of names to choose from. Some restriction will be placed on our choice if those palaeographers are right who date this document early in the first century BC: we might think of Simon and his two sons who were killed together at Jericho (1 Macc. 16:16), or of John Hyrcanus and his two sons Aristobulus and Alexander Jannaeus.

2. From the Zadokite Work
The Zadokite work reviews the background and early history of the community and finds allusions to this subject-matter here

and there throughout the scriptures. In the Song of the Well in
Num. 21:17f. the well is said to be the law, the 'princes' who
dug it are those noble souls in Israel who withdrew from
association with their fellow-Jews and sojourned in 'the land of
Damascus', while the 'staff' with which they dug it represents
the 'Expositor of the Law' (probably to be identified with the
Teacher of Righteousness), since mĕḥōqēq, here translated
'staff', may also mean 'lawgiver'. The 'land of Damascus'
(whether it is to be understood literally or figuratively)
designates the community's place of retreat at an early stage in
its history (CD 6.3-11).

A good example of the grouping of separate quotations so as
to yield a new and coherent interpretation is provided in CD 7.
10-20. Here Isa. 7:17 is cited: 'The LORD will bring on you and
on your people and on your father's house such days as have not
come since Ephraim departed from Judah' (where Ephraim or Jacob
is distinguished from Judah, Ephraim or Jacob denotes the
apostate majority and Judah the faithful remnant). The
statement that 'Ephraim departed from (sûr mēʻal) Judah' is
glossed thus: 'When the two houses of Israel separated, Ephraim
became ruler over (śār mēʻal) Judah, and all who hesitated were
given over to the sword (cf. Ps. 78:62), but those who held fast
escaped to the land of the north' (an apparent reference to the
withdrawal of the community). We note, incidentally, the
oscillation between homophones so as to produce a desired
interpretation, appropriate forms of sûr ('depart') and śārar
('rule') being pressed into service in this way.

There follows another oracle originally referring, like Isa
7:17, to the Assyrian invasion but similarly applied by the
Zadokite author to the community's withdrawal - Amos 5:26f.,
quoted in the form: 'And I have exiled the booth (sukkat as
against MT sikkût) of your king and the pedestals (kēne or kannê
as against MT kiyyûn) of your images (and the star of your god)
from my tent (mēʼohŏlî by metathesis for mēhālĕʼāh, beyond) to
Damascus.' The 'land of the north' in the gloss on Isa. 7:17 is
equated with 'Damascus' of Amos 5:27, whence the community's
place of retreat is called 'the land of Damascus' in the
application of the Song of the Well quoted above (CD 6.5). The
'booth of your king' is explained as referring to 'the books of
the law' and is linked with God's promise in Amos 9:11 to raise
up 'David's fallen booth'. The 'pedestals of your images' are
the books of the prophets, 'whose words Israel despised' (cf. 2
Chr. 36:16); the implication is that the law and the prophets

received due respect only in the seceding community. The 'star' is 'the Expositor of the Law who is coming to Damascus'; this is reinforced by the interpretation of Balaam's oracle about the 'star' from Jacob and 'sceptre' from Israel (Num. 24:17). The Zadokite author treats this text more cavalierly than do other Qumran writers: he distinguishes the 'star' from the 'sceptre', which he identifies with 'the prince of all the congregation' (cf. 4QpIsa^a V.3) who, when he arises, 'will strike through all the sons of Sheth (tumult)'. It looks as if the community thought at one time that the Teacher of Righteousness would survive until the end; after his death a later 'Expositor of the Law' was envisaged, whose advent would coincide with that of the 'Messiah of Israel'.

Further, the mention of 'striking' (qarqar) in Num. 24:17 suggests yet another oracle where the same idea occurs, though expressed by a different verb: 'Awake, O sword, against my shepherd, and against the man that is next to me, says God; smite (hak) the shepherd and the sheep shall be scattered, and I will turn my hand against the little ones' (Zech. 13:7). To this the Zadokite author adds a comment from another shepherd context in the same book: 'And those who pay heed to him are the poor of the flock' (Zech. 11:11) - the 'poor of the flock' being the members of the godly community.

So, by reason of coincidence in wording or similarity in subject-matter, a whole catena of biblical texts is viewed as presenting the origin, history and prospects of the community.

The same skilful combination of scriptures appears in the Zadokite interpretation of the law. To take one example: the marriage law was held to prohibit a man from having more than one wife at a time. This prohibition was based on 'the principle of creation' (yĕsôḏ habbĕrî'āh, with which cf. ἀπὸ δὲ ἀρχῆς κτίσεως in Mark 10:6) - 'God made them male and female' (Gen. 1:27), i.e. a man and a woman - and on the order of nature: the animals went into the ark two by two (Gen. 7:7). Moreover, plurality of wives is specifically forbidden to the Israelite king (Deut. 17:17), and if it be objected that David, for all his piety, had several wives, the explanation is that he did not know the law, for it was hidden from the death of Joshua and his fellow-elders until the time of Zadok (CD 4.20-5.5).

3. From the Rule of War

That the judgment of God will be executed against all nations by his elect people is affirmed repeatedly in the Qumran texts. Thus, expounding Hab. 1:12b, the Habakkuk *pešer* says that 'into the hand of his elect God will commit the judgment of all nations' (1QpHab 5.4). Just how the elect would execute divine judgment against the nations is set out in detail in the *Rule of War*.

Parts of the *Rule of War* have been regarded as a reinterpretation or fresh application of the closing paragraph of Dan. 11 and the beginning of Dan. 12. The outline of the career of Antiochus Epiphanes, traced in Dan. 11:21-39, gives way in verses 40-45 to a forecast of events which found no historical fulfilment in him. It is not surprising, then, that attempts should have been made in antiquity (as they are made to this day) to interpret these last verses in terms of some other person or persons, and one of the earliest of these attempts is made in the *Rule of War*.

The Roman occupation of Judaea seemed to provide a setting in which the concluding scenes of Daniel's last vision might be expected to come true in real life. A plan of action was accordingly drawn up for the 'time of trouble' foretold in Dan. 12:1. The sons of light were to take the field against the sons of darkness, the army of Belial, in the forefront of which stood 'the troops of the Kittim of Assur' - the Roman legions stationed in Syria. Among other contingents in the army of Belial are 'the violators of the covenant' (cf. Dan. 11:32) and also the nations mentioned in Dan. 11:41 (Edom, Moab and Ammon), together with the Philistines. 'The king of the Kittim in Egypt' - i.e. the commander of the Roman forces in Egypt (an explanation of 'the king of the south' in Dan. 11:40) - will be attacked by the sons of light as he goes forth to give battle to the 'kings of the north' (the singular 'king of the north' in Dan. 11:40 has designedly been made plural). The warfare will be long and fluctuating, and attended by unparalleled tribulation for the destined beneficiaries of divine redemption; but with heavenly aid - not least with the championship of Michael (cf. Dan. 12:1) - redemption will be secured and 'iniquity will be vanquished, leaving no remnant' (1QM 1.1-14; 17.4-9; 18.1-5).

Naturally, where the fulfilment of prophecy lies in the interpreter's future, a measure of creative imagination is called for because the interpretation cannot be controlled by positive knowledge of what has happened or is happening, as it can be when the fulfilment lies in the recent past or the present.

4. *From the Melchizedek text*

Similarly, a greater measure of creative imagination is called for when the scene of the interpretation is set in the heavenly world and not on earth.

The figure of Melchizedek, king of Salem and priest of *'Ēl 'Elyôn*, attracted mystical speculation in Judaism and Christianity. He appears briefly in the story of Abraham (Gen. 14:18-20) and receives one further mention in the Hebrew Bible, where the Davidic king is acclaimed in a divine oracle as 'a priest for ever after the order of Melchizedek' (Ps. 110:4). An early example of the speculation which he attracted is presented in a fragmentary document from Cave 11 at Qumran, published in 1965 (11QMelch).

This document begins by quoting the regulations for the year of jubilee in Lev. 25:13 and for the year of release in Deut. 15:1, and interprets both in terms of the end-time return from exile. In the tenth and last year of jubilee, Israel will finally be gathered home (cf. Isa. 61:1). The tenth jubilee is the last because Daniel's seventy weeks comprise ten jubilee periods of 49 years each./1/ The announcement of restoration and liberty at that time is assigned to Melchizedek, 'for that is the epoch of Melchizedek's "acceptable year"' (11QMelch 9).

Biblical authority for assigning this ministry to Melchizedek is found in Ps. 82:1, ''*'ĕlōhîm* stands in the congregation of *'ēl*; he judges among the *'ĕlōhîm*', and in Ps. 7:8, 'Above it (*'ālèhā*, i.e. above the congregation of the peoples) return thou (Melchizedek) on high; *'ēl* (so 11QMelch 11 instead of MT *YHWH*) will judge the peoples'. Ps. 7:8 is linked to Ps. 82 by the common theme of judgment and by the coincidence of the 'congregation of the peoples' (Ps. 7:8) with the 'congregation of *'ēl*' (Ps. 82:1). Melchizedek is promoted to be head of the heavenly court; the *'ĕlōhîm* on which he sits in judgment are the spirits of Belial's lot. But his ministry of liberation for the people of his own lot, the children of light, is adumbrated in Isa. 52:7, 'How beautiful upon the mountains are the feet of him who brings good tidings,... who says to Zion, Your *'ĕlōhîm* reigns!"'. As Ps. 82 is linked to Ps. 7 by *ɡĕzērāh šāwāh*, so by the same device is it linked to Isa. 52, for the *'ĕlōhîm* who stands in the congregation of *'ēl* in Ps. 82:1 is the *'ĕlōhîm* who reigns in Isa. 52:7, and the person intended in both places is Melchizedek, who by passing sentence

on the hosts of Belial inaugurates the age of release for the
righteous. This presentation of Melchizedek has nothing in
common with the part he plays in the argument of Hebrews, where
everything that is said about him is based on the two places in
which he is mentioned by name in the OT. Even the statement
that he has been 'made like Son of God' (Heb. 7:3) is based on
what is said, and on what is not said, of him in Gen. 14:18-20.
There is no real affinity between the identification of Jesus
with the ʾĕlōhîm of Ps. 45:6 in Heb. 1:8 and the identification
of Melchizedek with the ʾĕlōhîm of Ps. 82:1 and Isa. 52:7. Ps.
45:6 is expressly addressed to the Lord's Anointed, who for
Christians has been manifested as Jesus, and in any case Jesus,
as the Son of God (Heb. 1:2, etc.), has a special title to the
designation ʾĕlōhîm. For the rest, it may be observed that if a
pious Jew of this period could interpret ʾĕlōhîm in Ps. 82:1 and
elsewhere as meaning Melchizedek, the argument which our Lord
based on ʾĕlōhîm ʾattem in Ps. 82:6 should have met with little
objection from the pious Jews with whom he was engaged in debate
(Jn. 10:34-36).

        The angelology of the Qumran texts, to which 11QMelch makes
its contribution, is an important subject in its own right.
Another source of information about it is the liturgical
composition called Serek šîrôt ʿôlat haššabbāt, represented by
at least four manuscripts from Cave 4 and by a fragment from
Masada. Taking up the theme, 'Praise God, all ye angels' (cf.
Pss. 97:7; 103:20; 148:2), this composition exhorts the angels,
under many names, to various forms of the worship of God. The
exhortation formed part of the liturgy accompanying (or perhaps
replacing) the burnt-offering (ʿôlāh) for every sabbath
throughout the year, according to the Qumran calendar (i.e. the
calendar of the book of Jubilees). As in some NT documents
(Hebrews and Revelation especially), the heavenly temple is
viewed as the archetype of which the earthly temple is a copy,
and the earthly liturgy is designed to reproduce that presented
by the angels before the heavenly throne.

        More liturgical fragments from Cave 4 are included in the
newly published Discoveries in the Judaean Desert VII, ed. M.
Baillet (Oxford, 1982). While the Qumran community evidently ha
a rich calendrical liturgy, no provision appears to have been
made in it for anything like a fixed lectionary.

5. From the Genesis Apocryphon
Only five columns from the Genesis Apocryphon have been
published, because of the poor state of preservation of the rest

of the scroll. From what has been published, it appears that
the Genesis story is retold in the first person, in the mouth of
one or another of the principal characters (Lamech, son of
Methuselah, in column 2 and Abraham in columns 19-22). The
narrative is considerably embellished, partly along the lines
already familiar from Jubilees and from the 'book of Noah' which
has been incorporated in 1 Enoch.

Column 2 describes the birth of Noah. The infant's
unearthly appearance makes his father Lamech suspect his wife
Bathenosh (she is so called also in Jubilees 4:28) of
misconduct with one of the fallen angels, but when she swears
that this is not so, he consults his father Methuselah, who in
turn goes to interview his own father Enoch in Parvaim
(possibly the earthly paradise) to ask him what the birth of
his wonder-child portends (cf. 1 Enoch 106:1-19). There is no
close affinity between this account and the birth-narratives of
Luke's first two chapters, where nothing is said of the physical
appearance of John or Jesus - unless it be said that the angel's
proclamation in Luke 2:10-12 serves the same purpose as Enoch's
message in 1QGenApoc 2.22ff. and 1 Enoch 106:13-107:2. As for
Joseph's suspicion in Mat. 1:19, that is occasioned by the
simple fact of Mary's pregnancy and not by anything unusual in
the child himself. (Reference may be made to Richard Bauckham's
treatment in this volume of the birth-narratives in Pseudo-
Philo's *LAB*.)

Columns 19-22 retell the narrative of Gen. 12:9-15:4, with
a wealth of embellishment. Abraham tells how, on the eve of his
going down to Egypt, he was warned in a dream of what would
happen to him there. The biblical record says briefly that when
Pharaoh's princes saw Sarah, 'they praised her to Pharaoh' (Gen.
12:15), but 1QGenApoc makes them go into minute detail about her
beauty; they add that in addition she 'possesses abundance of
wisdom' (20.2-8). Abraham and his company spend seven years in
Egypt; during the first five he successfully conceals her and
then she is kept in Pharaoh's palace for two years until the
multiplication of plagues forces the king to release her.

In the story of Abraham and Lot's separation (Gen. 13:8-12)
the biblical record makes Abraham take the initiative; there is
no word of this in 1QGenApoc, but Abraham says he 'was grieved'
when Lot parted company with him (21.7).

Then, when Abraham is invited not only to survey the land
which is to be his but also to walk through its length and
breadth (Gen. 13:14-17), we are given a detailed itinerary:
setting out from the river Gihon (Nile?), Abraham travels north
along the Mediterranean shore until he reaches the Taurus
range; then he turns east to the Euphrates and follows its
southward course as far as the Persian Gulf; then, he says, 'I
journeyed along the coast of the Persian Gulf until I came to
the tongue of the Sea of Reeds' and so back to the river Gihon.
Then he returned to his base at Mamre (1QGenApoc 21.15-22). The
frontiers of a 'Greater Israel' are here delineated, a
territory which possibly takes in the whole Arabian peninsula.

The account of the invasion and rout of the four kings
from the east (Gen. 14) is told with less embellishment. Arioch
is described as the king of Cappadocia (1QGenApoc 21.23). No
attempt is made to amplify the Melchizedek incident, except for
a note identifying the Valley of Shaveh with 'the valley of
Beth ha-Kerem' (1QGenApoc 22.13f.).

The published text ends with an account of Abraham's
vision in Gen. 15.1-6. A chronological note (based evidently on
Jubilees 13:8-14-1)/2/ indicates that ten years have elapsed
since his first arrival in Canaan - two years in the land before
his descent into Egypt, seven years in Egypt, and a further
year since returning from there (1QGenApoc 22.27-29).

The literary *genre* of this document is disputed: at one
time Matthew Black, following a suggestion of Paul Kahle, was
disposed to classify it as an early Aramaic Pentateuch Targum,
whereas J. T. Milik expressed the view that it was 'no true
Targum'./3/ Much depends on one's definition of 'targum'.
Certainly there is nothing in its embellishment of the
patriarchal narratives that can properly be called exegesis, or
even exposition, and nothing to which the NT offers an analogy.
This kind of embellishment has more in common with the type of
sermon in which a biblical narrative is amplified so that its
main features may be brought more vividly before the hearers'
eyes. There is a difference between amplifying an ancient
narrative for this kind of purpose and imaginatively
supplementing historical events of the present or of the recent
past with details which have no factual basis. It is indeed
widely maintained that this has happened in the redaction of
our gospel material; but the Genesis Apocryphon cannot be
adduced as a parallel case.

E. CONCLUDING OBSERVATIONS

The main point of resemblance between OT exegesis in the Qumran texts and that in the NT is the principle of reading the OT in the light of a new situation - a situation in which the community concerned (whether the Qumran community or the primitive Christian church) recognized the age of fulfilment. At Qumran this new situation was effectively introduced by the ministry of the Teacher of Righteousness, who also taught his followers their principles of biblical interpretation. In the Christian story it is John the Baptist who in many ways plays a preparatory part analogous to that of the Qumran Teacher, but the basic principles of OT interpretation were laid down not by him but by Jesus. An important difference between the two situations is that there never came a point in the history of the Qumran community (so far as it can be traced) when it was held that the Messiah (or Messiahs) had come, whereas the church proclaimed from its inception that the Messiah had come in the person of Jesus. The fact that he had come gave the greater precision to the church's interpretation of scripture: 'to him all the prophets bear witness' (Acts 10:43).

Here was the key to the understanding of all that the prophets had spoken: in the idiom of Qumran, here was the pēšer to clarify the rāz. According to 1 Pet. 1:10f., 'the prophets ... inquired what person or time was indicated by the Spirit of Christ within them when predicting the sufferings of Christ and the subsequent glory'. Their own oracles remained a mystery to the prophets, but to the apostles and their associates they had become an open book. No need for further inquiry: the person was Jesus; the time was now. This knowledge made the OT a new book for them. They read Isa. 40-66, for example, no longer with reference to Judah's deliverance from the Babylonian exile but rather as the record of the greater deliverance procured by the sufferings of Christ and proclaimed in the gospel. As the Qumran commentators found in the prophetic oracles references to the Teacher's opponents as well as to the Teacher himself, so the early Christians, having found in the crucified and exalted Jesus the one who fulfilled the OT, had little difficulty in recognizing allusions to his enemies - to Judas in Pss. 69:25 and 109:8 (Acts 1:20) and to Herod and Pontius Pilate with their associates in Ps. 2:1,2 (Acts 4:25-28).

It was the Christ-event that made the OT a new book to the early Christians: their new interpretation of the OT did not create the Christ-event or the narratives in which they recorded it. In so far as the Qumran literature provides an analogy, it lends no support to the view that the evangelists engaged in free redactional activity uninhibited by historical fact.

If the men of Qumran, taught by the Teacher of Righteousness, looked for the appearance of three distinct figures at the time of the end - a prophet, a priest and a king - the NT writers saw these three rôles coinciding in Jesus: he is the prophet like Moses (Acts 3:22f.; 7:37), the perpetual priest after the order of Melchizedek (Heb. 5:6) and the anointed king, 'the root and the offspring of David' (Luke 1: 32f.; John 1:49; Rom. 1:3; 15:12; Rev. 22:16). This gave a further coherence to their interpretation of scripture. In becoming a new book for the church, the OT became quite a different book from that which was read and expounded in the synagogue, even if the text was the same. A common Bible will not be a bond of unity if its readers use differently-coloured spectacles./4/

Notes

/1/ Cf. R. T. Beckwith, 'The Significance of the Calendar for Interpreting Essene Chronology and Eschatology', *Revue de Qumran* 10 (No. 38, May 1980) 167-202.

/2/ Beckwith, ibid., pp. 168,169.

/3/ M. Black, *The Scrolls and Christian Origins* (London: Nelson, 1961), 192-198; J. T. Milik, *Ten Years of Discovery in the Wilderness of Judaea* (London: SCM, 1959) 31.

/4/ Among the abundance of literature on the subject-matter of this paper mention should be made of two chapters in J. A. Fitzmyer's *Essays on the Semitic Background of the New Testament* (London: Geoffrey Chapman, 1971): 'The Use of Explicit Old Testament Quotations in Qumran Literature and in the New Testament' (pp. 3-58) and '"4QTestimonia" and the New Testament' (pp. 59-89).

JEWISH HISTORIOGRAPHY, MIDRASH, AND THE GOSPELS

R. T. France
London Bible College
Green Lane
Northwood, Middx.
HA6 2UW

This title promises more than a single paper can hope to deliver, especially when its author cannot claim more than a superficial knowledge of either Jewish historiography or midrash. It will necessarily operate at a programmatic level rather than in technical detail. My aim is to ask some basic questions in relation to the comparisons often made between the Christian gospels and various documents or literary tendencies in the Jewish world of the first Christian centuries, and the conclusions sometimes drawn from these comparisons with reference to the historical character of the gospels.

To put the matter very crudely, the impression is getting around among those who have some acquaintance with current New Testament scholarship that there is a literary activity known as 'midrash' which flourished among first-century Jews, which included (indeed in the more extreme form of this popular impression could be said to consist of) the attribution to historical figures of fictional words and deeds whose origin may be traced to meditation on the Old Testament./1/ Thus the hopes and ideas of sacred scripture have become 'actualised' in the mind of the pious reader into ostensibly historical events which are then attached to some revered figure and related as if they had actually happened. (In this paper I shall for convenience refer to this alleged phenomenon as 'creative midrash', while acknowledging that such a term begs many large questions.) Parts of the Christian gospels, it is then claimed, belong to this genre, so that their contents may more plausibly be ascribed to 'midrashic' imagination than to traditions of the actual words and deeds of Jesus of Nazareth.

Now of course no responsible scholar would put the case
like that, but I believe this is how the matter is increasingly
perceived by those who are not themselves aware of the
complexity of the issues involved.   To discuss this question
therefore requires attention to several distinct but related
issues:

(a) Is there evidence that in the first century AD there
was such a genre in Jewish literature (whether or not the
term 'midrash' is an appropriate one by which to describe it
- and that is a big enough issue on its own!)?

(b) If such a genre existed, was it the dominant Jewish
approach to the writing of 'history', or were there other
more favoured approaches to historiography?

(c) If there were different approaches to history, with
which of them, if any, is it appropriate to compare the
Christian gospels?   Are there grounds for believing that
the Christian writers would naturally follow any such
accepted conventions, or were there factors which made their
approach distinctive?

(d) What in fact is the relationship between scripture and
tradition that can be discerned in the gospels?

Each of these questions covers a variety of important
issues, and each deserves at least a sizeable volume to itself.
What follows can only, therefore, attempt to map out the
ground for a possible evaluation of the presence and influence
of 'creative midrash' in the gospels.   Questions (a) and (b)
will be the subject of section I of this paper, and question
(c) of section II.   Question (d) is unfortunately too large an
issue to tackle in the same paper, though a responsible answer
to it is in fact the key to a proper answer to our basic
question, the other issues being only prolegomena./2/

In this discussion I shall be sparing in my use of the
term 'midrash' because of the ambiguities which now surround
it.   Some use it of 'every interpretation and application of
the Scriptures',/3/ others of 'exegesis of scripture which
attaches the exegesis to the text which it is expounding or
from which it has been derived';/4/ some will apply the term
only to a specific genre of literary work which can as a whole

be labelled 'a midrash', others use it of a specific
exegetical method, involving a creative use of apparently
unrelated parts of the Old Testament to throw light on the
passage under discussion, while for others it is a pointer to
the whole framework of hermeneutical axioms and procedures
which underlies such exegesis.   It will make for lucidity if
rather than using such a slippery term I specify at each point
which of these subjects is at issue.   It is particularly
important to avoid the covert shift from one to another of
these subjects merely on the ground of the current (or even
ancient) use of the term 'midrash' rather than on that of a
demonstrable connection between them in the literature with
which we are concerned.   This shift has not always been
avoided in recent discussion./5/

The question before us is, then, 'Did the gospel writers
share in a Jewish literary milieu which made it natural for
them to embroider or invent narrative and/or sayings of Jesus
on the basis of Old Testament passages?'/6/   We shall discuss
first the Jewish literary milieu, then the relevance of this to
the aims and methods of the Christian evangelists.

I   SCRIPTURE AND HISTORY IN JEWISH LITERATURE

This section does not pretend to a comprehensive coverage
of Jewish historiography and scriptural interpretation.
Important Jewish works (e.g. the Testaments of the Twelve
Patriarchs, of Abraham, and of Moses) are not included at all,
and those which are surveyed can be given only the most cursory
treatment.   Each demands a more detailed study, such as those
provided in this volume by Richard Bauckham on Pseudo-Philo and
by F. F. Bruce on the Qumran *pesharim*.   I aim here only to
illustrate the *variety* of approach which may be discerned in
extant sources of (or relevant to) the early Christian period,
so as to put a question mark against any assumption that there
was such a thing as *the* Jewish approach to the recording of
history./7/

Before mentioning those books normally termed 'midrashim',
I would like therefore to attempt a rough classification of
other types of non-biblical Jewish literature in terms of their
approach to the relation between scripture and history.   The
categories are not watertight, and in some cases the same work
may exhibit more than one of these approaches;   but the

approaches themselves seem to me sufficiently distinct to be
worth isolating in this way.

A. The retelling of biblical history

This important category accounts for a large part of the
writing of history in the literature with which we are
concerned.   It is not the telling of stories never told
before, but the retelling of sacred history already enshrined
in scripture, but now re-presented in order to emphasise
particular interpretations which the author wishes to draw
out of (or perhaps impose on) the biblical text.   It is thus
necessarily at the same time historiography and biblical
interpretation.

It is a common characteristic of these works that they
embellish the biblical narrative.   This embellishment may
take the form of an interpretative paraphrase, or of an
editorial comment of a moralising kind.   Sometimes, however,
the content of the story is itself affected, either by the
omission (or drastic compression) of events which the author
finds unacceptable or irrelevant to his purpose, or by the
addition of sometimes quite considerable sections of
narrative and/or sayings for which the biblical text
apparently supplies no warrant.

1. *The Targumim*
Within the targumim there is a fascinating range from an
exact correspondence with the biblical text (in so far as the
demands of translation allow) to the large-scale introduction
of additional material in parts of the Palestinian Targum.
Often the motive is to explain a puzzling aspect of the text,
as when God's apparently arbitrary command to Abraham to
sacrifice Isaac is explained in Pseudo-Jonathan as the outcome
of a dispute between Isaac and Ishmael, and the whole incident
is consequently turned from being purely a test of Abraham's
obedience to be a testimony to Isaac's dedication (the 'lad'
is, in this targum, 37 years old, and knows well what is going
on), and therefore a suitable basis for the developing Jewish
theology of the Aqedah.   There is also in this case a clear
desire to highlight Isaac as a moral example for the reader;
this too is a common motive for embellishment of the biblical
story in the targumim.   In this way the biblical story is

'actualised';   i.e. it is made relevant to the concerns of the author's own time./8/

It should be noted, however, that the motive for this expansion is not some other biblical text which produces a 'midrashic' combination of biblical themes, but rather the desire to interpret the biblical story in the light of the contemporary theological climate.   The starting-point for the interpretative process, in other words, is the history itself (which in these writings is necessarily itself 'scriptural') as it is perceived from the writer's own situation.   History is embellished indeed, but not on the basis of any scriptural text other than itself.

It would take many volumes to test how far this conclusion would be typical of the targumim in general, but I would hazard a guess that it is not untypical, and that in that case it is not correct to describe the targumic process as an embellishment of history *from scripture*.   We should not allow this issue to be clouded by the fact that the history is itself part of scripture.

2.   *The Book of Jubilees*

Among extant non-biblical works, Jubilees is the elder brother of the genre of the retelling of biblical history (though anticipated within the Old Testament canon by the Book of Chronicles).   Charles describes it as 'an enlarged Targum on Genesis and Exodus',/9/ and much of it is a relatively straightforward (though in places much abbreviated) repetition of the biblical accounts.   Here, as in the targumim, expansion may occur in order to explain puzzling or unacceptable features.   To take the same example, God's command to Abraham to sacrifice Isaac is again a cause of embarrassment./10/   In Jubilees, however, the explanation has a clearly scriptural origin;   it is found in a heavenly debate between God and Mastema which clearly reflects the role of Satan in the first two chapters of Job (*Jub.* 17:15ff).

It is perhaps typical of Jubilees, in a way that we have suggested is not generally true of the targumim, that passages of scripture other than the one being related are drawn into the interpretation and may add features to the narrative, as in the introduction of Mastema just mentioned.

The author's very prominent calendrical scheme itself, which constantly obtrudes into the narrative, owes its original inspiration to the jubilee legislation of Leviticus, even though it has clearly developed in his own mind or in the community to which he belongs far beyond its scriptural origins.   Similarly, the actions of the patriarchs are regularly made to conform to the legal regulations of the later books of the Pentateuch.   The breadth of the author's scriptural background is most strikingly illustrated in chapter 1, in the long 'opening speech' attributed to God on Mount Sinai and in the ensuing dialogue, in all of which the language is a mosaic of scriptural themes and expressions from many parts of the Old Testament (with a strong preference for deuteronomic language).

So Jubilees provides ample evidence of the embellishment of the biblical narrative with details based on other parts of scripture.   At the same time, it should be noted that the essential framework of the narrative in Genesis and Exodus is preserved.   The author does not invent whole stories, but rather explains, embellishes and interprets those which he finds in the text.   The imposition of his distinctive theological framework has not meant the abandonment of the biblical history, but only the addition of interpretative features and speeches.   Even with this author's rich scriptural background, there is no evidence of the invention *de novo* of scripturally-based narrative.

3.   *The Genesis Apocryphon*

The small part of this work that has survived and been published reveals it to be a writing with features reminiscent both of the Palestinian Targum and of Jubilees. Some of the extant part (especially that dealing with Genesis 14) is fairly literal targum, though the author is not averse to abbreviating his text in places (see the account of Lot's choice).   But he can also expand where it takes his fancy, as when God's command to Abraham to walk through the land (Gen 13:17) is developed into an actual journey with detailed itinerary.

The most striking expansion, of course, is that of Abraham's stay in Egypt.   This story clearly fascinated the author (he was not alone in this!), and he develops it not

only in order to explain away Abraham's deception (by a
dream), and to rescue Sarah's reputation (by stating, as
Genesis does not, that Pharaoh was unable to consummate the
marriage), but also in the interests of a sheer delight in
story-telling, with extravagant praise of Sarah's beauty,
details of the plagues which beset Pharaoh, and a variety of
prayers, discussions and consultations to draw out the
dramatic value of the story.

There was clearly an equally expanded treatment of the
birth of Noah, drawing on the tradition of Lamech's
suspicions about his parentage which is preserved in the 'Book
of Noah' (1 Enoch 106), but unfortunately too little of that
section has survived to give a clear picture.

We are nearer here to the world of popular story-telling
and the legends which increasingly clustered round the
biblical heroes, than to the scripturally-based interpretation
of Jubilees.   In the case of the Noah legend the author seems
to have abandoned the biblical text entirely, though the
attestation of the same legendary material in 1 Enoch shows
that he was not simply allowing his imagination free rein, but
following existing tradition, wherever this may have
originated.

4. *Philo*
As a first-century Jewish writer of 'biographies' Philo
is clearly important in discussing the literary background of
the gospels.   His *Life of Moses*, though a much longer and
more philosophical work than the Christian gospels, is the
most nearly comparable work, and may be taken as typical of
his approach to the writing of history.

Book II of the *Life of Moses* /11/ has less obvious
relevance to our study, as it is more a discussion of three
main aspects of Moses' importance, not set out in the form of
an account of his life, though including some relevant
incidents sparsely scattered in the text to illustrate the
points at issue.   Philo's main interest in the details of
the Old Testament accounts here is to draw out their
theological significance by extensive allegorisation of the
details of the cultic laws.   Thus the biblical text provides
the raw materials for his presentation of Moses as the ideal

lawgiver, priest and prophet; but for a more 'biographical' account of Moses' life we need to turn to Book I, the presentation of Moses as king.

F. H. Colson introduces his edition of the *Life of Moses* by commenting on the 'essential fidelity with which Philo adheres to the narrative of Scripture'. There is, he says, 'little or none of the legendary accretions' found in Jubilees, Pseudo-Philo, Josephus and the later rabbinic tradition. He goes on, however, 'There is, of course, any amount of amplification.'/12/ Fidelity which allows amplification but not legendary accretion: is this a distinction without a difference, or has Colson put his finger on something important?

To take an obvious example, the account of Moses' birth (*Vit. Mos.* I.8-17) does not move far from Exodus 2, though it 'amplifies' it into a more touching story, with the sort of details of the actors' motives, reactions, etc. which any reader of the Exodus account could provide from his own imagination. But the dreams and prophecies, and the specific competition between Pharaoh and Moses, which tradition had superimposed on the story by the time of Josephus and the Targum Pseudo-Jonathan, find no echo in Philo. Here we do apparently find 'amplification without legendary accretion'.

What Philo does add to the biblical account is not so much narrative detail, still less whole stories, but a character portrait of Moses as the perfect ascetic, the single-minded philosopher. The whole account is deeply and explicitly moralistic, and incidents which are either irrelevant or embarrassing to this aim are omitted, while those that are recorded are 'amplified' to make sure that the point is not missed. Usually Philo does his moralising *in propria persona*, though he is not averse to occasionally inserting short speeches of Moses for which the biblical text gives no warrant. (The crossing of the Red Sea is told twice, and the two accounts attribute quite different speeches to Moses at the same point: I.174; II.251-252.)

By and large I would judge Colson's distinction between Philo's 'amplification' and the 'legendary accretion' which his work does not display to be a valid and important one.

It should be noted also that the inspiration for the
considerable amplification is seldom, if ever, a 'midrash' on a
biblical text (other than the biblical story being retold), but
rather the moral and philosophical concerns of the author, and
particularly his apologetic aim.   If Philo's work is in any
way relevant to the literary genre of the Christian gospels, it
provides no encouragement for the discovery there of 'creative
midrash'.

5. 'Pseudo-Philo'
The *Liber Antiquitatum Biblicarum* is perhaps best
described as in the tradition of the Book of Jubilees (some
details from which reappear in this work), often retelling the
biblical stories fairly exactly, though abbreviating
drastically in the earlier period.   But the expansion of the
history is much more extensive than in Jubilees.   Much of it
is, like that of Jubilees, in the interests of the author's
particular theological concerns, especially in the areas of
eschatology, angels and demons, and the greatness of Israel.
Some consists in the liberal addition of names and numbers.

The most extensive narrative additions are the stories of
Abraham's opposition to the Tower of Babel, and of the exploits
of Kenaz.   The latter is, in M. R. James' words, 'a sudden
burst of inventiveness' for most of which no obvious source can
be suggested, scriptural or otherwise.   The story about
Abraham, however, while basically deriving from an imaginative
bringing together or unrelated parts of Genesis 11 (on the not
uncommon principle that juxtaposition in the biblical text
implies historical connexion),/13/ does seem to provide an
instance of a narrative feature derived from elsewhere in
scripture, in that Abraham is made to go through a fiery
furnace which apparently owes its origin to Daniel 3.   Even
here, however, it can be argued that Daniel 3 has provided
some of the content of the story, but is not itself its
origin./14/   Elsewhere in Pseudo-Philo there are numerous
examples of narratives influenced by other passages of
scripture, but it is usually a fine judgement as to whether
these passages are the origin of the narratives which echo
them./15/

6. Josephus
By far the most extensive 'retelling of biblical history'
is in Books I-XI of Josephus' *Antiquities*.   Here we have the

advantage of a useful recent study by F. G. Downing./16/
Downing's aim is to consider Josephus' redactional method as a
possible parallel to that of the gospels (especially Luke), so
his article is closely allied to our present purpose. On the
basis of a detailed study of Josephus' retelling of the stories
of Joshua-Judges and of the Letter of Aristeas, Downing
concludes that apart from the frequent interpolation of speeches
Josephus 'has added no story, no major event.... Josephus
certainly adds and excises details, and can give a quite new
colour and import to "the same" incident, so that it conveys
the impression he wants it to create (and avoids any he wishes
to eschew). But apart from speeches ... he does not create
events or incidents, either out of his head or by midrashic
exposition (and that despite being aware, as Thackeray and
others have shown, of the midrashic tradition).'/17/ Where
non-biblical materials came to Josephus in a source he was
using, he was prepared to include them, but imaginative or
'midrashic' creation of stories is quite foreign to his method.

     This is not, of course, to suggest that Josephus simply
copied his sources, scriptural or otherwise. They are
completely recast into Josephus' own words, and he may
rearrange them quite freely, as in the case of his classified
and selective analysis of the Mosaic legislation in
Antiquities IV.196-301. But even here, Downing concludes, in
terms of the *content* of the account 'the tradition remains in
control'./18/

     We shall return to Josephus in relation to his treatment
of more recent history, but in so far as his work is a
'retelling of biblical history' it seems it may properly be
described as a thorough reworking and re-presentation of the
biblical traditions, with the addition of much interpretative
and apologetic comment, particularly in the form of speeches,
but not as creative in relation to the sources used, still less
as 'midrashic'.

          B. Scripture applied to contemporary history

     We move now to a quite different type of literature, but
one which also impinges from a different angle on our subject
of the relation between scripture and history. Whereas in
the previous section we considered the treatment of history
which was *contained in* scripture, we deal now with the

interpretation of recent history and contemporary events *in the light of* scripture.

1. The Qumran pesharim

The rationale underlying the various 'commentaries' on scripture recovered from Qumran is that scripture in its entirety has a direct relevance to the recent history and present situation of the community. It is this conviction which makes possible a commentary on a verse-by-verse basis, since there is no part of the text which cannot be so applied, given the right key to its interpretation. The result is, of course, not what we would call exegesis of the text, and the application usually seems totally arbitrary. Sometimes the required contemporary relevance can be achieved only by modifying the text, to the extent of changing a suffix, rearranging a letter or two, or occasionally exploiting variant textual traditions. But this very fact suggests that while the biblical text is the framework on which the work is constructed, the controlling factor is the situation to which it is to be applied. To put it crudely, if the history were being created out of the text, there would be no need to adapt the text to fit the history.

The actual shape of the community's history and its contemporary concerns is not easy for us to reconstruct; but for the original readers it was common ground, the given factor on which the biblical exposition operated. For that reason they had no need to spell it out. Indeed there is little actual narration of historical events, but rather allusion to events presumed to be familiar to the readers. The whole concern is with how the biblical text may be perceived to predict or relate to these events.

The idea of 'creating' and narrating supposedly historical events and situations is therefore foreign to these works. They start at the other end, and any creative work is carried out on the biblical text and its interpretation rather than on the shape of the history. I am not aware of any point in the Qumran pesharim where it is demonstrable that the biblical text has provided the impetus for a fictional addition to recent history.

Of course the main concern of the Qumran exegetes was not with the past or the present but with the future. A large

part of the application of the pesharim is to what God is about
to do, and here of course they had no option but 'create' the
future events out of the biblical text.   The War Scroll is a
good example of this tendency, where scriptural texts
(particularly the last two chapters of Daniel) are used in the
construction of a detailed scenario of the coming conflict
(though the details generally owe more to the author's vivid
imagination as an armchair general than to scripture!).   But
the projection of future events on the basis of scripture is
clearly a quite different exercise from the rewriting or
embellishing of past history or of contemporary events, and
for this practice the biblical exegesis of the Qumran community
offers us no precedent.

2. Apocalyptic

In discussing the future hopes of Qumran we have already
begun to consider this genre.   The feature we have just noted,
the prediction of future events on the basis of scriptural
prophecies and patterns, is of course at the heart of the
apocalyptist's purpose.   But the recording of past history is
not their concern except in so far as it is necessary to
provide the build-up to the coming climax.

In this context historical descriptions are naturally
highly generalised and couched in language which makes them
unsuitable as sources for the prosaic reconstruction of the
course of events.   Thus the recapitulation of world history in
1 Enoch 85-90 is cast in the symbolic form of a vision of
animals, details of which can be identified with events known
from Old Testament and later history, but only in terms of the
most general outline.   The typical apocalyptist does not go in
for straight narration of past history.   Perhaps the nearest
approach to this is 2 Baruch 56-74, the interpretation of the
vision of the black and white rain.   Here the main phases of
biblical history up to the Exile are recapitulated and
classified as either good or bad (in a manner reminiscent of
1066 and All That!) but only in broad outline, which does not
offer promising material for the historical researcher.   The
sequence finishes, remarkably, with only two phases to cover
the whole period from the Exile to the coming of the Messianic
kingdom (i.e., assuming a late first century AD date for the
book, more than six centuries of recent history), in the
course of which the only historically identifiable event is the
restoration of the temple.   The focus here, as in all

apocalyptic, is thus firmly on the future; apocalypses,
therefore, while they may offer large-scale, schematic
interpretations of the course of history,/19/ are not in any
significant sense records of historical events, least of all in
recent history.

Of course literary genres are seldom as watertight as the
text-books would like them to be.   Jubilees, which we have
already considered as a retelling of biblical history,
occasionally verges on the apocalyptic and makes reference to
post-biblical events.   In *Jubilees* 23:11-32 the author
reflects on the progressive deterioration of human life since
the time of Abraham, leading on to a prediction of the woes
and conflicts which will precede the messianic age and the
blessings of that age itself.   But this too is all couched in
very unspecific terms, based no doubt on historical
experience, but in no sense a recording of historical events.
Similarly when the curse of Isaac on the Philistines (*Jub.*
24:28-32) is referred to the destruction of the Philistines by
the Kittim there is no question of rewriting history - rather,
as at Qumran, that history has been 'discovered' in scripture.

Apocalyptic, then, is not a promising ground in which to
look for light on 'creative midrash'.

C.   The recording of post-biblical history

The works considered in section A were concerned with
retelling history which was itself part of scripture, but
showed little interest in general in adding to that history
under the influence of other parts of scripture.   Those in
section B freely applied scriptural texts of all sorts to the
contemporary situation, but were not concerned with narrating
recent or contemporary events as such.   We turn now,
therefore, to Jewish works whose concern *was* to narrate more
recent historical events, to see whether here there is
evidence of the influence of scripture in creating fictional
accounts.

It is immediately striking that the works to be
considered here are few in number.   It may be an accident of
history, but the impression is easily gained that
historiography (other than the retelling of biblical history)
was not in itself a major interest of most Jews around the

early Christian period.

1. 1 and 2 Maccabees

A first century AD Jew wishing to write post-biblical
history had before him at least the model of the first two
books of Maccabees, both written within two or three
generations of the events they narrate.   (I take it the
so-called Third Book of Maccabees is more appropriately
classified with a historical romance like Judith than as a
recording of actual history.)

1 Maccabees writes in the style of an Old Testament
historian, his language heavily influenced by Old Testament
phraseology.   At times he is clearly concerned to point out
the links between the story he narrates and comparable Old
Testament events, most notably in the explicit comparison of
Mattathias with Phinehas in 2:26, backed up by the list of Old
Testament heroes in Mattathias' farewell speech.   But I am not
aware that anyone believes the content of the narrative to be
extrapolated from the Old Testament; 1 Maccabees, for all its
scriptural colouring, is regarded as a piece of responsible
factual historiography./20/   The one explicit
'formula-quotation' which occurs in 7:16-17 takes up a general
scriptural statement of the martyrdom of the people of God,
appropriate enough to the context to which it is applied, but
in no way itself a suitable *source* for the story of Alcimus'
preemptive strike.

2 Maccabees, for all the similarity of some of its
subject-matter, is of a quite different genre, more
Hellenistic than Jewish; it belongs to the class quaintly
described by literary specialists as 'pathetic historiography',
in which the goodies are very good and the baddies very bad,
and no pains are spared to enlist the reader's sympathies on
the right side.   Jason's epitomiser aims to be readable and
interesting rather than exhaustive (2:23-31; 15:38-39), and it
may be therefore that Jason's own work was less heavily
weighted towards the marvellous and the emotional; but the
epitomiser claims that while omitting much that was dull he has
added nothing (2:32), so it seems that Jason too was not
averse to stories of exemplary courage and of divine
deliverance by angelic horsemen.   All this, however, belongs
to the world of Hellenistic story-telling, and betrays no Old
Testament influence beyond the necessarily Jewish colouring of

the story.   When the author feels called on to give a
theological rationale for the events he records, he does so by
an explicitly homiletic digression (5:17-20; 6:12-17) which
owes nothing beyond its basic Jewishness to the Old Testament.

Whatever may be concluded then about the historical
veracity of the stories in 1 and 2 Maccabees (and in the case
of 1 Maccabees at least the verdict is likely to be very
positive), neither work shows signs of an influence from the
Old Testament beyond the provision of the theological
background against which the events of recent history are set,
and in the case of 1 Maccabees of the appropriate style and
language for writing the history of the people of God.

2. Josephus
The *Antiquities* does not finish with the Old Testament
canon, and the *Jewish War* deals with the events of the author's
own lifetime.   This is by far the most important example of
Jewish historiography within the period that interests us.
Nor does the fact that Josephus' works were written with an eye
to a non-Jewish readership reduce their significance for us,
for the same may be said of some if not all of the Christian
gospels.

We have seen above that F. G. Downing's study of
Josephus' method led him to the conclusion that Josephus set
great store by the faithful reproduction of the content (though
not the form) of his sources, and was not given to imaginative
additions except in the form of speeches.   This conclusion was
drawn largely from Josephus' history of the biblical period,
for which his sources are accessible to us.   For the
post-biblical period the sources are not so often available,
since much of Josephus' later material is drawn from his own
memory and researches, and his main source for the rather
earlier period, Nicolas of Damascus, is no longer extant.
However, we do still have one post-biblical source
extensively used by Josephus, the Letter of Aristeas, and this
too was taken into Downing's study.   Here too he finds the
same remarkable fidelity to the contents of the source,
despite a deliberate attempt 'to change whatever he can' in
terms of wording.   There are omissions, of course, but with
regard to the insertion of material not derivable from the
source the conclusions quoted above apply if anything more
strongly to the non-canonical Aristeas than to Josephus'

handling of the biblical history.

Beyond that we are left largely to speculation as to how
much, if any, of Josephus' history is his own invention.
Some is, no doubt, legendary, but that does not mean that it
was Josephus who started the legend.   I would hazard a guess,
and it can be no more, that his performance, if it does not
consistently match his promise 'neither to add nor omit
anything,'/21/ is at least governed by that ideal.   As for the
creation of recent 'history' out of scripture, it seems to me
that in the light of his handling of his biblical sources we
should be very cautious in assuming such a procedure, and I am
not aware that it has been demonstrated to be a significant
factor in his writing./22/

3. Stories of the Rabbis

While the rabbinic writings do not make it their business
to record recent history for its own sake, they offer many
brief anecdotes about individual rabbis which are related in
order to illustrate the point under discussion.   Among these
anecdotes, those concerning Ḥanina ben Dosa may be expected to
offer us one of the closest parallels to the gospels' stories
about Jesus, both in terms of date and location (Ḥanina was a
first century AD Galilean) and in terms of at least some
features of their respective characters (Ḥanina, like Jesus,
was something of a non-conformist, suspected of a loose
attitude to legal observances, living a life of poverty and
generosity, constantly available to help those in need,
usually by miraculous means, a man whose close relationship
with God became proverbial).

Here we have the advantage of a careful collection and
discussion of the relevant traditions (which are not, of
course, preserved together in documents about Ḥanina, like the
gospels) by Geza Vermes./23/   From his discussion it is clear
that this 'charismatic rabbi' was the sort of figure around
whom popular stories were likely to cluster, so that if ever
we might expect to find stories created out of scripture and
attached to a revered figure of recent history it ought to be
here.

Among the stories collected by Vermes I noticed only
three possible Old Testament sources:

(a) In two of the stories (*Ber.* 34b; *BK* 50a)/24/ the onlookers respond to a display of supernatural knowledge, 'Are you a prophet?', to which Ḥanina replies with the words of Amos 7:14, 'I am no prophet, nor am I a prophet's son'.   In neither case, however, does the story bear any resemblance to the Amos passage.   The formula is simply a scriptural phrase picked up and used on its own for a purpose which its original context could not have suggested.   The formula, in other words, is scriptural, but the narrative situation into which it is inserted came into existence independently of it.

(b) In *jBer.* 9a we find a formula reminiscent of Matthew's formula-quotations: God provided a spring of water under Ḥanina's feet 'to fulfil that which is written, "He implements the desire of those who fear him, he hears their cry and saves them"'.   If the event is specifically stated to have happened in order to fulfil Ps 145:19, is not this a clear case of a story created out of scripture?   Perhaps, but it is remarkable that the passage cited is couched in quite general terms, and neither the words cited nor their wider context suggest the specific provision of a spring of water.   Would it not be at least as plausible to suggest, as I would also wish to argue in the case of Matthew's formula-quotations, that a suitable Old Testament text has been added to draw out the scriptural significance of an existing miracle-story, however this may have originated?

(c) Vermes concludes from the general character of the miracles and other activity attributed to Ḥanina that he is portrayed in the likeness of Elijah./25/   Like Elijah, he prayed and God sent rain, *Ta'an* 24b (though the shape of the story is totally different).   Many other miracle stories relate to crises in everyday life (inadequate beams in a building, vinegar burning in a lamp when it was used in mistake for oil, provision of bread and a table to alleviate his poverty, disputes with neighbours over the behaviour of his goats, the theft of his donkey); the atmosphere is not unlike some of the Elijah and Elisha miracles (the widow's oil, the axe-head, etc.), but in none of these is the actual content sufficiently similar to suggest direct derivation.   It is rather a case of a general pattern of the miracle-working holy man, of which Elijah is the prototype and into which Ḥanina (among others) fits.   But if the actual stories about Ḥanina derive from this scriptural background, it is remarkable that

their specific content bears so little resemblance to that of
Elijah's miracles.

In all, the stories about Ḥanina bear more of the marks of
popular story-telling, involving often rather trivial
miraculous events, than of derivation from passages of the Old
Testament.   That specific incidents, or Ḥanina's life-style in
general, were then seen as fulfilling a scriptural pattern is
not surprising, hence the use of the Old Testament passages we
have noted./26/   But this is not at all the same thing as a
'creative midrash' which spins a story about Ḥanina simply out
of the biblical text;   that does not seem to have happened.

D.   The midrashim

In the discussion of all the above Jewish works I have
made little use of the term 'midrash' (beyond the use of my
question-begging shorthand label 'creative midrash'!).   Some
of them undoubtedly share some of the characteristics of the
works properly so-called, but none of them is, in terms of
literary genre, 'a midrash' in the sense in which the term is
applied to certain rabbinic writings.   It has been my aim to
show that a realistic reconstruction of Jewish literary
approaches to history around the first century AD will not
necessarily give a central place to midrash as such - indeed it
may find the midrashim proper of only peripheral interest, for,
as Vermes comments, 'historiography proper (is) a literary
genre completely alien to talmudic and midrashic writings'./27/
Let me then conclude this whistle-stop tour of Jewish
literature of the early Christian period with a few comments on
the possible relevance of the midrashim proper to the literary
milieu of the gospels as records of recent history.

The first comment must be in relation to their date.
While no one would suggest that the material contained in the
midrashim all derives from the period of their ultimate
literary composition, it is worth noting that with the
exception of the Tannaitic Midrashim (Mekilta, Sifra and Sifre)
few parts of the existing midrashim, if any, can be dated in
their literary form earlier than the fourth century AD, and
many are several centuries later. The dating of rabbinic
material is notoriously difficult, but at least there seems to
be a prima facie implausibility about using these works in
their final literary form as a source for reconstructing the

literary milieu of the first century, even though some of the
traditions they contain undoubtedly belong nearer to that
period.

As for the Tannaitic Midrashim, which approach closer in
their composition to the date with which we are concerned, the
remarkable fact is that very little of their material is
haggadic; they are in fact sometimes referred to as 'the
halakhic midrashim'. Haggadic midrash, the genre which is
usually appealed to as a background for creative tendencies in
the gospels, is a characteristic almost exclusively of the
later midrashim, not of those of the tannaitic period. In
other words, in so far as any dating is possible, the
impression is of a progression from halakhic to haggadic
midrash, the latter being primarily a characteristic of the
post-Mishnaic period./28/

So while individual traditions may indeed be recorded in
the midrashim, as also in the Talmud (see the passages about
Hanina cited above), which are relevant to the assessment of
first-century Jewish approaches to historiography, the
midrashim as literary works are not likely to aid us in
reconstructing the literary milieu of the gospels. In fact we
have seen that quite a full picture of the relevant Jewish
literary milieu can be constructed without invoking the later
phenomenon of the midrashim as a literary genre at all.

E. Conclusions

The aim of this brief survey, which was of necessity more
'impressionistic' than based on detailed study of all the
relevant documents, was to illustrate the *variety* of approach
to the relation between scripture and history in Jewish writing.

1. *Sacred history*

In retelling the stories of the Old Testament, we have
seen a wide range of degrees of fidelity to the original.
While many stories are retold, as in the Babylonian Targumim,
with little more than a paraphrase of the text, most writers
felt much more free to impose their own shape on the
traditions. The general tendency was to retain the essential
shape and order of the stories, though the omission or drastic
compression of parts found either unacceptable or uninteresting
was common. Some writers, however, were prepared to rearrange

and systematise the biblical material to suit a redactional
scheme of their own, notably Philo and Josephus.

     None of the writers studied were reluctant to interpret
or explain aspects of the stories in terms of their own
theological or moral stance - indeed this interpretation was
often the raison d'être of the retelling of the biblical
story.   In the case of Jubilees this interpretation was
sometimes clearly based on passages of scripture other than
the one being related, the writer's mind being saturated with
scriptural language and ideas.   Generally speaking, however,
the writer worked in his explanations from his own framework
of thought without specific reference to other biblical
passages.   Such interpretation and expansion, whether
explicitly based on scripture or not, could and usually did
take place without affecting the essential narrative content
derived from the Old Testament.

     There are, however, considerable additions to the biblical
narrative in some works.   In most cases the origin of the
additional material is unknown.   In the Genesis Apocryphon's
account of Abraham in Egypt it is apparently the writer's love
of a good story which has led him to fill out the brief
biblical account.   Sometimes a large complex of non-biblical
material will arise for no obvious reason other than inventive
story-telling, as with Pseudo-Philo's stories of Kenaz.
Hagiographic expansion of the stories of great men led to the
growth of a secondary tradition, which may appear in similar
form in different writings (e.g. the Genesis Apocryphon and the
'Book of Noah' on the birth of Noah, or Josephus and the Targum
Pseudo-Jonathan on the birth of Moses).   But again in very few
of these cases is there a clear derivation of the additional
material from other parts of scripture; Pseudo-Philo provides
some of the most likely instances, though even there the
distinction between a scriptural origin and a scriptural
colouring of the narrative is not easy to apply.

     We noted Colson's distinction between 'amplification'
which is consonant with 'essential fidelity to the narrative
of scripture' and the 'legendary accretion' with which he
charges Jubilees, Pseudo-Philo and even Josephus.   I do not
imagine that anyone would want to absolve Pseudo-Philo of the
charge, but we have seen that Downing's study of Josephus
indicates that he too displays an 'essential fidelity' to his

sources, though amplifying with speeches and moralising
comments, and that even where he records non-biblical
traditions it can be shown that he tends to follow sources
rather than to invent stories out of his own head.   What we
have not noted outside Pseudo-Philo, and less radically in
Jubilees, is any significant tendency to create or embellish
narratives out of other parts of scripture, in the way which
has come to be known as 'midrashic'.

2.   Recent history
In the case of ancient, sacred history we are able to
compare the later retelling with the biblical original.   With
regard to more recent history no such direct comparison with
the sources used (if any) is generally possible.   What is
remarkable is the lack of interest in most Jewish writings of
the period in relating recent history at all.   What Daniel
Patte says of the targumim could be written over most of the
literature we have been considering: 'There is not reference
in the Targumim, so far as I know, to *present* events (present
to the targumist, that is) which could be considered as having
this basic identity with the events of the sacred history.
To put it bluntly: it is as if for the targumist God acted (in
the past), will act (in the eschatological future), but is not
acting in between.'/29/

Even the writers of the Qumran pesharim, who took such
pains to relate scripture to their own situation, did so
primarily in view of their expectation of its imminent
fulfilment in the future;   'writing history' was not in itself
of interest to them, still less the creation of recent history
out of the texts they studied.   It was the texts that had to
be made to fit their situation, not vice versa.

In those books which do record post-biblical events, while
the aim is often clearly moral and hortatory, sometimes
apologetic, there is generally little sign of interest in
relating those events to scripture, though 1 Maccabees does
display this tendency quite markedly.   And even then it is
rather a matter of interpreting the events in the light of
scriptural patterns, as when Mattathias is likened to Phinehas
or Hanina appears as an Elijah-type holy man, than by any
discernible tendency to create narratives out of scripture.
In relation to recent, non-biblical history, therefore, there
is even less evidence of stories deriving from 'creative

midrash' than there is in the retelling of sacred history from
the distant past.

I would conclude, then, in relation to questions (a) and
(b) set out at the beginning, that it is dangerous to speak in
terms of a uniform 'Jewish approach to historiography' around
the early Christian period, and that it would certainly be
going far beyond the evidence to speak of the imaginative
creation of stories out of scripture as a characteristic of any
such approach, particularly with reference to recent,
non-biblical events./30/

II   THE GOSPELS AND THE JEWISH LITERARY MILIEU

It has long been fashionable to describe the Christian
gospels as constituting a literary genre of their own.   While
this is in important ways a true observation, it does not rule
out the value of enquiring in what ways they may be related to
existing literary practice in the environment to which they
belong, if not in terms of their literary shape as a whole, at
least in terms of some of their ideals and methods.   To which,
then, if any, of the variety of Jewish works we have been
considering is it appropriate to compare the gospels?

I limit the study to Jewish works because I do not believe
that C. H. Talbert,/31/ despite many interesting parallels, has
made out a strong case for classifying the gospels among
Graeco-Roman biographies.   The *primary* context not only of the
events recorded but also of the writing of the gospels is
generally agreed to be Jewish.   More importantly, in relation
to our particular question of the possible effects of Old
Testament scripture on the narrative, clearly no work from
outside the Jewish sphere of influence is likely to be relevant.

In their overall shape the gospels may perhaps be compared
to at least the first book of Philo's *Life of Moses*.   In each
case a great man of God is singled out as an object of
admiration and a source of instruction, by means of a roughly
chronological account of the main events of his life, together
with selections from his teaching.   The more systematic
discussion in Philo's second book, where the narrative content
is drastically reduced, while it may be compared in principle
with some of the collections on specific themes in John, and to
a lesser extent Matthew, is on a quite different scale and in a

much less 'biographical' form.

The principal difference between the gospels and Philo's *Life of Moses* from a literary point of view is that the latter has, in the first book, an existing framework into which it must fit, in that it is retelling a story which is already written in the Old Testament.   Philo is not bound to reproduce the scriptural material in its entirety, and on occasion chooses not to do so, but the basic shape of his work is that of a retelling of the biblical story.   The writers of the Christian gospels, on the other hand, had, at least at first, no such sacred structure laid down, and although Matthew, Mark and Luke chose to follow an essentially similar pattern both in terms of the interweaving of narrative and teaching and in terms of the overall development of the ministry, the freedom with which they operated within this pattern suggests that it did not yet have for them the status of 'scripture'.   Where scripture (that is, Old Testament scripture) came into their gospels it was because the story they were telling suggested a given passage or theme, not because there was an existing framework of scripture already laid down for them.

But any comparison of the gospels with those Jewish works which retell the stories of the Old Testament is in any case hazardous because of the nature of the history involved.   Even on the now conventional dates assigned to the gospels (which I do not regard as beyond question since John Robinson reopened the issue six years ago!) the time between the ministry of Jesus and the writing of the gospels is one or two generations. They are thus recent history, and as such in a different category from the retelling of the ancient history of the Old Testament around which centuries of pious meditation had had ample opportunity to weave elements foreign to the original story.   Even the stories of Ḥanina ben Dosa, which deal with comparatively recent history, were not recorded in their present form until centuries after his death.   In terms of the time-scale involved the closest parallels to the gospels would be Josephus' *Jewish War* and the First Book of Maccabees.

Downing's discussion of Josephus in relation to the gospels suggests that Luke in particular is both in his professed aim and in his performance 'following procedures similar to those discernible in Josephus';/32/ and those procedures, it will be recalled, do not encourage us to see

Luke as addicted to 'creative midrash'.   Thus in relation to
Luke's handling of the stories of Jesus' birth and childhood,
Downing believes that 'we would not expect him, if he were
following the conventions accepted by Josephus, simply to make
it up, even from scriptural meditation, or haggadic legends
attached to other figures.'/33/   At least where Josephus is
recording more recent history, he thus seems a more appropriate
model by which to evaluate the Christian evangelists than
those whose works related to the sacred history of the distant
past.

The interest of 1 Maccabees in drawing scriptural
parallels with the history he is relating may be very loosely
compared with the interest of the evangelists, particularly
Matthew, in the fulfilment of the Old Testament in Jesus.
In so far as there is value in this comparison, it suggests
that such an interest is quite compatible with the factual
reporting of events.

The above survey has suggested several other points at
which significant points of contact may be found, either in
overall genre or in detail, between the gospels and various
different Jewish approaches to the relation between scripture
and history, and we may reasonably expect useful light to be
thrown on the literary procedure of the evangelists by the
fuller studies which would result from an adequate discussion
of these points of contact.

But underlying all such attempts to trace points of
comparison and contrast between the gospels and any of the
various types of Jewish writing we have considered there lies
the more fundamental question of whether such comparison is
appropriate at all.   While we may reasonably assume that the
gospel writers were men of their times who will not
unnecessarily have cut themselves off from the accepted
conventions of writing in the culture in which they lived, we
must beware of making them mere imitators.   Even if we had
been able to find in non-Christian Judaism a unified approach
to the writing of history, does it follow that a Christian
writer would have felt obliged to follow suit?

The point was made forcefully by Samuel Sandmel in his
SBL Presidential Address of 1961 under the title of
'Parallelomania'./34/   In attacking those New Testament

scholars who on the basis of 'parallels' (sometimes more
superficial than real) explain elements in the New Testament as
'derived from' this or that Jewish source or tendency, he
protests against the idea 'that the writers of Christian
literature only copied sources and never did anything original
and creative'.   Early Christianity was, Sandmel believes, 'a
Jewish movement which was in particular ways distinctive from
other Judaisms. ... Only by such a supposition of such
distinctiveness can I account to myself for the origin and
growth of Christianity and its ultimate separation from
Judaism.'/35/

Foremost among the distinctive elements of early
Christianity was its sense of history.   Other Jews might
locate the decisive acts of God in the distant past of sacred
history, or, with the apocalyptists and the men of Qumran, in
the imminent future; but for the Christians the decisive work
of God was in Jesus the Messiah, whose recent life, death and
resurrection many of them had witnessed, and whose deeds and
words were the basis of their faith and the subject of those
writings they called 'gospels'.   So while other Jews looked
to the scriptures to discover and interpret the distant past,
or to understand their present situation with a view to
discerning what God was about to do, the Christians turned to
those same scriptures as the pattern and promise which had
already and recently been fulfilled.   Their interest, then,
was not in the Old Testament in itself, but in the Old Testament
as it is fulfilled in Jesus.

This total difference of orientation in relation to the
bearing of scripture on history cannot be left out of account
in any attempt to reconstruct early Christian literary practice
in the light of contemporary Jewish writing.   For all their
sharing in the same cultural milieu, and basing their religious
convictions on the same scriptures, their situation and outlook
was, by virtue of their being Christians, so fundamentally
different as to make it likely that parellels in literary and
exegetical method will be superficial rather than essential.
At least it cannot simply be assumed that a Christian writer,
because he was also a Jew, will have approached the scriptures
in the same way as the writer of Jubilees or of a Qumran pesher
or of the *Life of Moses*; indeed the difference of orientation
is such as to require that any such correspondence must be
specifically demonstrated from the text of the gospels

themselves.

This last consideration does not in itself rule out the discovery of, e.g., 'creative midrash' in the gospels. What it does demand is that the presence of this or any other literary or exegetical procedure must be shown not only by adducing 'parallel' non-Christian practices, but primarily by a study of the relation between scripture and history in the actual text of the gospels, interpreted within their own peculiarly Christian frame of reference.

And that is question (d) posed at the outset of this paper, a question to which I addressed myself briefly in a paper in *Gospel Perspectives II* in relation to the specific area of the infancy narratives of Matthew, but which is clearly far too large to begin to deal with here. It is, however, the really important question, to which the contents of this paper have been mere prolegomena, aiming only to clear the ground by pointing out the limitations of the approach which instead finds the key to the gospels in the literary practices of non-Christian Judaism.

Notes

/1/ For this popular impression see e.g. D. Winter, *The Search for the Real Jesus* (London: Hodder, 1982) 41.
/2/ See *Gospel Perspectives II* (Sheffield: JSOT, 1981) 239-266 for my attempt to take up this question in the limited area of Matthew's infancy narrative (especially pages 250-255). I believe that the case there argued, of a mutual interaction of historical tradition and scriptural comment, which necessarily requires that the narrative tradition has an origin independent of the OT texts which are used to throw light on it, could with appropriate modification be made in relation to much of the scripturally-influenced content of the gospels. A similar approach is found in the paper by Douglas Moo in this volume.
/3/ L. Hartman in M. Didier (ed.), *L'Evangile selon Matthieu: Rédaction et Théologie* (BETL 29. Gembloux: Duculot, 1972) 148.
/4/ J. W. Bowker, *The Targums and Rabbinic Literature* (CUP, 1969) 69.
/5/ See the introduction to Bruce Chilton's paper in this volume for a proposal to use 'Midrash' of the literary genre, and 'midrash' for 'the general process by which one "searches

out" the meaning of scripture'.   In those terms, only section
ID of this paper is concerned with 'Midrash', while the paper
as a whole is looking at the nature and importance of 'midrash'
in a wide range of Jewish works which are not generically
'Midrash'.

/6/   It should perhaps be emphasised that the scope of this
paper is limited to the question of the possible creation of
gospel material *out of scripture*.   Our study of Jewish
historiography will be limited to seeing how far the
elaborations of historical tradition were derived from
scriptural passages, and the application of these results to
the Christian gospels will observe the same limits.   The wider
question of whether there were, either in Jewish or Christian
'histories', imaginative elements inspired by other motives or
sources lies beyond our scope.   It is OT scripture as a source
of historical embellishment or outright fiction which is the
subject of this study.

/7/   In speaking of 'the recording of history' I am consciously
excluding those works which are apparently entirely fictional,
such as Tobit, Judith, or 3 Maccabees.   Such works are
typically set in a specific period of Jewish history, and to a
limited degree aim at verisimilitude in reconstructing the
historical milieu, but their specific content is not derived
from known historical sources, and they may be better
classified as 'historical romances'.   While no absolute
dividing line can be drawn between such works and the
embellishments of biblical and later history in some of the
works to be discussed in sections A and C below, it would be an
unhelpful dilution of the term to classify such works as 'the
recording of history'.

/8/   See the discussion of this theme by D. Patte, *Early Jewish
Hermeneutic in Palestine* (Missoula: Scholars Press, 1975) 76-81.

/9/   R. H. Charles, *The Apocrypha and Pseudepigrapha of the Old
Testament: vol. II Pseudepigrapha* (Oxford: Clarendon, 1913) 1.

/10/   For further variations in explanation of this command see
San. 89b; *Gen.R* 65:4.

/11/   Not that Philo himself would have regarded the two 'books'
as separable, but the division conveniently marks a change in
the style of composition which is relevant to our discussion.

/12/   F. H. Colson, *Philo* (Loeb Classical Library) vol. 6
(London: Heinemann, 1935) xvii.

/13/   See the paper of R. J. Bauckham in this volume, section
2.5.

/14/   *Ibid* section 3.2.

/15/   See the detailed discussion *ibid* section 3 as a whole.
/16/   'Redaction Criticism: Josephus' *Antiquities* and the
Synoptic Gospels', *JSNT* 8 (1980) 46-65; 9 (1980) 29-48.
/17/   *Ibid* vol. 8, 55-56.
/18/   *Ibid* vol. 8, p. 60.
/19/   For the apocalyptic view of history see especially
D. S. Russell, *The Method and Message of Jewish Apocalyptic*
(London: SCM, 1964) chapter VIII.
/20/   M. D. Goulder, *The Evangelists' Calendar* (London: SPCK,
1978) 132-138, has pointed out a series of 'parallels' between
1 Macc 3-16 and the stories in 1 and 2 Samuel and 1 Kings,
which he claims occur in 1 Maccabees roughly in the order of
the OT narratives.   He concludes that this is more than 'pious
colouring of a historical book', but it is not clear how far,
if at all, he regards the 'events' of 1 Maccabees as owing
their origin to reflection on the OT stories.   His interest in
context is in showing that 1 Maccabees was 'composing a history
as a series of fulfilments of the Law and the Prophets as read
in cycle' - i.e. as organising his work to correspond to an
existing lectionary.   Even if this contention is granted, it
does not by itself settle the question of whether the author
believed that he was recording actual events.
/21/   *Ant*. I 17.   Josephus sets out more fully his aims and
methods in relation to recent history in *B.J.* I 1-30; cf. *B.J.*
VII 454-455.   See also *Contra Apionem* I 47-52 for his claim
that his accuracy was endorsed by Titus, Vespasian and others!
/22/   *Cf*. A. W. Mosley, *NTS* 12 (1965/6) 23-24 for a collection
of favourable verdicts on Josephus' reliability as a historian.
/23/   'Ḥanina ben Dosa', *JJS* 23 (1972) 28-50;   24 (1973) 51-64.
/24/   See *JJS* 23, pp. 30, 33.
/25/   *JJS* 24, pp. 54-55.
/26/   *Cf*. the account of the martyrdom of Akiba in *Ber*. 61b,
which gives rise to a discussion in heaven of the relevance of
Ps 17:13-14 to the event;   there is no suggestion that the
story was itself derived from Psalm 17.
/27/   *JJS* 23, p. 28.
/28/   See further the introduction to Bruce Chilton's paper in
this volume.
/29/   D. Patte, *Early Jewish Hermeneutic*, 72.
/30/   *Cf*. the argument of A. W. Mosley, *NTS* 12 (1965/6) 10-26
that the better among ancient historians, Greek, Roman and
Jewish, 'did not feel free to invent stories of past events',
because 'people living then knew that there was a difference
between fact and fiction'.   He points out in particular that

he more recent the events, the clearer was the concern for
istorical accuracy.   In this he finds Josephus, the only
ewish historian he studies specifically, to be on a par with
he better Graeco-Roman historians.

31/ *What is a Gospel? The Genre of the Canonical Gospels*
Philadelphia: Fortress, 1977).
32/ *JSNT* 9, p. 30.
33/ *Ibid* 34.
34/ *JBL* 81 (1962) 1-13.
35/ *Ibid* 4-5.

THE GOSPELS AND THE JEWISH LECTIONARIES

Leon Morris,
17 Queens Avenue,
Doncaster,
Victoria 3108,
Australia.

There have been several lectionary hypotheses, some of which have not attracted wide support, for example, those of P. P. Levertoff/1/ and R. G. Finch./2/   More recently P. Carrington has argued that the Gospels were written to provide lections for use in Christian worship services: they 'were composed to give a Sunday-by-Sunday arrangement of the words and acts of Jesus to be announced or proclaimed at the proper point in the service'./3/ He has worked out his theory with particular reference to Mark. Many Greek MSS have forty-eight numbered sections in this Gospel (preceded by a *pro-oimion* lacking a number) and Carrington puts a good deal of emphasis on this as also on the fact that Codex Vaticanus has sixty-two sections./4/ He sees these as supporting his view that Mark was written to provide lections for a Christian year, with four sabbaths a month for twelve months plus fourteen lections 'for the special solemnity of the Pascha'./5/ His case is argued with sincerity and learning but it has not convinced many.

Professor Aileen Guilding has made out an impressive case for the view that the Jewish lectionaries lie behind our Fourth Gospel:

> The Fourth Evangelist seems to have preserved a tradition of Jesus' sermons which has not found a place in the Synoptic Gospels, and he has arranged these sermons against the background of the Jewish liturgical year, keeping to the regular order of the feasts without breaks or dislocations, and driving home the theological point of each discourse by linking with it the record of some carefully selected miracle, which he calls a *sign*./6/

he argues that John is following the three year Jewish cycle of readings, but she does not think that he followed it in order. t a given feast there might be a lection from the first, second or third year of the cycle and after having used one of the later years he may go back to an earlier year in a later part of the Gospel.

There is nothing inherently improbable about this and John certainly has more to say about the Jewish feasts than has any of the other evangelists. But the evidence scarcely supports the hypothesis. First, the range of the lections to which Guilding makes appeal is so wide as to be meaningless. For example, in discussing John 5, which she takes to refer to the Jewish New Year Festival, she appeals not only to the lections for that Feast but also to those for the two preceding sabbaths. With the three year cycle that makes a total of nine *sedarim* (lections from the Law) and nine *haphtaroth* (lections from the Prophets). The discussion is then widened to take in two more sabbaths with six more *sedarim* and six more *haphtaroth*. We now have thirty Old Testament passages in which to seek parallels. This is widened still further by including Psalms from a triennial cycle and a *seder* not in the regular readings but postulated on the basis of some statements in later Jewish writings. The number is then doubled with an appeal to a cycle beginning in Tishri as well as to the Nisan cycle./7/ With as wide a range as this it would be astonishing if there were not some contacts with a forty-seven verse chapter.

This is all the more the case in that the parallels are not necessarily frequent or close. For example when she deals with John 5 Guilding finds parallels only to verses 5 (Deut. 2:13), 20 (Deut. 3:24), 22 (Deut. 1:16), and 37 (Deut. 4:12)./8/ This total is less than impressive and the parallels are not close. Thus in v. 5 the only points are the use of the verb 'rise' of the lame man ('Arise...and walk') and of the nation ('rise up, and get you over the brook Zered') and the use of thirty-eight years for the duration of the man's illness and of the wilderness wanderings. Admittedly such parallels might be made by a first century writer, but there are not enough of them to indicate dependence. Guilding further emphasizes the theme of judgment. But judgment is found so often in the Old Testament and in John that it is not easy to think it shows dependence. A similar comment might be made at other points. Thus in examining John 6 Guilding finds it significant that we have the theme of faith both in the lections she adduces and in John 6. But John uses the verb *pisteuein* in all ninety-eight times (it is absent only from chaps. 15,18,21 in his whole Gospel). And the themes of belief and unbelief are found in many places in the Pentateuch.

It is not specially significant that they occur in a group of lections and a particular chapter of the Gospel.

Again, Guilding's case will not stand, at least in the form in which she sets it out. We have already noticed that she claims that John keeps 'to the regular order of the feasts without breaks or dislocations'. But John does not mention some feasts, e.g. Pentecost and Purim. And if he were following the Jewish liturgical year his omission of the great fast on the Day of Atonement is more than curious.

There are other difficulties with Guilding's view and perhaps I may refer to my fuller discussion in *The New Testament and the Jewish Lectionaries* (London, 1964), especially chapter II. Here I do no more than show that there are special problems in the way of Guilding's hypothesis in addition to those she shares with other upholders of lectionary theories.

Probably the most convincing case is that of M. D. Goulder. He sets out his view of the composition of our First Gospel in this way:

> The theory I wish to propose is a lectionary theory: that
> is, that the Gospel was developed liturgically, and was
> intended to be used liturgically; and that its order is
> liturgically significant, in that it follows the lections
> of the Jewish Year. Matthew, I believe, wrote his Gospel
> to be read in church round the year; he took the Jewish
> Festal Year, and the pattern of lections prescribed
> therefor, as his base; and it is possible for us to descry
> from MS. evidence for which feast, and for which Sabbath/
> Sunday, and even on occasion for which service, any
> particular verses were intended./9/

He adds, 'Such claims do not err on the side of modesty', a judgment from which few will dissent. He takes it for granted that Matthew used Mark, indeed he is considering 'the grounds for thinking that Matthew was writing a midrashic expansion of Mark'./10/ In a later book he argues that Mark was written to provide lections culminating in the passion to be read at Passovertide. But this gives lections only for half the year and there is no sale for six-and-a-half-month lectionaries'. So the other Synoptists provided what was needed, 'Matthew for a more conservative, Jewish-Christian, church with the accent on the festivals; Luke for a more Pauline, Gentile, church with the

accent on the Saturday O.T. lessons'./11/ Goulder is definite
that there was a Jewish cycle of readings so arranged that the
Pentateuch was read through each year. He brings considerable
learning to show that Matthew can be divided into a series of
lections which have their points of contact with the Jewish
lections throughout the year.

Manuscript Divisions

He finds support for his view in the divisions of the text
in Codex Alexandrinus, and indeed says it is 'the key to the
sub-division of Matthew into calendrical lections'./12/ There
are sixty-nine of them in Matthew and eighty-four in Luke which
at first sight seem a lot for the lections of a year. But for
Matthew Goulder's answer is that they are the readings for
'fifty Saturdays, and nineteen additional readings for the
extra holy days in Dedication, the watches of Passover night,
etc'./13/ As for Luke, he argues that this evangelist provided
three lections a week for twelve weeks leading up to Passover
for the instruction of catechumens on the Jewish model, not of
catechesis but of worship./14/

But, to make Matthew fit, Goulder has to argue that at
Passover the church read set passages at 6 p.m., 9 p.m.,
midnight, 3 a.m., and 'day'./15/ I suppose that this is not
impossible but I see no evidence for it other than that it
helps the lectionary hypothesis. But it seems highly unlikely
that the church was involved in such a complicated liturgical
process as early as the writing of Matthew. Indeed, earlier,
for Matthew would be writing for an existing pattern of
services, not creating a new one. Goulder finds in Luke
readings for 6 p.m., 9 p.m., midnight, 3 a.m., 6 a.m., 9 a.m.,
noon and 3 p.m./16/ His view of Lucan catechesis seems even
more improbable, for Luke repeatedly tells of people who were
baptized without any period of instruction, let alone a solid
three months of meeting three times a week. He tells of
crowds at Pentecost (Acts 2:41), some Samaritans (Acts 8:12-13),
the Ethiopian eunuch (Acts 8:38), Saul of Tarsus (Acts 9:18),
Cornelius and his friends (Acts 10:48), Lydia and her household
(Acts 16:15), the Philippian gaoler and his household (Acts 16:
33) and some converts in Corinth (Acts 18:8). If we relied on
Acts we would get the impression that no period of instruction
was needed. People believed and were baptized. Why then would
Luke precede his account of what he says actually happened with
a Gospel which not only envisages a period of instruction but

lists the actual readings to be used over a period of three months?   And why would he incorporate readings for catechumens in his lectionary for the whole church?

There are other problems.   As an example, Goulder holds that the divisions in Alexandrinus are 'substantially correct' though sometimes irrational.   Thus unit 66 is just one verse (Luke 19:12) while unit 67 is the rest of the story of the pounds./17/   Granted that first century people might not divide the text in the way we would, to take Luke 19:12 as the whole of a lesson for a service of worship is to abandon serious lectionary discussion.

Goulder holds further that the edentations in P75 correspond to lectionary divisions./18/   But he goes on to notice that only thirty-one agree exactly with his rubrics and another five nearly, while twenty-three are divergent.   When only 52.5% support the view and 39% are in contradiction we should surely look for some other explanation.   Indeed in another place Goulder himself makes so many concessions that the divisions of P75 seem not to prove anything./19/   It is more likely that they and the divisions in Alexandrinus were meant as means of making reference.   It may also be relevant that C. R. Gregory long ago maintained that when MSS were intended for liturgical use divisions and headings such as those in Alexandrinus were omitted./20/   A further point is that Goulder's position seems to mean that the divisions were original to the Gospels and that would be a bold claim.   Even though they are found in many ancient MSS they are absent from so many old ones that this is a precarious inference.

Writing 'In Order'

A further argument which I cannot but regard as curious is Goulder's treatment of Luke's statement that he wrote 'in order', καθεξῆς (1:3).   Goulder holds that this cannot mean 'in chronological order'./21/   He goes on to ask, 'why should it not mean "in liturgical order"?' and adds, 'There is in fact no satisfactory alternative interpretation.   Luke from his first paragraph authorizes the lectionary theory.'/22/   He further argues that the word always means 'in series' in Luke's five uses./23/   In this place he sees it as having emphasis.   He rejects the chronological meaning, Cadbury's 'as follows', the translations of RSV and NEB, the 'theological order' of E. Trocmé, G. Klein and E. Lohse, and the geographical emphasis of

the last mentioned. After all this the best he can come up
with is 'Why should καθεξῆς not mean "in *liturgical* order"?'
/24/ to which it is a fair retort, 'why should it?'. There is
nothing in Luke's other uses of the word to indicate such a
meaning and there is nothing in Luke's stylish preface to
indicate a liturgical concern. Goulder can be dogmatic.
'Others - Mark, Matthew (perhaps more, but we cannot trust
Luke's πολλοί too far) - have undertaken to order a narrative:
he has decided to make a thorough job of it, providing Gospel
fulfilments for the liturgical themes of feast and Sunday for
virtually the whole year.'/25/ This seems a lot to get out of
an innocent-looking adverb./26/ Is there no alternative to 'in
chronological order' other than 'in liturgical order'? The
argument is weak. Marshall's comment on the term is this: 'the
adverb may be taken to imply chronological exactitude or simply
an orderly and lucid narrative' and he goes on to notice that
Luke 'is broadly chronological in his treatment'./27/

Lectionary Difficulties

Quite apart from objections to a particular lectionary
view, such as that of Goulder or Guilding, there are problems
about the whole enterprise. Thus it is common to all the
lectionary hypotheses that appeal is regularly made to the
synagogue lections. It is accepted, almost without question,
that at the time the New Testament was written, the Jews read
the Torah in their synagogues according to a fixed lectionary
and, while the readings from the prophets are introduced more
cautiously, once introduced they are usually referred to with
confidence./28/ One would never gather from most of the
discussions that no one knows what the synagogue did about
readings during the first century.

Indeed, it is not clear how old the synagogue itself is.
The oldest mention of a synagogue so far attested appears to be
in an inscription in Egypt dated some time after 247 B.C./29/
E. L. Sukenik held that the oldest synagogue remains in
Palestine are 'not earlier than the first century C.E.'./30/ I
am not arguing that these are the first synagogues. The
institution may well be much older. Thus Joseph Gutmann thinks
it probable that the synagogue emerged at the time of the
Hasmonean revolution, about the middle of the second century
B.C./31/ But an early date has not been demonstrated and if
any lectionary hypothesis is to be plausible it must be shown
that synagogues had been in existence long enough for liturgical
development to have taken place.

Again, the oldest account we have of a synagogue service is
that in Luke 4 and it is not easy to see the use of a lectionary
there./32/ A lectionary takes time to develop. There are
experiments and mistakes and alternatives. Those who argue that
there was a lectionary in the first century should first
demonstrate that the synagogue had been in existence for long
enough for this to happen. It may be possible to do this but so
far it has not been done. Sidney B. Hoenig is sceptical. He
argues against the view that there was a synagogue in the temple
and goes on to say, 'these events in effect show definitely that
the beginnings of synagogue ritual and liturgy are to be dated
after 70 CE - not before'./33/ Even if the synagogue itself is
much older than Christianity the developed liturgy is quite
another thing. We should be clear that the development of
liturgical practices takes time/34/ and the working out of a
lectionary cannot be assumed to be the first task to be
undertaken. Hoenig is emphatic that the beginnings of the
synagogue are late. He concludes:

Only much later, after the Destruction in 70 CE, do we
witness the full emergence of synagogues, particularly in
Galilee. Their origin indeed may be traced to the
Maamadot, but their actual existence or functioning is
neither pre-Hasmonean, nor even post-Hasmonean; they are to
be found flourishing only in the post-destruction era.
Archaeological findings too have not uncovered any
synagogues in Judea of the period before 70 CE. The
liturgic (non-sacrifical) Synagogues (*i.e.* established
religious edifices or houses for standardized and
canonized prayer) did not exist in Judea during the Second
Commonwealth and surely not within the Temple precincts.
/35/

Hoenig may be wrong. The excavations at Masada and Herodium
have convinced many that there were synagogues at an earlier
time./36/ The Gospels and Acts show that there were
synagogues in many places in the earlier part of the first
century. I am building nothing on the correctness of Hoenig's
conclusion. I simply point out that he has made a careful
examination of the rabbinic material and that his view must be
refuted if the lectionary hypothesis is to be acceptable. So
far this has not been done.

Quite apart from the date of the synagogue there are very
real doubts about whether the Jews had a fixed lectionary

during the first century. The evidence, such as it is, makes
it unlikely. The Talmud records a dispute between R. Meir and
R. Judah b Ilai in the second century:

> Our Rabbis taught: The place (in the Torah) where they
> leave off in the morning service on Sabbath is the place
> where they begin at *Minḥah*; the place where they leave off
> at *Minḥah* (on Sabbath) is the place where they begin on
> Monday; the place where they leave off on Monday is the
> place where they begin on Thursday; the place where they
> leave off on Thursday is the place where they begin on the
> next Sabbath. This is the ruling of R. Meir. R. Judah,
> however, says that the place where they leave off in the
> morning service on Sabbath is the place where they begin
> on (Sabbath) *Minḥah*, on Monday, on Thursday, and on the
> next Sabbath./37/

Goulder maintains that R. Meir means that if, say, a sabbath
lection comprised Leviticus 1-5 it would be divided so that
when a morning reading finished at Exodus 40 the sabbath
afternoon *Minḥah* read Leviticus 1, Monday read Leviticus 2,
Thursday Leviticus 3 and the next sabbath Leviticus 4-5 so that
the whole was read through the week./38/ But it needs the eye
of faith to see this in the words of R. Meir. This is not what
he says. He has nothing about dividing the lections and
simply says that each reader takes up where the previous one
left off. There is no indication of a recognized lectionary.
/39/ Nor is there in the words of R. Judah, who simply
concerns himself with the sabbath lections and makes them
continuous. The fact of such a difference of opinion during
the second century makes it difficult to think of a fixed
lectionary as early as the first. J. Heinemann can say, 'the
very existence of the above ruling in the second half of the
second century makes nonsense of the assumption that one
single, fixed lectionary was in use at the time'./40/ If the
guide is that today's reader takes up where the last day's
reader left off neither appears to be reading a prescribed
passage. The words fit better in a situation where nobody
knew from sabbath to sabbath what would be read, but everyone
agreed that it was important that nothing be omitted. If this
was so each reader would simply start at the point where his
predecessor finished. G. F. Moore can say, 'It is clear from
this that the authorities recognized no division of the
Pentateuch into lessons of fixed length, or of a cycle of
lessons to be finished within a fixed time'./41/

It is not clear when the practice of continuous reading
began. The earliest attestation appears to be in the Mishnah
(*Meg.* 3:4), which is considerably later than the New Testament,
though, of course, the practice may well be much older than
this first mention in a written source.   Goulder, who has an
awe-inspiring capacity for sweeping hypotheses, thinks that 'it
goes back probably to Ezekiel and the Deuteronomistic community
in the 6th century B.C.'./42/ In the same note he says,
'Chapter 10 gives evidence for a continuous reading before the
Chronicler's time', but when we turn to Chapter 10 we find him
asking, 'why should we not suppose that sabbath practice in the
Chronicler's day already included a serial reading of the Law
round the year, as is first directly testified for the
synagogue by the Mishnah?'./43/ But why should we? Once again
our earliest *evidence* is the Mishnah.   Goulder argues in
another place that the sermons of the early Christian Fathers
indicate *lectio continua* and that this shows that the
Christians carried on Jewish practice./44/ But preaching
continuously through a book is no guarantee that a lectionary is
being used, as the practice of several of the Reformers shows.
Indeed, in modern times I have known more than one parish
priest preach through a book of the Bible on successive
Sundays while faithfully taking his Bible readings from a
lectionary which prescribed quite different passages.

There is a further problem in the length of the cycle. In
Babylon it was completed in a year, but in Palestine it took
three years. There is dispute as to which of these is the
older. Guilding based her work on a three year cycle; Goulder
based his on a one year cycle. But he can say, 'the first
rabbinic evidence of cyclical readings in units with which we
are familiar' shows that the annual cycle was 'firmly
established by the fourth century'./45/ Which is a long way
from the time when any of our Gospels was written. Elsewhere
he says that the lections used today go back at least to A.D.
300 and adds, '*I have merely claimed that the same* sidrôt *were
in use two centuries earlier*, and have adduced Philo and
other evidence'./46/ But a two centuries jump is quite a leap!
It does not demonstrate the point. The time gap is
unbridgeable with our present information. When he criticizes
the triennial cycle Goulder notes that it was in operation in
Palestine 'in A.D. 500' and adds, 'The evidence is all
centuries away'./47/ 'Perhaps the triennial system came in
with Jamnia: we do not know. The second-century evidence shows
only that the period between Passover and Pentecost was the

subject of calendrical meditation.'/48/ He is thus well aware
of the difficulties in the way of the triennial cycle, but he
argues quite firmly for the annual cycle as though there were
no doubts. But some are just as convinced about the triennial
cycle as he is about the annual cycle. Thus F. F. Bruce says
that the Hebrew text of the Bible

> is...divided into paragraphs which correspond to the
> natural sense; and the Pentateuch bears marks indicating
> the sections into which it was divided for the purpose of
> synagogue lessons. There were two such systems - an older
> one, used in Palestine, which divided the Pentateuch into
> 154 lessons, sufficient to last throughout a three years'
> cycle; and a later one, used in Babylonia, dividing the
> Pentateuch into fifty-four sections to serve as lessons
> for a one-year cycle...The latter, Babylonian, system
> finally prevailed and is used to the present time in
> synagogues throughout the world./49/

Until the point is cleared up all lectionary hypotheses are
under a cloud. A beautiful deduction from Matthew's use of the
annual cycle is useless if in fact his church used a triennial
cycle. The point needs more attention than the lectionary
people have given it so far.

So is it with the time of starting of the postulated
lectionary. Some hold that the sabbath cycle began in Nisan,
some in Tishri./50/ This six months time span makes a
considerable difference to the lections used on a given
sabbath. Some of the evidence favours one, some the other
hypothesis. Until the lectionary finally settled down it seems
that different synagogues may have had different starting
points.

This should perhaps be stated more strongly. J.
Heinemann agrees that L. Crockett and I are 'undoubtedly
right' in arguing that the existence of a fixed lectionary in
New Testament times is 'not proven', but thinks that it is
possible to go further and come to 'quite definite
conclusions that there was no single, generally accepted
Sabbath-lectionary in use in the first century, and that all
assertions regarding the reading of any particular weekly
portion at fixed times of the year are entirely unfounded
speculation'./51/ He surveys the available evidence and shows
that from the material available to us in such sources as the

Ḥilluqey Minhagim and the *qerovoth* of Yannai it is clear that in the fifth and sixth centuries there were cycles of about three and a half years with each new cycle starting at a different time of the year./52/ And in tannaitic times 'we find no mention of any fixed weekly readings at all'./53/ He concludes that 'it is not merely a case of being obliged to use caution in supposing that a fixed, triennial lectionary cycle was in existence in the second - or first - century; but rather that such a hypothesis contradicts all available evidence, and belongs clearly to the realm of fiction'./54/ He further says, 'the correlation of particular Pentateuch portions - other than those read on festivals and the 4 special Sabbaths - with any specific calendar dates is but the result of sheer guess-work'. /55/ These are strong words, but it is not easy to see how on the evidence they can be rejected. Those who advocate lectionary hypotheses should face the fact that, not only is the hypothesis in the first century not proven, but it flies in the face of a good deal of hard evidence.

Nor can we argue that the doubts simply leave it an open question where one opinion is as good as another. Against this is the fact that none of the evangelists makes any reference to a lectionary. This would be intelligible if there was a lectionary so well established that it was everywhere accepted and could be taken for granted. But the evidence shows that no lectionary could be taken for granted until centuries later. And if there was no universally accepted lectionary and if none of the evangelists says he was writing for a lectionary how could his readers (and how can we?) possibly know that he was?

Christians and Judaism

Even if there was an accepted lectionary among the Jews we face a further improbability. Why should we think that Christians, even Jewish Christians, would take it over? It is true that now and then New Testament Christians conformed to Jewish practice. Paul made a vow and cut his hair in connection with it (Acts 18:18). He associated himself with four men in Jerusalem who had made a vow and he assumed their expenses, purifying himself with them (Acts 21:23-6). Where no matter of principle was involved he was prepared to act as a Jew among Jews (1 Cor. 9:20). But references to 'the Fast' i.e. the Day of Atonement, Acts 27:9) and to Pentecost (Acts 20:16; 1 Cor. 16:8) appear to be no more than notes of time and do not form evidence that the Christians observed these days.

Evidence of conformity to Judaism is largely a matter of
worshipping in Jewish synagogues from time to time. It is, of
course, not improbable that Jewish Christians conformed more
closely to Jewish liturgical practices than did Gentile
Christians. But we have little evidence for this and we must
go on the evidence we have.

There is much more evidence that Christians distanced
themselves from Judaism. Thus there is a reference to 'Jewish
myths' from which believers should keep themselves and which
are linked with 'commandments of men turning away from the
truth' (Titus 1:14; cf. the singling out of them 'of the
circumcision', v. 10). There are derogatory references to
those who wish to be 'teachers of the law' (1 Tim. 1:7) and
those who misuse the law (vv. 8-11). There is probably at
least a glance at Judaism in the criticism of those who
'abstain from foods which God created to be received with
thanksgiving' (1 Tim. 4:3). Compelling Gentiles to 'judaize'
is rejected (Gal. 2:14) and it is insisted again and again that
the Jew has no advantage in God's sight over the Gentile (e.g.
Rom. 10:12 and the familiar 'the Jew first and also the Greek',
Rom. 1:16; 2:9 etc.). Christ crucified, the heart of the
Christian faith, is a stumbling block to the Jews (1 Cor. 1:
23). In John's Gospel 'the Jews' is an expression used
frequently of those opposing Jesus (John 5:16,18; 7:1 etc.).
The New Testament is not anti-Semitic. Many passages can be
cited to show that the Jews' place in God's plan is secure
(e.g. Rom. 11, and the 'to the Jew first' passages). But the
New Testament makes it abundantly plain that the Jewish way is
not the Christian way./56/

The first Christians were all Jews and Christians have
always regarded the Old Testament as sacred Scripture. So it i
not surprising that there are points of contact. But the
Christians had a distinctive position of their own which made
the gospel central, not the law. It is thus inherently
unlikely that they would have taken over a lectionary system
that made the reading of the law central (as do all the Jewish
lectionary systems known to us)./57/

The early Christians do not seem to have been keen on
anything like a liturgical year. It is generally held that,
from the first, Christians observed Sunday as their day of
worship (see Acts 20:7; 1 Cor. 16:2; cf. Rev. 1:10), an
opinion I share. But the evidence is not overstrong and it is

clear that the New Testament writers put no great emphasis on
it. There are no references in the New Testament to Christian
festivals (though there are a few to Jewish feasts). It is
usually held that from quite early days Christians observed
Easter (or Passover) and there is nothing improbable in the
thought that they gave liturgical emphasis to the time of the
year at which Christ suffered for the sins of the world and
rose triumphant over death./58/ But the New Testament does not
say so. We simply assume it and it is quite possible that our
assumption is wrong. New Testament Christians may have
preferred not to observe any time of the year liturgically./59/
There is no evidence and no likelihood that they observed any
other day. Paul could upbraid the Galatians with 'you observe
days and months and times and years' (Gal. 4:10) which looks
suspiciously like a repudiation of a liturgical year. In
similar strain he reminds the Romans that 'one esteems one day
above another, another esteems every day alike' (Rom. 14:5).
He commands the Colossians, 'let no one pass judgment on you...
in respect of a feast or new moon or sabbath' (Col. 2:16). I
suppose that it is possible that a Christian church which had
scant respect for a liturgical year of its own yet observed
meticulously lections from a Jewish year. But it seems
unlikely.

Further, the 'charismatic' nature of New Testament
Christianity as a whole is difficult to fit in with the
lectionary hypothesis./60/ Paul's picture of Christian
worship (1 Cor. 14) does not mention the reading of set
passages and is scarcely consistent with the use of a
lectionary. When nobody knew even who was going to give an
address why should we think that lections were read in an
orderly sequence? And, while Paul was all for peace and order,
his words show plainly that the Corinthians had not hitherto
restrained their tongues-speakers and that 'confusion' (or
'tumult', ἀκαταστασία, 1 Cor. 14:33) could justly be applied
to the way they comported themselves. At their communion
services, which ought to have been solemn and well ordered if
anything was, one could be in such a hurry to eat that his
neighbor was left hungry and another could drink so much that
he got drunk (1 Cor. 11:21). This is not the meticulous
observance of liturgical order. Whatever Paul's preferences
there is no denying that Corinthian practice had been to
conduct services in a somewhat free and easy manner.

It would, of course, be possible to argue that Paul is
irrelevant to the hypothesis that there was a lectionary
behind some or all of our Gospels. These days everyone agrees
that there were diversities in the New Testament church and few
would dispute that there were differences between Matthean and
Pauline Christianity. The apostle to the Gentiles may well
have taken a lighthearted attitude to the law, it might be
reasoned, but this is unlikely for Matthew. Goulder sees him as
a Christian scribe, trained in the methods and accustomed to the
thought patterns of the scribes. He understands him to have
written his Gospel not as an editor combining sources like Q and
M but by composing a midrashic expansion of Mark, his only
source. From this we might expect Matthew to have little in
common with Paul. Not so Goulder, 'For Matthew is not merely a
scribe, but a Christian scribe; and the rabbi to whom he owes
far and away the most is Paul.'/61/ He thinks that 'The
Pauline Christian went to church on Saturday night, and he
celebrated Passover and Pentecost, no doubt for a day apiece'
/62/ and further, that 'the Pauline churches retained the
traditional Sabbath readings of Law and Prophets in some form'.
/63/ He hopes to show 'that the Matthaean church read the
Pauline corpus in series round the year for the Epistle'./64/
On Goulder's view what happened in the Pauline churches was
very relevant.

And if we reject his view it is still the case that we
cannot dismiss the picture Paul gives of Christian worship when
we are considering Matthew. For, while there were probably
differences in liturgical practice in different parts of the
New Testament church, there is a limit. All Christians
professed to be following 'the Way' (to borrow the term in
Acts) and the New Testament clearly shows that there was a
certain amount of travel and interchange among the churches.
Nor should we overlook the fact that in his early days as a
Christian Paul spent a full year at Antioch (Acts 11:25-6) and
indeed was a delegate from that church when famine relief was
sent to the church in Judea (Acts 11:29-30). Our evidence is
that this church did not belong to any conservative group. It
was in Antioch that Gentiles were first evangelized and that
without reference to the church at Jerusalem (when the people
at headquarters heard about it they sent Barnabas to look into
it, Acts 11:19-24). The name 'Christian' originated in
Antioch, not in one of the older centres of the followers of
Jesus (Acts 11:26). The point of this is that for Goulder
Matthew was 'a bishop of a Syrian church',/65/ 'the community

school-master in a town in southern Syria' and 'a Christian out
of contact with the synagogue for a decade'./66/ He was 'a
sôphēr, a provincial schoolmaster/synagogue official'./67/ It
is, of course, not unlikely that the church in a southern
Syrian town would be somewhat more conservative than that in
the capital, Antioch./68/ But what it knew about Christianity
may well have been derived from Antioch and we have no reason
at all for saying that it was anything other than emancipated
from Jewish ways. There is no independent evidence for the way
the church of which Matthew was a member (or bishop) worshipped
but we have no reason for saying that it resembled a Jewish
synagogue. The practice of discipline in the Matthean church
(Matt. 18:15-20) differs in important respects from that
characteristic of the synagogue and we are justified in asking,
'Why should not the worship be different, too?' There are
Christian distinctives in worship. Sunday is a weekly reminder
of the Lord's resurrection. Baptism connects with his death
(Rom. 6:3-4), as of course does Holy Communion (1 Cor. 11:26).
We cannot assume that people who made Christ so central in
their worship happily accepted a way of worship from those who
rejected Christ.

Goulder sees Matthew as thoroughly Jewish. He sees that
evangelist as providing lections for such a minor festival as
Purim,/69/ though what Christians, even Jewish Christians,
would make of Purim is not easy to see. Goulder sums up
Matthew's achievement in this way: his Gospel 'is the readings
for a Jewish-Christian church, with a twenty-four hour
Pentecost and eight-days Tabernacles and Hanukkah, with
mourning on 9th Ab, and Purim the second week in Adar'./70/
Matthew had 'a full Holy Week use' with 'a lesson for each
week-day up to Passover'./71/ On 15th Nisan he provided
lections for 6 p.m., 9 p.m., midnight, 3 a.m. and 'day'./72/
Goulder finds it 'very difficult to think that these divisions
were not in the evangelist's mind, and in the tradition before
him'./73/ Locating this kind of thing in pre-Matthean
tradition takes it back to very early days indeed. But when we
ask for evidence we are given nothing but a brilliant
hypothesis.

Problems in Establishing a Lectionary Hypothesis

Goulder starts his lectionary view with the suggestion
that the resurrection story would be told on Easter Day./74/
There is nothing improbable about this. Indeed, it is highly

likely. But it is no argument for a lectionary. People who
insist on their right to read what they themselves choose and
who would refuse to accept a lectionary on the principle of the
freedom of the preacher to read his own selection from Scripture
yet read the Easter story on Easter Day (and the Christmas
story on Christmas Day). Such a lection proves nothing.

Much depends on the presuppositions we bring to the
subject. Goulder can say, 'could it be that the first
Christians remembered Judas' betrayal and Simon's supper the
day before Passover, and the Apocalyptic Discourse before
that?'./75/ Clearly Goulder's answer is, 'Yes, it could be'.
But there is no New Testament evidence that the first
Christians remembered any of these liturgically, not even the
Passover. For them 'Christ our Passover is sacrificed for us'
(1 Cor. 5:7). In the light of that how could they observe
another Passover?

Goulder goes on to raise the question, 'could it be that
the Gospels are in the order in which we have them because they
provided lessons for a whole primitive Christian Year, partly
Jewish in its background, but reaching its climax each year at
Passover and Easter?'./76/ He lists considerations that would
'be relevant to examining such a proposal'. There are quite a
few of them.

> We should need to know what were the themes, and if
> possible the readings, for the Jewish holy days at the
> period. We should need to know the way in which the
> synagogues read the Law and the Prophets on the intervening
> sabbaths. We should need evidence that the churches of the
> evangelists still observed Jewish festivals and
> traditional synagogue lections. We should need some
> external check on the subdivision of the Gospels into
> Nineham's 'stories or parables or groups of sayings', lest
> the whole topic break down into subjectivism. We should
> need some fairly striking correlation between the Jewish
> holy days and the passages in the Gospels which
> correspond with them; and a much more than random
> correlation between the individual pericopae and the
> sabbath readings. That is asking quite a lot./77/

These are Goulder's demands, not mine. I am not setting up an
impossibly difficult set of criteria and demolishing a
promising hypothesis because it does not meet my demands. They
are Goulder's own. But it can be fairly argued that not one of

them is met. We know the themes of the Jewish holy days only
in the most general sense. Obviously at Passover time it was
the deliverance from Egypt that was in mind and the
appropriate lections would be those telling of that
deliverance. On the Day of Atonement the themes were those of
repentance and forgiveness and the lections we assume would
stress these qualities. But this is the kind of thing we have
seen for the early Christians at Easter. We know the occasion
and we know accordingly the kind of thing that would be
suitable. But we do not know what in fact was read.

Goulder says, 'we should need to know...if possible the
readings'. The plain fact is that we do not. Another 'need to
know' is the way the synagogue read the law and the prophets
on the sabbaths, if that is what it did. We do not know this.
We need evidence that 'the churches of the evangelists still
observed Jewish festivals and traditional synagogue lections'.
There is not much evidence about the Christians and the Jewish
festivals and what there is is against. And, as we do not know
what the synagogue lections were at this time, we have no idea
whether the Christians followed them or not. We may agree with
Nineham that 'The natural thing would be for the preacher or
catechist to repeat *one* story, or parable, or group of sayings,
at each meeting and then go on to expound its significance for
his hearers.'/78/ But proving this is quite another matter
(1 Cor. 14 scarcely squares with it) so that Goulder's
'external check' is not easy to come by. Nor is his 'fairly
striking correlation between the Jewish holy days and the
passages in the Gospels which correspond with them'. We must
assume the lectionary hypothesis before there is any such
correspondence. Devout and learned Christians have read the
Gospels through the centuries without suspecting any such
thing. In the way most Christians read the Gospels still any
correlation with Jewish feasts is minimal and accidental. So
with Goulder's 'much more than random' correlation between the
Gospel pericopae and the synagogue lections. Since we do not
know what the lections were how can we possibly know whether
there is a correlation between them and the pericopae?

Goulder says frankly, 'we must be clear from the start
that there is never going to be enough evidence to "prove" the
case. I can never hope to achieve more than a plausible
reconstruction, and to reject this as "speculative" is to miss
the point; when we have no adequate evidence, our
alternatives are to speculate or to go ignorant'./79/ Fair

enough. My quarrel is with his contention that his
reconstruction is 'plausible'. What he seems to me to be
saying is: 'If the synagogue read the Law and the Prophets in
the way I lay down (here I interject: though nobody knows
whether it did or not), and if the Christian church retained
this hypothetical Jewish lectionary (against all the New
Testament indications), and if the evangelists wished to write
books to be used as lectionaries (without telling anyone that
this was what they were doing and without leaving indications
in their text to show it) this is the way they could have done
it.' Quite possibly, if we concede the three 'If's'. But they
are all highly improbable. I do not object to Goulder making
some daring speculations. But I have a problem when he says
quite definitely things like:

> In the first century A.D. the Western synagogue used an
> annual cycle of lections beginning in Nisan, in the
> spring. It had not only a fixed cycle of readings of the
> Law, which consisted of the 54 units which are in use to
> this day; it had also a series of fixed cycles for the
> Prophets and for the Writings. These were later broken
> up, but in Luke's time they were intact..../80/

All of these statements are at least doubtful; in my opinion not
one is correct. But they are stated with assurance as if they
were backed with irrefutable evidence. Constantly Goulder
gives the impression that we have knowledge which in fact we do
not have. He claims a firm base for his speculations when he
is building one speculation on another.

He prefers speculation to ignorance. But is it not better
humbly to face the facts? There are some not unimportant
matters about which we are in fact ignorant and a bold
speculation does not remove our ignorance. Goulder's work is
full of insights and there is no question about the depth and
width of his scholarship. Nor about his capacity for detailed
and painstaking work. As I am departing from his fundamental
position I would like it to be clear that I am full of
admiration for much that he has done. But a due recognition of
his learning, his talent and his sheer hard work does not carry
with it agreement that what he himself admits is speculation is
to be taken as fact. If the speculation lacks plausibility
then, despite the learning and the sincerity with which it is
argued, it must be rejected.

Goulder claims that breakaway movements tend to conservatism in matters of worship./81/ Perhaps. But it is a far cry from this to the assertion that Christians took over holus bolus a hypothetical Jewish lectionary in a time in which we do not know what either Jews or Christians did and abandoned it completely by the time of which we do have knowledge. What has become of their conservatism in this wholesale abandonment of the Jewish lectionary? And of reading the Gospels in the lectionary fashion in which on Goulder's view they were originally read? And why was all this so comprehensively forgotten when the church began to produce her own lectionaries?

'Luke developed his Gospel in preaching to his congregation' we read./82/ But no one knows whether Luke had a congregation or in fact whether anyone 'had' a congregation at the time Luke's Gospel was written. There is considerable evidence for a plurality of elders and it is quite a leap to a single preacher in a congregation and another to Luke's being one of them.

Goulder speaks of the Didascalia as belonging 'to the century when the Church was moving from keeping Passover-and-Easter to observing Holy Week'./83/ What then happens to the speculation that as early as the first century Matthew was providing lections for Holy Week? Another curious piece of reasoning comes from the citation of 1 Timothy 4:13, 'Till I come, attend to the public reading of scripture (τῇ ἀναγνώσει), to preaching, to teaching'. Goulder sees this as meaning that 'the readings were followed by exhortation and exposition in the liturgy' as in Justin. He goes on to cite Hegesippus: 'In every city that which the Law and the Prophets and the Lord preach is faithfully followed.' From this he concludes: 'Thus everything points, however tentatively, to the conclusion that the Church continued the Jewish practice of readings from Law and Prophets, followed by an expounding sermon; and that the expounding sermon in time gave birth to the liturgical gospel.' /84/ But appeal to Justin and Hegesippus to establish the reason for the writing of the Gospels seems curious. It is all the more so since neither is dealing with the topic and Hegesippus is not even writing about worship. His concern is with orthodoxy in doctrine which, he says, is found in both Corinth and Rome: 'In each list (of bishops) and in each city things are as the law, the prophets, and the Lord preach.'/85/ In any case the New Testament shows plainly that Christians did not stress the law as Jews did.

Sometimes even the proponents of lectionary theories recognize the possibility of being over-confident. Thus Goulder writes:

> It is not unnatural for those who have traced relationships between the Gospels and the Jewish calendar to be impressed with their discoveries, or inventions, Dr Carrington, in a moment of unhappy confidence, spoke of mathematical calculation, and I sense a similar note, *Heureka*, behind the work of Dr Guilding: yet neither does Guilding agree with Carrington, nor I with either, nor, I think, does any established scholar. Let the reader beware./86/

Or again he can say:

> Lectionary theories run the risk of explaining everything. I have argued that the prophetic books are in some way parallel with the Torah, and the Chronicler's work, and many of the books in the Writings, and St Luke's Gospel and St Matthew's. To offer so many explanations in terms of lectionaries must cast doubt upon the sanity of the theorist: perhaps he thinks Bauer's *Lexikon* was written as a lectionary.

But he points out that his method lends no support to the view that Paul's Epistles were written as a lectionary. This enables him to conclude, 'All is well: we belong to the day, and are sober'./87/ But perhaps the conclusion is premature. Such passages are a welcome recognition that lectionary views are far from having been proved. But unfortunately this humility is not sustained.

From all this it appears that there is still a long way to go before any lectionary hypothesis can be said to be probable. Generally speaking those who put such hypotheses forward emphasize the correlations they find between the Gospels and the lections they postulate. The strength of their case is that some of these correlations are impressive. But none of them has ever shown that we know what the Jews read in their synagogues in the first century. Even if this could be established, none gives a convincing reason why Christians who stressed the gospel should base their worship on lections which

stressed the law. And none squares the orderly lectionary view
with what the New Testament tells us of the charismatic
character of Christian worship. So far all lectionary
hypotheses simply build one hypothesis on another. They are
long on speculation and short on the kind of evidence that
would bring conviction. Until this is remedied they must
remain suspect.

All this has relevance to certain aspects of historicity in
the Gospels. Some of the lectionary hypotheses see the
Evangelists primarily as makers of edifying lectionary
readings. They were not interested in telling their readers
what happened, but in what would fit into a lectionary that
would serve the purposes of the church. The argument of this
paper means that such approaches should be rejected. There is
no real evidence that any of the Evangelists was aiming at
producing an edifying lectionary. Whatever their interests the
Evangelists were not lectionary-makers. The evidence is that
neither the Jews nor the Christians had lectionaries early
enough to meet the case.

Notes

/1/ C. Gore, H. L. Goudge and A. Guillaume, eds., *A New
Commentary on Holy Scripture* (London: SPCK, 1928), Part III,
128-9.
/2/ *The Synagogue Lectionary and the New Testament* (London:
SPCK, 1939).
/3/ *The Primitive Christian Calendar* (Cambridge: Cambridge
University Press, 1952) 44. He speaks of Luke as 'not...a
liturgical work' (62) but gives a table dividing it into
'lections' (103-6).
/4/ Ibid., 23-31.
/5/ Ibid., 70. He has been severely criticized. Thus C. F.
Evans, after outlining the way Carrington puts his thesis in
the introduction to his commentary on Mark, says: 'An analysis
of so precise and mathematical a kind can by its very nature
afford little margin for error. To carry conviction as a whole
it must do so in all its parts, and even one serious
dislocation would throw the whole out of gear. Serious doubts
do arise, however, at each point in the analysis' (*JTS*, n.s.,
14(1963) 142). As an example of the difficulties Evans points
to the fact that Carrington has fourteen lections attached to

Tabernacles, a feast whose celebration was unknown in the
church, but none in Pentecost, which at least was well
remembered, and he asks, 'Are we to suppose that the observance
died out early, despite its having fourteen special lections
assigned to it, which on this theory Pentecost did not?' (ibid.,
143). Cf. also Ralph P. Martin, *Mark: Evangelist and
Theologian* (Exeter: Paternoster, 1972) 85-87.

/6/ *The Fourth Gospel and Jewish Worship* (Oxford: Oxford
University Press, 1960) 1.

/7/ Ibid., chap. 6.

/8/ Ibid., 82,83.

/9/ *Midrash and Lection in Matthew* (London: SPCK, 1974) 172.
He later says, 'A Gospel is not a literary *genre* at all, the
study of Matthew reveals: it is a liturgical genre' (ibid.).

/10/ Ibid., 4. Cf. C. F. Evans, 'May Matthew have been the
first attempt to adapt Mark to a lectionary system?' (*JTS* n.s.
14 (1963) 144).

/11/ *The Evangelists' Calendar* (London: SPCK, 1978) 245.

/12/ *Midrash and Lection*, 455.

/13/ *Evangelists' Calendar*, 243

/14/ Ibid., 103-4. Goulder emphasizes the lack of Jewish
catechesis: 'there never was a Jewish catechism. Not only is
there no trace of it in all rabbinic literature, but Judaism
has no catechesis to this day' (ibid., 94); in the Talmud 'a
catechism in the sense of a course of instruction is ruled out'
(ibid., 95). But 'pious Jews went to synagogue three times a
week, Saturday evening, Monday and Thursday' (ibid., 92). He
holds that Christians took this as the model for their
catechesis.

/15/ *Midrash and Lection*, 432.

/16/ *Evangelists' Calendar*, 104.

/17/ Ibid., 76 and n. 1. An editorial review in *ExpTim* says,
'The whole lectionary theory has some weak spots. If one were
writing a book to serve as a lectionary one would aim to make
the readings roughly of similar length. But in the scheme
suggested some are as short as two verses and others longer
than two chapters. This discrepancy seems to be forced by the
need to establish links with the corresponding Old Testament
passage. Sometimes the parallels claimed are very forced, and
verses have to be treated in an unnatural way to make them fit
into the desired patterns' (*ExpTim* 86 (1974-75) 98).

/18/ Ibid., 76.

/19/ *Midrash and Lection*, 455, n. 6.

/20/ *Canon and Text of the New Testament* (Edinburgh: T. & T.
Clark, 1907) 469.

/21/ *Midrash and Lection*, 456.   Elsewhere he says that N.
Geldenhuys among others maintains 'without apology' that the
expression means 'a chronological order' (*Evangelists'
Calendar*, 9, n. 3).   But what Geldenhuys says is, 'By this he
does not mean that he intended to relate everything in strict
chronological order, but that it was his purpose to write a
narrative which would form a connected whole' (*Commentary on
the Gospel of Luke* (London: Marshall, Morgan & Scott, 1952) 53).
/22/ *Midrash and Lection*, 456.
/23/ *Evangelists' Calendar*, 8.
/24/ Ibid., 12.
/25/ Ibid., 13.
/26/ Goulder has another curious piece of linguistics when he
argues that Luke's παρηκολουθηκότι ἄνωθεν πᾶσιν ἀκριβῶς 'could
easily mean, "having followed all the Old Testament parallels
accurately from Genesis on"' (ibid., 15).   He further says that
Mark and Matthew both set out to draw up a series, 'but their
series were incomplete.   Mark started in October, and what is
the use of that?   Six-and-a-half-month calendars have no sale;
Luke followed everything through ἄνωθεν, from the beginning of
the cycle.   Matthew's stress on Jewish festivals is equally
inadequate for a Gentile church.   It is the fulfilments of the
Sunday-by-Sunday readings which count, every one taken
accurately in order...' (ibid., 16).
/27/ *The Gospel of Luke* (Exeter: Paternoster, 1978) 43.   He
cites other views, but none indicating an interest in liturgy.
Such a meaning is, of course, not found in standard lexicons of
the New Testament, nor for that matter in G. Lampe's *Patristic
Greek Lexicon*.   It did not appear in the early church.
/28/ Goulder can say, 'There are 54 *sidrôt* to be covered in
50/51 Sabbaths in a normal year.   But Lev. 16-18, the Atonement
sidrāh, is no. 29, and the 186 days before Atonement include
either 26 or 27 sabbaths.   Therefore one or two sabbaths in the
first half of the year will have had two *sidrôt* read together:
the end of Genesis, or the end of Exodus, to judge by
traditional synagogue practice, or both' (*Midrash and Lection*,
460, n. 10).   Cf. Guilding, 'The discourse on Jesus as the true
vine (John 15) contains allusions to several lectionary
readings for Tabernacles in which Israel is described as a
noble vine, planted by God, which has become worthless.   In
verse 21 of Jeremiah 2, haphtarah to Deuteronomy 9 we read...'
(*Fourth Gospel and Jewish Worship*, 117).   Such statements
convey the impression that there is no doubt about what was
read.

/29/ *TDNT*, 7, 811. Cf. also M. Hengel, *Judaism and Hellenism*,
2 (London: SCM, 1974) 54, n. 165.
/30/ *Ancient Synagogues in Palestine and Greece* (London:
British Academy/Oxford University Press 1934) 1; see also 69-70.
/31/ Joseph Gutmann, ed., *Ancient Synagogues: The State of
Research* (Chico, California: Scholars, 1981), 3-4. In n. 17 he
argues that 'The full development of the synagogue does not
come until after the destruction of the Temple in 70 C.E.'.
/32/ Jesus read from Isa. 61:1-2 followed by Isa. 58:6. This
is contrary to the rules for haphtaroth (where verses may be
omitted, but it is not permitted to go back to a previous
passage). There is no mention of a reading from the law, which
was central in all the lectionaries.
/33/ *JQR* 54 (1963) 129.
/34/ The oldest Christian liturgy extant is *The Apostolic
Tradition* of Hippolytus, usually dated early third century.
But even as late as this we read: 'It is not at all necessary
for him to utter the same words as we said above, as though
reciting them from memory, when giving thanks to God; but let
each pray according to his ability. If indeed anyone has the
ability to pray at length and with a solemn prayer, it is good.
But if anyone, when he prays, utters a brief prayer, do not
prevent him. Only he must pray what is sound and orthodox'
(G. J. Cuming, *Hippolytus: A Text for Students* (Bramcote
Notts.: Grove, 1976) 14). It takes a long time for forms to
become firmly fixed.
/35/ *JQR* 54 (1963) 130.
/36/ See, for example, Y. Yadin, *Masada, Herod's Fortress and
the Zealots' Last Stand* (London: Weidenfeld & Nicholson, 1966),
180-86.
/37/ *b.Meg.* 31b (Soncino translation).
/38/ *Evangelists' Calendar*, 57.
/39/ Elsewhere Goulder recognizes this: 'It is evident that
lectionary arrangements were in flux in the second century.
R. Meir laid down an arrangement under which it would take
rather over two years to read the Pentateuch, while his
contemporary, R. Judah b. Ilai's scheme would have taken $5\frac{1}{2}$
years' (*Midrash and Lection*, 227, n. 2).
/40/ *JJS* xix (1968) 45.
/41/ *Judaism*, 1 (Cambridge, Mass.: Harvard, 1958) 299. Moore
further points out that the Mishnah and the Tosefta regulate
the reading of the Law with great precision. But they say
nothing about a lectionary from which he infers 'that it was not
authoritatively established before the third century, though it
may have earlier become customary' (ibid., 300).

/42/ *Midrash and Lection*, 173, n. 8.
/43/ Ibid., 219.
/44/ *Evangelists' Calendar*, 54.
/45/ Ibid., 64-5.
/46/ Ibid., 105 (my italics). His claim is that Philo's
comments on Genesis divide into books corresponding 'almost
exactly' with the six opening sidrôt in the traditional cycle.
Philo's first book deals with Gen. 2:4-6:13; the *sidrā* with
Gen. 1:1-6:8; Philo's second with 6:14-10:9 omitting the
genealogies and the Babel story which the *sidrā* includes and
which goes on to Gen. 11 (ibid., 47-8). And so on. There is a
rough correspondence and Goulder holds that Philo's omissions
are due to the fact that he deals with these passages elsewhere.
But obviously all this falls well short of evidence that Philo
knew the lectionary.
/47/ *Midrash and Lection*, 227.
/48/ Ibid., he can refer to 'The vagaries of the calendar'
(ibid., 188).
/49/ *The Books and the Parchments* (London: Pickering & Inglis,
1963) 121. E. P. Sanders in a review of *Midrash and Lection*
comments, 'The rigidity of the hypothesis cannot take account
of the actual uncertainties' (*JBL* 96 (1977) 454). His review
is generally sympathetic but when he sums up he says: 'I
believe that it would be possible, for example, to separate the
study of Matthew's compositional habits from the lectionary
theory; the former decidedly deserves serious attention even if
the latter proves unpersuasive' (ibid., 455).
/50/ Cf. Goulder, 'We do not know whether the cycle ran for one
year or for three, or for some other span; and we do not know
whether it began in Nisan (April) or in Tishri (October)'
(*Midrash and Lection*, 173; he adds, 'It is even open to doubt
whether there was an accepted sabbath cycle before Jamnia').
/51/ *JJS* xix (1968) 41.
/52/ Ibid., 43-4.
/53/ Ibid., 45. I am grateful to Roger T. Beckwith for writing
to me about a work unavailable to me which supports my general
approach: 'Charles Perrot conjectures that there existed side
by side a precise 3-year cycle, beginning in Tishri, a $3\frac{1}{2}$
year cycle, beginning in Nisan and Tishri alternately, and also
other reckonings (*La lecture de la Bible dans la synagogue*,
Hildesheim, Gerstenberg, 1973, ch. 7).'
/54/ *JJS* xix (1968) 46.
/55/ Ibid.
/56/ Early in the second century Ignatius strongly condemns
living 'according to Judaism' which, he says, is a confession
that 'we have not received grace' (Mag. 8.1). He expressly

abjures sabbath observance (Mag. 9.1) and says forthrightly,
'It is monstrous to talk of Jesus Christ and to practise
Judaism' (Mag. 10:3; Loeb translation). This from the bishop
of Antioch, the very area in which Goulder claims that Matthew
and his conservative church still observed Jewish customs. Nor
can we say that Ignatius was trying to innovate for he
expressly says, 'Now this I say, beloved, not because I know
that there are any of you that are thus, but because I wish to
warn you...not to fall into the snare of vain doctrine' (Mag.
11.1).

/57/ Goulder says, 'Since the synagogue provided a daily
liturgy through the eight days (i.e. of Tabernacles), the
Church cannot but have desired to crown it with a daily measure
of the Lord's teaching' (*Midrash and Lection*, 365). But is
there any evidence that the early church slavishly followed
Jewish practice like this, even to the observance of an eight
day feast of Tabernacles? Or that it reasoned along the lines
of 'Anything you can do (liturgically) we can do better'?

It is sometimes said that the East Syrian (Nestorian)
church to this day uses a lectionary which simply appends New
Testament readings to a Jewish type lectionary. But the most
that can be said for this is that this church uses readings
from both the law and the prophets for many Sundays. It does
not follow the *lectio continua* principle but arranges the
readings topically. Further it completely lacks most of Exodus,
Leviticus and Numbers. It cannot be said that this church is
indebted to the synagogue for anything more than the idea that
there is value in reading from some parts of the law and the
prophets. The Lectionary is printed in A. J. Maclean, *East
Syrian Daily Office* (London: Rivington, 1894) 264-81 (I owe
this reference to Roger T. Beckwith).

/58/ Some suggest that the Quartodeciman controversy is evidence
that the early church observed Passover, affirming that the
dispute would never have been possible otherwise. The
controversy certainly shows that some Christians in the limited
area of the province of Asia followed the Jewish calculation of
the date of the Passover as they celebrated Easter (Eusebius,
HE V.xxiii-xxiv; the Palestinians are expressly included among
Christians who did not follow Quartodeciman practice, xxiii.3-
4). They used the term 'Passover' but whether this means that
they observed the Jewish feast is another matter. They may
simply be referring to the date of Easter (for that matter
Christians who would never dream of celebrating a Jewish feast
still use terms like 'paschal'). H. Lietzmann is not surprised
that some churches followed Jewish custom leading to

Quartodeciman practice, 'but it is remarkable that this custom
was by no means universal' (*The Founding of the Church
Universal* (London: Lutterworth, 1950) 133).   In fact it is not
attested outside the province of Asia.   Lietzmann thinks that
the Christians observed Pentecost (which depended on Easter)
but 'had no other annual festivals' (ibid., 136).

/59/ The discussion by Roger T. Beckwith, 'The Origin of the
Festivals Easter and Whitsun', *Studia Liturgica* 13 (1979) 1-20,
makes it very difficult to hold that either Easter or Whitsun
was of Jewish origin.

/60/ Cf. an editorial review of *Midrash and Lection*:   'On the
question of the use of liturgy in the early Church, one man's
guess is almost as good as another's.   We really know nothing
about it.   Such knowledge as we have is little more than
speculation based on ambiguous hints within the New Testament.
Some may think that one of the earliest acts of the earliest
Christians was to build up a formal and repetitive liturgy and
lectionary.   Others may feel that repeated forms of liturgy
belong to a later date in the story of the Church.   Our own
judgment would incline towards that of Conzelmann on this point:
'The primitive Church had other concerns than the construction
of a liturgy.   It concealed within itself tremendous energies
that could not be fettered to fixed forms"' (*ExpTim* 86 (1974-
75) 99).

/61/ *Midrash and Lection*,   153; see also 7.

/62/ Ibid., 453.

/63/ Ibid., 454.

/64/ Ibid., 389, n. 23.   The whole of chap. 8 is given over to
'Matthew and Paul'.   Cf. also *Evangelists' Calendar* chap. 8.

/65/ *Midrash and Lection*, 9.

/66/ Ibid., 22.

/67/ Ibid., 172.

/68/ But there is no reason for thinking it could have been as
conservative as Goulder holds Matthew's was.   He speaks of him
as 'presupposing Jewish ways at every step.   He officiated,
week by week, year after year, at worship that was Jewish in
root and mainly Jewish in branch.   He expounded Jewish readings
with Christian traditions in the Jewish manner' (ibid., 172-3).
This goes far beyond the evidence.

/69/ Ibid., 407.

/70/ Ibid., 453.

/71/ Ibid., 431.

/72/ Ibid., 432.

/73/ Ibid., 431.

/74/ E.g. *Evangelists' Calendar*, viii.

/75/ Ibid., ix.
/76/ Ibid.
/77/ Ibid., ix-x.
/78/ *The Gospel of St Mark* (Harmondsworth: Penguin, 1963) 22.
/79/ *Evangelists' Calendar*, x.
/80/ Ibid., 17. It is really extraordinary that he includes
the Writings, for the Talmud says definitely "Holy Writings may
not be read" and gives as an exception only the town of Neharde
(*Meg.* 116b). Cf. also *m. Šabb.* 16:1.
/81/ Ibid., 4.
/82/ Ibid., 7. Goulder sees him as perhaps 'the president of a
synagogue' (ibid., 159). For what it is worth Irenaeus says
that Luke 'always preached in company with Paul' (*Adv. Haer*,
iii.14.1) which does not look like the pastor of a
congregation at work.
/83/ *Evangelists' Calendar*, 8.
/84/ Ibid., 15.
/85/ Eusebius, *HE* IV.xxii.1-3; Loeb translation.
/86/ *Evangelists' Calendar* 101-2. Carrington repeatedly refers
to mathematical confirmation of his theory (*Primitive Christian
Calendar*, xiii, 27, 37, 59; cf. 'It fits our theory like a
glove', 26).
/87/ *Evangelists' Calendar*, 239-40.

TRADITION AND OLD TESTAMENT IN MATT 27:3-10

Douglas J. Moo
Trinity Evangelical Divinity School
Deerfield, Illinois   60015

Matthew's narrative of Judas' death is climaxed by the last, and perhaps the most complex of his *Reflexionszitate*. In keeping with other quotations of this type, uncertainties concerning the source(s) and textual basis exist, complicated in this case by the problematic reference to Jeremiah. The disparate elements of the quotation and their close relationship to the details of the narrative, along with apparent contradictions to the parallel narrative in Acts 1:17-20, suggest the existence of a creative exegetical procedure. And many would call this procedure a midrash./1/ The legitimacy of this designation can be determined only after the close-knit threads of narrative and quotation have been unravelled. It will be convenient to proceed by examining the quotation first and then the relationship of the narrative and the quotation.

I. The Quotation

The text of the citation is drawn mainly from Zech 11:13, although several important elements find no counterpart in Zechariah. In view of the ascription of the citation to Jeremiah, these extraneous elements are best explained by supposing that a passage from that prophecy has influenced the quotation./2/ It will be necessary to test this hypothesis by looking closely at the relationship between the quotation, the narrative and suggested background passages from Jeremiah. The complexity of the textual background and the freedom with which the texts are used warrant a phrase-by-phrase investigation of the citation. For convenience of reference, I include here the MT and LXX of Zech 11: 12b-13:

וישקלו את־שכרי שלשים כסף: ויאמר יהוה אלי השליכהו
אל־היוצר אדר היקר אשר יקרתי מעליהם ואקחה שלשים הכסף
ואשליך אתו בית יהוה אל־היוצר:

καὶ ἔστησαν τὸν μισθόν μου τριάκοντα ἀργυροῦς.
¹³καὶ εἶπεν κύριος πρός με Κάθες αὐτοὺς εἰς
τὸ χωνευτήριον, καὶ σκέψαι εἰ δόκιμόν ἐστιν,
ὃν τρόπον ἐδοκιμάσθην ὑπὲρ αὐτῶν. καὶ ἔλαβον
τοὺς τριάκοντα ἀργυροῦς καὶ ἐνέβαλον αὐτοὺς
εἰς τὸν οἶκον κυρίου εἰς τὸ χωνευτήριον.

καὶ ἔλαβον τὰ τριάκοντα ἀργύρια (Matt 27:9b) is a fairly
straightforward rendering of the beginning of the second major
clause in Zech 11:13. As in 26:15, Matthew uses the word
ἀργύριον, which may be a reflection of his Markan *Vorlage*
(cf. Mark 14:11)./3/ ἔλαβον is probably to be understood as
a third person ('impersonal') plural, as against the first
person singular of the LXX./4/ This modification may reflect
the tradition, since Matthew presents the priests as 'taking'
the money (v 6--λάβοντες τὰ ἀργύρια). Since ἀργύρια is perhaps
a reflection of Matthew's Markan source, no decision can be
reached regarding the textual background of the phrase.

τὴν τιμὴν τοῦ τετιμημένου (Mt 27:9c) is closer to MT
than to LXX, which deviates considerably from the Heb. The
personalized τετιμημένου perhaps depends on a vocalization of
הַיְקָר 'the price' as הַיָּקָר 'the honored one' (cf. the Pesh.)./5/
τιμή beautifully captures the irony inherent in יקר
('excellence'), while retaining the basic meaning of 'price,'
since τιμή can convey either of these ideas./6/ The freedom
with which Matthew treats his Zechariah source is already
evident, in the transposition of the two clauses, καὶ ἔλαβον
. . . and τὴν τιμήν . . . .

ὃν ἐτιμήσαντο ἀπὸ υἱῶν Ἰσραήλ (Matt 27:9d). The change of
person in the verb is a necessary translation modification,
since τιμάω is transitive, while יקר is intransitive, but
the change undoubtedly also commended itself to Matthew as
more closely approximating his tradition./7/ The phrase
clearly depends on MT since LXX has nothing comparable. ἀπό,
like its Heb. counterpart, מן has a partitive sense./8/
Matthew substitutes υἱῶν Ἰσραήλ for the Hebrew pronominal
suffix, a modification required because of the lack of an
antecedent for the pronoun./9/ In the following phrase,
the reading ἔδωκαν is generally preferred to ἔδωκα, the
following μου and the OT verse providing strong temptation to
assimilate to the first person./10/ On the other hand, the
following α may have led to the addition of the ν/11/ and
the narrative context would have exercised a powerful attraction
to the third person plural./12/ On the whole, ἔδωκαν is

more difficult and should probably be preferred. The less forceful δίδωμι (contrast LXX ἐνβάλλω, MT שקל) is perhaps used because the context '. . . calls for a less forceful action on the part of the Jewish leaders.'/13/

With the phrase εἰς τὸν ἀγρὸν τοῦ κεραμέως the major *crux* of the quotation is reached. No extant text or version gives any hint that a field is involved in the events narrated in Zechariah 11. While its presence in the quotation is no doubt due to the prominence of a field in the tradition associated with the death of Judas, the attribution of the citation to Jeremiah invites attempts to relate the mention of a field to a passage from that OT book. The passages usually suggested are Jeremiah 18 and 32./14/ The former passage features Jeremiah's visit to the house of the potter, while the purchase of a field figures prominently in the latter. ἀγγεῖον ὀστράκινον ('earthenware jar') in Jer 32:14 is often cited as the point of contact between Jeremiah 32 on the one hand, and Jeremiah 18 and Zechariah 11 on the other./15/ Torrey conjectures that the Hanamel of Jeremiah 32 may also have been the potter of Jeremiah 18, but this supposition is without evidence./16/ כסף and שקל are common roots and do not provide sufficient basis for the joining of Zech 11:13 with Jer 32:9./17/ Therefore, the only real parallels are found in the fact that a potter is featured in Jeremiah 18 and Zech 11:13 and the purchase of a field in Jeremiah 32 and the Judas tradition. The links between Jeremiah 18, 32 and Zech 11:13 are tenuous at best and it is difficult to reconstruct a process by which they would have been joined together. It is therefore necessary to ask if any other passage from the book of Jeremiah may provide a more relevant background for the narrative in Matt 27:3-8.

One's attention is immediately drawn to Jer 19:1-13. Two verbal links exist between Jeremiah 19 and Matt 27:3-10: 'innocent blood' (דם נקים [LXX: αἱμάτων ἀθῴων]--v 4) and 'potter' (יוצר [LXX: πεπλασμένον]--vv 1, 11). Even more striking is the thematic parallel: Jeremiah prophesies that a locality associated with potters (v 1) will be renamed with a phrase connoting violence (v 6) and used as a burial place (v 11), as a token of God's judgment upon Jerusalem (and in particular, upon the Jewish leaders (v 1))./18/ While a 'field' is not specifically mentioned in Jeremiah 19, the contextual similarity to Matt 27:3-10, taken in conjunction with the verbal connection (especially the key-word 'potter')

is a solid basis for associating Jeremiah 19 with the quotation
in Matt 27:9-10. If, as seems likely, the parallel between
the tradition of Zech 11:13 and Jeremiah 19 was first
discovered through the common mention of a 'potter,' the MT
has surely been the basic text employed, since LXX paraphrases
יוצר in Jer 19:1 and 11.

The last phrase of the quotation again has no counterpart
in Zech 11:13./19/ Based on the belief that the reference
to the field is from Jeremiah 32, Torrey feels that Jer 32:6
and 8 have given rise to the reference to God's command./20/
Lindars proposes a more complex background. The words καθὰ
συνέταξεν κύριος are found in Exod 9:12, where they indicate
the fulfillment of God's promise to Moses that, notwithstanding
the plague of boils, Pharaoh would continue to harden his
heart against the requests of the Israelites. This verse from
Exodus is related to Zech 11:13 through the mention of the
furnace used for the production of the ashes which caused the
boils (Exod 9:8; cf. LXX Zech 11:13: χωνευτήριον ['foundry']).
Thus, the 'ingenious' exegete 'expresses the idea of the divine
command, suggested to him by Jer 32 (39). 14, in the phrase
found in the Exodus passage.'/21/ The LXX word for 'furnace'
in Exod 9:8 is not the same one found in Zechariah, however,
and the whole reconstruction is generally too 'ingenious'
to be acceptable.

However, while dependence on Exod 9:12, mediated through
Jeremiah 32, does not seem sufficient to explain the phrase in
Matthew, an element of truth in this reconstruction can be
seen when it is recognized that the phrase καθὰ συνέταξεν
κύριος in Exod 9:12 is only one of a number of similar sayings
in the OT./22/ It is probable that Matthew draws on this
stereotyped expression as a paraphrase of the opening words
of Zech 11:13, 'and the Lord said to me.'/23/ That the words
must be an attempt to introduce Zech 11:13a into the citation
is demonstrated by the anomalous μοι. The verbal agreement
between the phrase in Matthew and the LXX rendition of many
of the 'obedience formulas' indicates that Matthew was aware
of the expression in its Greek form./24/

The formula quotation is therefore built up from several
OT elements: the foundation and essential structure is provided
by the phrases drawn from Zech 11:13, but the mention of the
field provides an important 'remodelling' of the quotation,
based on the Judas tradition and with reference to Jeremiah 19,

while the concluding phrase adds a 'decorative motif,' drawn from the traditional 'obedience formula.' Jeremiah is mentioned in the introductory formula because Jeremiah 19 was the least obvious reference, yet most important from the point of view of the application of the quotation./25/

Before turning to the narrative, a significant aspect of the text-form of the quotation should be emphasized: its close dependence on the MT. Several of the phrases from Zech 11:13 must depend on the MT, the influence of Jeremiah 19 is probably mediated through familiarity with the Heb., and no part of the quotation depends on the LXX against the MT. (The phrase καθὰ συνέταξέν μοι κύριος, while dependent on the Greek, is not an exception, since it is a stereotyped formula independent of any *one* OT passage.) It is not unlikely, therefore, that the MT is the sole *Vorlage* for the quotation./26/

II.   Narrative and Quotation

What now can be said about the relationship between this complex citation and the narrative which it interprets? On the one hand, there can be little doubt that the tradition has exerted considerable influence on the quotation. The introduction of the 'field' is, of course, the most notable example of this influence, but other minor deviations (the third person plural verbs, δίδωμι for שקל) are also best attributed to the impact of the tradition. What might be termed a 're-orientation of the text' has occurred—a phenomenon we will explore in more detail at a later point. But now it must be asked whether the reverse process has taken place. Have elements from the OT passages crept into or influenced the narrative?

The 'thirty pieces of silver' (v 3) is an allusive reference to Zech 11:13. That the idea of betrayal money is not taken from the OT is probable since Mark records the transaction without alluding to Zech 11:13. It cannot be finally determined whether the exact sum is an accommodation to the prophecy or an element in the tradition which helped direct Matthew's attention to Zechariah 11./27/ The latter alternative should not, however, be ruled out as summarily as it often is.

αἷμα ἀθῷον forms the first link in the chain of 'blood'

references which serve as an important literary motif in the
story (price of blood--v 6; field of blood--v 8)./28/
αἷμα ἀθῷον is, therefore, suspect as a subsequent addition
to the tradition, perhaps based on the OT (Jer 6:15 or 19:4,
especially)./29/ However, 'to shed innocent blood' is a
standard OT expression for a particularly heinous crime/30/
and is not, therefore, unnatural on Judas' lips./31/ If
Matthew himself is responsible for the expression, he has
probably been influenced by general usage rather than by a
particular OT passage.

The action of Judas described in v 5, ῥίψας τὰ ἀργύρια
εἰς τὸν ναόν, echoes the command in Zech 11:13 to throw the
silver pieces into the בית יהוה (οἶκον κυρίου). While the
verb is ἐνέβαλον in LXX, ῥίπτω is used in A' and Σ, so it is
thought possible that Matthew has added this detail to the
tradition on the basis of the OT text: 'It is known, as in
the Acts version, that Judas died suddenly and that the money
was used to buy land, but it is assumed that the money was
first thrown into the house of the Lord, because the prophecy
says so.'/32/ However, this interpretation is open to several
criticisms. It is, perhaps, unlikely that Matthew would have
presented Judas as throwing the coins into the sanctuary
(ναός)/33/ had he been creating the tradition. Moreover, if
the priest's role in the transaction is historical, their
involvement must have been precipitated by an action similar to
that described in v 4. At any rate, no OT text provides a
plausible basis for the addition of this element. It has even
been suggested that Judas' gesture should be understood as a
Jewish legal custom, apparently valid in the time of Jesus,
according to which a seller who wished to revoke a deal, but who
had been refused by the buyer, could deposit the money involved
in the transaction in the Temple, and so effect a revocation.
/34/ This historical context cannot be ruled out, but questions
concerning the date of the law and concerning its applicability
to this kind of situation mean that caution is necessary in
basing very much on it.

One further point might be raised with regard to the
appropriation of the prophecy as a whole by Matthew. It is
sometimes overlooked that the specific context of Zech 11:13 is
not as congenial to the function of the text as a prophecy of
Judas' dealings with the Jewish leaders as it might be. For the
'I' of Zech 11:13 is unambiguously identified as the prophet
himself, in the role of Yahweh's appointed good shepherd
(i.e., ruler), which role seems to be understood as a

refiguration of Christ's as the rejected shepherd par
xcellence. Matthew seems to be at pains to interpret Zech
1:13 so as to avoid the manifest absurdity of identifying
udas with the rejected shepherd while, at the same time,
ppropriating the passage as a prophecy of the history of
e betrayal money. This he can do only by substituting
rcumlocutory constructions for the first person verbs of
e OT passage. We have seen that, in fact, this is exactly
at is done: 'they' (the priests), rather than the rejected
epherd himself as the prophecy strictly requires, take the
lver coins and give them to the potter. The importance of
is insight for the specific question before us is obvious:
e necessity to avoid directly ascribing to Judas any of
e actions of the rejected shepherd in Zechariah renders it
likely that Matthew would introduce an action on Judas'
rt ('throwing the coins into the temple') that does just
at. Thus, although the verb used (ῥίπτω) may be taken from
e OT, it must at least be questioned whether the reference
Judas' throwing the coins into the temple in v 4 has been
troduced on the basis of the OT quotation./35/

    While v 5 is said to represent an attempt to introduce an
ement from Zech 11:13 into the narrative which was omitted
om the quotation, it is argued that εἰς τὸν κορβανᾶν in
6 is a doublet of εἰς . . . κεραμέως in the citation. Some
holars think this alleged dual understanding of the phrase
om Zech 11:13 is based on a variant reading of אוצר
reasury' for יוצר 'potter.'/36/ While no Heb. MS reads
אא the Pesh. ܐܨܪ seems to presume such a reading, which,
view of the verbal similarity, could easily have been
bsequently altered to יוצר ./37/ However, the translation of
e Pesh. is too slight a support for the suggested emendation
d יוצר must surely be retained as the *lectio difficilior*./38/
d it must also be noted that, in general, the evidence for
e use of variant readings in this way is slight. But if
ς τὸν κορβανᾶν cannot rest on a variant reading, it is
vertheless possible that the phrase is evidence of Matthew's
derstanding of Zech 11:13 in a dual sense. This
terpretation would have been facilitated by the word-play
יוצר-- אוצר /39/ and may, moreover, be based on the belief
at the יוצר in Zech 11:13 was a minor temple official
nnected with the treasury./40/

    The latter possibility is not, however, likely;/41/ so
e brunt of the argument must rest on the presumption that

Matthew was aware of, and utilized the word play אוצר -- יוצר
in the writing of Matt 27:3-10. Several indications speak
against this. To begin with, there is some doubt that κορβανᾶς
in v 6 actually means 'treasury.' This meaning for the word
is very poorly attested, a single passage in Josephus (Bell. 2.
175) being the only alleged example besides Matt 27:6./42/
Moreover, Gärtner has argued that the meaning of the word in
Josephus is 'sacred gifts,' a definition more in accord with
the meaning of the root קרבן elsewhere and appropriate in
the context./43/ κορβανᾶν in Matt 27:6 may therefore, denote
not the treasury, but sacred gifts, which were deposited in the
temple, to which the silver thrown by Judas could not be
added because of the profane purpose for which it had been
used./44/ A certain conclusion on this matter is probably
impossible, but even if κορβανᾶς is translated 'treasury,'
a serious objection can be raised against the supposed double
fulfillment of יוצר : the priests' decision *not* to put the
money into the treasury contradicts the explicit statement in
Zech 11:13 that the money was to be thrown אל־היוצר ./45/
This objection cannot be dismissed as demanding 'too rigid an
application of the quotation to the circumstances of the
context' or as failing to reckon with the 'more indirect
applications of the quotation.'/46/ An indirect application
is one thing, but the deliberate introduction of an element,
based on a variant interpretation, which expressly contradicts
the command of the prophecy is quite another. In other words,
were Matthew *inventing* details here in order to fulfill OT
prophecy, it is reasonable to expect that his creation would
be in strict accord with that prophecy.

Verse 7 introduces an important link between the narrative
and the mixed quotation of vv 9-10--ἀγρὸς τοῦ κεραμέως. The
fact that a field was in some manner involved in the tradition
associated with Judas' death is generally accepted in view
of the prominence of a field in the seemingly independent,
Semitic-colored account in Acts 1:16ff and the unexpected
addition of 'field' to the quotation in Matthew. However,
it is generally believed that the 'Field of Blood' mentioned
in v 8 is the historic kernel of the legend, while the
connection with 'potter' and the change of name has been
invented in order to bring the money into contact with a
'potter,' as Zech 11:13 indicates./47/ There is some basis,
however, for thinking that a potter's field was a part of
the original tradition. Benoit points out that the traditional
site for 'Hakeldama' was an area which was a source of clay

for the potters of Jerusalem and which, in view of its evil
reputation, was a natural location for the burial of
strangers./48/ The priest's purchase of the field for this
purpose would be in accord with rabbinic custom./49/ Moreover,
the fact that the linking of 'field' with 'potter' is not
found in any of the relevant OT texts and that this connection
does not correspond exactly to the role played by the 'potter'
in Zech 11:13 favors viewing the element as traditional rather
than as an OT-inspired creation./50/

We conclude, therefore, that there is reason to doubt
whether any important part of the narrative in Matt 27:3-8
has been created under the influence of OT passages. As we
have seen, several points in the pericope are not in complete
harmony with the OT prophecies cited, pointing to restraint
on the part of the transmitter of the tradition. Most
important, the unique features of the mixed quotation in
vv 9-10 constitute a strong evidence for the dominant role
played by the tradition in the process. As Benoit says,
'. . . the tradition recorded by Matthew in his gospel cannot
be explained by reference to the biblical texts alone, since
on the contrary, it governs the disconcerting use made of
them . . . .'/51/ In view of these considerations it is most
reasonable to think that the evangelist composed Matt 27:3-10
on the basis of a tradition that came to him substantially
in the form in which we now have it. It is probable that Jesus'
betrayal for a sum of money first led Matthew to Zech 11:13,
where the singular mention of a 'potter' reminded him that the
site of the 'Field of Blood,' purchased with Judas' ill-gotten
wages, was traditionally associated with the activity of
potters. This, in turn, led Matthew to the passage of
Scripture with a number of suggestive parallels to the
tradition, Jeremiah 19. Matthew collates Jeremiah 19 and
Zech 11:13, thereby indicating, at the same time, the
fulfillment of the prophecy regarding the wages of the rejected
shepherd and that concerned with the destiny of the Valley
of Topheth./52/

Presupposing this exegetical work is the identification
of Jesus as the rejected shepherd of Zech 11:4-14. Indeed,
the correlation of the destiny of Jesus, the God-appointed
leader of Israel, with the similar fate of Zechariah seems to
be the primary motivation for the narrative and quotation./53/
Thus, stress is placed on the fact that the money was the price
at which the 'precious one' was valued by the Jewish leaders.

This purpose is evident in Matthew's modifications of the
quotation, which, as we have seen, serve to involve Judas and
the priests in the action narrated in the text without
destroying the identification of Jesus with the Shepherd.

Thus, the wages given to the prophet in Zech 11:12 are
given to Judas in Matthew, the actions performed by the prophet
in Zech 11:13 are transferred to the priests, and the money
goes not to a potter directly but for the purchase of a
'potter's field.' While these changes are major enough, it
is important to note that there is no departure from the basic
thrust of Zechariah's prophecy. While Judas is the direct
recipient of the 'wages' in Matthew, Jesus is the one being
evaluated at this level--just as the prophet's worth is
evaluated in Zechariah 11. The verb changes serve to describe
the actions from the recipients' point of view, and the
addition of 'the field' extends the idea of the money being
given to the potter. Nevertheless, it is obvious that
the Matt 27:9, 10 quotation evidences a considerable
modification of text. Another important technique observed
here, for which there is ample precedent in Jewish literature,
is the combination of passages, based to some extent on the
use of similar words or phrases.

III. A Midrash?

In the current situation of terminological 'fuzziness'
with respect to terms like pesher and midrash, it is meaningles
and can be misleading simply to label a particular text with
these terms. Until generally accepted meanings of such terms
are forthcoming, it is essential that scholars carefully
state 'working' definitions and, beyond that, note *both*
similarities and differences between NT and various Jewish
exegetical procedures. Much of the confusion surrounding the
term 'midrash' for instance, is caused by its application by
different scholars to three different 'levels' of the
exegetical procedure: literary genre,/54/ exegetical
method,/55/ and hermeneutical axioms./56/ Thus the exegetical
methods of the rabbis (exemplified in the *middot* of Hillel
and R. Ishmael b. Elisha) may closely resemble the methods
employed by the Qumran sectarians/57/ or NT writers, but their
hermeneutical axioms or genre of writing may be entirely
different. Similarly, an eschatological orientation and
revelatory basis may characterize both Qumran and NT exegesis
(hermeneutical axioms), but exegetical methods may differ

appreciably.

In discussing midrash in Matt 27:3-10, then, it is crucial
to make comparisons at several levels./58/ In terms of *literary
genre*, the historical narration style of Matthew finds no close
parallel in rabbinic or Qumran literature. The rabbis exhibit
little interest in history *as such*; any narratives which are
found tend to be homilies based on biblical characters or
illustrations for halakic purposes. The detailed correspondence
of narrative and context is, of course, found in the Qumran
pesharim, but these, significantly, are written ostensibly
as commentaries on the text.

At the level of *exegetical method*, similarities with
the procedure of both the rabbis and the sectarians are
obvious: combination of texts based on possible word-plays
and modification of the OT text to suit its application are
well-known in both types of literature. But with respect to
that is for many the crucial characteristic of midrash--the
creation of narrative based on the OT--/59/ Matthew's
procedure is not, as we have pointed out, analogous to
rabbinic practice./60/

This last point leads us, finally, to say something
about hermeneutical axioms. For the NT authors, as in a
somewhat similar manner for the Qumran sectarians, the impact
of recent historical events was *the* decisive influence on
exegetical procedure. They were 'concerned not with
interpreting the OT, but with interpreting an *event* in terms
of the OT.'/61/ This fundamental datum is ultimately what
distinguishes NT exegesis from most rabbinic exegesis. The
latter functioned within the framework built up of tradition,
current community needs and Scripture and came to expression
in the form of detailed guidelines for behavior and edifying
stories, sometimes loosely linked to a biblical book. Granted
such a framework, creative influence on biblical narratives
from other OT texts is not unlikely. But in the NT, exegesis
functions within a framework dominated by very recent events
surrounding the life of Jesus of Nazareth, and came to
expression in, among other things, what are ostensibly
historical narratives. The creation of narrative under the
influence of the OT is *a priori* less likely in this kind of
framework simply because there is less interest in the OT
per se. In this respect, the NT situation is much closer
to that of the Dead Sea community, and few scholars have

suggested that the scrolls feature narratives *created* on the
basis of the OT.

In other words, resemblances between Matt 27:3-10 and
the rabbinic literature at the level of exegetical procedure
are outweighed by differences with respect to literary genre
and hermeneutical axioms. Whether one wants to speak of
midrash in Matt 27:3-10 depends, then, on the stage of
exegetical procedure about which one is speaking. But if the
term is used to designate, as it most often does today in
NT studies, a creative influence of the OT on the tradition,
I would think the term inappropriate here.

Notes.

/1/ See, most recently F. Mans, 'Un Midrash chrétien: le
récit de la mort de Judas' *RSR* 54 (1980) 197-203. The question
of historicity is closely bound up with this question. Many
agree with Montefiore (*The Synoptic Gospels* (2 vols.; 2nd ed.;
London: MacMillan, 1927), 2.329) who calls this narrative
'one of the clearest examples of history made up from bits
of Old Testament prophecy.'
/2/ This is preferable to other explanations which attempt
to account for the ascription to Jeremiah: (1) The variant
reading Ζαχαριου (22 Syr[hrg]) or Ησαιου (21 ϑ 33 157) should
be followed. (2) Since Jeremiah stands first of the prophets
in several OT books lists (J. P. Audet, 'A Hebrew-Aramaic
List of Books of the Old Testament in Greek Transcription,'
JTS n.s. 1 (1950) 136; Charles C. Torrey, 'The Aramaic Period
of the Nascent Christian Church,' *ZNW* 44 (1952-53) 222),
his name may be used here as a general reference to the
prophetic *corpus* (Str-B, 1, 1030; H. F. D. Sparks, 'St.
Matthew's References to Jeremiah,' *JTS* n.s. 1 (1950) 155;
Edmund F. Sutcliffe, 'Matthew 27,9' *JTS* n.s. 3 (1952) 227).
(3) An apocryphal book (which Jerome claims to have seen)
contained the conflated citation under Jeremiah's name
(Origen; Hieronymus; E. Lohmeyer, *Das Evangelium des Matthäus*
(rev. by W. Schmauch; Meyer K.; 4th ed.; Göttingen: Vandenhoec
& Ruprecht, 1967) 378; G. Strecker, *Der Weg der Gerechtigkeit
Untersuchung zur Theologie des Matthäus* (FRLANT 82; Göttingen
Vandenhoeck & Ruprecht, 1962) 80-81; (4) The quotation was
found in the 'Testimony Book' under Jeremiah's name (R. Harris,
Testimonies (with the assistance of V. Burch; 2 vols.:
Cambridge: University Press, 1916, 1920), 1. 59-60; J. A.
Findlay, 'The First Gospel and the Book of Testimonies,'

Amicitiae Corolla (ed. H. G. Wood; London: University of London: 1933) 65).   (5)   The ascription is due to a slip of memory (J. Finegan, *Die Uberlieferung der Leidens- und Auferstehungsgeschichte Jesu* (BZNW 15; Giessen: Töpelmann, 1934) 26; K. Stendahl, *The School of St. Matthew and its use of the Old Testament*   (Philadelphia: Fortress, 1958) 123).   (6)   The last part of the book of Zechariah was traditionally ascribed to Jeremiah.

/3/   Donald Senior, *The Passion Narrative According to Matthew: A Redactional Study* (BETL 39; Leuven: Leuven University Press, 1975) 354.

/4/   Lohmeyer-Schmauch, *Matthäus,* 378; Stendahl, *School,* 125. Senior (*Passion Narrative,* 353) and Gundry (*The Use of the Old Testament in St. Matthew's Gospel* (NovT Sup 18; Leiden: Brill, 1967) 126) are more hesitant, the latter pointing out that the influence of the LXX may have outweighed that of the context.   While relative degree of influence is difficult to assess, the probable reading ἔδωκαν (see below) is good reason to understand ἔλαβον as 3rd pl. as well.

/5/   Stendahl, *School* 125; Gundry, *Old Testament* 126; Senior, *Passion Narrative* 355; A. Baumstark, 'Die Zitate des Mt.-Ev. aus dem Zwölfprophetenbuch,' *Bib* 37 (1956) 302.

/6/   BAG 825.

/7/   Senior, *Passion Narrative* 355.

/8/   BDF (par. 164 (2)) note the unclassical use of ἐκ and ἀπό in this way.   Cf. GKC (par. 199w) for the Hebrew construction.

/9/   Gundry (*Old Testament* 127) notes that the targums often expand with the phrase 'the sons of Israel.' Senior (*Passion Narrative* 355) believes the change from indefinite to definite is characteristic of Matthew's redaction.

/10/   Cf. M-J. Lagrange, *Evangile selon Saint Matthieu* (EBib; 5th ed.; Paris: Gabalda, 1941) 513.

/11/   B. Metzger, *A Textual Commentary on the Greek New Testament* (New York: UBS, 1971) 67.

/12/   A. H. McNeile, *The Gospel According to St. Matthew* (London: MacMillan, 1928) 408; Gundry, *Old Testament,* 126. ἔδωκα is read by W. C. Allen, *A Critical and Exegetical Commentary on the Gospel According to St. Matthew* (ICC; Edinburgh: T & T Clark, 1907) 288; Montefiore, *The Synoptic Gospels,* 2. 343.

/13/   Senior, *Passion Narrative* 355.

/14/   F. F. Bruce, 'The Book of Zechariah and the Passion Narrative,' *BJRL* 42 (1960-1961) 341; C. C. Torrey 'The Foundry of the Second Temple at Jerusalem,' *JBL* 55 (1936) 252;

Stendahl, *School* 122; Strecker, *Weg* 77; R. S. McConnell,
*Law and Prophecy in Matthew's Gospel: The Authority and Use
of the Old Testament in the Gospel of Matthew* (Theologische
Dissertationen 2; Basel: Friedrich Reinhardt, 1969) 132;
B. Lindars, *New Testament Apologetic: The Doctrinal
Significance of the Old Testament Quotations* (London: SCM,
1961) 120; Jeremiah 32 only is mentioned by A. Schlatter
(*Der Evangelist Matthäus* (Stuttgart: Calver, 1957) 770;
A. Descamps ('Rédaction et Christologie dans le récit
matthéen de la Passion,'*L'Evangile selon Matthieu,* (ed.
M. Didier; Gembloux: Duculot, 1972) 389); Lohmeyer-Schmauch,
Matthäus 379).
/15/ Lindars, *Apologetic* 120; Stendahl, *School* 122.
/16/ 'Foundry' 252. Gundry (*Old Testament* 124) points out that
Hanamel, Jeremiah's cousin, was probably of a priestly family
and hence almost certainly not a potter.
/17/ Against J. Doeve, *Jewish Hermeneutics in the Synoptic
Gospels and Acts* (Assen: van Gorcum, 1954) 185-186. Doeve
characterizes Matt 27:3-10 as a *haggadah* and believes the
starting point of the complex was the connection between Matt
27:5 and Jer 26:15 through the phrase 'innocent blood.' Once
Jeremiah 26 was associated with Judas' death, the similar
theme of judgment against Jerusalem would have led the
Haggadist to Jeremiah 19 and 32, the entire Jeremiah tradition
then being tied into Zech 11:13 on the basis of the roots
כסף and שקל , found in Jer 32:9. The foundation of the
whole argument is weak, however; innocent blood is a common
expression that would not alone have provided a point of
contact between Matthew and Jeremiah 26. The motivation
for the joining together of Jeremiah 19, 26 and 32 is weak,
as well; practically the entire book of Jeremiah is
characterized by prophecies against Jerusalem.
/18/ See Gundry (*Old Testament* 124-5) and Senior (*Passion
Narrative* 360) for these specific points. Jeremiah 19 had
earlier been considered the background to this quotation by
A. Edersheim (*The Life and Times of Jesus the Messiah* (2 vols.;
London: Longman, Green and Co., 1883), 2. 596).
/19/ A few later LXX MSS have assimilated the phrase from
Matthew.
/20/ 'Foundry' 252.
/21/ *Apologetic,* 121; cf. also E. Schweizer, *The Good News
According to Matthew* (London: SPCK, 1975) 504.
/22/ The genre to which these sayings belong has been studied
by Pesch, who calls them 'Ausführungsformeln.' He notes
several instances of the obedience formula pattern in Matthew's

gospel ('Eine alttestamentliche Ausführungsformel im Matthäus-Evangelium: Redaktionsgeschichte und exegetische Beobachtungen,' *BZ* n.s. 10 (1966) 220-245).

/23/ Senior, *Passion Narrative* 361. Montefiore (*Synoptic Gospels*, 2. 343), Lohmeyer-Schmauch (*Matthäus* 379), Gundry (*Old Testament* 127) and Stendahl (*School* 123) think the phrase is an attempt to introduce the opening words of Zech 11:13. Stendahl's tentative suggestion that Matthew's phrase is an interpretation of בית יהוה as ביד יהוה cannot be maintained. As Gundry (127) points out in reply to a similar theory of Baumstark's, ביד is always used with an instrumental sense in association with the Word of God.

/24/ καθὰ συνέταξεν κύριος in Exod 36:8, 12, 14, 28, 33; 37:20; 39:10; 40:19; Lev 14:23; Num 8:3; 9:5; 15:23; 20:9, 27; 27:11; 31:31, 41. Matthew's dependence on this phrase is confirmed by the fact that καθά is used only here in the NT.

/25/ Gundry, *Old Testament* 125.

/26/ Allen, *Matthew* 288.

/27/ Strecker (*Weg* 77-9), who believes that Matthew has taken the story from oral tradition and added the quotation himself (as does also G. D. Kilpatrick, [*The Origins of the Gospel According to St. Matthew* (Oxford: Clarendon, 1946)]81), regards the 'thirty pieces of silver' as one of the rare Matthean additions to the tradition.

/28/ Lohmeyer-Schmauch, *Matthäus* 375; Senior, *Passion Narrative* 386-7.

/29/ Doeve, *Hermeneutics* 185.

/30/ Lohmeyer-Schmauch, *Matthäus* 375.

/31/ W. C. Van Unnik ('The Death of Judas in St. Matthew's Gospel,' *ATR* supp. ser. 3 (1974) 53-55) cites Deut 27:25 ('Cursed be whoever takes gifts [bribes] to take the life of innocent blood') and conjectures that Judas, in light of this verse, takes his own life to remove the curse. While the parallel is striking, it is doubtful that Judas would have acted so drastically on the basis of this verse alone.

/32/ Lindars, *Apologetic* 118; cf. also Senior, *Passion Narrative* 382. Stendahl (*School* 126) believes that Matthew adds the detail to utilize an element from Zech 11:13 that had been 'left hanging' after his changes to the text. But the freedom with which Matthew uses the OT text indicates that the retention of this phrase in the prophecy would have been no difficult matter. Lohmeyer-Schmauch (*Matthäus* 376) argue that Judas could not have thrown the coins into the Temple because the Sanhedrin was not there, but at the Roman trial (cf. Matt 27:1-2). But it is obvious that Matthew has added the Judas

pericope to the Marcan framework at a break in the material so
that the position of the narrative does not necessarily
represent a chronological indication.
/33/ While there is some dissent (Michel, 'ναός,' *TDNT* 4 (1967)
884-5), Matthew, at least, seems to distinguish ναός, the
sanctuary, from ἱερόν, the temple precincts (Compare 23:16, 17,
21, 35 with 4:5; 21:12, 14, 15; 24:1; 26:55).
/34/ J. Jeremias, *Jerusalem in the Time of Jesus* (3rd ed.;
London: SCM, 1969) 139.
/35/ Allen (*Matthew* 288) thinks the detail was a known fact
and has facilitated Matthew's use of the Zech 11:13 text.
/36/ As F. F. Bruce (*The New Testament Development of Old
Testament Themes* [Grand Rapids: Eerdmans, 1968] 110) paraphrases
the priests' thinking: '"How shall we fulfill the scripture?
Shall we give it to the 'ōsar or to the yōsar? We cannot give
it to the 'ōsar because it is blood money; let us give it to
the yōsar."' See also Allen, *Matthew* 288; Montefiore,
Synoptic Gospels, 2. 342; McNeile, *Matthew* 408.
/37/ T. Jansma, *Inquiry into the Hebrew Text and the Ancient
Versions of Zechariah 9-14* (Oudtestamentische Studien 7;
Leiden: Brill, 1950) 35; Sidney Jellicoe, *The Septuagint
and Modern Study* (Oxford: Clarendon Press, 1968) 320.
/38/ I. Willi-Plein, *Prophetie am Ende: Untersuchungen zu
Sacharja 9-14* (BBB 42; Cologne: Hanstein, 1974) 22. It is
improbable that אוצר was changed to יוצר because a scribe
felt the sum was too paltry to be placed in the treasury
(contra McNeile, *Matthew* 408).
/39/ Stendahl, *School* 124-5; Lindars, *Apologetic* 118 (who
does not dismiss the possibility that Matthew knew a variant
reading); Senior, *Passion Narrative* 357-8.
/40/ Stendahl, *School* 125. This understanding of יוצר in
Zech 11:13 is based on Torrey's thesis, according to which the
'potter' is identified as an official whose job it was to
melt down and mold (hence יוצר, in the sense of 'moulder')
the large amounts of metal that poured into the temple coffers.
The readings of LXX (χωνευτήριον--'foundry;' cf. also O'
and Σ'), A' (πλάστην--'moulder') and the targum (אמרכלא --
a minor temple official) are adduced as support for this
understanding of יוצר . Torrey regards the Pesh. reading
as an interpretive conjecture and denies any double
understanding of יוצר in Matthew ('Foundry').
Torrey's theory has been accepted by K. Elliger (*Das Buch der
zwölf kleinen Propheten* (ATD 25; 2 vols.; 2nd ed.; Göttingen:
Vandenhoeck & Ruprecht, 1951), 2. 154), P. Lamarche (*Zacharie
IX-XIV: Structure littéraire et messianisme* (EBib; Paris:

Gabalda, 1961) 65), P. Benoit ('The Death of Judas,' *Jesus and the Gospel I* (London: Darton, Longman & Todd, 1973) 198) Bruce ('Zechariah,' 341) and M. D. Goulder (*Midrash and Lection in Matthew* (The Speaker's Lectures in Biblical Studies, 1969-71; London: SPCK, 1974) 127).

/41/ No historical or archaeological evidence supports the thesis. The readings in the versions are not persuasive evidence since θ and A are no doubt dependent on LXX, which in turn seems to offer a conjectural emendation, according to which it was understood that the thirty pieces of silver were tested for their genuineness (cf. δόκιμον) in a furnace. The Targum completely transforms the meaning of the verse, referring to pious Israelites whose deeds are written down and deposited in the temple (Str-B, 1. 1030). Linguistic evidence is against Torrey, since יוצר always refers to a worker in clay in the OT and גזרה is used to designate a founder or moulder. Finally, the context seems to demand an ignominious destination for the 'lordly price' with which Zechariah was paid off, while Torrey's hypothesis would obscure this basic concept in the passage (Cf. Gundry, *Old Testament* 123).

/42/ . . . ἱερὸν θησαυρόν, καλεῖται δὲ κορβανᾶς, εἰς καταγωγὴν ὁδάτων ἐξαναλύσκων. BAG, 445; Karl Heinrich Rengstorf, 'κορβάν, κορβανᾶς,' TDNT 3 (1965) 861. κορβανᾶς is not found in LXX, and the Heb it transliterates is absent in DSS and rabbinic literature (Str-B, 1. 1028). The term has apparently been discovered in a pre-A.D. 70 Aramaic inscription, but with uncertain meaning (W. F. Albright and C. S. Mann, *Matthew* AB 26; Garden City, N.J.: Doubleday, 1971) 341).

/43/ 'The Habakkuk Commentary (DSH) and the Gospel of Matthew,' *JT* 8 (1955) 18-19. On the meaning of קרבן , see Rengstorf, 'κορβάν,' 860-66. The context in Josephus is concerned with Pilate's expropriation of the Jewish funds for the purpose of constructing an aqueduct. קרבנא is used meaning 'gift' in *b. Hul.* 8a and perhaps also in *b.Zebah* 116b and *Tg. Hos.* 12:2 Rengstorf, 'κορβάν' 861, n. 4).

/44/ This meaning is suggested as possible by M. Kohler in *The Jewish Encyclopedia* 1. 436 (mentioned by Rengstorf, 'κορβάν,' 861).

/45/ Gundry, *Old Testament* 123.

/46/ Senior, *Passion Narrative* 357-8, n. 34.

/47/ Strecker (*Weg* 80) speaks of Matt 27:3-10 as an etiological legend on the name 'field of blood.' While this is an extreme view (cf. criticisms by Senior, *Passion Narrative* 95-6), the belief that the 'Field of Blood' lies at the heart of tradition has good foundation (cf. Lindars, *Apologetic* 122;

Schweizer, *Matthew* 504; Senior, *Passion Narrative* 387-8). It
is often thought that the area was a cemetery, known as the
'Field of Blood' before the events of Judas' death were
associated with it (McNeile, *Matthew* 408; Stendahl, *School* 196;
Lindars, *Apologetic* 122) but Benoit ('Death,' 205-6)
characterizes this as a 'gratuitous assumption' in view of
the lack of mention of the name outside the NT.

/48/ Benoit, 'Death' 200-202.

/49/ Jeremias, *Jerusalem* 140. Allen (*Matthew* 289) feels
the name change was due to influence from Jer 19:11.

/50/ The 'potter's field' is regarded as a traditional element
by Stendahl (*School* 197), Montefiore (*Synoptic Gospels,* 2. 343),
Allen (*Matthew* 288), and Lagrange (*Matthieu* 517).

/51/ Benoit, 'Death' 206; cf. also Bruce, 'Zechariah' 324;
Lagrange, *Matthieu* 517; and R. T. France, "The Formula-
Quotations of Matthew 2 and the Problem of Communication,"
NTS 27 (1980-1981) 236.

/52/ Gundry, *Old Testament* 125.

/53/ Lohmeyer-Schmauch (*Matthäus* 380), Lagrange (*Matthieu* 517)
and Bruce ('Zechariah' 346) stress the fundamental importance
of the Shepherd motif in Matt 27:3-10.

/54/ A. G. Wright, 'The Literary Genre Midrash,' *CBQ* 28 (1966)
105-138, 417-456.

/55/ This seems to be assumed by, e.g., G. F. Moore, *Judaism
in the First Centuries of the Christian Era* (2 vols., London:
Cambridge, 1927), 1. 77; S. Horovitz, 'Midrash,' *JE* 8. 548.

/56/ Cf. especially R. Le Déaut ('Apropos d'une définition du
midrash,' *Bib* 50 (1969) 395-413) who says 'Le midrash est en
effect tout un univers que l'on ne découvrira qu'en acceptant
d'emblée sa complexité.' Cf. also D. Patte, *Early Jewish
Hermeneutics in Palestine* (SBL DS 12; Missoula, Mont.:
Scholar's Press, 1975) 117-124.

/57/ The basis for the hybrid term 'Midrash pesher' (cf. W.
H. Brownlee, 'Biblical Interpretation among the Sectaries of
the Dead Sea Scrolls,' *BA* 14 (1951) 64-65) which is probably
more confusing than helpful (cf. G. Vermes, 'Le "Commentaire
d'Habacuc" et le Nouveau Testament,' *Cahiers Sioniens* 5 (1951),
344-345).

/58/ These three levels are isolated and studied in my
dissertation, 'The Use of the Old Testament in the Passion
Texts of the Gospels' (U. of St. Andrews, 1980) 5-78.

/59/ This popular understanding of midrash appears to derive
from the first characteristic of midrash stated by R. Bloch:
it has its starting point in the text ('Midrash,' *DBSup* 5,
coll. 1263-1281 (c. 1265)).

/60/ For the same reason, R. E. Brown hesitates to speak of midrash in the Matthean infancy narratives (*The Birth of the Messiah: A Commentary on the Infancy Narratives in Matthew and Luke* (Garden City, N.Y.: Doubleday, 1977) 560-561).
/61/ X. Léon-Dufour, *The Gospels and the Jesus of History* (London: Collins and New York: Desclée, 1968) 215.

MIDRASH AND HISTORY IN THE GOSPELS
WITH SPECIAL REFERENCE TO R. H. GUNDRY'S *MATTHEW*

Philip Barton Payne,
Kyoto Christian Studies Center,
34 Sandan Nagamachi, Matsugasaki,
Sakyo-Ku, Kyoto 606   Japan.

Extensive analysis of Matthew as midrash has been undertaken by M. D. Goulder/1/ and most recently and thoroughly by R. H. Gundry's *Matthew: A Commentary on His Literary and Theological Art* (Grand Rapids: Eerdmans, 1982) 652pp. The work of Gundry is of particular interest because it is one of the most detailed redaction critical studies of Matthew ever done and because it is the work of someone who has already made very significant contributions to New Testament studies, not least in his insightful *The Use of the Old Testament in St. Matthew's Gospel* (Leiden: Brill, 1967). This commentary is the result of meticulous and painstaking research and contains many valuable insights both exegetical and theological, notably its articulate defence of authorship by the apostle Matthew (599-622). The main concern of this examination, however, is restricted to evaluating the thesis presented by Gundry that Matthew is a midrashic expansion and embellishment of Mark and Q. He argues that Matthew is a 'mixture of history and non-history' (630), an 'embroidering of history with unhistorical elements' (626), and that Matthew did not consistently intend to portray what actually happened in Jesus' life but freely embellished his sources midrashically with events that never happened and other creative additions.

Evaluation of Gundry's position is complicated since there is some ambiguity as to just what he means when he says that Matthew is midrashic./2/ He uses the term 'midrash' to refer both to particular elements of Matthew and to refer to Matthew as a whole. At times Gundry uses 'midrash' or 'midrashic' to refer specifically to those elements which he regards as unhistorical embellishments. This is evident in such statements as 'Matthew's gospel contains midrash . . . Matthew's midrash and haggadah were inspired as such, not as history . . . Classifying elements of Matthew as midrash' (637).

Yet at other times Gundry uses 'midrash' to refer to literature within which unhistorical embellishment occurs: 'by definition midrash and haggadah include unhistorical embroidery' (637). Thus he speaks of 'midrashic and haggadic literature of his [Matthew's] era' (629). He states that the gospels of Mark and Luke do not 'merit the descriptions "midrashic" and "haggadic"' and contrasts this with 'what we have discovered concerning Matthew' (628). 'First, it needs to be stressed again that we . . . call Matthew midrashic and haggadic . . . because free revisions and additions pervade the gospel and fall into tendentious patterns.' (637)

Gundry repeatedly refers to the importance of recognizing the literary genre of works and seems to indicate that he regards midrash as a common literary genre in Matthew's day. Thus, for example, he criticizes the view that 'embroidering history with unhistorical elements à la midrash and haggadah would be inappropriate to God's Word' of having a 'lack of appreciation for a literary genre that we think strangely ancient or personally unappealing' (626). He states that 'ancient midrashists' did not announce 'the genre' they were using (632). 'Genre' is used here in the technical literary sense that is recognized 'from the style and contents of what we say vis-à-vis shared knowledge and traditions of communication (cf. Hirsch, *Validity in Interpretation* 78-102, 262-64)'. (632)

Although Gundry does not explicitly state that he regards Matthew as a work of the literary genre midrash, various statements give that impression. After listing several categories of literary genre, 'history . . . fairy tale . . . poetry . . . historical novel . . . parables . . . proverbs', arguing that 'our identification of the kind of literature an author intended to write should depend on the data of his text studied in their historical setting', and speaking of 'a correlation between Matthew and extrabiblical midrash and haggadah', Gundry states 'our understanding of literary genres within the Bible is enriched and refined through comparison with literary genres outside the Bible' (639). He goes on to state that

Matthew edited historical traditions in unhistorical ways and in accord with midrashic and haggadic practices to which his first readers were accustomed . . . he intended not only to pass on historical information but also to

elaborate on its significance by embellishing it . . .
In sum, . . . *[we must]* enlarge the room given to
differences of literary genre and, consequently, of
intended meaning. (639)

Because of this ambiguity in Gundry's position we will
examine both of these related yet distinct positions: 1) that
Matthew though not of the literary genre midrash nonetheless
contains midrashic embellishments and 2) that Matthew as a
whole is a midrash genre work. Establishment of the latter
would, of course, add significantly to the argument that any
particular element of Matthew was intended as an unhistorical
midrashic embellishment.

Some Jewish works such as *Jubilees*, the *Genesis Apocryphon*,
and Pseudo-Philo's *Liber Antiquitatum Biblicarum*, which are
generally regarded as antedating the midrash literary genre,
freely embellished historical tradition with fictional events
and sayings. We will consider whether Matthew is analogous
either to midrash genre literature *per se* or to these earlier
writings in literary form, content, hermeneutical axioms, and
temporal standpoint and whether there is good evidence that
Matthew, like them, freely embellished historical traditions
with unhistorical material.

To do this we will consider first what evidence there is
for midrashic intent in Matthew, and second, what literary
problems confront the thesis that Matthew is midrashic. In
order to avoid terminological confusion 'midrashic intent' is
used in this essay to focus as Gundry does on the intent to
convey what is in fact unhistorical using historical narrative
form. We recognize, however, that this is merely one of many
ways in which the term 'midrash' has been used.

When referring to history in this essay we do not mean any
sophisticated science of history or strict requirements of
historical exactitude but simply the narration of events that
actually occurred. All historical writing is of necessity
edited, selective, and abbreviated. It is entirely possible
that Matthew, like Josephus, used a type of historical writing
that is interpretively edited but still conveys an impression
that is true to history. Gundry, however, goes significantly
farther than saying merely that Matthew's treatment of
historical traditions is interpretive and highlights
theological issues. He argues that Matthew intended to

embellish his story of Jesus with events that never actually
occurred and that free revisions and additions pervade the
gospel as in midrashic and haggadic literature of his era.

1.   Evidence for Midrashic Intent in Matthew

Gundry points to four things which he believes undermine
Matthew's historical reliability and consistently historical
intent and which indicate unhistorical midrashic embellishment
of his sources: the fulfilment quotations, the genealogy,
discrepancies with Mark or Luke, and tendentious changes.

1.1.   *The fulfilment quotations*
Gundry calls attention to Matthew's use of the OT as a
clue to his unhistorical intent, stating that 'Matthew converts
historical statements about the Exodus and the Babylonian Exile
into messianic prophecies (Hos 11:1; Jer 31:15; cf. Matt 2:15,
18) and negates what Micah affirmed about the smallness of
Bethlehem (Mic 5:1 [sic]; cf. Matt 2:16 [sic]' (632-33). These
and other examples are of questionable relevance to Matthew's
historical intent since, as has been well established in
various studies of fulfilment quotations and as Gundry himself
acknowledges (37, 469), fulfilment quotations were used to
introduce not only direct literal fulfilment of explicit
messianic prophecies, but also fulfilment along the lines of
corporate solidarity, typological correspondence, and historical
parallels (foreshadowing)./3/ Thus although in Matthew the
term 'fulfilment' is used in a broader sense than we might use
it, this usage was not unique to Matthew and need not be
regarded as indicative of Matthew's unhistorical intent.

Gundry writes that Matthew 'denies Bethelehem's leastness'
(29). Only, however, by isolating the comparison to the single
word οὐδαμῶς ('by no means') does he, as have other critics,/4/
derive a superficial formal negation. Taken as a whole,
however, the meanings are complementary. The idea of 'though
you are small . . . yet . . .' in Mic 5:2 corresponds in
meaning to 'you . . . are by no means least . . . for . . .' in
Matt 2:6. In both verses, apart from the Messiah's birth,
Bethlehem is reckoned insignificant; and in both verses because
of Messiah's birth insignificant Bethlehem becomes significant.
/5/

Matthew's use of the OT is the only clue Gundry suggests
that might indicate Matthew's unhistorical intent apart from a
detailed comparison of Matthew with his sources. The validity
of Gundry's assessment that such a use of the OT might lead to
the deduction of nonhistorical intent depends on Matthew's
readers distinguishing between literal and midrashic
interpretation. The extant literature, however, indicates that
'It is in the Babylonian Talmud, and during the early part of
the fourth century A.D., that midrashic exegesis is consciously
distinguished from literalist interpretation'./6/

1.2. The genealogy
Gundry asserts that Matthew has made 'the massive
transformation of a physical genealogy into a Christological
statement' (20). His own analysis, however, is based on
speculative probing into Matthew's mind and retracing the
thoughts that led him to create the genealogy:

> With "Eliezer" still in the back of his mind, Matthew now
> notices "Eliakim" in the genealogy of Joseph (see Luke 3:
> 30) . . . the name "Azariah" in the priestly genealogy
> (1 Chr 5:35-36 [6:9-10]) catches his eye. But Matthew
> shortens it to "Azor" . . . The obscuring of his priestly
> source protects Davidic Christology. His interest in this
> Christology leads to the name "Zadok," . . . The
> evangelist then goes quite naturally to Zadok's son
> Ahimaaz, . . . but shortens that name to Ἀχίμ . . .
> Still concerned to cover the traces of his priestly source,
> Matthew again introduces a reference to the royal tribe of
> Judah, this time with "Eliud" (cf. 1 Chr 12:21 LXXᴬ). . .
> His eye back on the genealogy of Joseph, Matthew leaves 1
> Chronicles to take up the name of Joseph's grandfather
> "Matthat" (Luke 3:24), which becomes "Matthan" . . .
> "Jacob" replaces "Heli" (Luke 3:23) to conform to the
> fathering of the patriarch Joseph by the patriarch Jacob
> . . . (18)

Unfortunately, Gundry gives no interaction with scholars
preferring less speculative and simpler explanations of the
data as historical./7/

1.3. Discrepancies between Matthew and Mark or Luke
Gundry states, 'Though they are not always so insuperable
as sometimes alleged, problems of harmonizing the stories in
Matthew and Luke support creativity on Matthew's part'. (36)

He perceives 'a number of outright discrepancies with the other
synoptics' (624); 'many of them rest, not on ambiguities or
arguments from silence, but on the plain, explicit wording of
the text'. (625)   In practice Gundry uses these as the clearest
sign of midrash, but in theory he recognizes that problems of
harmonization do not by themselves constitute adequate grounds
for calling Matthew midrashic (637). Because of space
limitations I will refer only to the five instances where
Gundry seems most clearly to allege outright unambiguous
discrepancies./8/

1.3.1.   Matt 2:13-23; Luke 2:39
Luke says that the Holy Family went back to Nazareth when
(ὡς) they finished the ceremonies in the Temple (Luke 2:
39), i.e., forty days after Jesus' birth (Leviticus 12).
This statement leaves no room for the Slaughter of the
Innocents, the flight to Egypt, and the residence there
til the death of Herod. In its other fifty-nine
occurrences throughout Luke-Acts, ὡς does not allow for
gaps like that. (36-37)

Gundry here seems to have assumed that the events of Matthew 2
must have preceded the return to Nazareth mentioned in Luke 2:
39. Eusebius, Epiphanius, and Patritius, however, maintained
that the events of Matthew 2 happened sometime after the return
to Nazareth mentioned in Luke 2:39./9/ A decision to move to
Bethlehem would be natural since it would allow Jesus to be
brought up in the city of David near the capital, would be
nearer to their relatives Zacharias and Elizabeth and their
baby John, and would avoid their living with gossip over Jesus'
birth so soon after their marriage. Thus, the house in
Bethlehem to which they moved after settling their affairs and
gathering their possessions in Nazareth would be 'the house' of
Matt 2:11 where the magi worshipped Jesus. The time this would
take explains why Herod 'gave orders to kill all the boys in
Bethlehem and its vicinity who were two years old and under,
in accordance with the time he had learned from the magi' (Matt
2:16). It also explains why after Herod's death Joseph
initially planned to return to Judea (where they would have
left many of their possessions in their hasty night departure,
Matt 2:14) rather than Nazareth (Matt 2:19-23). Gundry, too,
argues that 'In Matthew "the house" means Jesus' house' (31),
but he does not seem to appreciate that this interpretation
supports the view which regards the events of Matthew 2 as
following the return to Nazareth mentioned in Luke 2:39 and so

is historically consistent with Luke's account, which simply omits these subsequent events.

Even if Gundry were correct in his assumption that the flight to Egypt would have to precede the temple presentation and return to Nazareth, he has still overstated his case that the events of Matthew 2 are Matthew's creation. Luke does not say that the Holy Family went back to Nazareth *forty days after Jesus' birth* but simply: 'When everything was accomplished according to the law of the Lord, they returned to Galilee to their own town of Nazareth.' (2:39). Luke does not identify what he intends by 'when everything was accomplished', though presumably it includes at least Jesus' circumcision prior to his being taken to Jerusalem (2:21), his consecration to the Lord (2:22-23), and the offering of a sacrifice (2:24). Gundry's identification of 'when everything was accomplished' solely with the Temple ceremonies is his own supposition, one which unnecessarily excludes the circumcision and any other acts which Luke might have regarded as fulfilling the law of the Lord.

Gundry further states that ὡς does not allow for such time gaps, but the very next occurrence of ὡς with the aorist as a temporal conjunction (cf. BAG 906-7) reads: 'the heaven was shut up three years and six months, when (ὡς) there came a great famine over all the land' (Luke 4:25). The NIV translates ὡς here simply 'and'. The famine did not wait to begin until after the 3½ years were over, nor did it cease immediately after the first rain. It is incorrect, then to insist that ὡς cannot be used of somewhat indefinite periods of time. The flight to Egypt and residence there until the death of Herod could not have been very lengthy. From Bethlehem to Rhinocolure, the first Egyptian town, is only three or four days' journey,/10/ and Herod the Great died sometime between 12 March and 11 April, 4 B.C./11/

A further consideration favouring historical traditions of these events is that the more forced the connection between an event and the prophecy which is applied to it, the less likely it is that the event was fabricated. Since neither Hos 11:1 nor Jer 31:15 is predictive prophecy, it seems doubtful that Matthew would have fabricated events in Jesus' life to fulfil them. Rather, the more natural starting point for these theological reflections would be traditions of the flight to Egypt and of the slaughter of male children in Bethlehem (otherwise should not the slaughter have been of the infants of Rama?).

1.3.2.   *Matt 8:26; Mark 4:40; Luke 8:25*

> According to Matt 8:26 . . . the disciples had little
> faith when the storm raged on the Sea of Galilee; according
> to Mark 4:39-40; Luke 8:24-25, they had no faith. These
> statements are unambiguous. To pretend they are not - by
> suggesting, say, that no faith means not enough faith or
> that different kinds of faith are in view - is to open the
> door to somersaulting exegesis which could with equal
> legitimacy deny the clarity of scriptural statements
> expressing primary doctrines . . . and [to] forfeit our
> right to rest Christian theology on the clear teaching of
> Scripture. (625-626)

Actually, Luke 8:25 does not say that the disciples had no
faith, but simply asks, 'Where is your faith?'. Mark 4:40 is not
an assertion that they had no faith either, but is the question,
'Do you still have no faith?' or 'Have you no faith?'
(depending on the text preferred), a question which should be
understood in light of Mark 4:11, 'To you has been given the
secret of the kingdom of God' (cf. 3:14-15). Each of these
rebukes to the disciples is semantically equivalent and would
be a fair translation of a similar question in Aramaic. Any
slight shift in nuance cannot reasonably be called a
contradiction. Gundry himself says, '"Little faith" (17:20)
and "doubt" (21:21) are synonymous' (418).

1.3.3.   *Matt 14:16; Mark 6:37*

Gundry gives the impression that the simple omission from
Matt 14:16-17 of the question in Mark 6:37, 'Shall we go and
buy two hundred denarii worth of bread, and give it to them to
eat?', is one of Matthew's 'outright discrepancies . . . taking
away the disciples' misunderstanding' (624). Not only,
however, is there no contradiction inherent in the omission, but
the very statement of Matthew indicates the disciples'
misunderstanding: 'We have only five loaves here and two fish'
(Matt 14:17).

Here as frequently elsewhere Gundry downplays indications
in Matthew's text of the disciples' misunderstanding. Gundry's
view that discipleship 'by definition is "learning"' (7) and
his emphasis on the disciples' 'understanding Jesus' words'
(7) seems to follow the similar thesis of Gerhard Barth. This
thesis is vulnerable to criticism as exaggerated and
inconsistent with various passages in Matthew./12/

1.3.4. *Matt 21:41; Mark 12:9; Luke 20:16*

Gundry seems to include among Matthew's 'drastic changes', 'Making the chief priests and elders sentence themselves at the close of the parable of the tenant farmers (21:41), where in Mark 12:9; Luke 20:16 Jesus pronounces the sentence' (625). We agree with Gundry that Matthew has edited this section of his gospel guided by his redactional emphases, but not that this has resulted in a historical discrepancy with Mark and Luke. Note that the audience in Matthew seem to include a crowd of people (21:26,46, and ἔθνος in 43) as well as the chief priests and elders (21:23); and Matthew does not specify that it was the chief priests and elders who stated the response in 21:41. Only if Mark 12:9b and Luke 20:16a are read as statements actually verbalized by Jesus (as opposed to general summaries of what was communicated in the situation) and if Jesus' opponents did not give assent to this statement is there a discrepancy.

Here as so often elsewhere in the gospels it is impossible to distinguish exact quotations, loose quotations, and summaries of what was communicated. It was simply not customary to include specifiers of such fine distinctions. Ancient Greek manuscripts have no quotation marks specifying the start and finish of quotations. Even where the speaker is identified it is unwarranted to assume that a quotation is either exact or unbroken by editorial comment. A problem with quotation marks in our versions is that they give the false impression of tape-recorder type accuracy when in fact the gospel sayings of Jesus are often heavily edited and almost always translated into Greek.

1.3.5. *Matt 10:9-10; Mark 6:8-9; Luke 9:3*

Perhaps the best example Gundry produces of a discrepancy concerns the instructions in sending out the twelve. 'Remarkably, though Mark's text allows a staff "only", and then goes on to allow sandals as well, Matthew allows neither.' (187) The contradiction as Gundry states it here could hardly be more direct and obvious. Yet Gundry himself draws attention, as have many commentators, to Matthew's 'changing "take" (so Mark 6:8 and, similarly, Luke 9:3) to "acquire"' (186).

He argues 'that "acquire" has to do with benefits from ministry not with preparations for ministry' (187). Matt 10:10b, however, states 'the worker is worth his keep', implying that they could, indeed should, accept the hospitality offered them on this preaching journey. Furthermore, κτήσησθε governs all the accusatives in Matt 10:9-10 through ῥάβδον. Thus, on

Gundry's view the disciples were told not to acquire *as benefits from ministry* 'a bag for the journey, nor two tunics, nor sandals, nor a staff' (Matt 10:9). The bag, however, is specifically 'for the journey' (εἰς ὁδόν), not a benefit from it. And 'two tunics', 'sandals' and 'a staff' are unlikely benefits from ministry. All of these, however, including the specification of *two* tunics, fit naturally referring to preparations for a journey. Thus, it makes better sense to take the injunction in Matthew to mean: 'Go as you are. Do not make special *preparations* such as procuring sandals or a staff'. Consequently there is no contradiction between Matthew's prohibition of acquiring such things and Mark's permission to take only a staff (ῥάβδον μόνον) and wear sandals which were presumably already possessed. Gundry's objection, 'why should Jesus let those who already had a staff and sandals use them, but prohibit those who did not from getting such necessities?' (187) is based on the unlikely assumption that some of the twelve did not already have sandals or a staff. The improbability of this assumption is heightened in light of the extensive references in Matthew to Jesus travelling with his disciples prior to Matthew 10./13/

There is, it is true, a direct verbal disagreement between Mark 6:8, 'take . . . only a staff' and Luke 9:3, 'Take . . . no staff', even though it does not affect the overall thrust of either passage. Various explanations of this have been proposed. Grant Osborne, for example, suggests not implausibly that Luke was working with 'two traditions, one with respect to the sending of the twelve (take only sandals, so Mark 6:8) and one with respect to the sending of the seventy (take no sandals, so Luke 10:4)... Luke may have assimilated the two to avoid a seeming contradiction.'/14/ But, whatever the explanation, Luke's divergence from Mark is no basis for judging Matthew's treatment of his sources to be unhistorical midrashic embellishment. Gundry's own view is that Luke's version is post-Matthean, reflecting influence from Matthew (187).

Not only is Matthew's discrepancy with his sources open to serious question, so also is Gundry's assertion that Matthew has increased and intensified the rigorism of his sources (187, 625). If that were really *Matthew's* intention it seems odd that he deleted two of the most rigorous statements from Mark 6:8 (both are also in Luke 9:3): 'he instructed them that they should take nothing for their journey' and 'no bread'. Gundry also speaks of 'Matthew's dropping the prohibition of greetings along the road (Luke 10:4)'. (187) His explanation of this last omission, 'lest that seem to contradict the command to give greetings on entering a house (10:12)' (99), is weak, for Luke 10:4-5 puts the prohibition and command back to back without seeming to contradict himself: 'Do not greet anyone on the road. When you enter a house, first say, "Peace to this house".' Since Matthew, like Luke, specifies that a greeting is to be given 'as you enter the home' (Matt 10:12), there would be no contradiction for him as well to prohibit greeting people *on the road*. The fact that Matthew does not include these prohibitions makes it doubtful that he intended to make the tradition more rigorous. Furthermore, the shift from 'do not take' to 'do not acquire' is, if anything, a softening of rigorism. Matthew's remaining addition to this list, 'no gold, nor silver', hardly amounts to increasing rigorism since the real rigour lies in prohibiting even 'small change' (BAG 883), which is already specifically mentioned in Mark 6:8.

There are some differences between the gospels that are knotty problems, and some attempted harmonizations are insensitive to the nature of the texts, but most of the discrepancies Gundry alleges are only plausibly so designated by interpreting the passages in question as though the evangelists consistently and unambiguously expressed themselves with precision, a view inappropriate to the kind of loose informal language usage typical in the gospels. Similarly, unless it be thought that Matthew's readers made the kind of careful comparison Gundry has done (as Gundry on p. 635 suggests they may well have done) and also that they assumed strict chronology in Matthew, Mark, and Q, it is doubtful that they would have drawn the conclusions about Matthew's substantial nonhistorical intent and midrash genre that Gundry supposes.

1.4. *Tendentious changes*
The crucial issue in Gundry's assessment that Matthew is a midrashic work concerns what he calls 'the tendentious patterns of diction, style, and theology in the Gospel of Matthew' (624). He is convinced that these amount to 'a vast network of tendentious changes . . . drastic changes' (625). Gundry includes in these tendentious changes three categories of material: diction, Matthew's favourite vocabulary as shown by comparative word statistics; style, such as tight parallelism and conforming traditional phraseology to the OT; and theological emphases. Together these categories do cover a

great deal of the material of Matthew, but the vast majority of
these data fits into the first two categories, and any author
(historians included) has his own distinctive diction and
style. Such tendencies need have no bearing on the question of
historical versus unhistorical or midrashic intent unless their
application demonstrably distorts history. The comparatively
few points where Gundry alleges such distortion are rather
unconvincing (see discussion below).

Similarly, it is to be expected that each evangelist will
have his own particular theological concerns and emphases.
This in itself need have no bearing on the question of
historical intent. Only if Gundry could demonstrate that
Matthew's theological emphases so controlled his writing that
they eclipsed regard for what actually happened would he have
good evidence of unhistorical intent. It is only by using the
expression 'tendentious patterns' to include all of Matthew's
distinctive diction, style, and theological emphases, and then
by treating nearly all 'tendentious changes' from Mark and
Gundry's conjecturally inflated Q as unhistorical, that he is
able to give the impression of such a broad textual basis for
his thesis of unhistorical midrashic intent.

Gundry's depiction of Matthew's theology seems overly
pressed at many points. Frequently he alleges Matthew's
distortion by assuming that 'the Jewish crowds symbolize the
international church . . . disciples' (8). If, however,
Matthew had such a symbolic intention why does he contrast the
crowd with the disciples (13:36; cf. 23:1), sharply criticise
them (9:23-25; 20-31), say that Jesus sends the crowds away
(8:18; 13:36; 14:23; 15:39), and even have a large crowd
capture Jesus and cry, 'Crucify him!' (26:47,55; 27:20-24)? Or
to take another issue, Gundry finds implications of Jesus'
deity throughout Matthew, as the references to the 'Deity of
Jesus' in his topical index (649) show. Even in a statement
like Matt 4:24, 'people brought to him all who were ill', he
notes that the verb 'brought' 'may carry connotations of an
offering to God and thus of Jesus' deity' (64). Similarly
Gundry writes of Matt 2:11-12, 'Joseph has dropped out, the
child has come forward in order of mention, and Mary has gained
the designation "his mother" as in 1:18 - all to emphasize
Jesus' virgin birth and deity' (31). Even more extensive are
implications of Christology which Gundry detects, such as, 'For
a third time in the story Matthew inserts "behold" (34,9).
Each insertion plays a Christological role' (161) and 'To

increase the Christological emphasis Matthew adds Jesus' name again' (559).

The reading into the text of Matthew's church situation, too, seems overpressed. For example, if 'brother' in Matt 5: 21-26 (of which Gundry writes on p. 85, 'Matthew composed this antithesis') refers to a fellow disciple in a church court (84-87), why the mention of the Sanhedrin (5:22), the altar (5:22-24), and the prison (5:25)?

The weakness of Gundry's argument from 'tendentious changes' is most clearly seen when Matthew deliberately deleted from his sources the very tendencies which Gundry supposes were guiding his composition. If Matthew was so concerned to insert Christology that he would create new sayings, why did he delete Mark 3:11's 'You are the Son of God' (228) and, assuming its textual authenticity, the expression 'Son of God' in Mark 1:1 (13)? Similarly, if Matthew's creativity developed the gentile evangelism theme, why the deletion of Luke 2:30-32? Or why should Matt 8:34 omit a key reference to the church's mission to the gentiles found in both Mark 5:5 and Luke 8:27? It is doubtful that Matthew believed rebuff (Gundry's explanation of the omission, p. 157) was an adequate reason not to evangelize. Or if Matthew's creativity is the origin of his fulfilment of the Law theme, why delete all three references to fulfilling the Law in Luke 2:22-24?

One would think given the creative freedom Gundry posits for Matthew that he could have integrated such ideally suited sayings into his gospel. It is of course possible that Matthew did not adhere consistently to his tendencies, but to the degree that this is so the case that these tendencies led Matthew to create events and sayings not in his tradition is weakened.

Similarly as regards verbal tendencies, why would Matthew delete from Mark (e.g. 47, 63, 65, 139, 167, 237, 252, 266, 283, 317-18, 407, 531, 551-52, 574) and Luke (e.g. 95-96, 121, 167, 214, 407) his favourite terminology? The abundance of such examples shows that Gundry's verbal statistics unrealistically inflate his category of Mattheanisms.

A further problem with Gundry's analysis of Matthew's tendentious changes is that it does not depict Matthew's procedure as consistent: 'editorial fatigue set in . . . in the latter half of his gospel' (10)./15/

At the heart of Gundry's analysis of tendentious changes are his source assumptions, for without knowing what the author of Matthew changed it would be impossible to analyze his tendentious changes. Gundry defends his analysis of these tendentious changes from beginning to end with verbal statistics about Matthew's favourite vocabulary ('Mattheanisms') which he believes demonstrate that the tendentious changes throughout Matthew came from the imagination of its author. Gundry's analysis of tendentious changes, verbal statistics, and his entire detailed redaction critical analysis of Matthew as midrashic depend on two crucial source assumptions:

1.4.1. Source Assumption 1: An 'originally spare tradition' (627)

Apart from the assumption that only a scant amount of tradition was available to the writer of Matthew each of Gundry's midrashic interpretations could plausibly be attributed to other historical traditions or reminiscences. This assumption that Matthew was restricted to an 'originally spare tradition' contradicts Gundry's carefully reasoned defence of apostolic authorship and the years of personal experience with Jesus it implies. The probability of other traditions being available to Matthew than Mark and Q is evidenced by the use in Matt 5:37 of the tradition reflected in Jas 5:12 (which Gundry acknowledges, 91-93) and by Luke 1: 1-2's reference to the existence of many written accounts about Jesus' life. Gundry's The Use of the OT in St. Matthew's Gospel pictured the apostle Matthew as a careful note taker.

1.4.2. Source Assumption 2: 'The peculiarities of Matthew derive almost wholly from his own revisions of and additions to Mark and . . . Q' (2, e.g. 66, 127)

These two assumptions led Gundry successively to posit an inflated Q, then an inflated 'insertion' category, which led to an inflated 'Mattheanism' category and finally to the thesis that Luke used Matthew as an overlay.

1.4.2.1. An inflated Q

The only way Gundry can explain the whole of Matthew as a midrashic expansion of Mark and Q is to posit an inflated Q 'considerably beyond the limits usually imposed on Q' (xi). In order to explain Matthew's infancy narrative Gundry had to include Luke's infancy narrative in Q. He indicates Matthew's

ole dependence on the Lukan tradition in 340½ verses and often
sserts Matthew's use of the tradition behind Luke even where
ark covers the same event or saying (e.g. 58-59, 75). Gundry
requently writes things like, 'In this passage Matthew brings
ogether various materials scattered in Mark and Luke' (190,
37), including in his big Q source material which has very
ittle similarity with the Matthean passage which it supposedly
nspired. Although he nowhere states exactly how much of Luke's
ontent he thinks was available to Matthew, an examination of
he commentary proper indicates a corpus two to three times as
arge as scholarly consensus usually ascribes to Q. Contrast
. Kümmel's assessment: 'The special material of Matthew and
uke is much too dissimilar for the use of one or more written
ources to be proved as probable.'/16/

Furthermore, throughout his commentary Gundry treats
atthew's Q source as though its Greek wording corresponded
xactly to the wording found in Luke 'as usually seems to be so'
108, cf. 432). As regards the order of materials in Q Gundry
cites things such as, 'As can be seen from a listing of Luke's
arallels, Matthew rearranges his materials' (241). He even
ssumes that fairly large blocks of material from Q are
eproduced in Luke: 'Matthew desires fidelity to the eightfold
cheme still apparent in Luke . . .' (69).

Often Gundry's redaction critical analysis depends on Q's
aving precisely the form of words that occurs in Luke,
ncluding tense (e.g. 56, 197, 206, 212, 460), voice (e.g. 175),
nd number (e.g. 112), and even refinements like, 'Instead of
uke's first aorist ἐγενήθησαν we read the second aorist
γένοντο' (214). Although he frequently speaks of the
raditions behind Luke, Gundry's actual analysis is based
hroughout on the text of Luke. He gives the distinct
mpression of having searched Luke with a fine-toothed comb for
assages which might have given rise to the unexplained
ortions of Matthew and without any other evidence included
hem in his big Q.

Gundry's unproved assumption of extensive correspondence
etween Q and the text of Luke is an essential prerequisite of
is rigorously detailed redaction critical analysis of Matthew,
ithout such an assumption it would have been impossible to
roduce such a precise word-by-word analysis of how the entire
ext of Matthew was produced from its sources.

1.4.2.2. An inflated 'insertion' category

As a result of Gundry's inflated Q and 'by choosing to make whole passages rather than individual sentences our standard of judgment' (4) he derives an inflated category of words which Matthew 'inserted' into his sources. For instance, Gundry thinks Matt 1:2-17 to be based on the tradition recorded in Luke 3:23-38, yet according to his own criteria (3-4) Matt 1:2-17 has only 18 words paralleled in Luke 3:23-38, but 251 words are 'insertions'. Similarly, Matt 1:18-25 has only 6 words paralleled in Luke 2:1-7, but 155 words are 'insertions'; and Matt 2:1-12 has only 8 words paralleled in Luke 2:8-20, but 214 words are 'insertions'. The percentage of verbal parallel is so small in these 'parallels' that practically any two birth stories of a given person would have comparable shared terminology. Adding up all the figures listed in Gundry's Greek Index as 'insertions' and comparing the 'totals' for Matthew reveals that he designates *almost half*/17/ of the total occurrences of words in Matthew as 'insertions' which he says show 'with utmost clarity Matthew's fondness for the words inserted' (3)!

The very use of 'insertion statistics' entails substantial assumptions about our knowledge of Matthew's sources which must be examined. Reliable insertion statistics could not be given without detailed knowledge of what Matthew's sources were, so detailed that it is possible word by word to distinguish between what words are insertions and what words were in his sources. Gundry's statistics are based on a direct comparison of Matthew with Mark and Luke (641). It is conjecture, however, that the form of Q available to Matthew corresponded closely to the Greek wording of Luke's parallel passages. Kümmel insisted that 'nothing generally valid can be said about the wording' of Q. /18/ Also conjectural is the assumption that practically no other sources of the life of Jesus were used by Matthew other than Mark and Q. It is not even certain that the form of Mark which we have today was used by Matthew. These issues affect not simply the precision of 'insertion' statistics, a problem compounded by Gundry's inflated Q. They question the very validity of treating synoptic comparative word statistics as reliable guides to what Matthew inserted into his sources.

1.4.2.3. An inflated 'Mattheanism' category

Because to Gundry insertions reveal Mattheanisms 'with utmost clarity', his inflated insertion category produces an extremely broad definition of Mattheanisms. This category is s

broad that in passage after passage Gundry is able to include
practically every word as within Matthew's favourite diction.
These statistics do not prove Matthean creativity, let alone
fiction, for many passages from literature outside of Matthew
could be proved Matthean with them. For example, every
significant word in Eph 5:32 is 'typically Matthean' except
μυστήριον. Even where the vocabulary is distinctively Matthean,
are we to assume that Matthew was incapable of writing history
when using his favourite vocabulary?

   The fact that after citing 38 Mattheanisms in Matt 27:62-66
and 37 Mattheanisms in Matt 28:11-15 Gundry defends the
historical authenticity of Matthew's insertion about the bribing
of the guards at Jesus' tomb (584-85) shows the arbitrariness of
his use of statistics as a gauge of history and of his usual
assumption that insertions are unhistorical (635). Whether or
not Gundry's defence of the authenticity of this passage is
correct, this passage explicitly repudiates unhistorical
fabrication. This implies that unhistorical fabrication was
repugnant to the author of Matthew and at least brings into
question whether the writing of fiction in the form of
historical narrative à la midrash would be favoured by him. If
Matthew's original readers had perceived the gospel to contain
unhistorical creations throughout, this sharp criticism of the
Jewish leaders would (at the least) lose its punch.

   1.4.2.4. The thesis that Luke used Matthew as an overlay
   The conviction that occurrences of Mattheanisms can prove
Matthean creativity has led Gundry to think that 'we . . . have
to think of Luke's using Matthew as an overlay' (5) in order to
explain all the Mattheanisms in Luke. He affirms this even
though it contradicts some of his own statements such as, 'Had
"it is written" [Matt 4:7] formed part of the tradition here,
Luke [4:12] would certainly have kept it as he usually does'
(57, cf. 80). Since the extent of the overlay Gundry proposes
(e.g. 5, 41, 183, 187, 222, 227, 231, 233, 249, 253-59, 266-67,
291, 293, 295, 328, 337-38, 341, 346, 353, 354, 359-60, 371,
387-88, 420, 427-28, 429, 431, 443, 448, 449, 453, 531, 532,
544, 550-51, 559, 570, 578, 579, 581, 590, 595) would have
required a rewriting of Luke, in effect Gundry's overlay view
entails all the problems of the view that Luke used Matthew as
a source, including changes in order of material and the
difficulty of explaining the omission of much material which
seems ideally suited to Luke's themes. Furthermore, it
undermines Gundry's confidence both that Q is usually

reproduced in Luke and that Matthew consistently borrowed from
the traditions found in Luke rather than vice-versa. It even
tends to undermine the heart of Gundry's midrash theory, for if
Luke (whose historical intent Gundry affirms) so extensively
used Matthew, it indicates that Luke regarded Matthew as
historical narrative, not midrashic embellishment. All of these
problems result from Gundry's fixation on his inflated
'insertion' statistics which resulted from his inflated Q and
ultimately from his unrealistic source assumptions.

The only clues that Gundry suggests might have indicated
unhistorical midrashic intent to Matthew's early readers are
these four: the fulfilment quotations, the genealogy,
discrepancies with Mark and Luke, and tendentious changes. Yet
none of them either individually or together seems likely to
have given such an impression.

2.   Literary Problems with the Thesis that
Matthew is Midrashic

Gundry confidently asserts that midrash was familiar and
recognizable in Matthew's day. He refers not only to specific
elements of Matthew as 'midrashic' but also seems to indicate
that Matthew as an entire composition may be regarded as
belonging to the literary genre midrash (626, 638-39). In this
context (638) he refers to his earlier study, 'Recent
Investigations into the Literary Genre "Gospel"', where he
defines 'genre' according to standard usage: 'Genre has to do
with different strains of literary tradition in which
compositions as wholes share distinctive sets of traits, both
obvious and subtle, and consequently mediate certain holistic
meanings.'/19/ Gundry's commentary on Matthew also specifies
his concern with the literary genre of Matthew: 'Our
identification of the kind of literature an author intended
governs the criteria by which we judge the truthfulness as well
as the meaning of his work.' (638) His commentary throughout
seems to be based on the hypothesis that Matthew as a whole is
midrashic.

To establish the thesis that Matthew is a midrash genre
work one would have to 1) define the distinctive structure,
style, and content of the literary genre midrash; 2) establish
the existence before the time of Matthew of enough literature
with the distinctive structure, style, and content of midrash
to call it a familiar literary genre in that day; and

) demonstrate that Matthew is comparable, fitting the
istinctive structure, style, content and other characteristics
f midrash.

   2.1. The problem of the definition of midrash
   Gundry insists that 'the question whether midrash and
aggadah are to be found in Matthew is a question of
ermeneutics' (637). He specifies that we 'recognize genre from
he style and contents' (632), 'the shared structure', and
conformity to established conventions of writing' ('Recent
nvestigations', 113; cf. *Matthew*, 630) 'supported by adequate
xegetical and comparative data' (629). His previous studies
lso insisted on the importance of having a clear definition of
enre for it to be useful: 'The less specific the meaning of
genre," the easier a placement of the gospels in a prior
iterary tradition. But then the concept of genre regressively
oses its usefulness in our attempt to discover authorial
ntention.' ('Recent Investigations', 113)

   In spite of highlighting the importance of a careful
efinition of midrash and of specifying criteria which could
istinguish it from other genres, Gundry offers no careful
efinition of midrash as a literary genre. In fact the only
escription he attempts of midrash is that it is 'a mixture of
istory and nonhistory' (630, 637) with 'a high degree of
ditorial liberty . . . embroidering the OT' (628). He does
ot list any other criteria which might be used to distinguish
idrash from other genres.

   It must be granted that the definition of midrash is
omplicated by the variety of ways in which the word is used.
ouglas J. Moo has differentiated several categories of common
sage of the term 'midrash' in this volume, including its use to
efer to a literary genre, exegetical method, and hermeneutical
xioms. For Gundry to argue simply that Matthew used some
xegetical methods or hermeneutical axioms similar to what is
ound in midrashic literature would not seem to be an adequate
efence of his radical reinterpretation of Matthew. If he does
ot mean that Matthew is midrash in genre but simply that it
mbellishes history midrashically, he would need to define
unhistorical midrashic embellishment', its identifying
haracteristics, and the characteristics of the sorts of works
n which it occurs. Then he would need to argue that Matthew
as these characteristics.

2.2. Was midrash a familiar literary genre in Matthew's day?

A key to the plausibility of Gundry's thesis is that midrash involving a mixture of history and nonhistory was a recognizable literary genre in Matthew's day. Gundry himself has argued that the influence of a genre depends on its pervasiveness ('Recent Investigations', 113).

H. L. Strack, however, in delineating the history of midrash, states, 'The writing down of the Midrash, i.e. of Halachoth and Hagadoth, commenced with the second century of our era, and ended in the eleventh century. Of a more exegetical character are the oldest Midrashim: such as *Genesis Rabba, Mechiltha, Sifre, Sifra*.'/20/ Gundry, too, acknowledges 'the paucity of rabbinic materials . . . before A.D. 70' (601). Thus, use of the term *midrash* as a literary genre in Matthew's day would appear to be anachronistic. It may not be Gundry's intention to indicate that midrash *as a literary genre* was pre-Matthean, but his repeated references to midrash as 'a literary genre that we think strangely ancient' (626), 'ancient Jewish midrash' (625, 628, cf. 630, 632, 636), and 'ancient literary genres' (627) conceal the lateness of midrash as a literary genre. So also do his statements like 'his [Matthew's] readers were first-century Jews who were used to midrash and haggadah' (635) and references to 'midrashic and haggadic literature of his [Matthew's] era' (629, cf. 630, 639).

Gundry seems to be aware of this problem since his only list of examples from Jewish literature is qualified as follows

Of course, experts on such Jewish literature debate the exact definitions of "midrash" and "haggadah" and the applicability of these terms to particular pieces of literature. Semantics aside, it is enough to note that the liberty Matthew takes with his sources is often comparable with the liberty taken with the OT in Jubilees, the Genesis Apocryphon, the Testaments of the Twelve Patriarchs, 1 Enoch, the Targums, and the Midrashim and Haggadoth in rabbinic literature. In his *Antiquities* Josephus takes similar liberties, or includes materials in which they have been taken. (628)

When the terms 'midrash' and 'haggadah' are applied to 'particular pieces of literature' (i.e. their literary genre as

a whole) the only members of this disparate list that are
generally referred to as midrash in genre are the Midrashim and
of course the Haggadoth, insofar as they are one type of Midrash./21/
Thus, Gundry uses the term 'midrash' in an extremely broad way
to cover significantly more than has become generally accepted
by experts. He does the same thing with the term 'targum'.
Although 'targum' refers to the Aramaic paraphrases of the OT
which were used in synagogue worship, Gundry refers to
'Matthew's targum of Isa 58:7' (513).

Gundry's earlier work sharply criticized the kind of
approach which he has now adopted:

> The less authenticity we see in the canonical gospels, the
> more "pull" we require on the part of the literary genres
> . . . in order to account for the inauthentic material.
> The hugeness of the amounts of material attributed by
> trajectory critics to the "pull" of the genres almost
> necessitates reification of the genres. But close
> inspection fails to disclose the required strength of
> momentum for those genres during the period of the NT.
> ('Recent Investigations', 108, cf. 105, 109)

Gundry's commentary has failed to demonstrate that midrash was
a familiar literary genre in Matthew's day. In this volume
both R. T. France and Bruce Chilton argue that midrash was not a
literary genre familiar to first-century Jews.

2.3. *The alleged parallels are not really parallel to Matthew*

Gundry's alleged Jewish parallels to Matthew simply are not
parallel to Matthew in structure, style, and content. They
cannot reasonably be categorized with Matthew in literary genre.

Jubilees does embellish history, but unlike Matthew, it
has as its central focus the OT and corresponds closely to the
order of the narrative of Genesis and Exodus. In general its
embellishments are incorporated to conform those narratives to
the priestly code and Jewish legalism (cf. R. T. France's
essay in this volume).

F. F. Bruce concludes his contribution to this volume,
'there is nothing in its (1QGen Apoc) embellishment of the
patriarchal narratives . . . to which the NT offers an
analogy. Even Gundry has to admit that next to it Matthew's
procedure 'looks positively restrained' (632).

The Testaments of the Twelve Patriarchs according to Gundry's own reckoning were 'probably influenced by the NT' (513, cf. 387, 449). In any event they, like Jubilees, 1QGen Apoc, and the targums, narrate stories from antiquity, unlike Matthew's focus on the comparatively recent events of Jesus' life.

The targums are simply loose Aramaic paraphrases of the canonical Hebrew OT and provide no reasonable parallel to Matthew in genre.

Josephus surely did not intend his *Antiquities* to be understood as nonhistorical or a mixture of history and imaginative creation. While Josephus exercised some freedom in the writing of speeches, he stated his ideal in dealing with events of history 'neither to add nor omit anything' (*Ant.* 1.17; cf. *B.J.* 1.1-30). F. G. Downing's recent research concluded that Josephus did 'not create events or incidents, either out of his head or by midrashic exposition'./22/

The only undisputed examples of midrash as a literary genre are from the rabbinic period well after the time of the writing of Matthew. Haggadoth in particular are a late form of midrash./23/ These midrash genre works all have substantial differences in form, content, and hermeneutical axioms from Matthew.

Furthermore, Gundry has not given any evidence, let alone demonstrated, that the authors of any of the works he does list intended their readers to recognize that the events they narrate are fictitious and do not reflect historical actuality.

Since it would seem to be foundational to his thesis to establish that Matthew follows a familiar literary genre, it is unfortunate that Gundry gives practically no comparative supporting data. Compare his admission of this need on p. 629. But what besides the gospels is comparable to Matthew in form and content?/24/

2.4. *Differences in literary form between Matthew and Midrash*

Works of the literary genre midrash are quite unlike the literary form of the gospels. Gundry himself acknowledges, 'Matthew remains a literary anomaly' (599). He still has left unanswered the crucial question of his earlier article:

Where are the parallels to the shared structure and
information apparent in all four gospels - account of
introduction into public activity, record of authoritative
teaching and miraculous deeds, report of trial and death,
and indications of resurrection - all with the purpose of
edifying and/or converting readers religiously? ('Recent
Investigations', 113-14)

The critical consensus is that the four canonical gospels share
the same literary genre./25/ Gundry in his previous work drew
the following conclusion from this:

the gospels resist categorization in terms of prior and
contemporary genres of literature. But why? The more we
deny or doubt the historicity of the materials (including
the miracles) in the gospels, the more that question
becomes difficult to answer. We leave the gospels'
literary uniqueness without an adequate historical cause.

   On the other hand, high estimation of historicity
would supply the missing cause . . . the less conformity to
established conventions of writing, the greater the
likelihood of agreement between literary contents and
historical actualities. ('Recent Investigations', 112-23)

Now, however, that Gundry thinks that many of the events
described in Matthew never actually happened, he feels
compelled to explain this through established conventions of
writing, in particular, the literary genre midrash, or at least
the 'mode of communication [of] ancient midrash and haggadah'
(630).

   Gundry recognizes that 'There are differences between the
Gospel of Matthew and midrash and haggadah in ancient Jewish
literature. For one, those who produced midrash and haggadah
were embroidering the OT. Matthew was not' (628, cf. 41). The
centrality of the OT in midrash is a truism./26/ Gundry,
having cited what is probably the central characteristic of
midrash and admitted that Matthew at this crucial point is
strikingly unlike midrash - which virtually demolishes the
thesis that Matthew is a midrash genre work - immediately adds:

Or was he? In a way, we may regard his gospel as a
wholesale embroidering of the OT with the story of Jesus.
Nevertheless, Mark and the further tradition shared with
Luke remain Matthew's primary sources. But he treated

these sources, which, like the OT, were written and
venerated, in much the same way the OT was treated by
those who produced midrash and haggadah. (628)

Gundry's first statement in this quotation affirms that
Matthew is 'a wholesale embroidering of the OT with the story
of Jesus'. Any sense in which this is true, however, is far
removed from the embroidering of the OT found in the Midrashim.
In form rabbinic Midrashim typically 'work through consecutive
passages of Scripture, making comments and telling illustrative
stories which may have no historical referent. But the line of
continuity is the OT text, to which are appended the comments
and stories'./27/ This is also true of the Jewish works Gundry
mentions which preceded Matthew, such as Jubilees and the
Genesis Apocryphon. The line of continuity in Matthew, however
is not the OT but the life of Jesus. The OT is referred to as
it highlights the significance of Jesus Christ, but it is he,
not the OT, which is central. Delete the OT passages and the
structure and narrative continuity of Matthew is not altered.
/28/

Gundry's second statement in the above quotation seems to
be presenting a distinctly different thesis, namely that Matthe
embroidered Mark and Q, not the OT. This shift is defended by
the assertion that Mark and Q were venerated like the OT. This
position seems more plausible than the first since the basic
story line of Matthew parallels Mark, not the OT. Three
formidable problems, however, confront this thesis:
1) Matthew does not share the central characteristic of
midrash genre works, namely their character as commentary on th
OT. Many works of antiquity commented on revered books or work
regarded as sacred, but that did not constitute them as midrash
To call Matthew a midrash genre work because it comments on
Mark and Q, even if when Matthew was written they were venerated
as Scripture by a small minority of Jews, would not be in
accord with standard use of the term 'midrash'. This
characteristic of the centrality of the OT text applies not
simply to midrash as a rabbinic genre but also to the other
works Gundry cites which have been called 'midrashic'.
2) The point of authority for midrash works is the OT text;
the role of the midrash is secondary and subservient to the OT.
It is doubtful that Matthew was written to be secondary or
subservient to Mark and Q or even as primarily a commentary on
them. Gundry's own commentary proceeds with the understanding
that Matthew is a work of originality with its own distinct
theological authority, an authority he explicitly ranks higher

than Q (627).
3) Although Mark later was recognized as inspired and
canonical and may have been so recognized when Matthew was
written, there is no solid evidence that Q was ever so
recognized. If Q was so venerated why was it not preserved in
the early church? It is not particularly surprising that Q
and possibly other early written collections of traditions
about Jesus were lost, but if Q were venerated as Scripture its
disappearance becomes a major problem. M. D. Goulder avoids
this problem by treating Matthew as a midrash on a single
source, Mark.

2.5. Differences in content between Matthew and Midrash
In content, too, the midrash genre literature is
strikingly different from Matthew. Midrash clearly indicates
the OT *text which is being interpreted*. The purpose of the
midrash is to comment on, embellish, and apply the OT text.
/29/ In contrast, Matthew and the other evangelists were
'concerned not with interpreting the OT, but with interpreting
an *event* in terms of the OT'./30/ The Jewish works such as
Jubilees and the Genesis Apocryphon also differ from Matthew in
their primary focus on the OT text rather than an event.
Gundry's second suggestion that Matthew is a midrash on Mark
and Q also fails at this point since Matthew is not primarily a
commentary on Mark and Q, but rather on the Jesus event.

2.6. Differences in hermeneutical axioms between Matthew
and Midrash
In the midrash genre of rabbinic Judaism, 'the operative
hermeneutical axioms include a non-eschatological perception of
itself and a deep preoccupation with enunciating its identity
and directing its conduct, corresponding roughly to the two
forms haggadic midrash and halakic midrash'./31/ While less
preoccupied with enunciating Jewish identity than the rabbinic
Midrashim, the earlier works such as Jubilees and the Genesis
Apocryphon are similar to them in not exhibiting the
eschatological tenor of the gospels. Matthew, on the other
hand, is deeply eschatological. His theme, 'the messianic
kingdom has dawned', pervades everything, including the OT
fulfilments.

2.7. Differences in temporal standpoint between Matthew
and Midrash
Temporally the writers of midrash and works such as
Jubilees, the Genesis Apocryphon, and Pseudo-Philo's *Liber
antiquitatum Biblicarum* were far removed from the OT events they

embellished. Therefore it can be reasonably assumed that their
embellishments were not historical. Matthew, however, is
concerned with events in the recent past. Therefore it is not
proper simply to assume as Gundry so often does that Matthew's
alterations and additions to Mark and Q are unhistorical. Was
the author of Matthew capable of narrating events that actually
happened only when slavishly following Mark and Q?

Nevertheless, Gundry states that Matthew is
'indistinguishable from ancient Jewish midrash and haggadah in
distance from historical actualities, in liberties taken with
historical data'. (625) Yet even in the material which Gundry
reckons to be the most radically transformed, the birth and
infancy narratives, he has to qualify his midrash judgment:
'The recency of Jesus' lifetime may account for a certain
reserve in Matthew's version of the nativity, for we should
have expected a description of the star as bright, of the baby's
face as shining, etc., as in comparable Jewish literature.' (41)
At times Gundry even ascribes to Matthew a concern for minute
historical details: 'Matthew changes "they put him" to "he was
lying" because, strictly speaking "they" did not put Jesus
there - only Joseph did' (589); 'the substitution of Gadara for
Gerasa (8:28; cf. Mark 5:1; Luke 8:26) may show familiarity
with the region around Galilee, since Gadara was both smaller,
less well known, and closer to the lake than Gerasa. Such
familiarity agrees with authorship by Matthew, a Galilean'
(620, qualified to avoid the implication of authentic
reminiscence on 157-58). Such instances undermine Gundry's
working hypothesis that Matthew's alterations and additions to
the tradition are unhistorical. Furthermore, they point to the
crucial difference in temporal standpoint between midrashic
additions to the OT and Matthew's additions to his sources.

2.8. *The closest parallels to Matthew do not exhibit the
traits of midrash*
Undoubtedly the closest parallels to Matthew in literary
form are Mark and Luke. They are similar in narrative form,
content, the structuring of their material, and extensive
verbal parallels.

The nature of Mark's loosely joined collection of
traditions about Jesus has convinced most scholars of his
concern to record traditions about Jesus. Few have felt that
Mark is characterized by midrashic treatment. Such would in
any event be unexpected in a work written in Greek for a
primarily non-Jewish readership. The close parallels between

Matthew and Mark and the widely held consensus that Mark was
Matthew's primary written source make it probable that Mark
provided a paradigm for Matthew's gospel. Mark's probable
historical intent favours similar intent in Matthew.

Luke in his preface (1:1-4) states that his tradition was
handed down by eyewitnesses (αὐτόπτης) of the events (1:2) and
that he had carefully (ἀκριβῶς) investigated (παρηκολουθηκότι)
everything (πᾶσιν) from the beginning or for a long time
(ἄνωθεν, 1:3)./32/ A concern for historical evidence seems to
have characterized Luke's work./33/ For instance, the settings
of the parables in Jesus' life are explicitly stated far more
frequently in Luke (22) than in Mark (2) or Matthew (8)./34/
Of the nine parables J. Jeremias cites as having original
audience-situations, eight are from Luke./35/ Since Luke was
written by a Greek-speaking gentile for a non-Jewish readership,
midrashic style would not be expected.

Gundry affirms the historical intent of both Mark and Luke
(628). Thus, he supposes that Matthew is generically different
than Mark and Luke, with which works its similarity is obvious
- but generically similar to midrash, with which (even if works
such as Jubilees are included as midrash) any similarity is
tenuous.

On the other hand, some might argue that Matthew's lack of
historicity points to Mark's and Luke's lack of historicity.
Gundry himself asserts that questions of distinguishing 'the
historical and the unhistorical [are] . . . anachronistic [to]
the minds of a first-century author and his readers' (635). If
he really believes this was true, how does he so confidently
affirm the historical worth of Mark and Luke? He has no
objective evidence that Mark and Q treated their sources in a
qualitatively different way than Matthew. Perhaps they, too,
were theologically motivated, not historically, and embroidered
their sources unhistorically. If Luke's primary sources, Mark
and Q (or their sources) were unconcerned with history, can we
trust even Luke's attempt to record reliable history about
Jesus? By Gundry's estimation Luke follows Matthew extensively
in matters of detail (cf. above, pp. 10-11). Thus, on Gundry's
'midrashic Matthew' thesis Luke must not have been a very
discriminating historian either.

It is unlikely that Gundry's acceptance of such a
presumption in favour of midrash can be neatly isolated to
Matthew. It has already been applied by various scholars to

all the other gospels, and Gundry in seriously following the
implications of his approach has already explicitly rejected at
points the historical reliability of Mark (239) and questioned
the faithfulness of Luke to his traditions (87, cf. 58).   Even
in such theologically significant narratives as the
resurrection accounts he speaks of contradictions involving all
four gospels (594).

Since Mark and Luke, the closest literary parallels to
Matthew, do not exhibit the primary traits of midrash, the
position that Matthew is midrashic is lacking at precisely the
point where evidence of midrashic intent would be most
convincing.   Identification of literary genre is, after all,
most strongly influenced by the closest literary parallels.
Thus, any attempt to demonstrate similarities with midrashic
literature sufficient to indicate Matthew's unhistorical intent
will have to outweigh the 'generic pull' toward historical
intent of the closest literary parallels to Matthew.

2.9. Lack of evidence that Matthew was originally understood as midrash

Gundry, siding with many NT scholars, writes that 'earlier
generations of Christians did not have the question of
historicity on their minds' (633).   If this was true of the
early church which on Gundry's view did not recognize or
appreciate midrash and haggadah (634), one would expect that
the earliest conveyors of the Jesus tradition would have even
less interest in historicity - especially if they were 'first
century Jews who were used to midrash and haggadah' (635) and to
whom issues of 'distinguish[ing] the historical and the
unhistorical . . . were probably anachronistic' (635) as
Gundry alleges.   But in spite of such comments Gundry regards
Mark and Luke and the traditions incorporated in Matthew as
substantially historical.

Since this assumption that 'earlier generations of
Christians did not have the question of historicity on their
minds' (633) appears to lead many NT scholars (unlike Gundry)
to doubt the historicity of the gospel accounts, we will
consider some evidence for interest in the actual life of Jesus
in the earliest Christian records.   This evidence leaves many
questions unanswered about the exact nature of their perception
of history and the process by which traditions about Jesus were
preserved.   Nevertheless, the evidence is substantial that the
earliest church was interested in the life and teachings of
Jesus.

Before the writing of the gospels Paul was interested in what Jesus taught on such issues as divorce (1 Cor 7:10-11 parallels the content of Matt 5:32 and 19:3-19), remuneration for preaching (1 Cor 9:14 parallels Matt 10:10), giving to the needy (Acts 20:35), and eschatology (1 Thess 4:15-17 parallels the content of Matt 24:30-31). Gundry's statement on p. 489 that Matthew 'with a characteristic allusion to the OT, in particular Isa 27:13, . . . adds "with a great trumpet"' in Matt 24:31' seems to imply creative addition to the tradition. This is questionable since 1 Thess 4:16, written c. A.D. 50-51, already associates a trumpet blast with the parousia of Christ.

The very existence of the several gospels evidences interest in the life and teaching of Jesus. The continuation of this interest is evidenced throughout the earliest records of the apostolic fathers./36/ Not only did the apostolic fathers have a keen interest in the actual life of Jesus, their writings are replete with quotations from Matthew introduced as words or events of the life of Jesus./37/ If it were to be argued that these quotations came not from Matthew but from another source, they would still show that Matthew's contents were understood in the earliest records as sayings and events in the life of Jesus. In fact, if some of them did come from independent sources, this would further corroborate their historical reliability.

The consistent affirmation from the earliest of Paul's letters through all the apostolic fathers of the historical nature of material recorded in Matthew should not be dismissed simply by thinking that they were gullible or naïve (cf. 633, 'unthinking presumptions') in accepting any accounts of the life of Jesus Their rejection of the apocryphal gospels tells against this. In contrast to this consistent historical interpretation of Matthew is the total absence of interpretation of Matthew as midrash in the apostolic fathers. Such data led Gundry to acknowledge that Matthew's midrashic intent was 'lost sight of early' (634).

Gundry conjectures that the reference by Papias' elder that Matthew as written in a Hebrew διάλεκτος (Eusebius, *h.e.* 3.39.16) indicates 'style' and 'may show an early awareness of midrashic and haggadic characteristics' (634). While it is theoretically possible for this word to indicate 'style', such an 'awareness of midrashic and haggadic characteristics' seems to be incompatible with the preceding statements of Papias cited by Eusebius:

all things which I learnt from the elders with care and
recorded with care, being well assured of their truth.
. . . I took pleasure . . . in those that teach the truth
. . . in those who relate such precepts as were given to
the Faith from the Lord and are derived from the Truth
itself. Besides, if ever any man came who had been a
follower of the elders, I would enquire about the sayings
of the elders; what Andrew said, or Peter, or Philip, or
Thomas, or James, or John, or Matthew, or any other of the
Lord's disciples (*h.e.* 3.39.3-4).

Furthermore, the standard lexica of the NT and Patristic
literature do not even list the meaning 'style' for διάλεκτος.
All six NT occurrences clearly refer to 'language', and three
read ῾Εβραΐδι διαλέκτῳ (as does Papias) meaning 'Aramaic (or
possibly Hebrew) language' (Acts 21:40; 22:2; 26:14). F. F.
Bruce after examining Gundry's argument wrote, 'I have always
believed that when Papias spoke of Matthew as compiling the
logia in "Hebrew dialect" he meant either the Hebrew or the
Aramaic language, and I have seen no reason to change my mind'.
/38/ If Papias did mean to refer to style it could be
adequately explained as a reference to the extensive use of the
OT, parallelism, Semitic idioms, and Matthew's structuring of
his materials; it would not need to imply haggadic midrash.

According to Gundry the reason why the apostolic fathers
did not recognize Matthew as midrash is that about A.D. 85 they
were 'cut loose from the synagogue, where midrash and haggadah
were at home' (634) and so simply did not recognize this
literary genre. It is only by tying the knowledge of midrash
closely to the synagogues that Gundry can give a plausible
explanation why the early church, including the continuing early
Jewish churches, so quickly forgot about the literary genre
midrash.

It is untenable, however, that the cultural shift in the
early church from Jewish to gentile was as rapid and extensive
as Gundry's thesis requires. The earliest church including the
apostles was completely Jewish. Eusebius wrote: 'I have
received documentary proof of this, that up to Hadrian's siege
of the Jews [A.D. 135] there had been a series of fifteen
bishops there [in Jerusalem]. All are said to have been Hebrews
in origin . . . [He names each], all of them of the
Circumcision.'/39/ Ignatius used the OT extensively and was
concerned with the issue of Judaizers. Justin Martyr was born
in Flavius Neapolis (Shechem) in Samaria of Palestine and was

familiar with Judaism as is evident in his *Dialogue with Trypho*, which narrates Justin's dialogues with this leading Jewish scholar and some of his friends. It is devoted to persuading Jews of the truth of Christianity.

In light of such evidence it cannot correctly be said that Jewish Christianity disappeared so quickly that an element as familiar as Gundry supposes midrash to have been would be completely forgotten. The thesis that midrash was closely tied to the synagogue faces a further problem for those who, like Gundry, include as 'midrashic' some works which clearly had a setting outside of the synagogue. The Genesis Apocryphon was found at Qumran. Jubilees, the Testaments of the Twelve Patriarchs, and most of 1 Enoch are Maccabean Pseudepigraphal works. If midrash is recognized as a much wider cultural influence than something tied to the synagogue, Gundry's reason for it being forgotten in the early church loses its plausibility, and the lack of recognition of Matthew as midrashic in the earliest Christian writings remains an unexplained and serious problem for the view that Matthew is midrashic.

The supposition that the writer of Matthew was familiar with synagogue practice is undermined for those who, like Gundry (592, 620), believe that the author of Matthew was a tax collector. The available evidence has established as a scholarly consensus that tax collectors were excommunicated from the synagogues in Matthew's day for both social and religious reasons. Thus, although it is possible that synagogue methods might have been known to Matthew via Jesus and/or Jewish Christians, it must be considered improbable that Matthew the tax collector had been a regular synagogue attender or was highly influenced by midrashic literature if it was closely tied to the synagogue.

2.10. Interpretation of Matthew as Midrash has led to improbable reconstructions

The thesis that Matthew is a midrashic treatment has led Gundry to propose many improbable reconstructions such as: 'Matthew now turns the visit of the local Jewish shepherds (Luke 2:8-20) into the adoration by Gentile magi from foreign parts' (26).
'the star replaces the angel and the heavenly host in the tradition' (27).
'Matthew has transformed the praiseful return of the shepherds (Luke 2:20) into the magi's flight from persecution.' (32)

'Matthew changes the going up to Jerusalem by the Holy Family
(Luke 2:22) into a flight to Egypt.' (32)
'he changes the sacrificial slaying of "a pair of turtledoves
or two young pigeons", which took place at the presentation of
the baby Jesus in the Temple (Luke 2:24; cf. Lev 12:6-8), into
Herod's slaughtering the babies in Bethlehem' (34-35).
God sends rain on the righteous and the unrighteous (Matt 5:45)
'comes from the later saying about the raining of fire and
brimstone from heaven on Sodom (Luke 17:28-29)' (98).
Matthew adapted the parable of the wicked husbandmen to create
the parable of the labourers in the vineyard. (395)
Matthew transformed the parable of the prodigal son into the
parable of the two sons (Matt 21:28-32). (5, 365, 422)

        We will restrict comments to the last of these examples.
It is rather novel to include the parable of the prodigal son
in Q (5). If, indeed, Matthew used a tradition of this parable
it should be remembered that this parable is considered to
express the deepest human feeling of any of Jesus' parables.
It is without doubt one of the most outstanding parables ever
written. Is it likely that Matthew, whose artistry Gundry so
stresses, would transform this exquisite parable into the
comparatively unremarkable (though certainly crisp and telling)
one of Matt 21:28-30? The implausibility of such a
transformation is heightened since the parable of the prodigal
son fits well with Gundry's estimation of Matthew's
characteristic theology: the mixture of 'false' and 'true
disciples' (5), 'the condemnation of Jewish legalism' (6), 'the
necessity of confessing Jesus in public' (6), the rejection of
'any feeling of merit' (7), the special importance of 'the
commandment to love your neighbour as yourself' (7), 'the
association of Jesus with the Father' (8), and the portrayal of
'the church as a brotherhood...Its little ones [are] the poor
and persecuted outcasts . . . private judgments of
excommunication are prohibited . . . repentance by the
backslider needs to be met with forgiveness by the church that
matches divine forgiveness in heaven'. (9)

        Gundry does not state why Matthew did not use the parable
of the prodigal son in its traditional form. Presumably he
appeals to it because of his desire to explain everything in
the gospel from Matthew's creative use of Mark and Q, excluding
any historical reminiscences. Since Gundry found no more
suitable source for the parable of the two sons than the
parable of the prodigal son, he included it in his inflated Q.

The lack of felicity of this and many other applications of Gundry's thesis in specific reconstructions and the strikingly different interpretations of M. D. Goulder point to the arbitrariness of the 'midrash Matthew' thesis.

Summary and Conclusion

Gundry's commentary throughout is dependent on his view that Matthew's sources consisted almost entirely of Mark and a substantially inflated Q. Without this inflated Q and the further assumption that Q traditions appearing in Luke usually preserve the Greek wording that was available to Matthew it would have been impossible for Gundry to produce such a rigorously detailed redaction critical analysis of Matthew. The further assumption that Matthew treated his sources midrashically enables Gundry to explain Matthew's choice of practically every word in the first gospel. Whatever does not correspond to Mark or some part of Luke is regarded as Matthew's creative midrashic embellishment. The biggest gaps are filled by Matthew's artistic weaving into his material of events and themes from the OT.

Matthew's creativity is then confirmed through statistics of how often he used each word as an insertion. 'Insertions of words in paralleled materials show with utmost clarity Matthew's fondness for the words inserted.' (3) These statistics seem very convincing until examination of his Greek Index shows that he designates almost *half* of the total occurrences of words in Matthew as 'insertions'. As a result, what looks like statistical proof that a word is typically Matthean is often just an average random distribution into the 'insertion' category. Gundry's insertion statistics give the impression of massive support for his view that Matthew 'materially altered and embellished historical traditions . . . deliberately and often' (639). Note, however, that this conclusion is the inevitable result of his source assumption of an 'originally spare tradition' (627) and the corresponding assumption that Matthew's creative additions are almost always without historical grounding.

If, however, his commentary throughout had seriously considered the possibility that Matthew's additions to the tradition recorded in Mark and Luke could have come from other historical traditions or from personal reminiscences of the life of Jesus rather than Matthew's unhistorical creative embellishment, such negative conclusions about the historicity

of Matthew would not have resulted. The patterns of diction,
style, and theology Gundry notes are not in themselves
antithetical to historicity. Any writer, historians included,
has characteristic diction and style. Mark and Luke, just as
much as Matthew, have characteristic diction, style, and
theology. If we were to presume to identify the extent and
Greek form of their sources, they too would appear to have
tendentious patterns of diction, style, and theology.

Gundry struggled with the problem of integrating what he
believes to be substantial evidence for both historical and
unhistorical intent in Matthew. Supporting historical intent is
Matthew's historical narrative form, extensive and early
evidence that Matthew was originally understood as narrating
actual events and sayings from the life of Jesus, evidence for
historical intent in the comparable documents Mark and Luke,
and the apparent role of Mark as a paradigm which influenced
Matthew. Yet Gundry perceived 'a number of outright
discrepancies with the other synoptics' (624) which combined
with redaction critical conclusions about Matthew's pervasive
tendentious changes seemed to be incompatible with consistently
historical intent by Matthew.

To reconcile these data Gundry needed a literary genre
which would explain this mixture of history and nonhistory. He
recognizes that proper identification of the literary genre of
Matthew is vital since the establishment of an author's
intention is closely related to the genre of his writing. His
midrash solution has the apologetic value of defending Matthew
from the charge of making false historical claims. 'Since by
definition midrash and haggadah include unhistorical
embroidery, their message . . . could be falsified only by
means different from historical criticism.' (637)

What, however, is the evidence that Matthew in form and
content is similar to midrashic treatments of OT stories?
Gundry offers no comparative data or objective evidence of this.
Yet without evidence of such similarities it is arbitrary to
assert that Matthew intended to treat historical traditions
with the same kind of unhistorical embellishment they did.
Unless evidence can be given of close correlation between
Matthew and a genre which intended to embellish history
unhistorically the probability of any particular passage of
Matthew being so intended decreases significantly.

There is ambiguity whether Gundry means to go as far as to say that Matthew is a midrash genre work. Scholarly consensus identifies the midrash literary genre as post-Matthean. This rabbinic genre was not a familiar literary genre in Matthew's day, and so it could hardly have been his intention to write his gospel following the literary genre midrash. On the other hand studies of pre-Matthean 'midrashic' works have not yet established a consensus on how to categorize their literary genre, let alone on how to identify that genre's defining characteristics. The few comparative studies that have been done to date do not seem to indicate that Matthew fits a 'midrashic' genre.

In our opinion, then, Gundry's hope that his midrashic approach will restore historical credibility to the overall gospel tradition and save Matthew from the charge of historical error, although sincerely motivated, is unlikely to be fulfilled. To the contrary Gundry's thesis seems to undermine two key points he desires to preserve: the perspicuity and the historical reliability of the gospels. Hermeneutically, it invites confusion for the very reason that it gives no method for identifying unhistorical midrash by its formal characteristics.

Historically it treats as unreliable virtually all of the gospel tradition peculiar to Matthew. Of even more significant implication for the reliability of the entire gospel tradition is Gundry's estimate of the prevalence of midrash and of the lack of concern for historicity in the first century.

If he is correct in this, it becomes much more difficult to defend the historicity of Mark and Q (or their sources), though Gundry wishes to do so. In view of their similarity to Matthew they too could easily be regarded as midrashic in some degree, and, if they are so regarded, Luke would also be implicated. Gundry's working hypothesis is that practically every part of Matthew which is not corroborated by historical works (Mark and Luke) is unhistorical. If Mark and Luke are of the same midrashic genre, then virtually no historically acceptable record of the life and teaching of Jesus is left. Thus Gundry's midrash thesis threatens the historicity of not just parts of, but all 'that is the very center of the Christian faith, viz., the life and teaching of Jesus'. (623)

Notes

/1/ *Midrash and Lection in Matthew* (London: SPCK, 1974).
Since this work is examined in detail in this volume by Leon
Morris, it receives only passing reference in this study.
Goulder's *The Evangelist's Calendar* (London: SPCK, 1978) is
critically reviewed in this volume by Craig Blomberg.

/2/ I sent a copy of my analysis to Dr. Gundry and requested
that he correct any points of misunderstanding of his position.
He kindly responded, and the points he mentioned have been duly
revised. He did not, however, specify whether he intended to
depict Matthew as a midrash genre work or simply 'midrashic' in
some other sense.

/3/ Cf. Richard N. Longenecker, *Biblical Exegesis in the
Apostolic Period* (Grand Rapids: Eerdmans, 1975) 140-52, who
examines each of Matthew's fulfilment passages; R. Schippers,
'πληρόω' in *The New International Dictionary of New Testament
Theology* (3 vols.; ed. Colin Brown; Grand Rapids: Zondervan,
1975) 1.736-37; J. Barton Payne, *Encyclopedia of Biblical
Prophecy* (New York: Harper & Row, 1973) 135, 477.

/4/ E.g. Goulder, *Midrash and Lection in Matthew*, 128. Note
that Matt 2:5-6 reports the reply of the chief priests and
scribes without explicitly endorsing it.

/5/ Gundry pointed this out in his previous book, *The Use of
the Old Testament in St. Matthew's Gospel* (NovTSup 18; Leiden:
Brill, 1967) 91-92.

/6/ Longenecker, *Biblical Exegesis*, 32; W. Bacher, *Die
exegetische Terminologie der jüdischen Traditions-literatur*
(2 vols.; Leipzig: Mohr, 1889, 1905) 2. 112-13, proposes that
it was Abbaye b. Kahana in the fourth century who first
distinguished 'midrash' from 'peshaṭ' as stated in *b. Sanh.* 100b.

/7/ E.g. J. Gresham Machen, *The Virgin Birth of Christ* (New
York: Harper & Row, 1930) 202-9, 229-32; Norval Geldenhuys,
Commentary on the Gospel of Luke (Grand Rapids: Eerdmans, 1951)
150-55; F. F. Bruce, 'Genealogy of Jesus Christ' in *The New
Bible Dictionary* (ed. J. D. Douglas; Grand Rapids: Eerdmans,
1962) 458-59; E. Earle Ellis, *The Gospel of Luke* (London:
Nelson, 1966) 92-93; Leon Morris, *The Gospel According to St.
Luke* (Grand Rapids: Eerdmans, 1974) 100-101; Robert L. Thomas
and Stanley N. Gundry, eds., *A Harmony of the Gospels* (Chicago:
Moody, 1978) 313-19: D. A. Carson, *Matthew* in *The Expositor's
Bible Commentary* (12 vols.; ed. Frank E. Gaebelein; Grand
Rapids: Zondervan, 1981-) vol. 8 forthcoming.

/8/ Other issues Gundry raises, such as the problems relating
to the withered fig tree (Matt 21:17-22) are considered in
detail by D. A. Carson, 'Gundry on Matthew: A Critical Review'

Trinity Journal 3NS (1982) 71-91. Carson argues: 'Matthew
does no more than follow his typical pattern: he adopts a
topical grid. He gives the *impression* the discovery is the same
day, but in fact he does not actually specify: he simply says,
"When the disciples saw this . . .." . . . Matthew omits Mark's
"because it was not the season for figs" *[because]*. . .
Matthew's readers . . . would understand that if this event was
alleged to have taken place near Passover, then *of course* it
was not the season for figs. . . . Fig leaves appear about the
same time as the green fruit . . . This fig tree stood out as
one that was promising fruit; but in fact it was barren. . . .
How like Israel!', 79-80.

/9/ Cf. John W. Haley, *An Examination of the Alleged
Discrepancies of the Bible* (Grand Rapids: Baker, 1977) 413-14.
This view is supported e.g. by William F. Arndt, *The Gospel
According to Luke* (St. Louis: Corcordia, 1956) 97-98; Robert L.
Thomas and Stanley N. Gundry, *A Harmony of the Gospels with
Explanations and Essays* (Chicago: Moody, 1978) 30.

/10/ F. Godet, *A Commentary on the Gospel of St. Luke* (2 vols.;
Edinburgh: T. & T. Clark, 1881) 1.155.

/11/ Jos. *Ant.* xvii.6.4§167; xvii.8.1§191; xvii.9.3§213; *BJ*
i.33.8§665; ii.1.1§10. Cf. Harold W. Hoehner, *Chronological
Aspects of the Life of Christ* (Grand Rapids: Zondervan, 1977)
11-27.

/12/ Cf. Carson, 'Gundry on Matthew', 88, who refers to the
forthcoming dissertation of A. H. Trotter on the disciples'
understanding in Matthew.

/13/ E.g. Matt 4:18-23; 5:1; 8:21,23,25; 9:10,11,14,19,37; cf.
9.35. In 9:35 Jesus' actions, preaching the kingdom and
healing, are what he commands his disciples to model after him
in Matt 10:7-8. This implies that they were with him in his
travels, becoming familiar with the message of the kingdom and
how Jesus healed.

/14/ Osborne, 'The Evangelical and Redaction Criticism' *JETS* 22
(1979) 314. Osborne also suggests, 'Perhaps Matthew conflated
the two and stressed the negative side' (314), but as we go on
to show, it is doubtful that Matthew has in fact stressed the
negative side. For other discussions see, e.g. E. Power, 'The
Staff of the Apostles, A Problem in Gospel Harmony', *Biblica* 4
(1923) 241-66; M.-J. Lagrange, *Évangile selon Saint Marc* (9th
ed.; Paris: Gabalda, 1947) 151-53; U. Mauser, *Christ in the
Wilderness* (Naperville, Ill.: Allensons, 1963) 133-34.

/15/ This problem is encountered by J. Drury as well in his
attempt to depict Luke as midrashic, *Tradition and Design in
Luke's Gospel* (London: Darton, Longman & Todd, 1976) 96, 130,
137, 162. Drury's position is critically reviewed in this
volume by Craig Blomberg.

/16/ Werner Georg Kümmel, *Introduction to the New Testament* (London: SCM, 1966) 58.

/17/ The 'Matthean insertions in paralleled material' total is 3795 words. The 'total number of occurrences in Matthew' sum-total is 8572. Therefore over 44% of the total occurrences in Matthew of words listed in Gundry's (incomplete) index (641-49) are listed as insertions. Whenever Gundry lists two alternative figures for the same category the first one listed was used in these calculations.

/18/ Kümmel, *Introduction to the NT*, 54.

/19/ 'Recent Investigations', pp. 97-114 in *New Dimensions in New Testament Study* (ed. R. N. Longenecker and M. C. Tenney; Grand Rapids: Zondervan, 1974) 97. Here Gundry refers to genre as descriptive of 'the whole *as* a whole', p. 102, cf. 110.

/20/ 'Midrash', in *Schaff-Herzog Encyclopaedia of Religious Knowledge* (3 vols.; New York: Funk & Wagnalls, 1883) 2. 1504.

/21/ None of the others are included in H. L. Strack's list of Midrash works: 'Midrash', 1504-7.

/22/ 'Redaction Criticism: Josephus' *Antiquities* and the Synoptic Gospels', *JSNT* 8 (1980) 56; cf. R. T. France's essay in this volume.

/23/ Cf. Hermann L. Strack, *Introduction to the Talmud and Midrash* (New York: Jewish Publication Society of America, 1931) 203-4.

/24/ Ironically Gundry criticizes others for alleging parallels without adequate comparative data: 'hardly parallels' (173), 'too distant to merit discussion here' (220), 'superficial' similarities ('Recent Investigations', 99).

/25/ D. E. Aune, 'The Problem of the Genre of the Gospels: A Critique of C. H. Talbert's What is a Gospel?' pp. 9-60 in *Gospel Perspectives: Studies of History and Tradition in the Four Gospels, Volume II* (ed. R. T. France and David Wenham; Sheffield: JSOT, 1981) 44, 48.

/26/ Midrash is 'investigation and explanation of Scripture'; Strack, 'Midrash', 1504; Midrash is 'interpretation of Scripture'; Herbert Danby, *The Mishnah* (London: Oxford, 1933) 795.

/27/ Carson, 'Gundry on Matthew', 82; cf. Danby, *Mishnah*, 795 on the term midrash referring to 'systematic verse-by-verse commentary on Scripture'.

/28/ R. T. France in 'Herod and the Children of Bethlehem', *NovT* 21 (1979) 98-120, has demonstrated that the real continuity of Matthew 1-2 lies in the narrative of the birth and infancy of Jesus; OT quotations are appended.

/29/ Cf. Addison G. Wright, 'The Literary Genre Midrash', *CBQ*
28 (1966) 138.

/30/ X. Léon-Dufour, *The Gospels and the Jesus of History*
(London: Collins, 1968) 215.

/31/ Carson, 'Gundry on Matthew', 83.

/32/ For a careful examination of this passage cf. I. Howard
Marshall, *The Gospel of Luke* (Exeter: Paternoster, 1978) 39-44.

/33/ Cf. I. Howard Marshall, *Luke: Historian and Theologian*
(Exeter: Paternoster, 1970) 53-67, which includes extensive
bibliographical references.

/34/ Philip Barton Payne, 'Metaphor as a Model for
Interpretation of the Parables of Jesus, with Special Reference
to the Parable of the Sower' (unpublished Ph.D. dissertation,
Cambridge, 1975) 239-41.

/35/ Payne, 'Metaphor', 29.

/36/ Papias in Irenaeus, *haer.* 5.33.4, and in Eusebius, *h.e.*
3.39.1-4; Polycarp, *Phil.* 7.1, and in Irenaeus *ep. Flor.* ap.
Eus. *h.e.* 5.20.4; *1 Clem.* 42.1; Ignatius, *Smyrn.* 1-3 and *Trall.*
9; Apology of Aristides; Justin Martyr, *1 apol.* 42.4; 50.12;
53.3; 66.3; 67.7; *dial.* 53.1; 103.8; Tatian, *oratio ad Graecos*
and *Diatessaron*; Theophilus Antiochenus, *ad Autolycum*; Irenaeus,
haer. 1.8.1; 3.1.1; 3.5.2; 3.14.4; 4.33.8; Tertullian, *de*
praescr. 6 and 37.

/37/ Polycarp, *Phil.* 2.3 quotes the content of Matt 7:1; 6:14;
5:7; 7:2; 5:3,10 introduced with 'remembering what the Lord
taught when he said'; *Phil.* 7.2 cites the content of Matt 26:41
with 'even as the Lord says'. *1 Clem.* 13.1-2 introduces Matt
5:7; 6:14,15; 7:1,2, 'especially remembering the words of the
Lord Jesus which he spoke when he was teaching gentleness and
suffering. For he spoke thus'. *1 Clem.* 46.7-8 quotes the
content of Matt 26:24 and 18:6, . 'Remember the words of the
Lord Jesus; for he said'. Didache quotes the content of Matt
7:6, 'For concerning this did the Lord say' (9.5), and of Matt
6:9-13, 'as the Lord commanded in his gospel, pray thus' (8.2).
Ignatius testified to the actuality of the events recorded in
Matt 26:7 (*Eph.* 7.1), Matt 27:52 (*Magn.* 9.2), Matt 3:15; 1:1,23
(*Smyrn.* 1.1). *Barn.* 7.3 cites the content of Matt 27:34,48,
'when he was crucified he was given to drink vinegar and gall'.
2 Clem. quotes the content of Matt 10:32 (3.2), Matt 7:21 (4.2),
Matt 6:24 (6.1), Matt 16:26 (6.2), Matt 25:21 (8.5), and Matt
12:50 (9.11) as said by the Lord.

/38/ In a personal letter to me of April 3, 1982.

/39/ Eusebius, *The History of the Church from Christ to*
Constantine (tr. G. A. Williamson; Baltimore: Penguin, 1965)
156.

MIDRASH, CHIASMUS, AND THE OUTLINE OF LUKE'S CENTRAL SECTION

Craig L. Blomberg
Department of Religion
Palm Beach Atlantic College
1101 S. Olive Avenue
West Palm Beach, Florida 33401

No portion of the Synoptic gospels has proved as difficult to outline as Luke's central section./1/ Claims that Luke was either a reliable historian or a purposive theologian (or both!) must come to grips with this apparently 'amorphous' jumble of material./2/ J. Resseguie has recently surveyed the history of the interpretation of this section since 1856 and concludes that 'the important problem as to why Luke has gathered together this material into the central part of his gospel remains unsolved.'/3/ The most recent major commentary on Luke makes no attempt at all to outline this section, save for dividing it in thirds by the 'travel notices'./4/ The only recent monograph on Luke's central section concludes that its overarching theme is 'the confrontation between Jesus and the Jewish people as well as the concommitant [sic] conflict in which the fate of Israel as God's people is decided,' but it offers no outline of this material and relegates its parenetic sections to an unjustifiably subordinate role./5/ Within just the last few years, however, two very detailed approaches to the outline of Luke's central section have emerged which demand careful consideration. On the one hand, J. Drury and M. D. Goulder build on the previously neglected proposal of C. F. Evans/6/ to argue that Luke was constructing a midrash on the book of Deuteronomy./7/ On the other hand, C. H. Talbert and K. E. Bailey modify and expand Goulder's earlier but now apparently abandoned view that the central section forms one giant chiasmus/8/ with its climactic center in Luke 13:22-35./9/ Both approaches rely heavily on the rediscovery of methods of ancient historiography, especially within Judaism, which is currently illuminating many dark corners in New Testament studies.

Traditional Approaches

Chronological
For many years explanations of the arrangement of passages

in Luke's central section followed some chronological scheme,
taking Luke's claim in his preface to have written καθεξῆς and
interpreting it literally./10/ Yet most of the pericopes in
this section contain no geographical or chronological
information, and the little that Luke does supply scarcely
suggests that Jesus was seriously trying to travel from Galilee
to Jerusalem. Different writers tried to salvage Luke's
chronology by viewing the journey as a composite of more than
one trip to Jerusalem, sometimes trying to harmonize their
outlines with various trips of Jesus to Jerusalem in the gospel
of John. Dean Wickes viewed the central section as an
intertwining of two distinct sources of information about Jesus
traveling to Jerusalem./11/ C. J. Cadoux saw 10:25-13:9 as one
trip, 18:9-14 as the end of another, and the triumphal entry as
yet a third./12/ E. J. Cook modified Cadoux's scheme and added
a fourth journey, dividing Luke into 9:51-10:42, 11:1-13:9, and
14:25-19:28, and leaving the remaining material unassigned./13/
W. Gasse, finally, recognized the artificiality of all these
outlines but still wanted to interpret 9:51-56 as the start of
a literal journey. Gasse suggested that Jesus initially
intended to embark on a Samaritan ministry, but the reaction he
received at its outset dissuaded him from it. Gasse therefore
assigned all of 9:57-18:34 to Jesus' further ministry in
Galilee./14/

Non-Chronological

In 1938 C. C. McCown broke from these chronological
approaches and suggested that Luke was much more concerned with
logical order. Luke simply had 'a mass of other materials
which he did not wish to interpolate in the story of the
Galilean ministry, probably because much of it seemed to him to
be of a somewhat different type and to point toward the
approaching death of Jesus.'/15/ These materials showed what
following Jesus meant and also prefigured the spread of the
gospel among the Gentiles./16/ McCown's article, by turning
attention to questions of theology and literary style, began a
new trend which subsequent scholarship has almost unanimously
followed./17/ H. Conzelmann interprets the journey to
Jerusalem entirely from a theological perspective: 'Now the
destination is fixed as the place of suffering required
doctrinally....In other words, Jesus' awareness that he must
suffer is expressed in terms of the journey. To begin with he
does not travel in a different area from before, but he travels

in a different manner...'/18/   J. Schneider, E. Lohse, and B.
Reicke have all emphasized the didactic and parenetic aims
behind much of Luke's central section, with Reicke specifically
outlining the section in terms of alternating blocks of
material of either instruction for disciples or controversy
with opponents./19/ W. Grundmann builds on Conzelmann's
Christology to see not only Jesus' trip to Jerusalem but his
'wanderings' in general as suggestive of the suffering and
rejection which both Jesus and his disciples had to undergo.
Grundmann identifies three passages which especially highlight
this theme (9:51-10:32, 13:22-35, and 17:11-19) but assigns the
rest of the central section to three giant excurses, which
scarcely does justice to the importance of this material./20/
Similarly, J. H. Davies offers some keen insight into four key
passages (9:51, 13:31-35, 18:31-34, and 19:26-46), in light of
the goal of ἀνάλημψις first revealed in 9:51, but then jumps to
the conclusion that 'the journey sets the tone of the
teaching...not vice versa' (*contra* Reicke)./21/ W. C. Robinson
follows Schneider and Reicke, elaborating on the theme of
instruction for discipleship in terms of 'authenticated
witness,'/22/ while von der Osten-Sacken follows Conzelmann and
Davies, elaborating on the themes of suffering and
glorification in view of the delay of the parousia./23/
Neither, however, offers any fresh insights into the actual
structure of the central section./24/

        Many of the modern commentaries on Luke disclose this same
lacuna. Manson, Geldenhuys, Caird, Thompson, Morris, and
Schmithals all make no attempt to subdivide the central section
in any fashion save by individual pericope. Plummer, G.
Schneider, and Ernst, like Fitzmyer, simply break the material
into three periods or stages corresponding to the travel
notices in chapters 13, 17, and 19. A few nevertheless attempt
more detailed analyses. For example, E. E. Ellis divides
9:51-19:44 into six main sections, breaking at 10:42, 12:34,
13:21, 16:13, and 18:14. He entitles these sections,
respectively, 'The Meaning and Reception of the Kingdom
Message,' 'The Kingdom and the Power,' 'The Kingdom and the
Judgement,' 'Who Will Enter the Kingdom?' 'The Coming of the
Kingdom,' and 'Discipleship and the Rejected King'./25/ Each
of these sections in turn contains six subsections, a pattern
which Ellis discerns throughout Luke's gospel. Ellis admits,
though, that 'the intention of the Evangelist is less clear,'
and that his outline reflects 'some editorial shaping,'
although he stresses that 'the basic pattern is not

(consciously) the commentator's.'/26/ Yet his subheadings are
quite general and most of the gospel material could fit under
several of them./27/ Of course commentators as early as
Lagrange have grouped together pericopes in Luke's central
section in a topical way,/28/ and some of these groupings are
self-evident and have been widely noted--Luke 11:1-13 on prayer,
14:25-35 on the cost of discipleship, 15:1-32 on lost and found,
and 16:1-31 on the proper use of riches. These collections lead
one to look for similar patterns in the rest of the central
section even if they may be somewhat less obvious. Ellis,
therefore, appears to be on the right track in looking for a
topical outline, but he himself has not come up with a very
convincing one./29/ Better topical approaches will be
discussed further below./30/

At this point, however, a fundamental methodological
question arises. What textual indicators help to determine
where one section may end and a new one may begin, especially
where topical changes are not clearcut? Many introductory
hermeneutics texts list the basic indicators: changes in
audience, location, and style of writing, the use of
introductory and summary statements, the repetition of key
phrases and refrains, and other transitional words and
expressions./31/ Yet these features do not occur at all evenly
in Luke's central section, and the riddle of his outline
remains.

The Question of Method

Two recent articles attempt to break this impasse, but
come to diametrically opposite conclusions. G. Sellin divides
the text first at changes of location, second at changes of
audience, and finally at changes of form, arriving at a
detailed outline of the material with major subdivisions
beginning with 9:51, 10:38, 11:1, 11:14, 13:10, 13:22, 14:1,
14:25, 15:1, 17:11, 18:35, and 19:1, ending the central section
at 19:28./32/ This method certainly isolates some of the same
groups of passages noted above (e.g. 11:14-13:10, 15:1-17:10,
and 17:11-18:35), while at the same time setting apart two
single pericopes as entire major subsections (10:38-42 and
18:35-43). Furthermore, the two main travel notices in 13:22
and 17:11, which ought to signal the most dramatic breaks of
all, seem to come at singularly inappropriate places for a
change of theme. The healing of the lepers in 17:11-19 focuses
on the faith of the Samaritan, and faith is the explicit theme
of 17:5-6 and quite possibly the topic which unites all of
17:1-19./33/ The progression of thought in Luke 13 is less

clear, but it is striking that the parables in vv. 18-21 are
the only ones in the central section which explicitly mention
the kingdom of God, while the very next passage (vv. 22-30)
also deals specifically with the kingdom of God by discussing
who will and will not be sitting at table in it./34/ Despite
the importance of this theme throughout Jesus' ministry, its
fourfold occurrence here (vv. 18, 20, 28, and 29) stands out,
since βασιλεία τοῦ θεοῦ on Jesus' lips has not occurred since
11:20 and does not recur until 16:16.

Has Luke then simply scattered his travel notices
haphazardly about to keep the theme of Jesus' journeying before
his readers? David Gill suggests not. Gill views not only
13:22 and 17:11, but the shorter travel notices as well, as
consistently introducing passages which teach about true
discipleship and mission in a manner often contrary to
traditional Jewish expectations./35/ Gill recognizes that not
every passage on this topic has a travel notice, but he is
simply trying to establish a general pattern. While Gill seeks
to interpret the theological significance of Luke's central
section as a whole, his findings also suggest that the travel
notices do not necessarily signal a change of topic so much as
highlight passages of particular theological import for Luke.
Commentators should not feel compelled to use them as
indicators of major subdivisions within Luke's central section.
If a topical outline is to be found, then the only way left
lies in further attempts either to group passages of like theme
and build the whole from the parts or to discern some overall
pattern and deduce the parts from the whole, or to effect some
combination of the two. Both the midrashic and chiastic
approaches involve precisely such overall patterns.

A Christian Deuteronomy

C. F. Evans
In 1955 C. F. Evans argued that the sequence of passages
in Luke 9:51-18:14 closely parallels a selection of texts from
the book of Deuteronomy (Deut. 1:1-13:18, 14:28-18:22, 20:1-20,
21:15-22:4, 23:15-25:3, and 26:1-19). An adequate summary of
his synopsis of parallels would virtually require reproducing
his entire text because of the nature of his presentation, but
an idea of his method can be gained from the following
list:/36/

Luke	Deuteronomy	
10:1-3,17-20	1:1-46	sending forerunners

10:4-16	2:1-3:22	inhospitable kings and cities
10:21-24	3:23-4:40	special revelation
10:25-27	5:1-6:25	the summary of the Law
10:29-37	7:1-26	relations with foreigners
10:38-42	8:1-3	spiritual food
11:1-13	8:4-20	no privation
11:14-26	9:1-10:11	casting out wicked people and demons
11:27-36	10:12-11:32	keeping God's word, light, and frontlets
11:37-12:12	12:1-16	clean and unclean
12:13-34	12:17-32	richness toward God
12:35-53	13:1-11	reward/punishment for faithfulness/unfaithfulness
12:54-13:5	13:12-18	communal judgment and repentance
13:6-9	14:28	bearing fruit
13:10-21	15:1-18	Sabbath release from debt, slavery, disease
13:22-35	16:1-17:7	feasting in Jerusalem
14:1-14	17:8-18:22	food for Levites/banquet parables
14:15-35	20:1-20	excuses from battle and banquet
15:1-32	21:15-22:4	father and son, restoration of the lost
16:1-18	23:15-24:4	slaves, usury, and divorce
16:19-18:8	24:6-25:3	fair treatment of poor and oppressed
18:9-14	26:1-19	obeying the Law.

Luke has taken up the theme of a prophet like Moses (cf. Acts 3:22 and 7:37) and arranged large portions of his non-Marcan material to match the sequence of topics in the teaching of Jesus' forerunner. As does Deuteronomy, Luke's central section begins with some historical narrative, but continues almost exclusively with teachings. The parallels break off right where Deuteronomy's legal material ends.

Subsequent studies for the most part seemed not to know what to make of Evans' article and largely tended to ignore it. Yet even as cautious a critic as L. Morris could write that 'this is an interesting and suggestive approach and it may well give the truth of the matter...'/37/ More recently, though, Evans has won more unguarded acclaim. J. A. Sanders, one of

he pioneers in the field of comparative midrash, declares
hat Evans 'showed, beyond all doubt' the truth of his
ypothesis./38/   J. D. M. Derrett similarly endorses Evans,
requently building on his work in his innovative
nterpretations of the parables./39/ The Jesuit scholar, John
ligh, has even popularized Evans' approach by publishing a
ittle book of devotional readings from parallel texts in Luke
nd Deuteronomy./40/

Despite all this favorable attention, at least three
rucial questions raised by Evans' method pose problems for his
ypothesis. What parallels in ancient literature exist to the
pproach which he views Luke as employing? How close in fact
re the parallels which he has identified? To what extent do
hese parallels exclude other equally suggestive parallels
hat might be drawn between Luke and Deuteronomy but which
ould destroy his orderly sequence?

To answer the first question most of Evans' followers have
ppealed to the genre of Jewish midrash, although Evans himself
ever made that appeal explicitly. Deuteronomy itself involves
he restatement and elaboration of earlier portions of the
orah, and throughout Jewish tradition biblical texts were
requently rewritten in both canonical and extra-canonical
iterature./41/ This process of interpretation culminated in
he Rabbinic midrashim which date from Tannaitic and Amoraic
imes, but which contain some demonstrably pre-Christian
raditions./42/

It is not fair, however, to term the method which Evans
spouses midrashic. Regardless of disagreement on finer points
f definition,/43/ most agree that a fundamental characteristic
f Jewish midrash is that it interprets the Old Testament. The
iblical text is primary; the midrash merely comments on,
mbellishes and applies it./44/ This implies that the presence
f an Old Testament quotation or allusion in a piece of
iterature does not automatically make that writing midrashic,
lthough this restriction is not always observed./45/ Yet in
uke's central section only one passage, 10:25-37, can fairly
e interpreted as an elucidation of an Old Testament text./46/
ven then, of the two texts cited (Deut. 6:5 and Lev. 19:18),
t is the text from Leviticus, not Deuteronomy, which gives
ise to the question about one's neighbor and to the subsequent
arable of the good Samaritan. As for the allusions that Evans
inds, even if some or all were intended by Luke, they do not
urn Luke's pericopes into Old Testament commentary. Rather,

as both Sanders and Derrett repeatedly demonstrate, the Old
Testament references shed new light on the Lucan text, not
vice-versa as with midrash./47/

If Luke was not, strictly speaking, writing a midrash on
Deuteronomy, was he nevertheless conscious of the sequence of
parallels which Evans has adduced? Vermes has rightly
emphasized that few midrashim emerge in a vacuum,/48/ so Evans'
argument can be tested at least partially by comparing Luke
with early Jewish midrashim on Deuteronomy. The two main
extant works of this genre are *Debarim Rabbah* and *Sipre*. The
former was not compiled in its present form until perhaps
900 A.D., but many of its traditions are much older./49/ *Sipre*
stems from Mishnaic times, although unfortunately only the
commentary on Deuteronomy 1-6 has been translated./50/
Nevertheless if these works displayed some developments
identical to those Evans attributes to Luke, then his case
would be greatly enhanced.

In fact this is precisely not what happens. In *Debarim
Rabbah* one finds not a running commentary, but detailed and
often contradictory explanations of a choice selection of
texts, namely, those verses which begin one of the *sidroth* in
the triennial and annual lectionary cycles for the reading of
the Torah in the Jewish synagogues./51/ In the course of these
comments, other verses receive mention, but much more briefly.
Of forty-seven verses covered, only fifteen figure in Evans'
synopsis, and of these fifteen only nine have any commentary
similar to the type Evans sees taking place in Luke. Of these
nine, six suggest parallels between Deuteronomy and texts in
Luke other than those which Evans indicates./52/ If anything,
these 'parallels' point out how two texts covering a wide range
of topics and repeating themselves frequently may easily
converge in a number of places by coincidence.

The opening *parashiyoth* of *Sipre* prove no more helpful.
Unlike *Debarim Rabbah*, *Sipre* provides a running commentary on
long sections of Deuteronomy, but its primary emphasis is on
the legal stipulations of chapters 12-26, making it much more
halakic than haggadic./53/ This suggests at once that
substantive or generic parallels to Evans' synopsis will be
harder to find, and a reading of the first sections of the text
confirms this suspicion. The only striking parallel appears
in *par.* 26 (on Deut. 3:23) which remarkably resembles Luke's
parable of the asking son (Luke 11:11-13)./54/ But this

parallel does not support Evans, since he wants to link Deut. 3:23ff. with Luke 10:21-24.

Other ancient Jewish literature provides still less useful material for comparison. The *Pesikta Rabbati*, which contains fifty-three homilies on various texts from the Torah, avoids Deuteronomy almost entirely. Only two of its homilies treat passages from Moses' fifth book, and these passages fall outside the portions of Deuteronomy for which Evans finds Lucan parallels./55/ Of the 28 homilies of *Pesikta de Rab Kahana*, only one derives from Deuteronomy, this time from a passage which Evans skips over./56/ The targums on Deuteronomy for the most part adhere relatively closely to the original text and provide no parallels for Evans' hypothesis, either in content or form./57/

Christianity of course broke from Jewish tradition in many decisive ways, so the absence of parallels to a Christian Deuteronomy does not discredit the theory, *per se*. Convincing parallels would have greatly enhanced its plausibility, but their absence simply shifts the discussion to the other two questions noted above. How close in fact are the parallels which Evans has discerned? Can similar parallels not in his sequence be unearthed? As already noted, a fundamental principle of midrash is that its point of origin is in the Scriptural text. Even if it does not quote an entire verse, there is generally a verbal link of some kind with at least a given phrase or word in the verse./58/ Evans lists such verbal parallels wherever possible but only succeeds in finding them for fourteen of his twenty-two parallel pairs of texts./59/ In most instances, however, the words or expressions that he cites occur so often in Deuteronomy (and elsewhere in the Old Testament) that equally convincing parallels could have been drawn from a wide variety of other texts:

(1) Deut. 1/Luke 10:1-3--πρὸ προσώπου ὑμῶν   This phrase, also using the pronouns αὐτοῦ, ἡμῶν   and σοῦ recurs in Deut. 2:31, 33; 4:38; 6:19; 8:20; 9:3, 4; 13:14; 28:7; 30:1; and 31:3.

(2) Deut. 4:6/Luke 10:21-24--σοφός and συνετός.   This combination reappears only in 1:13, but in a form actually more parallel to the Lucan text (adjectival rather than substantival).

(3) Deut. 6/Luke 10:25-27--κληρονομέω.   This word occurs fifty times in all parts of Deuteronomy.

(4) Deut. 7/Luke 10:29-37--ἐλεέω.   This word is used also

in Deut. 13:17, 28:50, and 30:3.

(5) Deut. 8:4ff./Luke 11:1-13-- ἄρτος and ἐκπειράζω   The former word arises eight times in Deuteronomy; the latter, with its cognates, 12 times.

(6) Deut. 9-10/Luke 11:14-26-- ἰσχυρότερος and ἰσχυρός referring to Israel's enemies. This usage of these words is found also in Deut. 4:38, 7:1, and 11:23. An even closer parallel to the Lucan usage comes in 10:17, where the strong man is God himself. A striking link in favor of Evans, though, is the expression ἐν δακτύλῳ θεοῦ which occurs only here in Deuteronomy.

(7) Deut. 12/Luke 11:37-12:12-- κρίσις and ἐκχέω   Of the five usages of the latter, only the one in Deut. 19:10 refers, like the Lucan reference to the shedding of innocent human blood, rather than dealing with the prohibition against eating blood. The former occurs twenty-two times elsewhere in the book.

(8) Deut. 12-13/Luke 12:13-34-- εὐφραίνω, ψυχή, and ἔθνος All three words are quite common in Deuteronomy, arising twenty-one, thirty-three, and seventy-three times, respectively. The parable of the rich fool (Luke 12:13-21) is actually more reminiscent of Deut. 8:12-18.

(9) Deut. 13:13, 15/Luke 12:54-13:5-- πάντας τοὺς κατ- οικοῦντας This expression occurs only in these two Deuteronomic texts, but the use of πάντας could be coincidental, and the participial form of κατοικέω to refer to the inhabitants of Canaan recurs in twelve other places.

(10) Deut. 14:28/Luke 13:6-9-- τρία ἔτη   The phrase recurs only in Deut. 26:12, but a closer parallel than tithing legislation would be Lev. 19:23, on reaping the fruit of one's orchard only after three years.

(11) Deut. 17-18/Luke 14:1-14-- ἄρχων and ὑψόω   The former recurs nine times; the latter, only once. But this text (Deut. 8:14) offers an almost exact parallel (exalting one's 'heart').

(12) Deut. 20/Luke 14:15-35-- εἰρήνης   This is a good parallel. The word occurs only here in Deuteronomy, and its usage conceivably clarifies certain ambiguities in the parable of the warring king. /60/ But the closest parallel to the excuse of the newly-married man in Luke's great banquet parable comes in Deut. 24:5.

(13) Deut. 21:15-22:4/Luke 15-- 'sheep'. Only here do sheep 'go astray'. Interestingly, though, it is Matthew's parable of the lost sheep rather than Luke's which has the

verbal parallel with πλανάω (Luke says that the shepherd
'lost' the sheep.).
(14) Deut. 24:6-25:3/Luke 16:19-18:8-- λέπρα, ἄγρος, and
κριτής. Here the Lucan parallels appear out of sequence.
the words reappear in Deuteronomy once, nine times, and
eleven times, respectively. Only the first is noteworthy.

A few of the verbal parallels which Evans presents are
herefore suggestive, but only a few. Conceptually the set of
arallels fares little better. The series of parables in Luke
4:15-16:13 provides the best hope for confirming Evans'
ypothesis, at least in part; separate studies have plausibly
oncluded that behind the parables of the great dinner, the
arring king, and the unjust steward lie the very passages
vans has cited on holy war legislation and usury./61/ The
oincidence of the themes of wandering sheep and rebellious
hildren in the proper place in both sequences furthers the
ase for Luke (and Jesus/62/) having had Deuteronomy in mind at
his point.

Beyond these five cases, however, the parallels are
enerally quite vague. The sending of the seventy does not
atch the sending of the spies nearly as well as does Jesus'
rior commission of the twelve in Luke 9. The themes of
nhospitable people and special revelation recur throughout
euteronomy and Luke (cf. Luke 11:14-26, 42-52; 13:22-35). The
heme of relations with foreigners links Deuteronomy with the
arable of the good Samaritan only by stark contrast, while the
art of the summary of the Law which comes from Deuteronomy is
ot the part which the parable elaborates. The theme of
ependence on God's word for nourishment is a common Old
estament one, as is prayer, which at any rate is not
articularly in view in Deut. 8:4-20, the parallel Evans
upplies for Luke 11:1-13. The parallels to Deut. 10-13 are
till more vague. Evans' inability to pair Deut. 14, 19,
1:1-14, 22:5-23:14, and 25:4-19 with any Lucan texts weakens
is argument further. The Sabbath releases are not closely
elated; Deut. 15:1-18 speaks of an ἀφέσις of slaves every
eventh year which God commands, while Luke 13:10-17 describes
esus working to loose (λύειν and ἀπολύειν) a woman on the
abbath which the Jews prohibit. Reference to the fourth
ommandment (Deut. 5:12-15) would have been much more in order.
he parallel with feasting in Jerusalem is obtained only by
nachronistically interpolating the name of the city into the
euteronomic text. The issue of food for Levites has virtually

nothing to do with the banquet parables of Luke 14. Finally,
obeying the Law in Deut. 26 compares with the parable of the
Pharisee and publican only by contrast and again is very
general. The lack of close conceptual parallels thus combines
with the lack of noteworthy verbal parallels to render the
notion of Luke's use of Deuteronomy as a model for all of his
central section highly unlikely./63/ It is quite possible that
individual texts, especially some of the parables noted above,
may have drawn on themes from Deuteronomy./64/ But the evidence
does not justify any more sweeping claims than this.

J. Drury

J. Drury nevertheless applauds Evans' study and builds on
it in order to defend his view that Luke's entire gospel, but
expecially his non-Marcan material, is midrashic. Luke has
creatively altered and embellished his sources, which Drury
restricts to Mark, Matthew, and the Old Testament./65/ Drury
emphasizes that this type of historiography seriously discredits
Luke as a reliable historian, though not as a good historical
novelist. Drury does not view this as a loss, however, for he
sees Luke as a paradigm for all generations of Christians of how
to adapt the gospel message to the changing circumstances of
history and culture./66/

An analysis of Drury's entire thesis lies outside the scope
of this essay, but a few brief comments deserve mention./67/
First, Drury depends highly on the approach to the Synoptic
problem which dispenses with Q (or which at least makes Luke's
texts differ greatly from Q's), so that most of the differences
between Luke and Matthew can be attributed to Luke's fertile
imagination. Despite the vigorous attempts of Farmer and a few
others to support such a stance with solid arguments,/68/ most
New Testament students still find some sort of Q hypothesis
necessary/69/ and conclude that Luke has regularly reproduced
this source without introducing major conceptual changes./70/
Second, if the parables of Jesus are substantially authentic,
again as most would still maintain,/71/ then Drury cannot be
right in the procedure he assigns to Luke throughout much of the
central section where parables predominate./72/ But if Luke
depended on tradition for his parables, most of which come from
L,/73/ and if he carefully preserved much of the tradition
which he obtained from Q, then not a lot of material remains for
Drury to utilize in speculating about Luke's midrashic
creativity, since he admits that Luke has not been nearly so
inventive in his Marcan sections as in his non-Marcan ones./74/

Third, Drury's excuses for those parts of Luke's gospel which
do not easily fit his hypothesis border on special pleading. In
one case Drury describes Luke's editorial method as 'the dark
before the dawn, the flagging of energy before the last
stretch.'/75/   Elsewhere he comments: 'Luke's creative powers
are at a low ebb in this section,' 'He seems to have forgotten
his editing work,' or ' There are signs of the writer's fatigue
precisely where we would expect them.'/76/ But why should Luke
so often be tired or absent-minded? Was he working long hours
day after day to meet a publisher's deadline, or what? Drury's
approach, in short, is more ingenious than plausible.

As for Luke's central section, Drury follows Evans very
closely. But if one is not convinced by Evans' careful pairing
of the Lucan and Deuteronomic texts, he will find Drury's less
detailed discussion even more unsatisfactory. Nevertheless
Drury offers some helpful insights in the preface to his
discussion of Luke's central section. There he notes its
thematic structure:

> As we might expect of Luke, it is set in an historical
> order. First things are put first by a beginning with
> calls to discipleship. Last things are put last by a
> conclusion which teaches the coming of the kingdom and
> judgement. Hopes are thus raised that the intervening
> material is also in an historical order, and the hopes
> are fulfilled. The call of the disciples is followed
> by their successful mission, the basic things of the
> disciples' life are illustrated by the Good Samaritan
> loving his neighbour and Mary's love of God developing
> into teaching about prayer. Then with its historical
> and spiritual basis established, the Beelzebul controversy
> brings the kingdom up against its enemies.../77/

And so he continues. Drury of course means by 'an historical
order' what most would call a topical or logical order. Yet to
the extent that a topical order can explain the sequence of
passages in Luke's central section, recourse to the 'Christian
Deuteronomy' hypothesis becomes unnecessary. Had Drury applied
his ingenuity to developing this topical approach, instead of
only sketching these introductory outlines, he might never have
needed to fall back on Evans' theory.

M. D. Goulder

M. D. Goulder goes well beyond both Evans and Drury to
claim that Luke's central section, like the rest of his gospel

(and all of Matthew and Mark as well), follows the Jewish cycle
of lectionary readings for both Torah and *haphtarah* as well as
other scattered portions of the Old Testament. Even Goulder's
predecessors balk a little at this point. Drury reviews *The
Evangelists' Calendar* very favorably, but nevertheless
entertains two reservations: (a) as Goulder himself admits,
some of his parallels fit much better than others, and (b) even
granted his parallels, they do not exclude more traditional
historiographical concerns. One can admit the influence of the
lectionary in some passages without having to find it
everywhere./78/ Evans similarly concludes that this 'all or
nothing character' of Goulder's thesis is its main weakness,
adding that 'the Old Testament is a long and repetitive book.
It is hardly surprising if echoes of its quasi-sacrosanct
diction and its comparatively limited stock of themes should be
heard in almost any section of the gospels.'/79/ One could only
wish that Drury and Evans had applied these criticisms to their
own works as well.

Again a critique of Goulder's overall theory lies far
beyond the present scope of discussion./80/ Perhaps the most
important lesson to be drawn just from his analysis of Luke's
central section is the one which confirms how the parallels
between Luke and Deuteronomy are often so general as to allow
for equally plausible (or implausible) parallels to be drawn
elsewhere. Goulder's set of parallels, in summary form,
proceeds as follows:/81/

Luke	Deuteronomy	
9:51–10:24	1:1–3:22	sending forerunners
10:25–11:13	3:23–7:11	summary of Law, including prayer
11:14–54	7:12–11:25	stiffneckedness of Israel
12:1–13:9	11:26–16:17	apostasy vs. prosperity
13:10–14:24	16:18–21:9	rejection of God's message, banquet/battle excuses
14:25–16:13	21:10–25:19	same sequence of parallels as Evans
16:14–17:4	26:1–29:9	(parallels break down)
17:20–18:14	29:10–30:20	repentance or else wrath
18:15–43	31:1–30	the new generation
19:1–20:18	32:1–52	threats of destruction

As is apparent, the points of comparison are quite general and
introduce themes which reappear regularly throughout many parts
of Scripture. Goulder does not even try to list the types of

verbal parallels which Evans offered./82/ Moreover his sequence
of lections contradicts Evans' synopsis in several places,
especially toward the end of Luke's central section. Goulder
can claim some support from *Debarim Rabbah*, since its set of
lections corresponds exactly to the textual divisions which
Goulder proposes. Yet *Debarim Rabbah* follows the standard
midrashic practice of dwelling primarily on the first verse of
each lection, while Goulder's parallels almost never involve the
opening verses of the lections in which they occur. Either one
has to assume that the divisions of the hypothesized first-
century lectionary were not the same as later on, in which case
Goulder's outline finds no Jewish or Christian precedent, or
else one assumes an early origin for Goulder's divisions, in
which case the omission of comment on initial texts is
unprecedented. Either way Goulder's thesis is weakened.
Finally, as the above list indicates, at one point the parallels
break down altogether, since the main parallel after the
sequence of parables in Luke 14:15-16:13 is the correspondence
between the passages on divorce in Luke 16:18 and Deut. 24:1-4.
Yet according to Goulder's lectionary scheme, Deut. 24:1-4
belongs with the previous Lucan passages./83/ In short, Goulder
has produced an even less convincing set of parallels than did
Evans or Drury. Of the three hypotheses, Goulder's seems least
likely of all.

    Goulder himself seems to sense this when he concludes his
chapter on 'Luke and the Annual Torah Cycle' by cautioning:

    Let the reader beware. Such correspondences...are heady
    stuff. Each correspondence is a double selection,
    sometimes only a verse or two out of five chapters with a
    verse or two from a lection of ten or twenty. Sometimes no
    sidra text can be alleged, sometimes only a general
    parallel of thought. It is too early to speak of
    demonstration./84/

Goulder decides that only if he can also match *haphtaroth* with
the Lucan passages will he allow himself to claim that 'it would
take a hardened sceptic to refuse the thesis.'/85/ Yet,
contrary to his own estimation, this attempt to compile an
additional set of parallels fails altogether. Again limiting
the discussion to Luke's central section, his list of
correspondences can be summarized as follows:/86/

    Luke   *2 Kings*
    9:51-10:24   1-3   fire from heaven (2 Kg. 1:10),

		leaving parents (1 Kg. 19:20), not greeting those met (2 Kg. 4:29).
10:25–11:13	4:1–6:23	asking of neighbors (2 Kg. 4:1–3) good Samaritans (2 Chr. 28:15).
11:14–54	6:24–8:29	destruction of strong men, Beelzebul (2Kg. 1:1ff.).
12:1–13:9	9–10	slaying at sacrifices, rising cloud (1 Kg. 18:44), feeding of birds (1 Kg. 17:4).
13:10–14:24	11–12	not entering house (2Chr. 23:6ff.), stoning prophets (2 Chr. 24:18–21).
14:25–16:13	13–14	suing for peace (2 Sam. 8:4ff.), temple/tower building (2 Kg. 12:10).
16:14–17:19	15–17	leper cleansing (2 Kg. 5:14).
17:20–18:14	18–19	Hezekiah/Mannasseh contrast like publican/Pharisee (2 Chr. 31:5ff. 33:12ff., Pr. Man. 4:8).
18:15–43	20–21	(no parallels)
19:1–20:18	22–23	evil Jehoiakim/Archelaus/throne claimant.

This list virtually disproves Goulder's thesis singlehandedly. In only two instances does Goulder actually cite a parallel text from the appropriate *haphtarah* (2 Kg. 1:10 and 4:1–7). Six times his parallels come from passages elsewhere in Samuel-Kings; four times they come from Chronicles. One (Pr. Man. 4:8) turns completely outside the canon for its parallel, and the final parallel requires a comparison between an Old Testament character, a historical figure from the days of Roman occupation, and a king in a parable of Jesus. Goulder can conjecture all he wants about Luke reading 'the whole Histories through the Chronicler's glasses,'/87/ or about how the early church might have gotten off schedule in its Scriptural readings./88/ The simple fact remains that Goulder set out for himself rigid restrictions on the texts into which he could look for parallels to the gospel material,/89/ yet abandons these restrictions in all but two instances in the actual course of his study. Goulder concludes, nevertheless, that all of these parallels are 'credible,'/90/ and that these ten, plus at least six of the Luke/Deuteronomy parallels, comprise part of his total of 'forty-nine exact landfalls' between Luke and the Old Testament./91/ How any of these sixteen 'landfalls' in Luke's central section can be termed 'exact' defies explanation.

Discussion of the other thirty-three is out of place here, but a
straightforward reading of Goulder and the texts he cites does
not suggest that they are significantly different in kind./92/

Conclusion

The 'Christian Deuteronomy' hypothesis has commendably
drawn attention to possible new Old Testament texts which may
shed light on Lucan passages. The method of comparative
midrash, while probably a misnomer, has suggested innovative and
sometimes persuasive interpretations of several of the Lucan
parables. Present Lucan research in general is recognizing more
and more how steeped both Luke and Acts are in Old Testament
thought./93/ Contrary to much of this research, though, Luke is
not one of the most conservative New Testament writers in his
view of the role of the Law in the early church. I have
elsewhere argued precisely the opposite; while Luke emphasizes
fulfillment of the Law, Prophets, and Psalms, he repeatedly
stresses how Christianity has broken away from the Law./94/ To
imagine Luke depicting Jesus as simply repeating the themes and
sequence of the teaching of Moses, even if creatively
reinterpreting it, does not at all do justice to Luke's concern
for the freedom from the Law which Christians enjoy. The Old
Testament themes and allusions serve to highlight by contrast
Luke's redactional concerns and can best be explained by assuming
that they reflect genuine historical reminiscences of the
sayings and events from the days of Jesus and his disciples./95/
They do not solve the problem of the outline of Luke's central
section, and it is improbable that they can illuminate Luke's
overall structure elsewhere. In fact one can almost at random
compile lists just like those of Evans, Drury, and Goulder for
other sets of Lucan passages coupled with Old Testament texts.
The appendix to this essay supplies one such example. In it,
the first ten psalms are matched with the first ten *sidroth* of
Luke according to Goulder's divisions. At least two parallels
emerge for every pair of texts, though seldom are they
significant verbal parallels. Yet all this demonstrates only
how frequently Luke, especially in his non-Marcan material,
develops themes common to most parts of the Old Testament.

Chiastic Structures

Initial Studies

Another innovative explanation of the structure of Luke's
central section invokes the stylistic figure known as chiasmus,
or inverted parallelism. Old Testament students have long

recognized a wide variety of types of poetic parallelism, and
A. DiMarco has recently cataloged a long list of canonical and
apocryphal texts in which chiasmus has been seen./96/ N. Lund
pioneered the modern study of New Testament chiasmus and leaned
heavily on its Old Testament background to conclude that it
reflected a peculiarly Semitic form of thought./97/ Talbert,
however, has documented the widespread use of chiasmus in
classical texts, while Bailey has pointed out how often it
occurs even in ordinary conversation./98/ Nevertheless it is
perhaps more frequent in Semitic texts, and it certainly merits
careful attention in a study of ancient Jewish historiography.

The use of chiasmus can be aesthetically, mnemonically, or
conceptually motivated. Perhaps the origin of the device lies
in its mnemonic function./99/ In antiquity groups of stories
or teachings might be arranged in inverted parallel form to aid
in their memorization and transmission./100/ The inversion also
introduced 'movement and variation into the fixed patterns of
reiteration.'/101/ At the literary level, chiasmus created an
artistically pleasing sense of symmetry and also focused
attention toward its center where the climax or most important
ideas occurred. Additional 'laws' of chiasmus involve the
function of the center as a turning point and as the locus for
introducing an antithetical thought, the parallelism often
found between center and 'extremes,' and the use of frame
passages to introduce and conclude the chiasmus./102/

Luke's writings in particular lend themselves to outlines
involving parallelism at either the traditional or redactional
stages. Commentators have often noted correspondences between
the infancy narratives on John and Jesus in Luke 1-2,/103/
between the transfiguration and ascension in Luke 9, 24, and
Acts 1,/104/ between two parallel sources in Acts 1-5,/105/ and
between the two 'halves' of the book of Acts (chaps. 1-12 and
13-28)./106/ W. Radl and G. Muhlack have both devoted entire
monographs to ways in which Luke's gospel and the Acts parallel
each other./107/ Talbert adds to this list of parallels Luke
4:16-7:17 and 7:18-8:56, 9:1-48 and 22:7-23:16, Luke 3 and 4,
and finds a chiasmus in Acts 15:1-21:26./108/ The value of
these various sets of correspondences varies greatly.
Morgenthaler's discoveries of doubling phenomena in almost
every passage in Luke-Acts show how a method can be carried to
extremes./109/ At least some of the correspondences seem
undeniable, though, and it would not be surprising if some such
principle of 'balance' lay behind Luke's central section.

Morgenthaler himself perceived a chiastic outline spanning
Luke 5:27–19:10, although he only included a few passages in
it:/110/

5:27–32	19:1–10	call of tax-collectors (Levi and Zacchaeus)
7:36–50	18:9–14	Pharisees and sinners
10:29–37	17:11–19	compassionate/thankful Samaritans; evil/thankless Jews
10:38–42	16:19–31	Martha and Mary/rich man and Lazarus
14	15	series of three parables.

Morgenthaler, however, ranges well outside of Luke's central
section for his first two sets of parallels, and his fourth set
of parallels is linked only by the fact that in John's gospel
Mary and Martha have a brother named Lazarus!

Goulder, before proposing his lectionary hypothesis, also
suggested a chiastic outline for Luke's central section:/111/

10:25	18:18	how to inherit eternal life
11:1	17:5	faithful prayer, illustrated by
11:14	17:11	a healing
11:37	16:14	Pharisaic hypocrisy, illustrated by
12:1	16:1	the love of money
12:35	15:1	repentance
13:10	14:1	rejection of Israel and invitation to the outcast.

This outline, though, is not entirely chiastic, since the third
set of parallels breaks the sequence in the second column. Most
of the parallels are also very general. As with the Christian
Deuteronomy theories, the texts in the first column might be
equally well-matched with several other parallels. For example,
11:1ff. fits at least as well with Luke 18:1–8 or 9–14 which
deal with faithful prayer. Pharisaic hypocrisy reappears in
13:10–17 and 14:1–14, and both of these texts contain healings
as well. Luke 18:18 actually falls outside the boundaries of
the central section as Goulder defines it (9:51–18:14).
Finally, not one of Goulder's parallels matches any of the five
found by Morgenthaler.

Already it is clear that specific criteria will again be
required to help evaluate the validity of the various chiastic
theories and to ask in each case, therefore, if significant
verbal as well as conceptual parallelism is present and if the
parallelism adduced is close enough to exclude other equally
reasonable parallels being drawn./112/   Only then may a chiastic

outline be judged plausible.

C. H. Talbert

Talbert builds on Morgenthaler and Goulder but adds much
more detail. His outline falls into eleven parts:/113/

(a)	10:21-24	18:15-17	kingdom revealed to children
(b)	10:25-37	18:18-20	inheriting eternal life
(c)	10:38-42	18:9-14	de-emphasizing good works
(d)	11:1-13	18:1-8	God's willingness to answer prayer
(e)	11:14-36	17:11-37	healing, kingdom signs, judgment warning
(f)	11:37-54	17:1-10	brotherly rebuke and meals
(g)	12:1-48	16:1-31	hell, riches, and stewardship
(h)	12:49-13:9	14:25-15:32	family loyalties, prudence, repentance
(i)	13:10-17	14:1-6	Sabbath healing, people more important than animals
(j)	13:18-30	14:7-24	kingdom parables, banqueting, and the outcasts
(k)	13:31-33	13:34-35	perishing in Jerusalem.

Again two of the passages in the second column break the
necessary sequence for a complete chiasmus. Apart from this,
how do these parallels fare against the above criteria? In (a)
the only real point of similarity is the reference to children,
but in 10:21 Luke uses νήπιος, while in 18:15 he employs
βρέφος./114/ In (c) Martha's concern for Jesus' physical well-
being hardly compares with the Pharisee's self-adulation. As
noted above, much of chaps. 13 and 14 could fall into (e).
Over half of Luke's parables deal in some way with eating, and
Jesus hardly considered the Pharisees as 'brothers,' so (f) is
very weak. In (j) only 13:18-21 are explicit kingdom parables,
and banqueting and the invitation to outcasts reappear
throughout Luke's gospel. Almost half of Talbert's outline is
therefore quite unimpressive.

The other six parallels stand out a little more. In (b)
both passages begin identically with a questioner asking Jesus,
'What shall I do to inherit eternal life?' The subsequent
answers, however, bear little resemblance to each other. In
one case Jesus poses a counterquestion and then a parable. In
the other he quotes the Law and adds a direct command. In the
first he deals with the broad question of neighborliness; in the
second he declares specifically, 'Sell all that you have...'

The center of the chiasmus, (k), if there is a chiasmus, is
perhaps left better undivided. In (g) and (h) multiple
correspondences arise of varying weight. The threat of hell
would be stronger if the same expressions were used in both
cases but they are not./115/ The theme of riches prevails
throughout Luke 12 and 16 so that 12:13-34 and 16:9-15 are not
obviously the two closest parallels on that topic. 12:35-48
and 16:1-13 also fall under the subheading 'prudent action
taken ahead of time'. Finally, the fruitless tree and
tasteless salt are not closely related and in any case break
the order of parallels.

This leaves (b), (i), and those portions of (g) and (h)
which deal with faithful and unfaithful stewardship,
transcendence of family loyalties, and repentance. Several of
these parallels prove more striking and will be discussed
further below. For now one must conclude that Talbert has
failed to fit all of Luke's central section into a chiasmus.
Talbert stresses the importance of attributing chiastic
structures to the final redactor of a work whenever
possible./116/ In this case, however, since much of the
material does not easily fit a chiastic outline, then perhaps
some pre-Lucan chiasmus underlies the central section involving
only a fraction of it.

K. E. Bailey

Bailey has constructed just such a pre-Lucan outline and
goes into much more detail than any of his predecessors. Unlike
Talbert, he freely admits that some material simply cannot fit
his proposed chiasmus. Bailey therefore identifies the chiasmus
as the work of a pre-Lucan Jewish-Christian theologian. With
Talbert he identifies 13:31-35 as the center. The repetition of
Jerusalem at the extremes and in the center of 9:51-19:48 gives
the city an unmistakable prominence. 'Death and the
eschatological day are the climax of the document.'/117/
Bailey's outline falls into ten main sections, each of which
contains subdivisions which often contain further parallels.
Again a mere list of section headings does not do justice to his
outline, but briefly it can be summarized as follows:/118/

(a)	9:51-56	19:10, 28-48	Jerusalem: eschatological events--day, death, fulfillment, judgment, salvation, (vision).
(b)	9:57-10:12	18:35-19:9	Follow me: people come to Jesus, Jesus goes out.

(c)	10:25-42	18:18-30	What shall I do to inherit eternal life?
(d)	11:1-13	18:1-14	Prayer: assurance, steadfastness, right approach.
(e)	11:14-32	17:11-37	Signs and the (present/ coming) kingdom: Son of man.
(f)	11:37-12:34	16:9-31	Conflict w/ Pharisees: money, heavenly treasure.
(g)	12:35-59	16:1-8, 16	The kingdom is not yet and is now.
(h)	13:1-9	14:12-15:32	The call of the kingdom to Israel (and outcasts).
(i)	13:10-20[*sic*]	14:1-11	The nature of the kingdom: love and not law--Sabbath healings, humility.
(j)		13:22-35	Jerusalem: eschatological events-- salvation, judgment, vision, fulfillment, death, day.

The number of details Bailey succeeds in pairing cannot fail to impress, and at first glance his thesis seems irrefutable. Nevertheless not all of the parallels carry equal weight. Is it possible that even Bailey has overestimated how much of Luke's central section can be squeezed into a chiastic mold?/119/ Bailey estimates that 90% of this section fits his outline; the figure is actually closer to 86%./120/ Yet these are strange percentages. If Luke valued the chiasmus so highly as to retain this much of it intact, why did he then disrupt it at all, making it so much less obvious to his readers? If he didn't value the chiasmus that highly, then why did he preserve so much of it? A fit of almost 100% *or* one in the range of, say, 30% to 50% would be more understandable. In the former case, it would show that Luke wanted his readers clearly to perceive the chiastic outline; in the latter, that he valued the chiastic source as a source, but not to the exclusion of other equally important sources, for example, Q.

Bailey does not discuss the correspondences in his outline in any detail, but simply remarks that they 'are very strong and need no comment.'/121/ In fact they do need comment, for not all are by any means self-evident.

(a) Very general. Jerusalem occurs eleven times between 9:51 and 19:48, /122/ five of which fall outside the center and extremes of Bailey's chiasmus. /123/

(b) No noteworthy parallels. People come to Jesus in virtually every chapter of Luke. Jesus' sending of the seventy has nothing to do with Zacchaeus' call.

(c) No parallels apart from the introductory questions discussed above.

(d) One excellent parallel (11:5-13 and 18:1-8) and one less striking one (11:1-4 and 18:9-14). Commentators have often noted the first parallel, but Marshall has pointed out that 18:9-14 probably begins a new subsection in Luke's outline and is not primarily about how to pray./124/

(e) Very general. Present and coming kingdom do not really match. The title Son of man recurs also in 9:56, 58; 12:8, 10, 40; 18:8, 31; and 19:10.

(f) Suggestive. Luke 12:13-21 probably belongs more closely with 16:19-31.

(g) Good. The link between these servant parables is actually quite strong, as the discussion below will note.

(h) One excellent parallel (Luke 13:1-9 and 15:1-32). To include 14:12-35 along with all of chapter 15, however, too greatly overbalances the nine brief verses of chapter 13 and adds no additional verbal parallels.

(i) One good parallel (the two Sabbath healings) and one very poor one. The parables of the mustard seed and the leaven do not urge humility, but depict the growth of the kingdom and the contrast between its eventual magnitude and insignificant origins.

(j) Same as with Talbert. The overall chiastic structure of 13:22-35 is hard to perceive. 'Salvation' appears in only one half, 'vision' and 'judgment' do not appear in the same sequence in the two halves, and 'fulfillment' is only present by contrast. Without this frame vv. 32-33 become synonymously rather than chiastically parallel: vv. 32a and 33a - 'I cast out demons and perform cures/I must go on my way,' vv. 32b and 33b - 'today, tomorrow, and the third day/the day following,' vv. 32c and 33c - 'I finish my course'/perishing in Jerusalem.

Bailey's attempt to outline most of Luke's central section thus falls short of demonstration. Yet some of the parallels remain striking, especially between pairs of parables. Perhaps a better outline would restrict the chiasmus to these parallels

and view Luke's chiastic source as simply one of several sources
used in the composition of his central section. Specifically,
five pairs of parables, all peculiarly Lucan,/125/ taken in the
order in which Luke presents them, suggest just such a source.
In every instance there is significant verbal as well as
conceptual parallelism. The five pairs of parables are Luke
10:25-37 and 18:9-14, 11:5-8 and 18:1-8, 12:13-21 and 16:19-31,
12:35-38 and 16:1-13, and 13:6-9 and 15:11-32.

A Chiastic Parable Source

At least as long ago as 1927, R. S. Franks observed that
the parable which most resembles the parable of the Pharisee
and publican 'in method and character' is that of the good
Samaritan./126/ Both parables portray members of the Jewish
religious establishment in a surprisingly poor light. In both
cases, they are identified by name (priest/Levite; Pharisee).
No other parable of Jesus does this. Both parables have been
regularly termed 'example-stories,' and the only two others
usually grouped with them in this category are the third pair
of parables listed above!/127/ Both have unlikely heroes, the
Samaritan and the tax-collector, who were particularly despised
by the average Jew. Both draw a sharp contrast between their
expected heroes and their actual heroes. Schlatter observes
that only these two parables take place in a fixed location,
each time for the same reason, to show that God's service is not
localized in the temple along lines of conventional
understanding./128/ Verbally, the parables are linked by the
important theological theme of justification (δικαιόω). The
parable of the good Samaritan addresses the lawyer's concern
that he be justified, while the Pharisee and publican both
receive Jesus' verdict on whether or not they went home
justified. This verbal link is striking since δικαιόω occurs
in no other parable of Luke's central section and in only three
other distinct gospel pericopes (Luke 7:29, 35par. Matt. 11:19;
Matt. 12:37; and Luke 16:15). Closely related to the theme of
justification is that of mercy. The good Samaritan shows mercy;
the publican prays, 'God be merciful to me...' The Greek
reveals that the parallels are not verbal (ἔλεος, ἱλάσκομαι),
but the thoughts remain quite similar. Both the wounded man and
the publican are powerless to overcome their predicaments and
must rely utterly on the help of someone else.

The parallelism between the parables of the friend at
midnight and unjust judge proves even closer. Commentators have
often paired these two parables./129/ Both depict two main

characters, one of whom has an urgent request which only the
other can grant. In each case the second character at first
refuses to grant the request, but eventually relents, though
not for the proper motives. Both parables apply to God's
people, assuring them that he will answer their prayers.
Verbally, an important parallel arises in 11:7 and 18:5 with
the idiom παρέχω κόπον . This expression occurs in no other
parable of Jesus and in only one other Synoptic passage (Mark
14:6 par. Matt. 26:10), but it is central to the two parables
here. Neither the sleeping man nor the unjust judge wants to
be bothered. In both cases, this unwillingness to help leads
directly to an *a fortiori* contrast with God's willingness to
grant his people's requests.

The parables of the rich fool and the rich man and Lazarus
match the two remaining 'example-stories'. Both begin with the
verbal parallel ἄνθρωπός τις πλούσιος, found elsewhere in the
Synoptics only in the parable of the unjust steward. But there
the rich man is not the central character and is not the one
judged but the one judging. The rich fool and the rich man of
Luke 16:19-31, however, parallel each other closely. Besides
being wealthy, each seems unconcerned with anyone except
himself. The rich fool ignores God; the rich man ignores
Lazarus. Both die; no other parables of Jesus relate the death
of one of their characters. Both parables continue by
recounting the tragic consequences of the rich men's deaths.
Both conclude by disclosing not that riches, *per se*, are evil,
but that earthly treasures apart from heavenly ones lead only to
ruin (cf. 12:21 and 16:30).

The next set of passages matches the parables of the
watchful servants and unjust steward. Both are servant
parables, /130/ and in each case the servants are faced with the
urgent need to plan for a potentially tragic future. In each
case too the key future event is an accounting or reckoning with
their master. Both parables further focus on the successful
preparation for that reckoning by the servants. In the one
case, the servants prepare to receive the master into their
house; in the other, the servant prepares to be received into
the houses of his master's debtors. In this pair of parables,
however, the potential verbal parallelism in the use of servant
figures never materializes. Luke 12:37 uses δοῦλος, while 16:1,
3, and 8 employ οἰκονόμος. The only verbal links are supplied
by the parallel references to the master as κύριος (12:36, 37;
16:8), but this term appears frequently in the parables of L

(cf. 13:8; 14:21-23; 19:16-25). In light of the previous and
subsequent parallels, however, the conceptual similarities here
seem close enough to warrant their inclusion in the
chiasmus./131/

    The final set of parallels joins the parables of the fig
tree and prodigal son. Farmer points out how the parallels
actually extend to cover all of 13:1-9 and 15:1-32. He lists
six structural characteristics which these two passages share:
(a) an introductory setting (13:1, 15:1-3), (b) three closely
related sayings comprising the main body of the passage (13:2-3,
4-5,6-9; 15:4-7, 8-10, 11-32), (c) nearly exact structural and
semantic parallelism between the first two passages, (d) the
transitional ἤ linking the first two passages, (e) a rhetorical
question introducing and an emphatic λέγω ὑμῖν concluding each
of the first two passages, and (f) the third passage as a longer
story illustrating in more detail the point of the first two
passages./132/ Farmer concludes that these observations,
coupled with the non-Lucan style and vocabulary of these
passages, verify that Luke 13:1-9 and 15:1-32 have both come
from the same pre-Lucan source./133/ Verbally, the most
significant parallel is the refrain of repentance. The four
shorter 'parables'/134/ all conclude with a moral about
repentance, and the longer two expound this theme in synonymous
language./135/ Surprisingly, μετανοέω or μετανοία occurs in
only one other parable of Jesus (Luke 16:30).

    The only other passage in the gospels which closely
resembles Luke 13:1-9 and 15:1-32 in structure falls squarely
between these two passages. That text is Luke 14:7-24. These
verses could very plausibly form the center of the proposed
chiastic source of peculiarly Lucan parables./136/ They contain
an introduction (v.7), two closely related sayings (vv. 8-11 and
12-14), and a third passage which elaborates on the common theme
of the rejection of the exalted and the invitation to the
downtrodden (vv. 15-24). The transitional καί replaces the ἤ,
and no rhetorical questions or λέγω ὑμῖν's appear. Instead vv.
8 and 12 both introduce their sayings with a ὅταν + subjunctive
construction, followed by a negative prohibition and then a
strongly contrasting positive command (cf. the use of ἀλλά in
vv. 10 and 13). Each passage ends with a generalizing
conclusion (vv. 11, 14, and 24)./137/

    Luke 14:7-24 would form a very fitting center for a
chiasmus of Jesus' parables. Its theme is central to any

presentation of Jesus' teaching and characterizes the 'extremes'
of the chiasmus as well (Luke 10:25-37 and 18:9-14). An
antithetical thought also occurs here--the extension of the
kingdom invitation to include outsiders. The subsequent
parables of Luke 15 dramatically illustrate this new thought.
P. M. Laconi has underlined how the length and frequency of
parables increase the nearer one gets to the center of Luke's
travel narrative, which further suggests that the dominant
themes occur in chapters 13-15./138/

These five pairs of closely paralleled passages, along with
Luke 14:7-24, can hardly have found their way into Luke's gospel
in this precise order by sheer accident. All of the passages
are peculiarly Lucan; all fall within his central section. The
only parables peculiar to this part of the gospel not contained
in this chiasmus are 14:5, 14:28-33, and 17:7-10./139/ All
three of these passages begin with the formula τίς έξ ὑμῶν, but
otherwise have little in common. Yet remarkably 14:5 and 28-33
fit opposite each other in the gap between the final set of
parallels and the center of the chiasmus. Furthermore, 17:7-10
fits opposite the only other τίς έξ ὑμῶν parable so far
unaccounted for in Luke (11:11-13)./140/ This latter parable of
course has a close parallel in Matthew, but a good argument can
be made that in Luke it originally stood with 11:5-8./141/ Are
these two additional correspondences coincidental? Perhaps, but
one wonders. Conceivably the proposed source could have
contained these extra parables as well, in which case every
parable and only those parables peculiar to Luke's central
section would be embraced. The chiasmus would then appear as
follows:

10:25-37	18:9-14
11:5-8	18:1-8
11:11-13	17:7-10
12:13-21	16:19-31
12:35-38	16:1-13
13:1-9	15:1-32
14:1-6	14:28-33
14:7-24

Whether or not these last short parables be added, enough
evidence has emerged to make very plausible the hypothesis that
Luke utilized a chiastically structured parable source
independent of the other gospel strata and preserved its
sequence of material even while combining it with other sources.
The peculiarly Lucan parables comprise 41.5% of Luke's central
section (less than 5% of which is subtracted if the four τίς έξ

ὑμῶν parables are omitted), which falls well within the range
suggested above for a source which strongly influenced Luke but
which by no means governed the arrangement of all his
material./142/   The idea of such a source preserves the
integrity of the Q material and fits in with previous theories
that Luke's peculiar material, especially his parables, came
from one or more special sources./143/   Talbert's concern that
chiasmus be attributed to the editor rather than to the sources
of work is here at least partially cancelled out by Luke's
apparent disinterest in chiasmus elsewhere.   Lund, for example,
points to Luke 11:42-48, 49-52, and 13:34-35 as three places
where Luke has destroyed chiasmus in his source material./144/
Studies of vocabulary and style also suggest that much of Luke's
non-Marcan material is pre-Lucan./145/

   The Source as a Basis for a Topical Outline
   The entirety of Luke's central section nevertheless remains
unexplained.   Luke did not want to arrange all of his material
chiastically, and the chiastic sequence of parables is actually
disguised by the intervening material even while left fully
intact.   At this point the quest for a topical outline resumes.
The most plausible and detailed outline of Luke's central
section comes from I. H. Marshall's commentary.   Marshall
identifies the following section headings:/146/

9:51-10:24	duties and privileges of discipleship
10:25-11:13	the characteristics of disciples
11:14-54	controversy with the Pharisees
12:1-13:21	readiness for the coming crisis
13:22-14:35	the way of the kingdom
15:1-32	the gospel for the outcast
16:1-31	warnings about wealth
17:1-10	teaching for disciples
17:11-18:8	the coming of the Son of man
18:9-19:10	the scope of salvation.

   A few modifications can make this outline a little more
detailed and precise.   9:51-10:24 falls nicely into two parts,
the introduction to the journey (9:51-62) and the mission of the
seventy (10:1-24).   Similarly 10:25-11:13 breaks down into
10:25-42, expounding the double commandment which summarizes the
Law,/147/ and 11:1-13, addressing the topic of prayer./148/   The
fourth subsection perhaps ends not at 13:21 but at 13:9, since
vv. 10-21 have nothing to do with judgment.   Vv. 18-21,
moreover, link closely with vv. 22-35, and since the travel
notices need not indicate major breaks,/149/ one may propose

13:10-14:24 as the next major subsection. All of the passages
in this subsection deal with the theme of kingdom reversals:
the 'illegal' Sabbath healings, the end vs. the beginning of the
life of mustard seed and leaven, the closed doors at the
Messianic banquet with strangers inside, Jerusalem as the center
of destruction instead of salvation, and the parables of
reversal in 14:7-24./150/ Further evidence for the boundaries
of this subsection emerges from the way it unfolds into two
parallel 'halves':

13:10-17	14:1-6	Sabbath healing
13:18-21	14:7-24	pair of brief, parallel parables
13:22-35	14:15-24	longer discourse on who will enter the kingdom./151/

14:25-35 then forms a separate short subsection on the theme of
counting the cost of discipleship./152/ Finally, 17:11-19
probably belongs not with 17:20-18:8 but with 17:1-10. The
story of the healed lepers makes no reference to the Son of man,
but it does emphasize the faith of the foreigner. Similarly,
17:5-6 treats the disciples' request for increased faith;
πίστις surprisingly occurs elsewhere in Luke's central section
only in 18:8. The rest of 17:1-10 can then be viewed easily as
explaining the nature of faith. Faith does not tempt others
(vv. 1-2), it is forgiving (vv.3-4), and it does not merit
reward (vv. 7-10).

The resulting outline of Luke's central section looks like
this:

9:51-62	Introduction to Following Jesus
10:1-24	Mission of the Seventy
10:25-42	The Double Commandment
11:1-13	Prayer
11:14-54	Controversy with the Pharisees: A Series of Contrasts
12:1-13:9	Preparing for Coming Judgment
13:10-14:24	Kingdom Reversals
14:25-35	Cost of Discipleship
15:1-32	Joy of Repentance
16:1-31	Use and Abuse of Riches
17:1-19	Teachings about Faith
17:20-18:8	When and How the Kingdom Will Appear
18:9-30	How to Enter the Kingdom
18:31-34	Conclusion to Following Jesus.

The parables peculiar to Luke play a significant role in the

subsection of this outline in which they occur. The good
Samaritan suggests the addition of the story of Mary and Martha;
the double commandment is thus illustrated by an example of love
for neighbor and one of love for the Lord. The parables on
prayer suggest the juxtaposition of the Lord's prayer. The
parables of the rich fool and fig tree illustrate the need to
prepare for the coming judgment as graphically as any passages
in that section, and the 'Tischreden' of Luke 14 do the same for
the theme of kingdom reversals. The tower builder and warring
king form the center of 14:25-35. The parables of Luke 15 and
16 obviously dominate their subsections in the outline. The
apparent harshness of 17:7-10 might have brought to Luke's mind
the similarly extreme demands of 17:1-6. 18:1-8 climaxes the
discussion of the days of the Son of man. Finally, 18:9-14
aptly introduces the qualifications for justification, entering
the kingdom, and eternal life, which the three pericopes of that
subsection specify--humility, childlikeness, and a willingness
to abandon one's wealth. The only subsections not represented
by at least one parable are 9:51-62, 10:1-24, 11:14-54, and
18:31-34. The first and last of these require no explanation,
forming obviously appropriate introductions and conclusions to
Jesus' 'journey'. 10:1-24 also fits naturally at the beginning,
and may be in its correct historical setting, as Drury
suggested. Drury may also be right about 11:14-54, or Luke may
simply have had additional material he wanted to include which
didn't fit obviously with one of the parables of his chiastic
source. Otherwise one can readily reconstruct how Luke could
have gathered the material for his central section together,
arranging it around his parable source via topical links.
Although he did not create any new chiasmus, he nevertheless
preserved the chiastic structure of his source. This chiasmus
seems likely to have originally served a mnemonic purpose, for
since a parable document would not have been a connected
narrative, it is less likely that a chiastic arrangement could
have served profound theological or aesthetic purposes. Further
support for the mnemonic use is provided by some catchwords and
phrases which appear to link consecutive parables, for example,
διασκορπίζω in Luke 15:13 and 16:1, ἄνθρωπός τις πλούσιος in
16:1 and 19, and προσεύχομαι in 18:1 and 11.

Finally, one may note how the parable source in every
instance matches parables of like audience. While Jesus
frequently faces both disciples and opponents in the same
crowd, Luke generally suggests for each parable that a
particular part of that audience is primarily in view:

10:25-37	18:9-14	controversy	(lawyer-10:25; self-righteous-18:9)
11:5-8	18:1-8	discipleship	(disciples-11:1, 17:22; cf. 11:5, 18:1)
11:11-13	17:7-10	discipleship	(disciples-11:1, 17:5; cf. 11:11, 17:7)
12:13-21	16:19-31	controversy	(one of multitude-12:13; Pharisees-16:14)
12:35-38	16:1-13	discipleship	(disciples-12:22,16:1)
13:1-9	15:1-32	controversy	(some present-13:1; Pharisees-15:2)
14:1-6	14:28-33	controversy	(Pharisees-14:1; great multitudes-14:25)
	14:7-24	controversy	(Pharisees-14:1).

Parable research, of course, does not generally place much trust in the accuracy of the audiences which the evangelists assign to Jesus' parables./154/ Yet if this information was already present in Luke's source--and six correspondences seem unlikely to be coincidental--then the case for its historicity must be enhanced./155/

Conclusion

The hypothesis of Luke's chiastic parable source combines with the proposed topical outline to help show how Lucan and pre-Lucan stages of the tradition grouped and joined the various pericopes of Luke's central section. No longer need this section be deemed disjointed or amorphous; Luke was neither confused nor disorganized. He was not attempting to trace Jesus' journey either chronologically or geographically and so cannot be accused of being a bad historian on either account. Of course Jesus' early ministry was in Galilee while his last weeks were spent in and near Jerusalem, so that he obviously had to travel from the one area to the other at some point. Many of the teachings of Luke's central section may well have been uttered by Jesus on this journey, but they need not have been, and certainly not necessarily in the order in which they now appear. These teachings reflect Jesus' consciousness of his impending destiny, regardless of his precise geographical location at any given time. Neither has Luke followed the sequence of the book of Deuteronomy to create a 'Christian midrash,' although if he had, this would not automatically demonstrate the inauthenticity of the various sayings and teachings of Jesus involved, unless one follows Drury and excludes the possibility of Luke's having utilized written sources for his L material. It would, however, make it highly

unlikely that *all* the material went back to Jesus, so that Luke
simply happened on traditions which fit his pattern every step
of the way. But it is no doubt much better, at least for his
parables, to assume that Luke has drawn on very early tradition
which was structured in such a way so as to facilitate accurate
transmission. And while labelling something pre-Lucan in no way
demonstrates its authenticity, the probability of it being
authentic can only be enhanced. The parables of course have
often been regarded as an authentic part of the gospel
tradition, but the peculiarly Lucan parables have recently come
under repeated fire for being inventions of the third
evangelist./156/ Here is some additional evidence to uphold the
traditional view./157/ Finally, if Luke has correctly
identified the audiences of these parables, then at least here
interpreters need not resort to the types of tradition-critical
dissection which the rejection of Luke's contextual information
requires. In short, the chiastic parable source not only
unlocks the secrets of the outline of Luke's central section,
but opens a door out of the confusing maze of interpretations of
the parables themselves./158/

Notes

/1/ Most agree that Luke 9:51 introduces a new major section of
the gospel, but suggestions as to its end include 18:14, 31, 34;
19:10, 27, 28, 44, and 48. I have elsewhere argued in favor of
18:34 as the best terminus and adopt that position here. See
Craig L. Blomberg, 'Tradition History in the Parables Peculiar
to Luke's Central Section,' (Ph.D. Diss.: Aberdeen, 1982)50-58.
/2/ Cf. J. M. Creed, *The Gospel according to St. Luke* (London:
MacMillan, 1930) 139; Joseph Blinzler, 'Die literarische
Eigenart des sogenannten Reiseberichts im Lukasevangelium,' in
Synoptische Studien, ed. J. Schmid and A. Vögtle (München: Karl
Zink, 1953) 42-52. William Hendriksen, *The Gospel of Luke*
(London: Banner of Truth, 1979) 541, even tells of a seminarian
who abandoned his study because of his inability to make any
sense of this section!
/3/ James L. Resseguie, 'Interpretation of Luke's Central
Section (Luke 9:51-19:44) Since 1856,' *StudBibetTheol* 5 (1975):
36.
/4/ Joseph A. Fitzmyer, *The Gospel according to Luke*, vol.1
(Garden City: Doubleday, 1981) 138-40.
/5/ Helmuth Egelkraut, *Jesus' Mission to Jerusalem* (Frankfurt:
P. Lang, 1976) 213.
/6/ C. F. Evans, 'The Central Section of St. Luke's Gospel,' in

Studies in the Gospels, ed. D. E. Nineham (Oxford: Blackwell, 1955) 37-53.

/7/ John Drury, *Tradition and Design in Luke's Gospel* (London: Darton, Longman & Todd, 1976); M. D. Goulder, *The Evangelists' Calendar* (London: SPCK, 1978).

/8/ Strictly speaking, 'chiasmus' refers only to a simple ABB'A' pattern, but it will be used here, as frequently elsewhere, to refer to more extended forms of inverted parallelism as well.

/9/ C. H. Talbert, *Literary Patterns, Theological Themes and the Genre of Luke-Acts* (Missoula: SBL, 1974) 58-65; Kenneth E. Bailey, *Poet and Peasant* (Grand Rapids: Eerdmans, 1976) 79-85; M. D. Goulder, 'The Chiastic Structure of the Lucan Journey,' *TU* 87 (1964):   195-202.

/10/ More recently, many other possible interpretations have been recognized. See esp. Gerhard Schneider, 'Zur Bedeutung von καθεξῆς im lukanischen Doppelwerk,' *ZNW* 68 (1977): 128-31; Richard J. Dillon, 'Previewing Luke's Project from His Prologue (Luke 1:1-4),' *CBQ* 43 (1981):   219-23.

/11/ Dean R. Wickes, *The Sources of Luke's Perean Section* (Chicago: UCP, 1912).

/12/ C. J. Cadoux, 'The Visits of Jesus to Jerusalem,' *Exp*, ser. 9, 3 (1925):   175-92.

/13/ E. J. Cook, 'Synoptic Indications of the Visits of Jesus to Jerusalem,' *ExpTim* 41 (1929-30):   121-23.

/14/ W. Gasse, 'Zum Reisebericht des Lukas,' *ZNW* 34 (1935): 293-99.

/15/ C. C. McCown, 'The Geography of Luke's Central Section,' *JBL* 57 (1938):   63-64.

/16/ Ibid., 66.

/17/ Two exceptions are Louis Girard, *L'Évangile des Voyages de Jésus* (Paris: Gabalda, 1951) 65, who divides the section into three journeys (9:51-11:13, 11:14-13:35, and 14:1-18:14), and George Ogg, 'The Central Section of the Gospel according to St. Luke,' *NTS* 18 (1971-72): 39-53, who sees two streams of tradition about Jesus' last journey (9:51-10:42 and 17:11-19:28) with leftover material gathered in between.

/18/ Hans Conzelmann, *The Theology of St. Luke*, trans. Geoffrey Buswell (London: Faber & Faber, 1960) 65.

/19/ Johannes Schneider, 'Zur Analyse der lukanischen Reiseberichtes,' in *Synoptische Studien*, 207-29; Eduard Lohse, 'Missionarisches Handeln Jesu nach dem Evangelium des Lukas,' *TZ* 10 (1954):   1-13; Bo Reicke, 'Instruction and Discussion in the Travel Narrative,' *TU* 73 (1959):   206-16. Cf. also G. W. Trompf, 'La section médiane de l'Évangile de Luc: l'organisation des documents,' *RHPR* 11 (1973-74):   141-54.

/20/ Walter Grundmann, 'Fragen der Komposition des lukanischen Reiseberichts,' *ZNW* 50 (1959): 252-58.
/21/ J. H. Davies, 'The Purpose of the Central Section of Luke's Gospel,' *TU* 87 (1964): 169. Cf. Reicke, 'Instruction,' 110, 117.
/22/ William C. Robinson, Jr., 'The Theological Context for Interpreting Luke's Travel Narrative (9:51ff.),' *JBL* 79 (1960): 20-31.
/23/ Peter von der Osten-Sacken, 'Zur Christologie des lukanischen Reiseberichts,' *EvT* 33 (1973): 476-96.
/24/ Similarly unhelpful for these purposes are Floyd V. Filson, 'The Journey Motif in Luke-Acts,' in *Apostolic History and the Gospel*, ed. W. W. Gasque and R. P. Martin (Exeter: Paternoster, 1970) 68-77, and Frank Stagg, 'The Journey Toward Jerusalem in Luke's Gospel,' *RevExp* 64 (1967): 499-512.
/25/ E. Earle Ellis, *The Gospel of Luke* (London: Oliphants, 1974) 35-36. The middle four sections are also labeled 'Teachings of Messiah;' and the final section, 'The Road to Jerusalem'.
/26/ Ibid., 32-33.
/27/ E.g., 10:25-37 under 'Who Will Enter the Kingdom?' 11:37-54 under 'The Kingdom and Judgment,' and 9:51-56 under 'The Rejected King'.
/28/ M. J. Lagrange, *Évangile selon Saint Luc* (Paris: Gabalda, 1941) xxxixxli. Cf. also the partial outlines of Schneider, 'Reiseberichtes,' 220; Josef Schmid, *Das Evangelium nach Lukas* (Regensburg: Pustet, 1960) 8.
/29/ The same is true for the section headings of Eduard Schweizer, *Das Evangelium nach Lukas* (Göttingen: Vandenhoeck & Ruprecht, 1982) 109-76, which are equally general; and of Philippe Bossuyt and Jean Radermakers, *Jésus: Parole de la Grâce selon saint Luc*, vol. 2 (Bruxelles: Institut d'études théologiques, 1981) 260, who adopt the highly implausible boundaries of 9:18-17:10 for Luke's central section.
/30/ See below, pp. 22-24.
/31/ See e.g. Walter C. Kaiser, Jr., *Toward an Exegetical Theology* (Grand Rapids: Baker, 1981) 71-77; Grant R. Osborne and Stephen B. Woodward, *Handbook for Bible Study* (Grand Rapids: Baker, 1979) 69-72.
/32/ Gerhard Sellin, 'Komposition, Quellen und Funktion des lukanischen Reiseberichtes (Lk. IX 51 - XIX 28),' *NovT* 20 (1978): 105-13
/33/ See below, pp. 22-23.
/34/ See below, p. 22.
/35/ David Gill, 'Observations on the Lukan Travel Narrative and Some Related Passages,' *HTR* 63 (1970): 119-221.

/36/ Evans, 'Section,' 42-50.

/37/ Leon Morris, *The New Testament and the Jewish Lectionaries* (London: Tyndale, 1964) 53. More recently, however, Morris has become more sceptical of this approach.

/38/ James A. Sanders, 'The Ethic of Election in Luke's Great Banquet Parable,' in *Essays in Old Testament Ethics*, ed. J. Crenshaw and J. T. Willis (New York: KTAV, 1974) 254.

/39/ J. Duncan M. Derrett, *Law in the New Testament* (London: Darton, Longman & Todd, 1970) 100, 129, 226.

/40/ John Bligh, *Christian Deuteronomy* (Langley, Bucks: St. Paul, 1970).

/41/ E.g. Chronicles/Kings, Jubilees/Genesis-Exodus, and the Genesis Apocryphon. Cf. further Geza Vermes, *Scripture and Tradition in Judaism* (Leiden: Brill, 1973); Renée Bloch, 'Midrash,' trans. Mary H. Callaway, in *Approaches to Ancient Judaism: Theory and Practice*, ed. William S. Green (Missoula: Scholars, 1978) 38-48.

/42/ Cf., however, Jacob Neusner, *The Rabbinic Traditions about the Pharisees Before 70*, 3 vols. (Leiden: Brill, 1971).

/43/ Cf., e.g., Moshe D. Herr, 'Midrash,' *EncJud* 11, 1507; Addison G. Wright, 'The Literary Genre Midrash,' *CBQ* 28 (1966): 120-22; Daniel Patte, *Early Jewish Hermeneutic in Palestine* Missoula: SBL, 1975) 117-18.

/44/ Wright, 'Midrash,' 438; Bloch, 'Midrash,' 31-33; Gary G. Porton, 'Defining Midrash,' in *The Study of Ancient Judaism*, vol. 1, ed. Jacob Neusner (New York: KTAV, 1981) 55-92. This is true both for 'midrash' and for 'Midrash,' following Bruce Chilton's distinctions elsewhere in this volume.

/45/ E.g. Merrill P. Miller, 'Targum, Midrash and the Use of the Old Testament in the New Testament,' *JSJ* 2 (1970-71): 44; R. Le Déaut, 'A propos d'une définition du midrash,' *Bib* 50 (1969): 406-7; Lars Hartman, *Prophecy Interpreted*, trans. Neil Tomkinson (Lund: Gleerup, 1966), 174-77.

/46/ Cf. Luke 18:18-30 which falls outside the scope of Evans' study. Luke 12:35 (cf. Exodus 12:11) is one other possible, but not obvious, quotation.

/47/ Sanders, 'Ethic;' Derrett, *Law*; idem, *Studies in the New Testament*, 2 vols. (Leiden: Brill, 1978).

/48/ Vermes, *Scripture*; cf. Jeffrey R. Sharp, 'Comparative Midrash as a Technique for Parable Studies' (Ph.D. Diss.: Southern Baptist, 1979) 44.

/49/ Emil Schürer, *The History of the Jewish People in the Age of Jesus Christ*, vol. 1, rev. & ed. G. Vermes, F. Millar, and M. Black (Edinburgh: T & T Clark, 1973) 94.

/50/ *Sifre zu Deuteronomium*, trans. Henrik Ljungmann, vol. 1 (Stuttgart: Kohlhammer, 1964). The full text is available in unpointed Hebrew in Louis Finkelstein, ed., *Sifre on Deuteronomy* (New York: Jewish Theological Seminary of America, 1969).

/51/ 'Deuteronomy,' trans. J. Rabinowitz, in *The Midrash Rabbah*, vol. 3, ed. H. Freedman and M. Simon (London: Soncino, 1977).

/52/ The forty-seven verses are: 1:1, 9, 10, 11, 12; 2:3, 4, 31; 3:2, 23, 24, 26, 27; 4:7, 25, 27, 30, 31, 41, 42; 6:4, 5; 7:12, 14; 9:1; 10:1; 11:26; 12:20; 16:18; 17:14; 20:10; 21:10; 22:6, 8; 24:9; 28:1, 3, 6, 12; 29:1, 3, 4; 30:11, 14; 31:14; 32:1; 33:1. The nine parallels are:

Deb. R.	Deut.	Luke	
1:21	2:31	10:29-37	Jew, journeying, overtaken, helped by foreigner, money
1:22	2:31	11:14-23	binding of kings, angels/demons
2:1	3:23	11:1-13	extensive discussion of prayer
2:15	4:7	10:17-20	certainty of victory over enemies
2:24	4:31	15:11-32	father yearning for son to repent
3:9	9:1	11:14-23	dispossession of enemy kings and armies
4:4	11:26	11:33-36	soul/Torah are lamp/light
4:9	12:20	11:42	justice for oppressed, bread for hungry, tithes
5:6	16:18	18:1-8	requiring impartiality of judges.

/53/ Hermann L. Strack, *Introduction to the Talmud and Midrash* (Philadelphia: Jewish Publication Society of America, 1931) 204-8. *Sipra* skips over Deut. 1:31-3:22, 4:1-6:3, 6:10-11:25, 26:17-31:13, and 31:15-30.

/54/ Ljungmann, *Sipre*, 58: 'Wenn schon diese, die die Welt durch ihre guten Werke aufrecht halten konnten, den Heiligen, g. s. E., baten, dass er ihnen nur umsonst gäbe, um wieviel mehr muss der, der nicht zum tausendmaltausendsten oder zum zehntausendmalzehntausendsten Teil Schüler ihrer Schüler ist, den Heiligen, g. s. E., bitten, dass er ihm nur umsonst gebe!'

/55/ *Pesikta Rabbati*, 2 vols., trans. William G. Braude (New Haven: YUP, 1968), *pars*. 12 and 25.

/56/ *Pesikta de-Rab Kahana*, trans. William G. Braude and Israel J. Kapstein (London: Routledge & Kegan Paul, 1975) xi-xiii.

/57/ In Neophyti I, e.g., only 1:1, 5:6-7, 5:17-21, 6:4, 27:15, 32:1, and 33:2 show substantial expansions of the original text; none parallels anything of Evans.

/58/ Birger Gerhardsson, *The Testing of God's Son* trans. John Toy (Lund: Gleerup, 1966) 14; J. W. Doeve, *Jewish Hermeneutics in the Synoptic Gospels and Acts* (Assen: Van Gorcum, 1953) 118.

/59/ The parallels are always in the Greek. One wonders if comparison should not also be made with the Hebrew versions, since synagogue readings almost always required use of the mother tongue.   Cf. Morris, *Lectionaries*, 31:34.

/60/ See J. Duncan M. Derrett, 'Nisi Dominus Aedificaverit
Domum: Towers and Wars (Lk XIV, 28-32),' *NovT* 19 (1977):   241-
61.

/61/ Derrett, *Law*, 126-55; ibid., 48-77; idem, 'Nisi,'
respectively.

/62/ *Contra* Drury, *Tradition*, 182-83, Sanders and Derrett use
comparative midrash to further the case for these parables'
authenticity, since Jesus would have been more likely familiar
with such a method than Luke.

/63/ Glenn. H. Wilms, 'Deuteronomic Traditions in St. Luke's
Gospel' (Ph.D. Diss.:   Edinburgh, 1972) 17-32, conducts a
similar survey and concludes that 16 of the 22 'parallells' show
no correspondence of subject matter at all.

/64/ However, for dissenting views, on 14:15-24, see Humphrey
Palmer, 'Just Married, Cannot Come,' *NovT* 18 (1976):   241-57; on
14:28-33, H. St. J. Thackeray, 'A Study in the Parables of the
Two Kings,' *JTS* 14 (1912-13):   390-3; on 15:4-32, H. B. Kossen,
'Quelques remarques sur l'ordre des paraboles dans Luc XV et sur
la structure de Matthieu XVIII 8-14,' *NovT* 1 (1956):   75-80; and
on 16:1-9, J.-P. Molina, 'L'Injuste Mamon,' *ETR* 53 (1978):   372.

/65/ Drury, *Tradition*, 12.

/66/ Ibid., 182-83.

/67/ For representative reviews, see H. Benedict Green, *ExpTim*
88 (1977):   314-15 (positive and fairly uncritical); John Fenton,
Theol 80 (1977):   65-66 (extremely partisan); Graham Stanton,
JTS 30 (1979):   270-3, and C. H. Talbert *JBL* 98 (1979):   151-53
(both critical but not unappreciative); Brian McNeil, 'Midrash
in Luke?' *HeyJ* 19 (1978):   399-404 (generally unappreciative).

/68/ E.g. William R. Farmer, *The Synoptic Problem* (New York:
Macmillan, 1964); E.P. Sanders, 'The Argument from Order and the
Relationship between Matthew and Luke,' *NTS* 15 (1968-69):   249-
61; and for more recent developments, Bernard Orchard, 'The
Two-Gospel Hypothesis,' *DownRev* 98 (1980):   267-79.

/69/ See esp. Joseph A. Fitzmyer, 'The Priority of Mark and the
"Q" Source in Luke,' in *Jesus and Man's Hope*, vol. 1, ed. D. Y.
Hadidian (Pittsburgh: Pickwick, 1970) 131-70; Howard Bigg,
'The Q Debate Since 1955,' *Themelios* 6 (1981):   18-28; Kazuhiko
Uchida, 'The Study of the Synoptic Problem in the Twentieth
Century: A Critical Assessment' (Ph.D. Diss.:   Aberdeen, 1981).

/70/ See esp. Siegfried Schulz, *Q: Die Spruchquelle der
Evangelisten* (Zürich: Theologischer Verlag, 1972); Paul
Hoffmann, *Studien zur Theologie der Logienquelle* (Münster:
Aschendorff, 1972).

/71/ See esp. Norman Perrin, *Rediscovering the Teaching of Jesus*

(London: SCM, 1967); Joachim Jeremias, *The Parables of Jesus*,
trans. S. H. Hooke (London: SCM, 1972); Hans Weder, *Die
Gleichnisse Jesu als Metaphern* (Göttingen: Vandenhoeck &
Ruprecht, 1978).
/72/ Drury, *Tradition*, 75-80, concedes that the parables could
go back to Jesus, but his discussion concentrates exclusively on
their Lucan characteristics and hypothetical Old Testament
sources.
/73/ This siglum refers to Luke's singly-attested material
without presupposing any particular source-critical explanation
of its origin.
/74/ Drury, *Tradition*, 120-21, cautioning against overstressing
this point.
/75/ Ibid., 162.
/76/ Ibid., 96, 130, 137.
/77/ Ibid., 144.
/78/ John Drury, *JSNT* 7 (1980): 71-73.
/79/ C. F. Evans, 'Goulder and the Gospels,' *Theol* 82 (1979):
431-32.
/80/ A brief but incisive critique appears in Morna Hooker's
review, *EpwRev* 7 (1980): 91-93. Several of Hooker's criticisms
appeared already in Morris' *Lectionaries*, concerning similar
hypotheses for John's gospel. It is hard to understand how
Goulder can endorse this demolition work (*Calendar*, 20-21), and
yet not see that his own work on the Synoptics involves many of
the identical problems.
/81/ Goulder, *Calendar*, 95-101.
/82/ Goulder refers to the Greek only twice, noting the very
general links between Deut. 6:16 and Luke 10:25 (ἐκπειράζω) and
between Deut. 13:4 and Luke 12:5 (τοῦτον φοβέω).
/83/ Goulder, *Calendar*, 100.
/84/ Ibid., 102.
/85/ Ibid.
/86/ Ibid., 146-53.
/87/ Ibid., 151.
/88/ Cf. his comments, ibid., 174, on the unevenness of fit
between Luke and Isaiah: 'It is a common human tendency to go
rather too slowly at any large task, and to have to speed up at
the end.'
/89/ Ibid., 141.
/90/ Ibid., 153.
/91/ Ibid., 154-55.
/92/ Discussion of Goulder's further comparison with Isaiah and
Ecclesiasticus is unnecessary, since he finds only one
'influential' parallel with Luke's central section (ibid., 171,
206-11). For more general comments on Goulder's latest work,

see Leon Morris' article elsewhere in this volume.

/93/ See esp. Jacob Jervell, *Luke and the People of God* (Minneapolis: Augsburg, 1972). David R. Catchpole, 'Paul, James and the Apostolic Decree,' *NTS* 23 (1977): 428-29 speaks of a 'quite remarkable consensus' which sees Lucan theology as 'fundamentally Mosaic,' citing *inter alios* T. W. Manson, W. G. Kümmel, F. Hahn, L. Goppelt, G. Bornkamm, and H. Conzelmann.

/94/ Craig L. Blomberg, 'The Law in Luke-Acts,' unpublished essay delivered to the Tyndale Fellowship NT Study Group (Cambridge, 1981). Cf. Max Turner, 'The Sabbath, The Law and Sunday in Luke-Acts,' in *From Sabbath to Lord's Day*, ed. D. A. Carson (Grand Rapids: Zondervan, 1982) 99-157.

/95/ Blomberg, 'Law,' 20.

/96/ Angelico DiMarco, 'Der Chiasmus in der Bibel,' trans. Wolfgang Meyer *LingBib* 36 (1975): 21-97; 37 (1976): 49-68. One of the Old Testament books which employs extended chiasmus several times is Zechariah. Cf. Joyce G. Baldwin, *Haggai, Zechariah, Malachi* (Leicester: IVP, 1972) 74-81.

/97/ Nils W. Lund, *Chiasmus in the New Testament* (Chapel Hill: UNCP, 1942) 296; idem, 'The Influence of Chiasmus upon the Structure of the Gospels,' *ATR* 13 (1931): 27-48.

/98/ Talbert, *Patterns*, 67-70; Bailey, *Poet*, 50.

/99/ Talbert, *Patterns*, 81.

/100/ Ibid. Cf. Albert B. Lord, *The Singer of Tales* (Cambridge, Mass.: HUP, 1960) 119.

/101/ George Howard, 'Stylistic Inversion and the Synoptic Tradition,' *JBL* 97 (1978): 389.

/102/ Lund, *Chiasmus*, 40-41. Cf. Bailey, *Poet*, 50.

/103/ See esp. René Laurentin, *Structure et théologie de Luc I-II* (Paris: Gabalda, 1964).

/104/ See esp. J. G. Davies, 'The Prefigurement of the Ascension in the Third Gospel,' *JTS* 6 (1955): 229-33.

/105/ See esp. Bo Reicke, *Glaube und Leben der Urgemeinde: Bemerkungen zur Apostelgeschichte 1-7* (Zürich: Zwingli, 1957).

/106/ See esp. M. D. Goulder, *Type and History in Acts* (London: SPCK, 1964).

/107/ Walter Radl, *Paulus und Jesus im lukanischen Doppelwerk* (Bern: H. Lang, 1975); Gudrun Muhlack, *Die Parallelen von Lukas-Evangelium und Apostelgeschichte* (Frankfurt: P. Lang, 1979).

/108/ Talbert, *Patterns*, 39-44, 26-29, 45-48, and 56-58, respectively. Donald R. Miesner, 'The Missionary Journeys Narrative: Patterns and Implications,' in *Perspectives on Luke-Acts*, ed. C. H. Talbert (Edinburgh: T & T Clark, 1978), 199-214, modifies the last of these to embrace all of 12:25-21:16.

/109/ Robert Morgenthaler, *Die lukanische Geschichtsschreibung als Zeugnis*, 2 vols. (Zürich: Zwingli, 1948).

/110/ Ibid., vol. 1, 156-57.

/111/ Goulder, 'Structure,' 196.

/112/ Cf. Mary Tolbert, *Perspectives on the Parables* (Philadelphia: Fortress, 1979) 98-101.

/113/ Talbert, *Patterns*, 51-52.

/114/ Talbert argues that Luke deliberately altered Mark's παιδία in the latter verse to bring the text closer into line with 10:21 (ibid., 53), but if this was Luke's motive, surely he could have used the identical word in both places.

/115/ In 12:5 the term is γέεννα; in 16:23, ἄδης.

/116/ Talbert, *Patterns*, 8-9.

/117/ Bailey, *Poet*, 79-85.

/118/ Ibid., 80-82.

/119/ Cf. Russell P. Shedd's review in *Themelios* 3 (1977): 27. Schweizer, *Lukas*, 108-9, accepts five of Bailey's ten divisions as plausible.

/120/ Bailey, *Poet*, 79, who omits 10:13-15, 21-24; 11:27-28, 33-36; 12:1-12; 16:17-18; 17:1-10; 18:15-17, 31-34; and 19:11-21, a total of 1011 out of 7334 words, following the totals of Robert Morgenthaler, *Statistische Synopse* (Zürich: Gotthelf, 1971) 107-12.

/121/ Bailey, *Poet*, 82-83.

/122/ Luke 10:30, 13:4, 17:11, 18:31, and 19:11.

/123/ The only verbal link (σῶσαι in 9:55b and 19:10) depends on the adoption of a rather poorly attested textual variant in 9:55.

/124/ I.H. Marshall, *The Gospel of Luke* (Exeter, 1978), 677.

/125/ Luke 12:35-38 is sometimes viewed as a variant of Mark 13:33-37. But even if this be so, Mark is best seen as having used a pre-Lucan tradition, so that no problem is posed for our hypothesis. See David Wenham, *Gospel Perspectives IV: The Rediscovery of Jesus' Eschatological Discourse* (unpublished monograph in preparation).

/126/ R. S. Franks, 'The Parable of the Pharisee and the Publican,' *ExpTim* 38 (1926-27): 373.

/127/ Rudolf Bultmann, *The History of the Synoptic Tradition*, trans. John Marsh (Oxford: Blackwell, 1963) 178; A. M. Hunter, *Interpreting the Parables* (London: SCM, 1960) 11; Simon Kistemaker, *The Parables of Jesus* (Grand Rapids: Baker, 1981) xiv.

/128/ Adolf Schlatter, *Das Evangelium des Lukas* (Stuttgart: Calwer Verlag, repr. 1960) 288-89.

/129/ E.g. A. R. C. Leaney, *The Gospel according to St. Luke* (London: Black, 1958) 188; Wilhelm Ott, *Gebet und Heil*

(München: Kösel, 1965) *passim*; Schlatter, *Lukas*, 298; Marshall,
Luke, 462; Walter Schmithals, *Das Evangelium nach Lukas*
(Zürich: Theologischer Verlag, 1980) 131.
/130/ Cf. the detailed study of this class of parables by Alfons
Weiser, *Die Knechtsgleichnisse der synoptischen Evangelien*
(München: Kösel, 1971).
/131/ Interestingly enough, the very similar servant parables
immediately following Luke 12:35-38 do display very striking
verbal links with the parable of the unjust steward. Luke 12:42
also utilizes οἰκονόμος; this reference plus the three in Luke
16 account for all of the appearances of the term in the
gospels. Luke 12:42 also terms the steward φρόνιμος, a word
which recurs in the gospels only in Luke 16:8!
Several explanations of this phenomena are possible: (1) It
could indicate that the chiasmus postulated here is Lucan rather
than pre-Lucan. All the rest of the evidence, though, points
against this conclusion. (2) It could indicate that a pre-Lucan
document has already combined the chiastic parable source with
other material. A parallel procedure is involved in the various
proto-Luke hypotheses. While very plausible, such a theory is
virtually impossible to demonstrate because of the extra
hypothetical stage of tradition the has to be postulated. (3)
It could indicate that Luke 12:35-48 stood together in Luke's
special source right from the start. Vv. 39-46, however,
contain as nearly exact verbal parallelism between Luke and
another gospel as is found anywhere among his parables. Some
type of dependence, either on Q or Matthew, must be involved.
(4) It could indicate that Luke simply found a very appropriate
place to insert vv. 39-46 which elsewhere belongs to the end of
Jesus' ministry (Matt. 24:43-51). This alternative is perhaps
best. It fits the procedure postulated for Luke for the rest of
his central section below, pp. 22-24, and meshes with the
process of dissolution of Jesus' original eschatological
discourse suggested by Wenham, *Gospel Perspectives* IV.
/132/ William R. Farmer, 'Notes on a Literary and Form-Critical
Analysis of Some of the Synoptic Material Peculiar to Luke,' *NTS*
8 (1961-62): 305. Several of these parallels are also noted by
Bossuyt and Radermakers, *Jésus*, 347.
/133/ Farmer, 'Notes,' 316. Luke 15:4-7 is of course generally
seen as a variant of Matt. 18:12-14, but a good case can be made
for viewing these traditions as literarily independent. See
Joachim Jeremias, 'Tradition und Redaktion in Lukas 15,' *ZNW* 62
(1971): 181; cf. Marshall, *Luke*, 600.
/134/ 13:2-3 and 4-5 are of course not parables in their present
form. But Kenneth E. Bailey, *Through Peasant Eyes* (Grand

Rapids: Eerdmans 1980) 74-80, terms them 'parabolic speech'. Might they have been 'de-parabolized' in a later stage of the tradition, as seems to have happened elsewhere? Cf. Richard Bauckham, 'Synoptic Parousia Parables and the Apocalypse,' *NTS* 23 (1977): 167.

/135/ By bearing fruit in 13:9 (cf. 3:8--'bear fruits that befit repentance'), and by admitting sin in 15:18 and 21.

/136/ Again 14:16-24 is often considered to have a parallel (Matt. 22:1-10), but it is better to view these traditions as independent literarily (and probably historically as well). See Palmer, 'Married,' 255; E. Galbiati, 'Gli invitati al convito (Luca 14, 16-24),' *BeO* 7 (1965): 130; Leon Morris, *The Gospel according to St. Luke* (Grand Rapids: Eerdmans, 1974) 233; Kistemaker, *Parables*, 100, 198.

/137/ Rinaldo Fabris, 'La parabola degli invitati alla cena: Analise redazionale di Lc. 14, 16-24,' in *La parabola degli invitati al banchetto*, ed. Jacques Dupont (Brescia: Paideia Editrice, 1978) 138-39, also emphasizes the close parallelism between Luke 14:1-24 and 15:1-32.

/138/ P. M. Làconi, 'La parabole in San Luca,' *Parole di Vita* 6 (1971): 427-36.

/139/ 14:5 is considered too short to be a parable by some, but formally it matches 11:5-8, 11:11-13, 14:28-32, 15:4-10, and 17:7-10, as a rhetorical question with metaphorical imagery introduced by τίς ἐξ ὑμῶν.

/140/ Gerhard Sellin, 'Lukas als Gleichniserzähler: die Erzählung vom barmherziger Samariter (Lk 10:25-37),' *ZNW* 65 (1974): 166-89, rightly stresses the importance of this distinct category of parable.

/141/ See David Flusser, *Die rabbinischen Gleichnissen und die Gleichniserzähler Jesu*, vol. 1 (Bern: H. Lang, 1981) 85.

/142/ Again the word counts follow Morgenthaler, *Synopse*, 107-12. The percentage derives from 2682/6471, using 18:34 as the end of the central section.

/143/ See esp. Étienne Trocmé, *Jesus and His Contemporaries*, trans. R. A. Wilson (London: SCM, 1973) 91. Cf. the earlier discussions of Vincent H. Stanton, *The Gospels as Historical Documents*, vol. 2 (Cambridge: CUP, 1909) 231; and J. Vernon Bartlett, 'The Sources of St. Luke's Gospel,' in *Studies in the Synoptic Problem*, ed. W. Sanday (Oxford: Clarendon, 1911) 349.

/144/ Lund, *Chiasmus*, 282-95.

/145/ See esp. Joachim Jeremias, *Die Sprache des Lukasevangeliums* (Göttingen: Vandenhoeck & Ruprecht, 1980); and cf. Blomberg, 'Tradition History,' 312-41.

/146/ Marshall, *Luke*, 9-10.

/147/ Cf. Bailey, *Poet*, 80: vv. 29-37 illustrate love for one's neighbor; vv. 38-42, love for the Lord.

/148/ Lagrange, *Luc*, xxxix-xl, similarly separates these two sections.

/149/ See above, p. 4.

/150/ So too Charles L'Eplattenier, 'Lecture d'une séquence lucanienne: Luc 13/22 à 14/24,' *ETR* 56 (1981): 283-87.

/151/ Cf. also Fabris, 'invitati,' 139-40, on the parallelism between 13:18-35 and 14:7-24.

/152/ So too Lagrange, *Luc*, xli.

/153/ Cf. further Jean Pirot, *Jésus et la richesse: Parabole de l'intendant astucieux (Luc XVI 1-15)* (Marseille: Imprimerie Marseillaise, 1944) 36-49; Gerhard Schneider, *Das Evangelium nach Lukas*, vol. 2 (Gütersloh: Gerd Mohn; Würzburg: Echter Verlag, 1977) 363.

/154/ So classically Jeremias, *Parables*, 33-42, and followed by almost all students of the parables.

/155/ For further support for this position, see J. Arthur Baird, *Audience Criticism and the Historical Jesus* (Philadelphia: Westminster, 1969); Philip B. Payne, 'Metaphor as a Model for Interpretation of the Parables of Jesus with Special Reference to the Parable of the Sower' (Ph.D. Diss.: Cambridge, 1975) esp. 239; Paul S. Minear, 'Jesus' Audiences, according to Luke,' *NovT* 16 (1974): 81-109.

/156/ See e.g. Sellin, 'Gleichniserzähler;' M. D. Goulder, 'Characteristics of the Parables in the Several Gospels,' *JTS* 19 (1968): 51-69; Drury, *Tradition*.

/157/ Cf. further Philip B. Payne, 'The Authenticity of the Parables of Jesus,' in *Gospel Perspectives*, vol. 2, ed. R. T. France and David Wenham (Sheffield: JSOT, 1981) 329-44.

/158/ See further Blomberg, 'Tradition History,' 390-93.

APPENDIX: COINCIDENTAL PARALLELS BETWEEN
LUKE 1:1-4:37 AND PSALMS 1-10

Psalm 1
delight in Law of Lord

yielding fruit in season
wicked will perish

Luke 1:5-25
Zach. & Eliz. walk in all
commandments
Zach. gets his turn to serve
Zach. is punished for
faithlessness

Psalm 2
"you are my son...begotten"
nations, ends of earth for
possessions
serve the Lord with fear

Luke 1:26-56
"you will bear a son"
he will reign over house of
Judah
Mary acquiesces

Psalm 3
rising foes; God answers
deliverance belongs to the
Lord
blessing upon thy people

Luke 1:57-80
Zach. is freed from his muteness
Zach. declares God's promised
deliverance
Zach. blesses God

Psalm 4
commune with your own hearts

offer right sacrifices
lifting up the Lord's light

sleeping, lying down in peace

Luke 2:1-40
Mary ponders everything in her
heart
purification and sacrifices
Lord's glory shines; light for
Gentiles
Jesus sleeps, Simeon departs in
peace

Psalm 5
entering, worshipping in
Lord's house
there is no truth in their
mouths

Luke 2:41-52
Jesus in temple, father's house

Jesus confounds the teachers

Psalm 6
"turn, O Lord,...turn back"

flood and drench
"Depart, all you workers of
evil"

Luke 3:1-20
baptism of repentance (implies
turning)
baptism
"You brood of vipers"

Psalm 7
  psalm of David
assembly of the peoples,
  regnancy

Luke 3:21-38
Jesus is son of David
genealogy, births and children

Psalm 8
God is majestic over all the
earth
God delegates his dominion

God alone is worthy of worship

Luke 4:1-13
devil tempts Jesus with world's
kingdoms
Satan given authority over
earth
worship God only, so Jesus

Psalm 9
enemies turned back, perished
Lord is stronghold for
oppressed, poor

Luke 4:14-30
crowd fails to destroy Jesus
Jesus preaches good news for
poor, oppressed

Psalm 10
emphasis on actions of wicked
Lord doesn't forget afflicted

Luke 4:31-37
emphasis on actions of demon
Jesus frees man from affliction

POSTSTRUCTURALISM AND BIBLICAL STUDIES:
FRANK KERMODE'S, *THE GENESIS OF SECRECY*

D. S. Greenwood
St. Catharine's College
Cambridge, CB2 1RL

> 'You can talk to Miss Quested about the Peacock
> Throne if you like - she's artistic, they say.'
> 'Is she a Postimpressionist?'
> 'Postimpressionism indeed!   Come along to tea.
> This world is getting too much for me altogether.'

> 'Derrida will have his day, even among the Biblical
> texts.'

I.   Introduction

Whenever the 'isms' of modern scholarship acquire the
prefix 'post' - as they do with an almost inevitable
regularity - those who are not properly acquainted even with
the original 'ism' tend to throw up their hands in a mixture
of amusement and despair, as does E. M. Forster's character
Fielding in the above piece of dialogue./1/   At the risk of
provoking this reaction, I want to attempt to describe some
of the beliefs held - some of the assertions made - by a
growing number of literary-critical theorists, who, with
varying degrees of commitment, adhere to the particular 'ism'
in my title - Poststructuralism.   My intent is to try and
provide something of a supplement to the useful surveys and
assessments of Structuralist thought and practice produced
for those in biblical studies by, among others, D. Patte,
J. Calloud and A. M. Johnson./2/   My mode of exposition
combines a consideration of four crucial Poststructuralist
'preoccupations' with frequent reference to one exemplary
and highly popular book, Frank Kermode's, *The Genesis of
Secrecy*./3/   Kermode discusses the practice of midrash,

guided by the work of G. Vermes, M. D. Goulder, J. Drury and
D. Stern./4/   He also raises more general and perennial
problems of historicity and in so doing pays close attention
to the Gospel of Mark.   As I will indicate below, Kermode
has some trenchant criticisms to make of modern professional
New Testament scholarship.   He firmly believes that,
(Preface, p.ix) 'the gospels need to be talked about by
critics of a quite unecclesiastical formation'.   This
remark does not mean that he is in any way unaware and
unappreciative of the contemporary proliferation of literary
approaches to the gospel narratives; he is to be found, for
instance, drawing frequently upon the last decade of
American parable studies.   Yet his work is, to some extent,
sui generis, in that he displays his customary ability, 'to
assimilate, connect and communicate in a crisp, epigrammatic
style information and ideas from a host of specialisms,
literary and non-literary'./5/   Consequently, Kermode's
criticism cannot be had wriggling and sprawling on any
familiar pin.   Therein lies its appeal and my justification
for this article./6/

   Why then make the effort to come to terms with the
techniques and claims of yet another 'Post-ism', given that
some of the controlling presuppositions of the 'ism' in
question are atheistic and even hedonistic?   In the course of
his recent massive and highly readable book dealing with some
of the challenges facing Christian theologians and exegetes
in a 'Culture of Pluralism', David Tracy suggests that the
bemused and sceptical biblical scholar should exert himself
to confront those readings and analyses of his institution's
'classic' texts made by those outside his discipline.
Taking his assimilative cue from the theorist Paul Ricoeur,
Tracy says that positive benefits will result if we

   recognise that semiotic and structuralist explanations of
   codes, deep and surface structures (can) enrich our
   understanding of the text by developing that
   understanding further, by challenging our former
   complacent understanding, by compelling us to think
   again, by suggesting analogies that provoke our attention
   and expose our sloth.   This is the case even when a
   particular reader disowns the sometimes imperialist
   claims of the methods while still finding their readings
   of the texts illuminating and transformative./7/

It may be that, 'biblical study will no longer be conducted under the exclusive or even dominant hegemony of one discipline such as historical philology...but will be studied through a multitude of disciplines inter-reacting mutually'.   Perhaps 'Field Criticism' is here to stay./8/ It is certainly the case that from their side of the fence, professional literary critics are turning with more and more relish to the sacred texts, although often admitting as they do so that they feel 'like knights errant, who find themselves in the middle of a tournament' with their lances unaccountably left at home!/9/   Frank Kermode himself, reviewing Raymond Brown's, *The Birth of the Messiah*, encouraged his fellow critics to cross over into pastures new:

> The subject (biblical studies) is dauntingly vast, and there is a learned argument at practically every point along the way... The outsider is struck with something close to awe at the meticulous industry of the Biblical scholars and his reaction may well be to let them get on with it, since there seems to be no easy way in... However ill-equipped we may feel, we must get some sense of it, and not allow it to become an institutional preserve./10/

The Genesis of Secrecy sees Kermode making just such an endeavour.   Reviewing the book from the biblical studies' side of the fence, Amos Wilder of the Harvard Divinity School had this to say:

> Those who would differ with (Kermode's) readings will need to come to terms not only with his impressive literary analysis but also with the influential views of language and narrativity to which he appeals... At various points he shows himself in agreement with much current linguistic theory and literary discussion of fiction according to which narrative has only intertextual meaning and little transparence on the real world./11/

It is to some of these influential preoccupations that I now want to turn.

II.   The Death of the 'Absolute Signified': the
      radical implications of the semiological
      'world-view'

In what is perhaps the most unsettling chapter of his
book, No. V, 'What Precisely Are The Facts?', Kermode,
quoting Jean Starobinski and Roland Barthes, says the
following (p. 117)

> We cannot escape the conclusion that 'the fact can
> exist only linguistically, as a term in a discourse',
> although 'we behave as if it were a simple reproduction
> of something or other on another plane of existence
> altogether, some extra-structural reality'.

Another equally assertive use of the 'we' plus negative verb
can be found just a few pages before this, after a brief
consideration of a passage from Thomas Pynchon's novel
The Crying of Lot 49 (p. 108).

> We can, indeed, no longer assume that we have the
> capacity to make value-free statements about history,
> or suppose that there is some special dispensation
> whereby the signs that constitute an historical text
> have reference to events in the world.

For the more extreme advocates of this kind of dogmatic
'Indeterminacy', God, the 'Absolute Signified' is dead, and
his 'death' is an event of unprecedented dimension.   On the
older view, now presumed impossible, signs, words and things
were united by an intrinsic resemblance principle, an
alliance willed by God himself./12/   As a result, a given
signifier did not simply refer to its immediate signified,
but to the author of this divinely instituted principle of
resemblance, God, who acts as the 'Absolute Signified'.
(If there is a single theme which draws together the
otherwise disparate field of 'structuralist' thought, it is
the principle - first enounced by Ferdinand de Saussure -
that language is a differential network of meaning.   There
is no self-evident or one-to-one link between 'signifier'
and 'signified', the word as (spoken or written) vehicle and
the concept it serves to evoke.   Both are caught up in a
play of distinctive features where differences of sound and

sense are the only markers of meaning.)   It used to be
believed that, by addressing and treating man as a 'Thou' at
Creation, God granted him ontological status and dignity and
constituted him as a subject able to subdue creation, to
make the signs speak, to interpret.   Now that its divine
centre has apparently collapsed, according to our
Poststructuralist theorists, language appears hollow and
arbitrary, a disoriented chain of void signifiers.
Nietzsche famously compared this situation to that of coins
having lost their imprints and which, therefore, are no
longer considered coins but mere metal./13/   Thus the 'death
of God', as conceived by Nietzsche, decisively conditions the
setting out of the semiological task - a task consisting of
showing 'what constitutes signs, what laws govern them', as
Saussure put it.   Rather than 'making the signs speak', man
must stand aside and allow the signs to speak for themselves!
A potentially infinite number of combinations between
different signifiers may give birth to countless shades of
signification.   The door is firmly closed to all traditional
meaning and reference and left open to the disquieting
possibility of ambiguity or even silence.   Kermode interacts
with this kind of general scepticism at every turn,
although he does seek to distance himself at times from the
'flourishing radical party' of critics whose Poststructuralist
outlook is very much of the Nietzschean kind just discussed
(p. 125)./14/

        The thinker who with his programmatic questionings of
what has come to be thought of as 'Classical Structuralism'
has most excited the avant-garde literary-critical
imagination is Jacques Derrida.   In his editor's
introduction to *Semeia* 23 (1982) 'Derrida and Biblical
Studies', Robert Detweiler voices his conviction that
Derrida (p. 1) 'poses perhaps the greatest contemporary
threat to traditional biblical scholarship'.   Herbert
Schneidau, writing in the same issue, is surely correct in
asserting that the vast majority of those critics who have
used the techniques of structural analysis for the
exploration and exegesis of biblical texts have to date
appeared 'blithely unconcerned about their own
metaphysical presuppositions'./15/   Their Proppian and
Greimasian analyses have been thoroughly positivist in
orientation.   Lévi-Strauss himself notoriously remarked in
an essay on the Oedipus Myth that he was not trying to

achieve an interpretation of the text concerned - an
interpretation, 'acceptable to the specialists' -, but only
to demonstrate, like a 'street pedlar' the 'functioning of
the mechanical toy which he is trying to sell to the
onlookers'./16/   D. A. Carson could therefore write in 1980
that, 'most structural analysts....have not developed an
exclusive approach to Structuralism which turns more on
ideology than method'./17/   The advent of the prefix 'post'
is surely indicative that this very 'shift' has in fact taken
place.   To persist for a moment with this too catastrophic
metaphor 'shift', *The Genesis of Secrecy* straddles this
'fault-line', with its clever domestication of many Derridean
ideas.   Schneidau believes that 'Derrida will have his day,
even among the Biblical texts', and goes on to warn us that,
'the first task for us is to make educated guesses about how
his proposals will be deployed and what series of effects we
can expect among the other elements'./18/   One of Derrida's
most important contentions is therefore that the
disciplines known as linguistics and Structuralism -
best exemplified for him in the work of Saussure and
Lévi-Strauss - still rely on fundamentally idealist
assumptions which are never questioned and which are
reflected in their conception of the sign itself as a
reliably transcendent Archimedean point above chaos.   He
argues repeatedly that there is no origin, no end, no place
outside discourse from which to fix, make determinate and
establish metaphysical boundaries for the play of linguistic
signifiers.   Promulgating what amounts to one of the most
virulent forms of philosophical 'materialism' to have arisen
in the history of Western thought, Derrida dismisses all
notions of a metaphysical 'presence' beyond language and
writing as fictions, whether they have been formulated under
such heads as subject, substance, eidos (idea), transcendence,
conscience, spirit, or under the ultimate fiction of God!
I quote the far-reaching opening statement from his often
cited and influential essay, 'Structure, Sign and Play in the
Discourse of the Human Sciences', to illustrate his
subversive materialism, not to mention his typically
convoluted syntax:

    ...the structurality of structure...has always been
    neutralised or reduced, and this process of giving it a
    centre or referring it to a point of presence, a fixed

> origin, also.   The function of this centre was...above
> all to make sure that the organising principle of the
> structure would limit what we might call the freeplay of
> the structure... The concept of the centred structure is
> constituted upon a fundamental immobility and a
> reasoning certitude anxiety can be mastered./19/

Elsewhere, Derrida states that there 'never has been and
never will be a unique word, a master name'./20/   Man's
constant return, consciously or not, to the perennial and
endemic illusion of 'logocentrism' must be exposed - the
metaphysical strongholds of both the classical and the
Christian Logos are to be ruthlessly torn down.   Yet, to his
credit, no philosopher has ever been more conscious of the
double-bind - the paradox inherent in all negatively
destructive philosophical critiques.   To those of his
detractors who would charge him with 'bad faith' because he
makes propositional statements at all - given that he
'doesn't believe in "truth" ' - his own notoriously difficult
French style is in itself an eloquent answer.   It is replete
with puns, unacknowledged literary allusions and ironic echoes.
This is his very personal way of confessing that all writing -
including his own - is irredeemably figural, that all
philosophers, despite their vehement protestations to the
contrary, are actually sophists in disguise.   In attempting
then, like Nietzsche before him, to remove all vestiges of
idealism from thought, he finds that he is constrained to
'remove' philosophy, to be left only with language.   The 'lie
of language' for both Nietzsche and Derrida consists of what
they see as the pretence that language is able to relate the
world of men to some wider, benevolent cosmic scheme.   'What
then is truth?', asked Nietzsche, echoing Bacon's 'jesting
Pilate':

> (it is) a mobile army of metaphors, metonymics,
> anthropomorphisms - in short, a sum of human relations
> which, poetically and rhetorically intensified, became
> transposed and adorned and which after long usage by a
> people seem fixed, canonical and binding on them.
> Truths are illusions which one has forgotten are
> illusions./21/

It follows that for Derrida and the growing number of
literary critics who practise the derivative revolutionary

mode of literary criticism known as Deconstruction, all
stratagems designed to establish an objective or scientific
hermeneutics can only be acts of defensive mastery.   All
interpreters seek to keep an unruly, maverick band of wild
words within the bounds of intelligibility.   Eugenio Donato
expands upon this basic axiom with a helpful clarity and an
obvious relish:

> Each sign is in itself not the thing that offers itself to
> interpretation but interpretation of other signs.   There
> is never an interpretandum which is not already an
> interpretans, so that a relationship of both violence and
> elucidation establishes itself with interpretation.
> Interpretation does not shed light on a matter that asks
> to be interpreted, that offers itself passively to
> interpretation, but it can only seize violently an
> interpretation that is already there, one which it must
> overturn, overthrow, shatter with the blows of a hammer...
> Interpretation, then, is nothing but sedimenting one layer
> of language upon another to produce an illusory depth
> which gives us the temporary spectacle of things beyond
> words./22/

Kermode's *The Genesis of Secrecy* 'consists', as he himself
remarks in his Preface 'of a number of approaches to general
problems of interpretation'.   His invocation of Hermes as
the ancient patron of thieves and tricksters as well as of
interpreters should therefore not surprise us;   it is
completely in keeping with the spirit of Derrida's teasings
and Donato's reflections.   That readers misinterpret
literature has probably been recognised as long as literature
has existed.   Poststructuralism, taking as read the
'contributions' of many another sceptical 'ism', turns this
human deficiency into a law - into a binding philosophical
tenet.   With what implications for textual criticism we must
now go on to examine.

III.   Intertextuality and Freeplay

Kermode's interest in these Poststructuralist concepts
partly accounts for his attraction to the practice of
midrash - 'the narrative interpretation of narrative', as he
terms it.   So it is that midrash becomes just one

compelling historical example of the 'inescapable fact' that
narrative can only have 'intertextual' meaning, with little, if
any transparence on the real world.   Plots are found, he says
(p. 86), 'on occult connections between the new narrative and
many old ones'.   This rage for reuniting is supposedly
incurable.   In his recent book, *The Pursuit of Signs*, Jonathan
Culler remarks that Intertextuality has the effect of calling
'our attention to the importance of prior texts, insisting that
the autonomy of texts is a misleading notion and that a work has
the meaning it does only because certain things have previously
been written'./23/   Roland Barthes warns that from this
perspective, 'the quotations of which a text is constructed are
anonymous, irrecoverable, and yet already read; they are
quotations without quotation marks'.   For Barthes, the text
(as opposed to the 'work') therefore becomes an indefinite
field in permanent metamorphosis, where language is seen as
being continually at work, endlessly deferring any closure of
meaning.   A plurality of interpretations of an already
Connucopian Text is therefore highly desirable, and so it is
no accident that Barthes suggests that the 'Text' might well,
'take as its motto the words of the man possessed by devils:
"My name is legion, for we are many." (Mark 5:9)'./24/
Narration will always drive us deeper and deeper into its own
secret structure, but will also simultaneously send us back to
previous narratives, previous works.   Because of this,
interpretation is forever filling in the gaps to produce
meaning.   Narrativity acquires a capital 'N' - a worryingly
autonomous existence - just as writing is invested with an
ontological status as 'Text', the ultimate source of meaning.
When Kermode speaks of (p. 144) 'the meshes of a text', he
would seem to be echoing some of the kinds of metaphors used
to characterise Intertextuality by a number of American
Poststructuralists, notably Geoffrey Hartman, Paul de Man and
J. Hillis Miller./25/   One particular figure keeps occurring:
that of the labyrinth.   Here is Miller operating on a poem by
Wallace Stevens called, 'The Rock':

> The multiple meanings of the word 'cure', like the meanings
> of all key words and figures in *The Rock*, are incompatible,
> irreconcilable.   They may not be followed, etymologically,
> to a single root... The origin rather is bifurcated, even
> trifurcated, a forking root, which leads the searcher for
> the ground of the word into labyrinthine wanderings in the
> forest of words./26/

In the face of this intolerable situation, where literary
texts seem to take on a life of their own and where single
words of single poems patently resist the critics' most valiant
efforts to end their reverberation and oscillation, despair
might seem to be the only option.   Yet it is at this point
that the very Nietzschean concept of 'Freeplay' is usually
invoked and personalised.   Kermode can be found alluding to
this notion as well, in what is perhaps his most elegant and
entertaining chapter, No. III, 'The Man in the Macintosh, The
Boy in the Shirt', where the puzzling character of Mark
14:51-52 is set beside James Joyce's equally bewildering 'Man
in the Macintosh' from *Ulysses*.   Kermode speaks of bolder
opinions held by the avant-garde critics on how one ought to
treat a puzzle in a text (pp. 54-55):

> Newly liberated from conventional expectations first
> formulated by Plato, solidified by Aristotle, and
> powerfully reinforced over the past two centuries, we are
> no longer to seek unity or coherence, but, by using the
> text wantonly, by inattention, by skipping even...by
> encouraging in ourselves perversities of every sort, we
> produce our own senses.

Kermode's enlightened reader of Mark is perhaps left with
Freeplay as his only choice, fated as he is (like Bunyan's
Christian in the Valley of Humiliation as it were) to
traverse a path filled with pitfalls, strange lacunae,
peculiar interruptions and seemingly pointless reiterations!
Since by definition the reader/interpreter cannot say
anything 'about' the text, he can only busy himself round
about its margins and borders.   Should a text have alternate
endings, as does Mark, (to Kermode's obvious delight), then
the reader has the liberty to select which one satisfies and
pleases him the most, as if he were at the cinema, watching
the film version of John Fowles' *The French Lieutenant's
Woman*!   Geoffrey Hartman, commenting on Derrida's work *Glas*
puts the matter very starkly, and in terms that are almost
unashamedly hedonistic:

> The fulness of equivocation in literary structures
> should now be thought about to the point where Joyce's
> wordplay seems normal... A 1001 nights of literary
> analysis lie before (us)./27/

Never in the history of modern literary criticism has
the freedom of the reader been more strongly advocated.
Painstaking historical criticism is frowned upon,
intentionalism is laughed out of court, and any attempts to
defend 'Validity in Interpretation' /28/ are dismissed as
foolishly quixotic, even ideologically repressive.   In an
earlier book *The Classic*, Kermode can be seen already siding
with those who maintain that textual interpretation is a kind
of fiction-making in its own right.   Kermode here argues
that Nathaniel Hawthorne's ambiguities in his works *The House
of The Seven Gables* and *The Scarlet Letter* are deliberate
'evasions of narrative authority' and 'imply that each man
must make his own reading...the old contracts between the
authoritative maker and the reader confident that there is a
correct interpretation are boldly broken'./29/   It is only
to be expected that many Poststructuralist critics should look
to the past to find 'precursors' with a similar hermeneutic,
hence their interest in Kabbalistic paradigms, Gnosticism and
the allegorical interpretation of Scripture./30/   In *The
Genesis of Secrecy*, Kermode seeks to collapse any distinction
between pre-scientific exegetes and modern biblical critics
by archaeologically cataloguing the excesses of each.

The wholehearted championing of Freeplay is perhaps
nowhere more obvious than in the recent work of J. D. Crossan,
a scholar who has for some time been contributing in a very
lively fashion to the burgeoning discipline of parable
studies.   In his book, *Cliffs of Fall: Paradox and
Polyvalence in the Parables of Jesus* /31/ he employs such
eyecatching phrases as 'the Permanence of Paradox', 'Primal
Grammatology' and the 'Ubiquity of Metaphor'!   In seeking to
radicalise Johan Huizinga's definition of 'play' (from his
classic study *Homo Ludens*) he helpfully distinguishes the
Structuralist 'basis' from that of Existentialism and
Classicism.   'The difference may be caught', he announces,
'through the metaphor of the labyrinth', reminding us of
Miller's reflections on Wallace Stevens' poem 'The Rock':

Classicism had a labyrinth with a centre almost impossible
to find... *Theseus has Ariadne*.   Existentialism moans that
there is no centre, or there is nothing in it, or one can't
get in, or one can't get out.   *Theseus loses Ariadne*.
Structuralism says that we create the labyrinth ourselves,

that it has no centre, that it is infinitely expansible,
that we create it as play and for play, and that one can
no more consider leaving it than one can envisage shedding
one's skin. *Theseus is Ariadne*./32/

For Crossan, just as for Kermode, the science of
hermeneutics 'has returned at last to its etymological
origins as the act and gift of Hermes'. Consequently, he
too undertakes a long 'exposition' of the parable of the
Sower, describing it as 'a parable about the process of
parabling'. Citing articles by D. Wenham and T. J. Weeden,
he develops his analysis 'without any presuppositions about
the four texts of the parable', and yet initially draws
attention to the basic units isolated by source and form
criticism./33/ His strongest criticisms are reserved for
what he sees as the previous commentators' deliberate
avoidance of 'the presence of the triadic yield from the very
beginning of the parable's existence', and so the parable is
to be considered 'a metaparable of hermeneutical polyvalence,
as a mirror rather than a window parable'. Having
maintained that paradox is 'a destiny to be enjoyed rather
than a difficulty to be avoided', he concludes by inviting
his readers to 'leave the safe havens of Mimesis for the
dangerous seas of play'./34/

Freeplay therefore means that there can be no such thing
as an accurate reading of a text, only different kinds of
misreadings. Paul de Man defines what he means by a good
misreading:

By a good misreading, I mean a text that produces
another text which can itself be shown to be an
interesting misreading, a text which engenders
additional texts./35/

By implication, boredom and restriction become the twin evil
fates cramping the Poststructuralist quest for stimulation
and liberty. Another prominent literary critic, Stanley
Fish, has even gone as far as to say, quoting A. N.
Whitehead, that the critic need no longer be concerned with
being right, but only with being interesting!/36/ For
these men, criticism has clearly become an activity whose
chief measure of success lies in its power to trigger our
pleasures and whose principal value resides in its capacity

to keep pleasurable experience going in a hopefully infinite
variety of ways./37/

    IV. The self-deconstructive power of literary
        discourse - the notion that 'every text
        performs its own self-dismantling'.
        (J. Hillis Miller)

    This third Poststructuralist preoccupation depends very
much on the ideas of Intertextuality and Freeplay discussed
above.   If texts can only refer to other texts, then this
same 'referral' is also to be noted within individual works.
Since language is deemed incapable of referring to anything
external to its own systems, it follows almost
tautologically that any talk of literary representation or
mimesis is senseless./38/   It also follows that virtually
any work of any period can be read as an exemplification of
the fictive relation of language to reality.   In this sense,
Tracy is correct to see *The Genesis of Secrecy* as
'deconstructive'./39/   But before returning to Kermode,
let us listen to our group of critics as they
seek to defend the thesis that indeterminacy is itself to be
found rooted in the 'drama' of certain literary works - that
all literature is by definition 'about' its own textual
problematics.   Here is a passage from de Man's book,
Blindness and Insight:

    Literature...is the only form of language free from the
    fallacy of unmediated expression.   All of us know this,
    although we know it in the misleading way of a wistful
    assertion of the opposite.   Yet the truth emerges in the
    foreknowledge we possess of the true nature of literature
    when we refer to it as fiction.   All literatures,
    including the literature of Greece, have always designated
    themselves as existing in the mode of fiction;   in the
    Iliad, when we first encounter Helen, it is as the emblem
    of the narrator weaving the actual (Trojan) war into the
    tapestry of a fictional object.   The self-reflecting
    mirror-effect by means of which a work of fiction asserts,
    by its very existence, its separation from empirical
    reality, its divergence, as a sign, from a meaning that
    depends for its existence on the constitutive activity of
    this sign, characterises the work of literature in its
    essence./40/

The thrust of this dense passage seems to be that literature
differs from everyday language in its refusal to claim
innocence, its unwillingness to take the easy road and
disguise its compromised nature.   It is thus by
problematising itself that literature becomes 'the only form
of language free from the fallacy of unmediated expression' -
it is characteristic of 'literature in its essence' to put a
sign of cancellation upon its own apparent referentiality.
A similar procedure can be found in J. H. Miller's reading of
Charles Dickens's, *Sketches by Boz*.   The *Sketches*, Miller
notes at the outset, 'seem firmly attached to the social facts
of London in 1836'./41/   'Here, even if nowhere else,
Dickens seems to have been practising a straightforward
mimetic realism.'   We soon realise that for Miller 'mimetic
realism' is a term of abuse, and so he goes on to argue that
this seeming realism in Dickens is merely an 'inevitable
misreading' invited by literature, and that the *Sketches by
Boz*, like *Oliver Twist*, express both the illusion and its
deconstruction'.   Boz, the narrator, 'must tell lies, employ
fictions, in ways that expose the fact that they are lies'.
Miller adduces massive textual evidence to show that the
Sketches 'do put their own status in question - theatrical
metaphors, references to other literary works and forms,
hints that social reality, far from being solid and
determinate, is itself a kind of 'text' that persistently
eludes interpretation'.   Thus, 'the *Sketches* are not mimesis
of an externally existing reality', Miller concludes, 'but
the interpretation of that reality according to highly
artificial schemas inherited from the past'./42/   Since both
de Man and Miller foreclose the very possibility of
languages referring to the world, any text they deal with will
automatically turn out to be a dramatisation of its own
problematics.   Thus not only Homer and Dickens, but all
writers of all times and places become readable,
as if they were self-regarding writers of postmodern
fiction./43/

          To return to *The Genesis of Secrecy*.   Just as the
parable 'Before the Law' seems to be the place for Kermode
(pp. 27-28 where Kafka's novel *The Trial* 'deconstructs' or
dismantles itself, so, by extension, Mark's Parable of the
Sower with its *hina/hoti* crux of 4.11-12 is taken to be
crucial for our understanding of the Gospel as a whole, (p.
59).   'We should not be unduly surprised', he says if, 'the

Gospel, like its own parables, both reveals and conceals.'
He states in another chapter (p. 134), that 'the Little
Apocalypse...is a model of the whole... All Mark's minor
intercalations reflect the image of a greater intervention
represented by the whole book.   And all such lesser
interventions deepen and complicate the sense of the
narrative;   or, they are indications that more story is
needed, as a supplement, if the story is to make sense.'/44/
It is however when Kermode turns his attention to a passage
from John's gospel that we find him at his most perplexing.
He prefaces a consideration of chapter 19.31-37 with these
rather lugubrious reflections (p. 101):

> If so many causes act in concert to ensure that texts are
> from the beginning and sometimes indeterminately studded
> with interpretations...what should we expect when the
> document in question denies its own opacity by claiming to
> be a transparent account of the recognizable world?   In
> practice we may feel that we have no particular difficulty
> in distinguishing between narratives which claim to be
> reliable records of fact, and narratives which simply go
> through the motions of being such a record.   But when we
> think about it...the distinction may grow troublesome.

Kermode then takes the passage and 'deconstructs' it by
revealing what he sees as the glaring discrepancy between its
own strident claims to be (p. 105) 'an accurate and
dependable account of what actually happened' - "the one who
has seen has witnessed, and the witness of him is true, and he
knows that he speaks truly" - and its obviously figural
literary, 'intertextual' nature.   The Old Testament texts
concerned have, he believes (p. 105), 'manifestly generated
the new narrative'.   After citing C. H. Dodd, he finishes by
saying (p. 111), 'it must appear, then, that the historical
record as we have it is constructed in considerable measure
from the testimonies'./45/   In some respects then, Kermode's
stratagems here and in his sixth chapter, 'The Unfollowable
World', resemble those of the Deconstructionist critics
considered here./46/

      This third Poststructuralist notion that has just been
examined - the idea that, 'every literary text performs its
own self-dismantling' - obviously depends upon the first

concept, that of Intertextuality.   If texts can only refer to
other texts that have 'generated' them, then different kinds
of layers of discourse can be peeled apart by the agile,
freeplaying critic.   For each, the radical implications of
semiological world-view are taken as read - the belief,
namely, that the world of signs is closed in upon itself.

     Can these three rubrics and the Poststructuralist outlook
in general be subjected to some kind of Christian
philosophical analysis?   In many ways the semiological
world-view, if we can call it that (and many of its
proponents do not shirk from styling it so!), must be exposed
as being virulently anti-Christian, with its assault on the
Logos-idea and its insistence that there is a great gulf
fixed between language and reality.   As Crossan puts it in
another of his books, 'We must live within story... God must
either be a product of human language (in which case an idol),
or, totally beyond language and hence unknowable.'/47/
Presumably this must be unacceptable to an 'Incarnational'
Christianity.   Thinking along lines suggested by V.
Poythress, it might prove possible to demonstrate in detail
how the philosophical presuppositions that undergird the
semiological world-view are involved in self-contradiction.
/48/   I leave the task of producing a sustained Christian
critique (or should I call it a 'deconstruction'?!) of this
type to those better qualified than myself, and use this
observation to impel my reader to my fourth and final
Poststructuralist battle-cry - The Institutional Control of
Interpretation.   On the one hand, the deconstructive
critic believes in the possibility of Freeplay,
advocates a new allegorism and generally 'strives
for' the creative autonomy of the reader/critic/interpreter.
Yet - and here is the contradiction - he also has to admit
that the idea of a free subject is really a fiction, and that
meaningful Freeplay is impossible because of the ways in
which institutions control and limit the production of
interpretation.   We can, after all, only read in certain
ways at a given point in time because of the coding we have
received.   (We might also comfort ourselves with the
observation that the very fact that interpretation has a
history tends to undermine the much-vaunted anti-historical
orientation of most varieties of Poststructuralism.)/49/

V.   The Institutional Control of Interpretation

In an amusing piece written in 1977, Kermode urbanely
asked the question, 'Can we say absolutely anything we like?'/50/
and proceeded to demonstrate, to his own satisfaction at least,
that we could not, by citing examples from the history of
Shakespearean criticism.   He draws parallels between it and
the history of biblical interpretation, setting the innovative
and charismatic individual over against the institution -
'tradition and the individual talent', to invoke T. S. Eliot's
catchphrase for the same opposition.   'The institution', he
writes, 'will characteristically be concerned with such
matters as canon, and with anathematising incompetent, that is,
heretical or unorthodox, interpretation.   The individuals will
characteristically do whatever the spirit moves them to do.'
He goes on to offer us a piece of autobiography about his
Arden edition of Shakespeare's, *Tempest*, first published in
1954.   A reviewer noted with some hilarity that if the pages
on Caliban were representative of the 'new approach to
Shakespeare, we might as well head straight for the madhouse
and give ourselves up!'   In 1974, Kermode read a new article
on the play which began with the author's brief account of the
'conventional' views he was about to dismiss.   The author
added a footnote to say that these views were usefully
summarised in Kermode's own Introduction to the text of the
play!   Kermode contends throughout *The Genesis of Secrecy*
that judgements, assessments and interpretations of all kinds
are historically conditioned by the sets of assumptions
available to given institutions.   Jonathan Culler called this
phenomenon 'Institutionalised Competence', in the course of
putting his highly influential case for a 'Structuralist
Poetics'./51/   Some central assertions from Culler's sixth
chapter, "Literary Competence", will perhaps help us to
understand Kermode's contentions.   In the first place, Culler
dismisses the idea that a poem can have 'meaning' of and by
itself:

...The semiological approach suggests rather that the poem
be thought of as an utterance that has meaning only with
respect to a system of conventions which the reader has
assimilated./52/

Culler then quotes the narratologist Gerard Genette, a thinker
whose ideas on narrativity Kermode uses when discussing Mark's

intercalations.   'Like any other activity of the mind,
reading is based on conventions of which, with some
exceptions, it is not aware'./53/   It follows from this that
the critic will naturally find it a most fruitful activity to
consider works which are read differently in different
periods, because these furnish the most decisive evidence
about the system of operative conventions.   On this view,
any literary work can be rendered intelligible if one invent
the relevant conventions.   This is why Kermode makes much,
(p. 18), 'of the moment when the Old Testament finally
became joined to the New... This new form of interpretation,
whereby...a previously non-existent book called the Old
Testament is created out of an old one, the Torah, by a
hermeneutical fiat is a model of our own procedures, of the
way we go about our higher initiate reading'.   Later, having
summoned up Joyce's enigmatic Man in the Macintosh, he comes
back to the same theme (p. 53).

> There must be supra-literary forces, cultural pressures,
> which tend to make us seek narrative coherence, just as we
> expect a conundrum to have an answer, and a joke a point.
> Our whole practice of reading is founded upon such
> expectations, and of course, the existence of genres such
> as the pointless joke and the deviant conundrum depends
> upon the prior existence of the normal sort./54/

Going in tandem with Institutionalised Competence is what has
been called the law of 'tacit exclusion'.   Kermode makes the
connection between the two at the end of his third chapter
(p. 71).

> The conviction that Mark cannot have meant this or that is
> a conviction of a kind likely to have been formed by an
> institution, and useful in normal research;   the
> judgements of institutional competence remove the
> necessity of considering everything with the same amount
> of minute attention, though at a risk that a potential
> revolution may be mistaken for a mere freak of scholarly
> behaviour.

So it was that Austin Farrer's 'reading' of Mark was tacitly
excluded by the consensus of New Testament scholars, Kermode
reports. In his essay 'Can we say absolutely anything we like?'

Kermode cited the similar case of Gregor Mendel, the pioneer
geneticist, whose formulations and discoveries were rejected
by the scientific consensus of his day./55/   Kermode would
undoubtedly agree with a remark made by Jürgen Habermas in his
book *Knowledge and Human Interests*, 'true interpretation is,
in fact, a consensus among partners'.   Repeatedly, Kermode
allies himself with the powerful German hermeneutical
tradition.   At one point (p. 39) he quotes two oracular
remarks by H.-G. Gadamer: 'One understands differently when
one understands at all', and, 'the meaning of a text goes
beyond its author not sometimes but always'./56/

> VI.   Conclusion. Kermode's strictures against
>   professional New Testament scholars

Given that we may wish to disagree sharply with many of
the theoretical assumptions that inform *The Genesis of
Secrecy*, are there assertions and accusations in the book that
we should be taking to heart, as professional exegetes and
interpreters or as educated lay-readers of the New Testament?
Kermode announces (p. 119) that one of the purposes of his
book is to encourage attempts to try and attend to 'what is
written' rather than 'what it is written about'.   He
believes that the story of modern biblical scholarship tends
to confirm his view, 'that it takes a powerful mind' to do
this.   He often has some hard things to say to biblical
scholars, accusing them of having little acquaintance with
even elementary forms of disciplined literary analysis.
After calling Mark's sequence of Betrayal, Desertion and
Denial 'a literary construction of sophistication, one that
has benefited from the grace that often attends the work of
narration', he says that, 'this grace (is) not always taken
into account by scholars who seek to dissolve the text into
its elements rather than to observe the fertility of their
interrelations'.   Discussing the interpolated account of the
death of John the Baptist (p. 130), he speaks of the
'remarkable naïveté of professional exegesis when confronted
with problems of narrative'./57/   As for ordinary
'lay-readers' of the gospels, he accuses them of rarely
considering the differences between them (p. 69).   'We are
so used to mixing the gospels up in our memory into a smooth
narrative paste', that we rarely reflect, 'that if we had
only Mark's account, there would be no Christmas, no loving

virgin mother, no preaching in the temple'.

When he does get down to his sustained 'readings' of
Mark, Kermode can be very stimulating.   (Like all good
reviewers I encourage the readers of this article to
'respond' to these at first hand - aware as I am that I have
perhaps not taken sufficiently careful heed of Milton's sage
counsel: 'Unlesse warinesse be us'd, as good almost kill a
Man as kill a good Book...we see a kinde of homicide may be
thus committed'! (*Areopagitica*)).   Suffice it to say here
that his section on intercalations is excellent precisely
because, contrary to the Poststructuralist critical outlook
that he at least in part endorses at a theoretical level, he
talks in terms of a controlling author, who has cleverly
organised his gospel so that each part reflects the whole
(pp.127-134).   Is Kermode's view of the hermetic in Mark and
the general 'Unfollowability' of the gospels dictated by more
than the literary-critical preoccupations I have tried to
examine here?/58/   I hope that by trying to give an account
(however brief) of some 'of the influential views of language
to which Kermode appeals' (Wilder's review), I have, at
the very least, cleared the way for professional New
Testament scholars (the 'insiders'!) to be able to engage
with his detailed readings.

Notes

/1/ Taken from E. M. Forster's novel, *A Passage to India*.
See the Abinger Edition of E. M. Forster, ed. O.
Stallybrass, vol. 6 (London: Edward Arnold, 1978), p. 60.
/2/ See, D. Patte, *What is Structural Exegesis?*
(Philadelphia: Fortress, 1976);   J. Calloud, *Structural
Analysis of Narrative* (Missoula: Scholars, 1976);   A. M.
Johnson, Jr., ed. and transl., *The New Testament and
Structuralism* (Pittsburgh: Pickwick, 1976).   Article length
treatments include, A. C. Thiselton, 'Keeping up with Recent
Studies II. Structuralism and Biblical Studies: Method or
Ideology?', *ExpTim* 89 (1977-8) 329-335;   C. Armerding,
'Structural Analysis', *Themelios* 4 (1979) 96-104.
     Among recent accounts of the ways in which 'Classical
Structuralism' has metamorphosed into its even more protean
successor, Poststructuralism, also known as Deconstruction,
are, J. V. Harari, ed., *Textual Strategies: Perspectives in
Post-Structuralist Criticism* (Ithaca: Cornell U.P., 1979);

R. Young, ed., *Untying the Text: A Post-Structuralist Reader*
(London: R.K.P., 1981);   D. Donoghue, *Ferocious Alphabets*
(London: Faber, 1981);   Annette Lavers, *Roland Barthes:
Structuralism and After* (London: Methuen, 1982).   Handiest of
all is C. Norris, *Deconstruction: Theory and Practice* (London
and New York: Methuen, 1982).   J. Culler's *On Deconstruction*
(London: R.K.P.) (forthcoming) promises to be the
authoritative guide.   Armerding's 'new star'('Structural
Analysis', p. 96)   has become a veritable supernova!
/3/   Cambridge, Mass.: Harvard U.P., 1979.
/4/   See *The Genesis of Secrecy* (hitherto referred to in the
notes as G.S.) notes to pages 80-82, p. 154.
/5/   This compliment came from David Lodge in his *Twentieth
Century Criticism: A Reader* (London: Longman, 1972) p. 661.
Kermode himself, writing very recently in response to an
assessment of his career as a critic (published in the same
periodical), states that 'what one is always looking for in
criticism' is 'a power to connect an occasional interpretation
with a rich source of information'.   See both J. Arac,
'History and Mystery: The Criticism of Frank Kermode', and
Kermode's 'Reply to Jonathan Arac' in *Salmagundi* 55
(1982), pp. 135-155, 156-162.
/6/   In the Preface to his *Moses and the Deuteronomist: A
Literary Study of the Deuteronomic History* (New York: Seabury,
1980) R. M. Polzin salutes Kermode's work, and presents his
own study as a similar effort, 'to end a centuries old eclipse
of biblical narrative...in Old Testament studies' (p. xi).
        For a typical Poststructuralist treatment of a classic
English poet and his works see J. Goldberg, *Endlesse Worke:
Spenser and the Structures of Discourse* (Baltimore and London:
John Hopkins University, 1981).   Goldberg quotes Kermode's
concluding palinode before beginning his treatment of
Spenser's, *The Faerie Queene*.
/7/   D. Tracy, *The Analogical Imagination: Christian Theology
and the Culture of Pluralism* (London: SCM, 1981) 117.
/8/   These words and this slogan are those of J. D. Crossan.
See his article 'Perspectives and Methods in Contemporary
Biblical Criticism', *Biblical Research* 22 (1977) 39-49.
/9/   This remark is just one of several confessional asides
penned by Northrop Frye, as he prefaces his new and very
important book on the Bible, *The Great Code: the Bible and
Literature* (London: R.K.P., 1982).
/10/   From *New York Review of Books*, 29.6.1978, p. 39
/11/   In *Interpretation* 34 (1980) 297.

/12/ The most compelling delineation of this 'older view'
from a Poststructuralist perspective is perhaps that of
Michel Foucault in his *The Order of Things: An Archaeology of
the Human Sciences* (New York: Vintage, 1973), ch. I, 'The
Prose of the World'.
/13/ See Nietzsche's essay, 'On Truth and Falsehood in an
extra-Moral Sense', reprinted in W. A. Kaufmann, ed., *The
Portable Nietzsche* (New York: Viking, 1954), 42-47.
/14/ For one examination of the 'New Nietzsche', see,
D. Allison, ed., *The New Nietzsche* (New York: Dell, 1977).
/15/ Herbert Schneidau, 'The Word against the Word', in R.
Detweiler, ed., *Semeia* 23 (1982) 21.
/16/ C. Lévi-Strauss, *Structural Anthropology* (New York:
Doubleday, 1967) 209. Quoted by Schneidau ('The Word',
p. 22).
/17/ D. A. Carson, 'Hermeneutics: a brief assessment of
some recent trends', *Themelios* 5/2 (1980) 18.
/18/ Schneidau, 'The Word', pp. 1, 6.
/19/ To be found in R. Macksey and E. Donato, eds., *The
Structuralist Controversy: The Languages of Criticism and the
Sciences of Man* (Baltimore and London: John Hopkins
University, 1972) 247.   J. Culler's article on Derrida in
Sturrock, ed., *Structuralism and Since*, pp. 154-179, is
perhaps the most accessible and rigorous one chapter
introduction to his thought yet available.   Full
bibliographical details of Derrida's works are given there,
as they are in C. Norris, *Deconstruction: Theory and
Practice* (see note 2) pp. 143-145.
/20/ J. Derrida, *Speech and Phenomena and Other Essays*
(Evanston: Northwestern U.P., 1973) 159.
/21/ See note 13 for details.
/22/ E. Donato, 'The Two Languages of Criticism', in *The
Structuralist Controversy*, p. 96.
/23/ J. Culler, *The Pursuit of Signs* (London: R.K.P., 1981)
103.
/24/ R. Barthes, 'From Work to Text', reprinted in J.
Harari, ed., *Textual Strategies*, 77-81.
/25/ An excellent general guide to the twenty-five years,
1952-1977, in American criticism is F. Lentricchia's *After
the New Criticism* (Chicago: University of Chicago, 1980).
Lentricchia is particularly astute in pointing out the
continuities between 'New Criticism', with its idea of the
'Verbal Icon' ('A poem should not mean but be'), and

American Poststructuralism with its Barthesian
'hypostasisation of the Text'.   I have drawn freely from
Lentricchia's survey throughout this article.
/26/ J. Hillis Miller, 'Stevens' "Rock" and Criticism as Cure',
Georgia Review 30 (Spring, 1976) 10-11.   Compare his essay
'Ariadne's Thread: Repetition and the Narrative Line' in
Interpretation of Narrative, M. J. Valdes and O. J. Miller,
eds., (Toronto, University of Toronto, 1978) 148-167; in
this volume, as in many such others increasingly, approaches
to narrative from the German hermeneutical tradition can be
found together with those from the Derridean perspective.
/27/ G. Hartman, 'Monsieur Texte: On Jacques Derrida, His
'Glas' ', *Georgia Review* 29 (Winter, 1975) 783.   In his
recent book, *Criticism in the Wilderness* (New Haven: Yale
U.P., 1980), Hartman can be found carrying this kind of
polemic much further.   Like Derrida, he has also recently
tried his hand at literary analysis of the Bible: see R. M.
Polzin and E. Rothman, eds., *The Biblical Mosaic: Changing
Perspectives* (Semeia Studies: Philadelphia: Fortress, 1982)
ch. 10, 'Jeremiah 20.7-12: A Literary Response with M.
Fishbane',pp. 184-195.
/28/ Itself (of course!) the title of a well-known and
controversial defence of Intentionalism, namely, E. D.
Hirsch, *Validity in Interpretation* (New Haven: Yale U.P.,
1967).   For two challenging critiques of Hirsch's positions,
see P. D. Juhl, *Interpretation: An Essay in the Philosophy
of Literary Criticism* (Princeton: Princeton U.P., 1980), and
F. Lentricchia's chapter 'E. D. Hirsch: The Hermeneutics of
Innocence', in *After the New Criticism*, 256-280.
/29/ F. Kermode, *The Classic* (London and New York: Faber,
1975) 107-108.
/30/ D. Tracy has a brilliant analysis of how various
'postmodern' thinkers (including literary theorists such as
Roland Barthes and Harold Bloom) seek to 'retrieve
hermeneutically' previous 'uncanny' traditions of thought.
See his ch. 8, 'The Situation: The Emergence of the Uncanny'
in *The Analogical Imagination*, 339-370.   Tracy admits his
debt to Kermode's *The Classic* for his own wide-ranging use
of the concept of the 'classic' religious text.
/31/ New York: Seabury, 1980.
/32/ *Cliffs of Fall* , p. 72.   Jorge Luis Borges turns out to
be the unsurprising postmodern source of this 'labyrinth'
preoccupation.   Compare the references to J. H. Miller's

criticism at note 26!
/33/ *Cliffs of Fall*, ch. 2, 'Sower and Seed', pp. 25-64.
/34/ Ibid., pp. 70, 86.
/35/ P. de Man, 'Nietzsche's Theory of Rhetoric',
Symposium 28 (Spring, 1974) 51. For the contemporary
critical notion of 'misreading', see Harold Bloom's *A Map of
Misreading* (New York: Oxford U.P., 1975), together with his
decidedly outlandish *Kabbalah and Criticism* (New York:
Continuum, 1975), both saturated by a terminology drawn from
the occultist traditions noted by Tracy.
/36/ Stanley Fish, 'Interpreting the Variorum', *Critical
Inquiry* 2 (Spring, 1976) 465-485. This is reprinted in
Fish's recent volume, *Is there a Text in this Class?*
(Cambridge, Mass.: Harvard U.P., 1980) 147-173.
/37/ For the most extreme of all protracted defences of
Freeplay, see Roland Barthes *The Pleasure of the Text* (New
York: Hill and Wang, 1975), trans. R. Miller.
/38/ Deconstructive criticism therefore opposes itself
violently to the kind of exercise carried out classically by
Eric Auerbach, in his famous book, *Mimesis*. For a useful
consideration of some of the implications of this opposition,
see, Robert Alter, 'Mimesis and the Motive for Fiction',
Tri Quarterly 42 (Spring, 1978) 228-249.
/39/ Tracy, *The Analogical Imagination*, 262.
/40/ P. de Man, *Blindness and Insight: Essays in the
Rhetoric of Contemporary Criticism* (New York: Oxford U.P.,
1971) 17.
/41/ J. H. Miller, 'The Fiction of Realism: "Sketches by
Boz", "Oliver Twist", and Cruikshank's Illustrations', in
A. Nisbet and B. Nevius, eds., *Dickens Centennial Essays*
(Berkeley: University of California, 1971) 89.
/42/ Ibid., 115-122. Miller's very recent, *Fiction and
Repetition: Seven English Novels* (Oxford: Blackwell, 1982),
finds him extending these deconstructive strategies to such
classic English novels as Hardy's *Tess of the d'Urbervilles*,
and Conrad's *Lord Jim*.
/43/ For recent attacks on these kinds of deconstructive
procedures see, for example, M. Mudrick, 'Adorable Ideas and
Absent Plenitudes', *The Hudson Review*, XXX, (1977-78) pp. 587-95
and C. Norris, 'Deconstruction and the Limits of Sense',
Essays in Criticism XXX, 4 (1980) 281-92.
/44/ Lecturing in Cambridge on 13.2.1982, Derrida himself
took Kafka's 'Before the Law' as his subject, using its

despairing message for theoretical reflections similar to
Kermode's.   His way with Kafka's text resembled his toyings
with a fragment of Nietzsche's in his *Spurs: Nietzsche's
Styles,* trans. B. Harlow (Chicago: Chicago U.P., 1979) 123-139.
He floats the possible interpretations that one might put on
the fragment 'I have forgotten my umbrella', only to mock them
all.   For him it is a statement at once hermetic and
totally open.   See Norris, *Deconstruction,* ch. 4, 'Nietzsche:
philosophy and deconstruction', pp. 70-73.
/45/   His reference is to Dodd's, *Historical Tradition in the
Fourth Gospel* (Cambridge: Cambridge U.P., 1963); none of
this is to suggest that the unsettling questions about John's
claims are a product of Kermode's approach.   They have been
present ever since conventional historical and literary
analysis have worked on the gospel.
/46/   For Derrida's own first sustained encounter with a New
Testament book, namely, Revelation, see his 'Of an
Apocalyptic Tone Recently adopted in Philosophy',   *Semeia* 23
(1982) 63-99.   (The whole issue of *Semeia* is entitled
'Derrida and Biblical Studies'.)   H. Schneidau's words again
come as a warning to us of a possible approaching spate of
Derridean criticism of the biblical texts.   For him, as we
noted previously (see above, n. 15, and the relevant section
in this article), the techniques of 'Classical Structuralism'
had little to offer: 'The texts of the Bible are from this
new viewpoint most intriguing; their resistance to past
categorizations is a sign that they are readier for
Derridean analysis than for the methods of those who derive
their notions of genre from Propp, or from Northrop Frye.'
('The Word', p. 23).
/47/   *The Dark Interval: Towards a Theology of Story* (Niles:
Argus, 1975) 40-41.
/48/   V. Poythress, 'Philosophical Roots of Phenomenological
and Structuralist Literary Criticism', *WTJ* 41 (1978-9) 165-
171.   Much more substantial as a guide to the interaction
between hermeneutical thought and Poststructuralism - an
interaction at the heart of *The Genesis of Secrecy* - is T. K.
Seung's *Structuralism and Hermeneutics* (New York: Columbia
U.P., 1982).   Seung castigates Poststructuralism for its
relapse into an extreme and debilitating relativism,
unconstrained by any recognition that there are constants as
well as variables in the texts with which it engages.
/49/   But see E. W. Said's essay, 'The Text, the World, the
Critic', in Harari ed., *Textual Strategies*, 161-189.

/50/   In Q. Anderson et al., eds., *Art, Politics and the Will: Essays in Honour of Lionel Trilling* (New York: Basic, 1977), 159-172.

/51/   J. Culler, *Structuralist Poetics* (London: R.K.P., 1975).

/52/   Ibid., 116.

/53/   Ibid., 116.

/54/   Kermode has a fascinating footnote on genre and generic expectations with reference to the gospels at 'Notes to Pages 135-143', no. 20, p. 162.   On this whole matter see D. E. Aune's substantial 'The problem of the genre of the gospels: a critique of C. H. Talbert's *What is a Gospel?*' in R. T. France and D. Wenham, eds., *Gospel Perspectives: Studies of History and Tradition in the Four Gospels, Volume II* (Sheffield: JSOT, 1981) 9-61.

/55/   The work of Michel Foucault has centred around these kinds of 'exclusions'.   See especially his *Madness and Civilisation: A History of Insanity in the Age of Reason* (London: Tavistock, 1971).   For a serviceable introduction to Foucault see J. Sturrock ed., *Structuralism and Since*, 81-115.   The essay is by Hayden White.

/56/   A. C. Thiselton's *The Two Horizons* (Exeter: Paternoster, 1980) is the most detailed examination of this German hermeneutical tradition.   Most notable among literary theorists writing from this perspective is perhaps Wolfgang Iser.

/57/   Tracy, *The Analogical Imagination*, 296, n. 81, has a lengthy excursus on current issues in narratological theory, with some highly suggestive questions for the future study of biblical narrative.   He refers to a forthcoming book by Paul Ricoeur. For a refreshingly different study of Old Testament narrative see R. Alter's *The Art of Biblical Narrative* (New York/London: Basic/Allen & Unwin, 1981/1982).   Alter is suspicious of Structuralist and Poststructuralist procedures and believes strongly that narrativity cannot be considered and discussed as a concept in isolation from moral and spiritual issues.   For him, Old Testament narratives are an intricate interweaving of fiction and history.   See David Lodge's highly appreciative review, *Times Literary Supplement*, 5.11.1982.

/58/   Among literary critical reviews of *The Genesis of Secrecy* are E. D. Hirsch's polemical, 'Carnal Knowledge', *New York Review of Books* 14.6.1979 and Helen Gardner's extended attack in her own Charles Eliot Norton Lectures of 1979-80, published as *In Defence of the Imagination* (Oxford: Clarendon, 1982).   See her chapter V 'Narratives and Fictions, pp. 111-137.

POSTSCRIPT - WHERE HAVE WE GOT TO, AND WHERE DO WE GO FROM HERE?

R. T. France
London Bible College
Green Lane
Northwood, Middx.
HA6 2UW

The aim of these pages is not to repeat or even to summarise all that has gone before. Much of the preceding papers will be taken for granted, and no further reference will be made to it. I aim now only to draw out some main lines of thinking which have emerged which bear on the overall theme of these volumes, 'History and Tradition in the Four Gospels', and to ask what may be the implications for further study in this area.

The papers in this volume vary in character and in the direction of their thrust, but all have been written in the context of a current tendency to judge the aims and methods of the Christian gospels by reference to supposedly parallel literary phenomena in non-Christian Judaism. Three areas of concern have arisen:

1. Are the 'parallel' Jewish phenomena in themselves correctly understood and described by New Testament scholars?

2. How relevant are they to the Christian gospels? Has a significant generic similarity been established?

3. What does study of the gospels themselves indicate as to their attitude to tradition and their approach to history?

The third question is clearly the most important. The ultimate witness to the aims and methods of the gospel writers must be the text of the gospels themselves. Of course that text must be studied with a due awareness of their literary and historical context, but it cannot be assumed that the conventions and attitudes of non-Christian Jewish writers will be found unaltered in the Christian gospels. If our studies

have in fact, as I believe they have, shown the need for
at least a doubtful verdict on the first two questions,
it becomes all the more important to attempt a responsible
answer to the third.   On this task we have, I trust, in various
ways made a beginning, but much more work is needed.

These three questions form a suitable framework for this
post-script.   References to papers in this volume will be by
the author's name with either the number of the section, where
given, or the page number.   Reference will also be made to my
article in *Gospel Perspectives II* on 'Scripture, Tradition and
History in the Infancy Narratives of Matthew' (abbreviated to
France *GP2*), which belongs with the subject-matter of this
volume, and forms part of its argument.

1.   Midrash and history in first-century Judaism

It is by now commonplace to complain about the varied and
misleading uses of the term 'midrash' especially by New
Testament scholars who are not themselves specialists in Jewish
literature.   We have perhaps been more consistent in our
complaints than in our own usage.   Bruce Chilton's proposal to
use 'Midrash' of the genre of 'specific rabbinic documents'
purporting to be exegetical treatments of the Old Testament,
and 'midrash' of 'the general process by which one "searches
out" the meaning of scripture' (Chilton p. 9), would, if
universally adopted, help to sort out the confusion.   But
unfortunately we have no proprietary rights over scholarly
usage, and the danger of a slippery use of the term remains.

It is well exemplified when Payne (p. 177) attributes to
Gundry a use of 'midrash' as a term for 'those elements which
he regards as unhistorical embellishments'.   This is indeed
the idea the term is coming to convey in popular usage, but it
has nothing to do with either of Chilton's meanings mentioned
above.   Nor would Gundry accept this as a *definition*;   but his
constant emphasis on this theme does threaten to give the term
this value in his usage if not in his dictionary, so that Payne
can go on (p. 179) to propose to use 'midrashic intent' 'to
focus as Gundry does on the intent to convey what is in fact
unhistorical using historical narrative form'.   It is such
shifts of meaning which cause some specialists in Jewish
literature to despair of New Testament scholarship!

Even within the more 'correct' meaning of the term adopted

by Chilton, his paper emphasises the *variety* of types of
midrash, not only in the methods employed in interpreting the
Old Testament but also in the aims of the enterprise (see his
section III, especially pp. 24-25).   Even within this 'proper'
usage of the term, in other words, it is hard to see what is
the basic generic pattern with which the gospels are being
compared.

But in any case very little that can confidently be traced
back to the first century AD is 'midrash proper'.   When one
takes into account the broad range of relevant Jewish literature
(see the survey in my paper, which itself is very far from
complete), there is cause for real surprise that 'midrash' has
been taken to be a major factor in the search for the literary
affinities of the gospels.   Far more prominent in Jewish
literature of the relevant period is the important category of
'rewritten Bible' (*cf.* my 'Retelling of Biblical History',
France section IA), works which have been called 'narrative
Midrashim', but 'their lack of an exegetical programme suggests
they are not best treated as a species of Midrash' (Chilton
p. 10).   Yet it is in this category, rather than among the
Midrashim, that there may be more promising grounds for
discovering generic similarities with the gospels.

We noted with some surprise the small number of Jewish
works of the relevant period which are devoted to recording
recent, non-biblical history.   Jewish historiography of the
first century seems to have concentrated more on the ancient,
sacred history of the Old Testament; and even here the interest
was often more in drawing appropriate morals than in the events
for their own sake.   Nonetheless, where a scriptural narrative
is taken as the basis for comment, it exercises a decisive
control on the writer.   It may need to be explained,
illustrated, even apologised for, but it is the story as
written which remains the fixed basis for the explanation.
The explanation may involve expansion and embellishment of the
story, sometimes drawing on what is clearly a long-developing
tradition of interpretation, but it is seldom that the writers
display a willingness to create whole stories which have no
apparent basis in either scripture or tradition.   Even in the
case of Pseudo-Philo, perhaps the most imaginative story-teller
among those discussed, for all his delight in tracing the
fulfilment of prophecy, his 'ingenuity in this field of exegesis
is displayed not in creating events to fit prophecies, but in
finding prophecies to fit events' (Bauckham p. 60).

It is interesting to note here the contrast in the Qumran
texts between their freedom in inventing *future* or heavenly
events on the basis of Old Testament prophecy (Bruce pp. 92-93)
and the lack of evidence for any tendency to invent *past*,
earthly 'history' on the same basis (Bruce p. 87).

All this, and much more in the preceding pages, throws
grave doubt on any suggestion, whether advanced in the name of
'midrash' or not, that the narration in historical form of
unhistorical events, whether derived from scriptural
meditation or from pure imagination, was typical of most first-
century Jewish literature, the more so when it is *recent*
'events' which are in question. The whole literary scene is
much more complex than that, and an approach to the gospels on
the basis of possible literary parallels must take due account
of this complexity. Where, within the wide range of Jewish
approaches to history, if at all, may a relevant parallel be
found?

2. The Gospels and Jewish literature

'In terms of *literary genre*, the historical narration
style of Matthew finds no close parallel in rabbinic or Qumran
literature' (Moo p. 167). The same could be said of the other
gospels, and it is questionable how far an extension of the
area of comparison would alter the verdict. Of course
historical narration is an essential feature of 'rewritten
Bible' books and of historians like 1 Maccabees and Josephus
(as it is also of the 'historical romances' like Tobit and
Judith); but to be a close generic parallel a Jewish work
would need to be a self-contained book of somewhere around
20,000 words (preferably in Greek) presenting with a mixture of
narrative and discourse (ranging from single sayings to quite
long speeches) a selective biographical portrait of a religious
leader of the recent past (two or three generations at most),
with a view to winning followers. Obviously there is nothing
of the sort extant outside Christian circles, for even Philo's
life of Moses, besides being very much longer, records not
recent history but the well-rehearsed events of many centuries
ago as already enshrined in scripture.

But perhaps to insist on such a close generic similarity
to the gospels as a whole is to miss the point. Are there
significant ways in which they are engaging in a similar
enterprise to other Jewish writers of the day, even if in a

different literary context?   In particular, even if they are
not Midrashim, are they in any significant sense 'midrashic'?

That the gospels are not, in any proper sense of the word,
Midrashim may surely be taken for granted, in that they are not
commentaries on any given scriptural 'text', whether an Old
Testament book as a whole or even any pre-existing collection
of Old Testament material.   This rather obvious point will be
developed in the next section.

But what of the suggestion that the 'text' commented on
was not a part of the Old Testament, but the Gospel of Mark
and/or other early gospel material, treated by Matthew as a
sacred text requiring a midrashic treatment?   Quite apart from
questions about the order of composition and degree of literary
dependence of the synoptic gospels, this proposal raises the
probably unanswerable question of how soon any account of the
life and teaching of Jesus was accorded a widely recognised
status as 'scripture'.   But even if we may assume that Mark
could have been so regarded by Matthew, what sort of 'midrash'
would Matthew then be carrying out on the text of Mark?
Certainly nothing like a rabbinic Midrash with its extended
comments (consecutively) on individual verses and phrases.
If there is a Jewish literary parallel to this supposed
procedure of Matthew, it must be in the area of 'rewritten
Bible', where some sections of the 'scriptural' narrative are
retold with little change, some abbreviated or passed over in a
brief summary, and some expanded with explanatory or apologetic
material.   Probably the closest analogy among the works we have
studied would be Pseudo-Philo, with his sometimes quite
extensive additions to the stories he is retelling.   Here
Bauckham's study has some important observations (sections
6.2-3; 6.8), concluding that the inventiveness postulated for
Matthew and Luke by some recent New Testament scholarship would
make Matthew a 'radical innovator' engaged in 'a far more novel
and audacious enterprise than Pseudo-Philo's' (Bauckham p. 65).
And yet we have seen that Pseudo-Philo is more free in this
regard than most producers of 'rewritten Bible'.   Where such a
conclusion can be drawn it is clear that we have moved away
from the possibility of judging the gospel writers' methods by
analogy with contemporary literature.

Nor should it be forgotten that the 'scripture' used by
Matthew on this hypothesis was one written less than a
generation before his own writing.   The rationale behind much

of the expansion in books of 'rewritten Bible' was the need to
interpret the ancient texts to a context several centuries
removed from its origin, during which time interpretative
tradition had had opportunity to weave quite considerable
haggadic embellishments around the scriptural text.   The
situation is in no way parallel to Matthew's use of a text
written less than a generation earlier, which in its turn
recorded the events of only a generation ago.   In terms of
proximity to the events narrated, a closer analogy to the
gospels would be 1 Maccabees or the later history of Josephus.
But this analogy moves us still further away from any
meaningful use of the term 'midrashic', and into an area where
the evidence suggests a less inventive approach to the contents
of the narrative than that of Pseudo-Philo (see France sections
IC, IE2).   Josephus, as a Hellenistic historian, seems to
model his approach on the careful historiography of Thucydides
(and of course the same has been suggested for Luke), and there
is no reason to believe that, for all his clearly partisan
views, he sat light to historical fact.   Where Josephus does
allow himself some inventiveness is in many of the speeches he
inserts into his narrative; but it is interesting that it is
precisely in the *sayings* of Jesus in the gospels that scholars
tend to be more confident of an underlying tradition rather
than free invention by the evangelists, so that here any
analogy between Josephus and the evangelists breaks down.

We would suggest, then, that much more care is needed in
applying terms like 'midrash' to the gospels on the assumption
that there is a demonstrable analogy between their situation
and literary procedures and those of Jewish writers, whether of
Midrashim proper or of 'midrashic' works.   Payne's article
emphasises this question in relation to Gundry's constant
appeal to 'midrash and haggadah' as the context within which
Matthew's literary practice is to be understood.   Until the
area of comparison in Jewish literarure is more precisely
defined, and the parallel is shown to be a significant and
relevant one, we are right to treat such categorisation with
great caution.

3.   The evidence of the gospels themselves

How may we determine what the gospel writers themselves
thought they were doing?   We may, as the previous sections
have indicated, try to reconstruct what non-Christian authors
of the period were doing, and assume that the gospel writers

had similar aims.   That approach has turned out to be full of
problems, both in the analysis of contemporary literature and
in determining the appropriateness of the comparison.   Or we
may try to reconstruct the historical interests of the
first-century *Christian* community.   This is in principle a
more promising approach, if we begin with the direct evidence
of, for example, Paul's epistles, and try from them to deduce
what were the attitudes of first-century Christians to the
Jesus of history.   (A future volume of *Gospel Perspectives* will
attempt this approach by studying the Jesus tradition outside
the gospels.)   The New Testament provides ample evidence that
the focus of early Christian interest was on the fulfilment of
God's purposes in very recent events, and it is clear that such
an orientation will necessarily produce a quite distinctive
approach to history.   But even here there is an inevitable
element of speculation in our view of what 'must have been'
their attitude.   Ultimately the only solid evidence for the
historical interests of first-century Christians is the sort of
history they did in fact write, in the gospels and Acts.

Thus if we want to know what the gospel writers thought
they were doing, our primary line of approach must be to
analyse what we actually find in the gospels.   Perhaps this is
too obvious to mention, but some recent scholarship has not
obviously given the appropriate weight to this primary evidence.
Indeed this volume too is perhaps at fault here, in that we have
devoted so much attention to the ground-clearing exercise of
establishing the limitations of the indirect approach via
Jewish literature that we have not dealt adequately with the
actual data of the gospel text.   It is surely here that future
work must be focused.

The role of a 'midrashic' use of the Old Testament in the
formation of the gospel text has necessarily been in the
forefront of our discussion.   We have, particularly in our
studies of specific passages (see especially Moo and France
GP2), noted the full and frequent use of Old Testament material
in drawing up the narratives of the life of Jesus (and of course
the same would have been true in a parallel study of the
tradition of Jesus' *sayings*).   We have noted the strong
interest (particularly of Matthew) in tracing the fulfilment of
Old Testament themes and passages in the events of Jesus' life,
often resulting in an imaginative application of Old Testament
texts in ways which we would have difficulty in recognising as
'scientific exegesis'!   We have no doubt that the Old

Testament was a very important formative influence on many of
the stories of Jesus as they appear in the gospels.

But the point where we have found it necessary to dissent
from the attribution to the gospel writers of a 'creative
midrash' which produced unhistorical stories in historical form
out of Old Testament texts is in the observation of the
secondary role of the Old Testament texts in relation to the
gospel traditions.   In our studies of Matthew's infancy
narrative and of the Judas-pericope, Moo and I, while agreeing
that the wording and even the structure of the passages has
been decisively influenced by Old Testament texts (both those
explicitly cited as 'fulfilled' in these events and, in the
case of the infancy narratives, an even more important
substratum of Moses-typology), have found it more satisfactory
to explain these features as the result of a deliberate
presentation of existing traditions in the light of a perceived
'fulfilment' than as indicating that the story itself was
created out of the Old Testament texts.

To observe a strong scriptural colouring, in other words,
is not to settle the question of the *origin* of the traditions.
The question remains, which came first, the tradition or the
scripture?   We have not seen good reason for assuming the
latter answer in any case.

Nor is this surprising when we recall that the gospels are
not structured as a 'midrash' on any given Old Testament text.
The framework is that of a tradition of the words and deeds of
Jesus, not of a text or series of texts from the Old Testament
which in themselves invited a commentary.   The texts are
there because the stories suggested them, and not *vice versa*.
The point is usefully summed up in Chilton's proposal (p. 27)
to describe the Transfiguration not as 'haggadic midrash' but
as 'midrashic haggadah', 'because the story is the primary
vehicle of the ideas involved, while scripture is used in a
subsidiary manner'.   The same point is developed by Bauckham
in discussing the gospels in relation to Pseudo-Philo (sections
6.4-7), leading to a warning 'against too readily concluding
that the Evangelists would have created events to fulfil
prophecies.   If they did so, they had, so far as I can tell,
no precedent in Jewish "midrashic" literature' (p. 64).

This question of the plausible *starting-point* for the
gospel traditions (i.e. did they arise out of actual events or

out of scripturally-inspired imagination) must be discussed in
due awareness of the difference between the situation of a
gospel writer, dealing with events well within living memory,
and a compiler of 'rewritten Bible'. Bauckham develops this
point in his section 6.10, where he points out the tendency of
Jewish writers to use traditional material (rather than sheer
invention) to explain the Old Testament text where they had
any available and notices that if Matthew acted similarly, as
he probably did, it is far more likely than in the case of the
'rewritten Bibles' 'that an Evangelist's traditions, however
"midrashic" his procedure in using them may be, could be
historical in origin' (p. 67).

   Blomberg's paper has taken this question a stage further
to suggest that not only the individual incident but also the
literary structure of a whole major section of a gospel (Luke's
central section) finds a more plausible origin in a carefully
structured pre-existing collection of Jesus' teaching than in a
'midrashic' framework created by the evangelist. To push the
origin of this structure back to a stage before the final
composition does not in itself, of course, guarantee the
historicity of the material. But it does cast further doubt
on the radically innovative 'midrashic' role sometimes
attributed to Matthew and Luke. The underlying
parable-collection postulated by Blomberg may be assumed to be
a deliberate systematisation of traditional material at some
stage in the development of the church's teaching. This still
leaves open the question of the origin of the individual
parables, but the further back they are traced, the more
implausible becomes the suggestion of an origin independent of
the teaching of the historical Jesus.

   But to argue, as we have repeatedly done, that the gospels
do not provide evidence of a tendency to 'create history out of
scripture' is not necessarily to rule out creativity altogether.
Even if the inspiration was not meditation on an Old Testament
passage or theme, is it not possible that the tradition of
Jesus' words and deeds could be expanded with additional stories
and sayings in the course of the church's worship and teaching
by its own inner dynamic? It is clear that this did happen to
the Old Testament stories within Jewish tradition, as every
example of 'rewritten Bible' in its own way illustrates. Even
if it is true that writers like Jubilees, Pseudo-Philo or
Josephus did not generally create stories *de novo* out of other
parts of the Old Testament, and whenever possible used

traditional material as a basis for their explanatory
additions, it remains clear from the very fact that such
traditional material was available that someone at some time
did add considerably to the original scriptural stock.   Is not
a similar process plausible in the formation of the gospels?

Of course it is possible.   But before such a process is
assumed by analogy with the 'rewritten Bible', we should
remember a point frequently noted in this volume, that is the
difference between the retelling of ancient, sacred history and
the recording of contemporary or recent events (see e.g. France
especially section IE; Payne section 2.7; Moo pp. 167-68).
The difference in time-scale alone is surely a major problem
for such an analogy: the development of supplementary material
over many centuries within the folk-tradition of a nation is
not at all the same thing as the addition within the Christian
community of new material to the stories of their leader within
the lifetime of many who were present during the actual events.
In addition,the *explicitly* 'scriptural' status of the Old
Testament stories may be supposed to have rendered them more
subject to devotional and apologetic elaboration than is likely
to have been the case with the stories of Jesus.   As Bruce
comments on the Genesis Apocryphon, its embellishment of the
Old Testament 'has more in common with the type of sermon in
which a biblical narrative is amplified so that its main
features may be brought more vividly before the hearers' eyes.
There is a difference between amplifying an ancient narrative
for this kind of purpose and imaginatively supplementing
historical events of the present or of the recent past with
details which have no factual basis'.   For this latter
practice, he concludes, the Qumran literature provides no
analogy (Bruce pp. 96, 98).   Of course early Christians did
preach about Jesus, and no doubt much of the theological
interpretation of the stories of Jesus which we find in the
gospels owes its origin to such preaching.   But to observe a
process of theological interpretation is not at all the same
as to postulate the development of new elements of narrative.

We return then to the question whether the contents of
the gospels themselves provide any evidence of such
creativity.   The studies in this volume do not offer enough
detailed material to venture a firm answer.   One possibility,
that stories had to be created in order to fulfil the demands
of a lectionary, has been firmly discounted in Morris' paper
(see his conclusion, pp. 148-49).   In our studies of the

suggested role of the Old Testament in inspiring new traditions
we have frequently come back to the recognition of a respect
for tradition as such among first-century Christians which
makes any tendency to free creativity improbable.   Many other
studies have been undertaken in this area, including some of
the papers in our earlier volumes, but there is room for many
more.   At least we feel able to claim on the basis of what
this volume has shown that a creativity in the gospels which
sits loose to the historicity of the events and sayings
recorded would need to be proved from the gospels themselves
rather than assumed on the basis of 'how Jews wrote history'.

As for 'midrash' and its relevance to this question, I hope
we have effectively ruled out the simplistic syllogism which
runs:

> Midrash is unhistorical writing in the guise of history
> The gospels (or parts of them) are midrash
> Therefore the gospels (or those parts of them) are not to
>   be taken seriously as history.

I believe the foregoing papers make both premisses of this
syllogism illegitimate, or at least subject to such drastic
qualification as to destroy their relevance to such an
argument.   Whether or not the same conclusion could be drawn
from other premisses, this particular line of approach does not
prove the case.